MASON CITY

CHARLES CITY

DECORAH

MC GREGOR

STATE UNIVERSITY OF IOWA
FORMER STATE CAPITOL
IOWA CITY 1840-1857

INDEPENDENCE

EPISCOPAL SEMINARY
FORMER DUBUQUE
FEMALE COLLEGE
SAND SPRINGS

DUBUQUE

GALENA

ELDORA

MONTICELLO

ANAMOSA

AGRICULTURAL COLLEGE
MARSHALLTOWN

CEDAR RAPIDS

MT VERNON

CORNELL COLLEGE

CLINTON

DE WITT

UNIVERSALIST
CHURCH

GRINNELL

MARENGO

IOWA CITY

TIPTON

GRINNELL COLLEGE

OSKALOOSA

WASHINGTON

DAVENPORT

MUSCATINE

K COUNTY
RT HOUSE

ITON

ALBIA

OTTUMWA

MT PLEASANT
IOWA WESLEYAN
COLLEGE

DON

CENTERVILLE

BLOOMFIELD

KEOSAUQUA

BURLINGTON
UNIVERSITY

FARMINGTON

FORT MADISON

1870

KEOKUK

STATE CAPITOL   1857-1884
DES MOINES

DRAWN BY Bill Wagner   10/69

STRONG-MINDED WOMEN

AMELIA BLOOMER/*Council Bluffs*

ARABELLA MANSFIELD/*Mount Pleasant*

MARY NEWBURY ADAMS/*Dubuque*

ANNIE SAVERY/*Des Moines*

AUGUSTA CHAPIN/*Iowa City*

MARY DARWIN/*Burlington*

STRONG-MINDED WOMEN

❊

The Emergence of the
Woman-Suffrage Movement
in Iowa

❊

LOUISE R. NOUN

❊

The Iowa State University Press

LOUISE R. NOUN is chairman of the Iowa Civil Liberties Union, a board member of the American Civil Liberties Union, and a member of the Iowa Capitol Planning Commission. She was graduated from Grinnell College—which honored her in 1964 with its Alumni Award for contribution to her community and to her college—and received her M.A. degree in art history and museum management from Radcliffe College. She was awarded the National Municipal League Distinguished Citizen Award in 1956. Mrs. Noun has held offices in the League of Women Voters at the state and local levels. She has been a member of the Council of the National Municipal League and the Des Moines Plan and Zoning Commission and has been a trustee of the Des Moines Art Center.

© 1969 The Iowa State University Press
Ames, Iowa 50010. All rights reserved

Composed and printed by
The Iowa State University Press

First edition, 1969

Standard Book Number: 8138–1602–5
Library of Congress Catalog Card Number: 72–83322

IN MEMORY OF

BABETTE FRANKEL

My Matriarchal Grandmother

ROSE FRANKEL ROSENFIELD

My Strong-minded Mother

MARGUERITE NEFF

My Friend in the League of Women Voters

CONTENTS

List of Illustrations ✧ *page ix*
Preface ✧ *page xiii*
Chapter 1 ✧ 1848–1860 ✧ *page 3*
Chapter 2 ✧ 1861–1865 ✧ *page 23*
Chapter 3 ✧ 1866 ✧ *page 35*
Chapter 4 ✧ 1867 ✧ *page 67*
Chapter 5 ✧ 1868 ✧ *page 79*
Chapter 6 ✧ 1869 ✧ *page 101*
Chapter 7 ✧ 1870 ✧ *page 125*
Chapter 8 ✧ 1871 ✧ *page 167*
Chapter 9 ✧ 1872 ✧ *page 199*
Chapter 10 ✧ 1872–1920 ✧ Carrie Chapman Catt ✧ *page 225*
Biographical Notes ✧ 1872–1920 ✧ *page 263*
Appendix A ✧ Report of 1870 Woman-Suffrage Convention at
Mount Pleasant ✧ *page 279*
Appendix B ✧ Woman's Declaration of Independence, 1948
page 283
Bibliography ✧ *page 289*
Index ✧ *page 309*

LIST OF ILLUSTRATIONS

❧

Ninth national woman's rights convention, New York City, May 12, 1859 (*Harper's Weekly,* June 11, 1859) ❖ *page 2*

Lucy Stone (Stanton, Anthony, and Gage, *History of Woman Suffrage,* vol. 2, 1882) ❖ *page 4*

A Natural Consequence: Proper Prudence (*Harper's Monthly,* November 1852) ❖ *page 6*

Elizabeth Cady Stanton (Parton, *Eminent Women of the Age,* 1869) ❖ *page 7*

Susan B. Anthony (Stanton, Anthony, and Gage, *History of Woman Suffrage* vol. 1, 1881) ❖ *page 9*

The Great Republican Reform Party Calling on Their Candidate (Currier and Ives, publisher, 1856) ❖ *page 11*

Amelia Bloomer (Stanton, Anthony, and Gage, *History of Woman Suffrage,* vol. 1, 1881) ❖ *page 12*

The Bloomer Polka (Lithographic title design, New York Historical Society) ❖ *page 14*

Turkish Costume (*Harper's Monthly Magazine,* July 1851 ❖ *page 14*

Woman's Emancipation (*Harper's Monthly Magazine,* August 1851) ❖ *page 15*

American and French Fashions Contrasted (*Water-Cure Journal,* November 1851) ❖ *page 18*

Letter for Home (Lithograph by Winslow Homer, 1863) ❖ *page 23*

Lizzie Bunnell Read (Andreas' *Illustrated Atlas of Iowa,* 1875) ❖ *page 25*

"The Mayflower," March 1, 1862 (Louise Noun) ❖ *page 26*

Annie Wittenmyer (Hanaford, *Daughters of America,* 1882) ❖ *page 27*

The Wife and Mother at a Primary; The Father Stays at Home Attending to the Children (Brockett, *Woman,* 1870) ❖ *page 34*

Women in the Army—The Dress Parade (Brockett, *Woman,* 1870 ❖ *page 51*

Anna Dickinson's receipt for payment for special train, March 10, 1869 (Library of Congress) ❖ *page 59*

Front-page story about Anna Dickinson's special train (*Des Moines Register,* March 11, 1869) ❖ *page 59*

Anna Dickinson (Parton, *Eminent Women of the Age,* 1869) ❖ *page 59*

Some Popular Lecturers in Character (*Harper's Weekly,* November, 15, 1873) ❖ *page 66*

Theodore Tilton (Brockett, *Men of Our Day,* 1868) ❖ *page 72*

Annie Savery (Pastel portrait by Napoleon Sarony, Iowa State Department of History and Archives) ❖ *page 78*

Advertisement for "female medicine" (*Cedar Rapids Times,* April 27, 1865) ❖ *page 82*

Julia Ward Howe (Stanton, Anthony, and Gage, *History of Woman Suffrage,* vol. 2, 1882) ❖ *page 89*

Mary Darwin (Iowa State Department of History and Archives) ❖ *page 96*

The Age of Brass, or the Triumph of Woman's Rights (Currier and Ives, publisher, 1869) ❖ *page 100*

The Age of Iron. Man as He expects to Be (Currier and Ives, publisher, 1869) ❖ *page 102*

Mary Livermore (Stanton, Anthony, and Gage, *History of Woman Suffrage,* vol. 2, 1882) ❖ *page 106*

Mary Walker (Walker, *Hit,* 1871) ❖ *page 109*

Letter from Amelia Bloomer concerning Mary Walker's dress, (*The Agitator,* October 23, 1869, Vassar College library) ❖ *page 109*

Mary Newbury Adams (Iowa State Department of History and Archives) ❖ *page 113*

Home of Lucy Graves (Andreas' *Atlas of Iowa,* 1875) ❖ *page 114*

Rowena Guthrie Large (Iowa State Department of History and Archives) ❖ *page 115*

Caroline Ingham (Iowa State Department of History and Archives) ❖ *page 120*

Joseph and Ruth Dugdale (Iowa State Department of History and Archives) ❖ *page 124*

Hannah Tracy Cutler (*Woman's Journal,* September 26, 1896) ❖ *page 139*

Henry O'Connor (Gue, *History of Iowa,* vol. 4, 1903) ❖ *page 140*

John Irish (Iowa State Department of History and Archives) ❖ *page 142*

Arabella (Belle) Mansfield DePauw University) ❖ *page 144*

Augusta Chapin (Hanson, *Our Women Workers,* 1881) ❖ *page 147*

Martha Callanan (Gue, *History of Iowa,* vol. 4, 1903) ❖ *page 150*

Home of Martha and James Callanan (Iowa State Department of History and Archives) ❖ *page 151*

Maria Gray Pitman (Iowa State Department of History and Archives) ❖ *page 152*

Mary Jane and John Coggeshall (Iowa State Department of History and Archives) ❖ *page 153*

Elizabeth Boynton Harbert (Stanton, Anthony, and Gage, *History of Woman Suffrage,* vol. 3, 1887) ❖ *page 158*

Victoria Woodhull presenting her memorial to the House Judiciary Committee (*Frank Leslie's Illustrated Newspaper,* February 4, 1871) ❖ *page 166*

Victoria Woodhull (New York Historical Society) ❖ *page 169*

Keziah Anderson (Photo supplied by Wallace D. Eubanks, grandson) ❖ *page 175*

Victoria Woodhull asserting her right to vote (*Harper's Weekly,* November 25, 1871) ❖ *page 176*

Advertisements placed by Victoria Woodhull's first two husbands (*Muscatine Journal,* December 25, 1863; *Mount Pleasant Home Journal,* June 9, 1865) ❖ *page 179*

Get Thee Behind Me (Mrs.) Satan (*Harper's Weekly,* February 17, 1872) ❖ *page 198*

Phoebe Couzins (Stanton, Anthony, and Gage, *History of Woman Suffrage,* vol. 3, 1887) ❖ *page 204*

Carrie Chapman Catt leading woman-suffrage parade, New York City, 1917 (Library of Congress) ❖ *page 224*

Carrie Chapman Catt at the time of her marriage to Leo Chapman, 1885 (Iowa State Department of History and Archives) ❖ *page 224*

Iowa Woman Suffrage Association convention, Oskaloosa, 1889 (Iowa State Department of History and Archives) ❖ page *233*

Program and menu for the Mississippi Valley woman-suffrage convention, Des Moines, 1892 (Iowa State Department of History and Archives) ❖ *page 238*

Carrie Chapman Catt during California referendum campaign, 1896 (Library of Congress) ❖ *page 240*

Woman-suffrage flag (Iowa State Department of History and Archives) ❖ *page 242*

Once More the Castle Is Being Stormed ("Ding" cartoon, *Des Moines Register,* February 20, 1909) ❖ *page 245*

Woman-suffrage parade, Boone, 1908 (Iowa State Department of History and Archives) ❖ *page 246*

Anna Howard Shaw speaking at street meeting, Boone, 1908 (Iowa State Department of History and Archives) ❖ *page 247*

Flora Dunlap (Iowa State Department of History and Archives) ❖ *page 249*

Hooray for Mother; Aw Susie, Be Them Dishes Washed?; Women Marching (John Sloan drawings, 1912; Louise Noun; Ben and Beatrice Goldstein Foundation; University of Michigan Museum of Art) ❖ *page 251*

Woman-suffrage parade, New York City, 1915 (Library of Congress) ❖ *page 252*

Iowa Equal Suffrage Association board of directors, 1915 (Iowa State Department of History and Archives) ❖ *page 253*

Propaganda for woman suffrage: When a Fellow Needs a Friend; On the Road to Woman Suffrage (Iowa State Department of History and Archives) ❖ *page 255*

Antiwoman-suffrage propaganda: Population Diagram (Iowa State Department of History and Archives) ❖ *page 255*

Antiwoman-suffrage advertisement (*Iowa Homestead,* May 25, 1916) ❖ *page 258*

PREFACE

⚏

To UNDERSTAND FULLY the history of the woman-suffrage movement in the United States, it is necessary to know how it developed within the various states and to trace the effect of the
personalities and actions of nationally known suffrage leaders on
the emerging state organizations. The Iowa story (which could
be paralleled by similar stories in any one of the northern states)
poignantly reveals the hopes and disappointments of a small band
of idealistic women, who were encouraged by politicians to believe that suffrage would be granted to their sex as soon as the
Negro was enfranchised, and recounts their first faltering steps
toward organization and their courage in the face of ridicule. It
is a story of vain attempts to avoid involvement with the dissensions dividing the woman-suffrage movement in the East, of a
notorious and alluring free-love advocate who attained high position in the suffrage movement, of vain efforts to please critics by
purging woman's rights ranks of "undesirable" advocates, and of
an infant movement torn asunder by internecine warfare.

Although this book is primarily a study of the history of
woman suffrage in Iowa during the Reconstruction period, it also
covers the years 1872–1920 as reflected in the life of Carrie Chapman Catt in order to give an overall view of the suffrage movement. Basic material for this book has been gleaned from a
thorough study of newspapers and periodicals published during

the years 1866–1872 as well as letters and diaries of the period. Source material is listed in the Bibliography. Librarians wherever I have worked have been most helpful to me. My special thanks go to Miss Helen Aten, head reference librarian of the Iowa Traveling Library, for her untiring efforts in helping me with this study; to Lida Lisle Greene, director of the Iowa Historical Library; and to Mildred K. Smock, director of the Council Bluffs Free Public Library.

My appreciation also goes to Jack Musgrove, curator of the Iowa State Department of History and Archives, for his cooperation in making available the numerous photographs and other materials which furnished many of the illustrations for this book. I am also grateful for permission to use the following material:

❖ Illustrations from the *Harper's Weekly* files of the Drake University and University of Iowa libraries.

❖ Illustrations from the *Harper's Monthly* file in the Iowa State Traveling Library.

❖ The Dr. Woodhull and Dr. Harvey advertisements from the collection of the State Historical Society of Iowa.

❖ The *Water-Cure Journal* illustration from the National Library of Medicine secured by the Iowa State Medical Library.

❖ The picture of Keziah Anderson Dorrance furnished by her grandson, Wallace D. Eubanks.

❖ The photograph of Belle Mansfield furnished by DePauw University.

❖ The Currier and Ives prints, the photograph of the 1915 suffrage parade, and the 1896 and 1917 photographs of Carrie Chapman Catt from the Library of Congress collections.

The John Sloan drawing, "Hooray for Mother," is in the author's private collection. The reproduction of *The Mayflower* of March 1, 1862, is from one of 31 copies of this paper given to the author by Mr. and Mrs. Sidney Macmullen.

Most of the Iowa material is reproduced for the first time in this book; other pictures which I have never seen reproduced except in the original source include the John Sloan drawings; the illustrations from Brockett's *Woman: Her Rights, Wrongs, Privileges, and Responsibilities;* the cartoon from the November

1852 issue of *Harper's Monthly;* the dress reform illustration from the *Water-Cure Journal;* the picture of Hannah Tracy Cutler from the *Woman's Journal;* and the engraving of Theodore Tilton from Brockett's *Men of Our Day.*

Searching out and putting together the story of the Iowa woman-suffrage pioneers has been an exciting adventure. It is interesting to learn that the problems they faced and the choices they had to make were in many ways as difficult as those which challenge women today. May we take courage from their courage and learn from their mistakes.

LOUISE R. NOUN

STRONG-MINDED WOMEN

Yᴱ MAY SESSION OF Yᴱ WOMAN'S RIGHTS CONVENTION—Yᴱ ORATOR OF Yᴱ DAY DENOUNCING Yᴱ LORDS OF CREATION.

The ninth annual national woman's rights convention, New York City, May 12, 1859, as caricatured in Harper's Weekly. *Note the jeering crowd in the balcony. The disturbances at this and other woman's rights conventions were not so much that the mob objected to the doctrine of woman's rights as that they were addressed by men who were leaders in the antislavery movement. The women therefore also had to bear the odium attached to that hated cause.*

1

1848-1860

Four women, born between 1815 and 1820 and in the vanguard of the woman's rights movement in the United States in the first half of the nineteenth century, were to play important roles in Iowa in the post-Civil War years. One of these women—Amelia Bloomer of reform dress fame—was a resident of Iowa when the war ended in 1865, having moved there from Seneca Falls, New York, ten years before. The other three—Lucy Stone, Elizabeth Cady Stanton, and Susan B. Anthony—were national leaders to whom Iowa woman's rights advocates looked for guidance and help. Each of them visited the state in the years between 1869 and 1872.

The story of the lives of these women before the Civil War embodies a history of the founding and development of the woman's rights movement in the United States and provides a background for their activities in the postwar era.

LUCY STONE

THE MOST WIDELY KNOWN of these woman's rights advocates in the pre-Civil War years was Lucy Stone, who was notorious because she did not use her husband's name. Born in 1818 on a small farm some twenty miles north of Worcester, Massachusetts, Lucy Stone was the eighth of nine children, and much of her childhood was spent in helping her overburdened mother. Despite the opposition of her father, who did not believe in education for women, Lucy managed by dogged determination to earn enough through teaching to enable her at the age of twenty-five to enter Oberlin College in Ohio, the only institution of higher education in the United States which admitted women. Following her graduation in 1847 Lucy Stone was hired as a lecturer for the Massachusetts Anti-Slavery Society, an occupation so unfeminine that it filled her parents with dismay. Soon Lucy was regularly lecturing on woman's rights as well as the evils of slavery and facing bitter opposition, ranging from verbal attacks by the clergy to rowdies who broke up her meetings.

Lucy Stone began her woman's rights campaign prior to and independently of the crusade which formally emerged with the first woman's rights convention at Seneca Falls, New York, in 1848; she is often called the morning star of the woman's rights movement. In

1850 she joined with other advocates in New England in signing a call for the first national woman's rights convention held at Worcester, Massachusetts, in November of that year. From this time until the birth in 1857 of her only child, Alice Stone Blackwell, her magnetic and emotional appeals were a prominent part of many woman's rights meetings.

A petite, feminine girl with a winsome expression and a quiet, almost shy manner, Lucy Stone was the antithesis of the stereotype of the manly woman's rights advocate. She had brown hair, large gray eyes, a short almost pug nose, and a florid complexion which was indicative of the rugged life she led as a child. She was noted for her soft, musical voice which could easily be heard in even the largest halls, and for her ability to sway audiences with incidents from the lives of suffering women. Since she spoke extemporaneously, her lectures have been preserved for posterity only through brief newspaper reports.

In 1855 at the age of thirty-seven Lucy Stone married Henry Blackwell, a devout woman's rights advocate and the brother of the pioneer woman doctor Elizabeth Blackwell. The unorthodox ceremony was performed by Thomas Wentworth Higginson, minister of the Free Church in Worcester, and commenced with the reading of a protest composed by the bride and groom. This was entered as an official part of the marriage contract and objected under six headings to the common-law system which denied a married woman control of her person, her children, and her property (including the money she earned) and suspended her legal existence during marriage. Newspapers from coast to coast carried comments about this protest.

After living in the Midwest a short time, the Blackwells settled in a Gothic cottage in Orange, New Jersey. In this house—placed in Lucy Stone's name—her only child, Alice, was born in 1857. When the first tax bill on the house arrived, Lucy returned it to the collector with a note stating that as a protest against taxation without representation she refused to pay it. As a consequence several pieces of furniture (some accounts say Alice's cradle was included) were sold at auction to satisfy the claim of the state, and Lucy Stone again received widespread publicity.

From the time of the birth of Alice until after the Civil War, Lucy Stone was relatively inactive in the woman's rights movement, although she kept up her contact with other woman's rights advocates and did what she could from home base.

A NATURAL CONSEQUENCE.

Miss Lucy (*blushing extensively*).—"Miss President and Ladies, It is my painful duty to resign my office as Corresponding Secretary of the Woman's Rights Association—for I am to be married to-morrow."

Only ugly, unmarried women attended woman's rights meetings, according to these cartoons from Harper's Monthly, *November 1852.*

PROPER PRUDENCE.

Miss Prudence (*emphatically*).—"Miss President, I repeat it—No conscientious Woman will ever marry until she is in a condition to support her Husband and Children in a suitable manner."

ELIZABETH CADY STANTON

ALTHOUGH LUCY STONE began lecturing on woman's rights a year before Elizabeth Cady Stanton became active in the campaign, Mrs. Stanton has earned the title of mother of the woman's rights movement because she was the prime mover in organizing the first woman's rights convention at Seneca Falls in 1848. Although only local in nature, this meeting gained nationwide attention, and soon women in other parts of the country were organizing similar conventions.

Mrs. Stanton, three years older than Lucy Stone, was born in 1815 in Johnstown, a village in upstate New York. Her father, Daniel Cady, was a wealthy and socially prominent lawyer with extensive landholdings both in New York State and in western Iowa, where Mrs. Stanton's son, Gerrit Smith Stanton (also her sister and brother-in-law, Madge and Duncan McMartin), settled after the Civil War. Elizabeth had a superior education for a girl of her time, studying Latin, Greek, and mathematics along with the village boys at Johnstown Academy. Despite the fact that she graduated at the head of her class, she could not go to college because none admitted women in 1830 (Oberlin was opened three years later). Instead she was sent to Troy Female Seminary, the first endowed school for women in the United States, run by the pioneer educator Emma Willard. Here she spent two unhappy years rebelling at her fate as a girl. "If there is any one thing on earth from which I pray to God to save my daughters," Mrs. Stanton said in later life, "it is a girl's seminary."

When she was twenty, Elizabeth married Henry B. Stanton, a pioneer abolitionist; and their wedding journey was a trip to London to attend a world antislavery convention. Here Mrs. Stanton met forty-seven-year-old Lucretia Mott, a well-known Philadelphia Quaker who was denied her seat as a delegate because of her sex. Living in the same boarding house in London, the two women spent many hours discussing the injustices which women suffered, including the possibility of someday holding a woman's rights convention.

From 1842 until 1847 the Stantons lived in Boston, where Henry Stanton practiced law and Mrs. Stanton's lively mind was stimulated by the intellectual life of this city—a life enriched by such men and women as Ralph Waldo Emerson, the philosopher; Bronson Alcott, the educator (and father of the future author, Louisa May Alcott); William Lloyd Garrison, the abolitionist; Margaret Fuller, author of *Woman in the Nineteenth Century;* and Theodore Parker, the rebel Unitarian minister. She visited Brook Farm when this utopian experiment in communal living was flourishing—a community which set her to dreaming of an associative world where all men and women would be equal and love and mutual respect would replace all laws regulating marriage.

When the Stantons moved to Seneca Falls, New York, in 1847, Mrs. Stanton found little outlet for her energies in this small upstate factory village. The following summer when she learned that Mrs. Mott was visiting the nearby community of Waterloo Mrs. Stanton sought her out and enlisted her help in organizing the woman's rights convention which the two women had talked of in London eight years previously. This meeting, which formally launched the woman's rights movement in the United States, was held in the Wesleyan Chapel at Seneca Falls on July 18 and 19, 1848. The Declaration of Sentiments adopted here set forth the injustices and indignities suffered by women in all areas of life—social, educational, economic, legal, and political—and constituted the women's Declaration of Independence. This declaration and a series of resolutions demanding redress of grievances which were also adopted by this meeting were never replaced as the platform of the woman's rights movement. (See Appendix A.) The immediate effect of the Seneca Falls meeting, however, was general public ridicule and widespread denunciation by the press.

Because of her fast-increasing family—five sons and two daughters were born between 1842 and 1859—Mrs. Stanton's public appearances in the years prior to the Civil War were limited. She lectured in the vicinity of Seneca Falls and delivered two addresses before New York legislators in the capitol at Albany. In addition she sent carefully reasoned woman's rights arguments to any paper which would print them, as well as composing long controversial letters and resolutions to be read at woman's rights meetings. She personally was able to attend only one of the annual national woman's rights conventions— in New York in 1860—the tenth, and the last one held before the Civil War. Here she created a furor by presenting a series of radical resolutions on the subject of divorce.

Mrs. Stanton, 5 feet 3 inches tall, was a plump young woman who became increasingly heavy with age. Her black curly hair, which she cut short at the time of the Bloomer rage in 1851, was a mass of snow-white ringlets by the time she was fifty. She had a clear, fresh complexion, a merry twinkle in her light blue eyes, and a benign expression—characteristics which allowed her to express the most radical thoughts with relative impunity. She was a brilliant conversationalist and an accomplished writer whose lively style soon made her the leading publicist for the woman's rights movement. Mrs. Stanton's patrician background was revealed in her gracious manner and her boundless self-assurance which sometimes bordered on arrogance. Reared a Presbyterian, as a young woman she rejected association with any organized religion. Her children were free to attend the church of their choice or no church at all if they wished. During the Civil War the Stantons moved to New York City, where Henry Stanton had been appointed to a government job. In 1868 the family settled in a spacious Victorian mansion at Tenafly, New Jersey.

SUSAN B. ANTHONY

TWO YEARS YOUNGER than Lucy Stone and five years younger than Mrs. Stanton, Susan B. Anthony was born near South Adams in western Massachusetts in 1820. Her father, a well-to-do manufacturer of cotton goods, lost his fortune in the 1830's; in 1845 the family moved to a farm near Rochester, New York. Here Miss Anthony began teaching at the age of fifteen, an occupation which she pursued until she was thirty. While in her late twenties, she was drawn into active participation in the reform agitation which was sweeping upper New York State—first as a temperance worker and then into the more radical (and unladylike) antislavery and woman's rights movements. In May 1851 she went to Seneca Falls (a village ninety miles from Rochester) to attend an antislavery rally. Here she was the guest of her fellow temperance worker Amelia Bloomer, who introduced her at this time to Elizabeth Cady Stanton. This was the beginning of a lifelong friendship and a close working relationship between the two women. In 1852 Miss Anthony attended her first woman's rights meeting, the third national convention which met at Syracuse, New York. She brought with her both a controversial letter and a series of resolutions written by Mrs. Stanton, which she read to the assembly.

Since Miss Anthony was neither a fluent writer nor an accomplished public speaker, she relied in her early years almost entirely on Mrs. Stanton for the preparation of woman's rights ammunition. In turn Mrs. Stanton, tied down at home with her large family, looked upon Miss Anthony as her connecting link with the world—"the reform scout who went to see what was going on in the enemy's camp" as well as the stouthearted henchman who was willing to deliver to reform meetings her most explosive bombshells.

Miss Anthony was a tall, slender woman (her contemporaries called her angular), who dressed in a plain manner consistent with her Quaker upbringing. Although she had a biting and sardonic humor, she was a deadly serious person who seldom smiled. Thoroughly honest and sincere but often irritatingly blunt and tactless, she was universally looked upon as the perfect stereotype of the "strong-minded" woman.

In contrast to the quixotic and ebullient Mrs. Stanton, Miss Anthony was a persistent plodder—willing to do the routine work of organizing meetings, distributing tracts, raising funds, and recruiting workers. Since she was unmarried and relatively free from family responsibilities, she soon became the workhorse of the woman's rights movement. Along with Mrs. Stanton, Miss Anthony abandoned the temperance movement in 1853; and once the slave was emancipated and the Civil War ended, she devoted the rest of her life exclusively and wholeheartedly to the elevation of the rights of women.

THE GREAT REPUBLICAN REFORM PARTY,
Calling on their Candidate.
For Sale at No 2 Spruce St N.Y.

"The first thing we want is a law making the use of Tobacco, Animal food and Lager-ier a Capital Crime—"

"We demand, first of all, the recognition of Woman as the equal of man with a right to Vote and hold Office—"

"An equal division of Property that is what I go for—"

"Col. I wish to invite you to the next meeting of our Free Love association, where the shackles of marriage are not tolerated & perfect freedom exist in love matters and you will be sure to Enjoy yourself, for we are all Freemounters—"

"We look to you Sir to place the power of the Pope on a firm footing in this Country—"

"De Poppylation ob Color comes in first—arter dat, you may do wot you pleases—"

"You shall all have what you desire—and be sure that the glorious Principles of Popery. Fourierism, Free Love, Woman's rights, the Maine Law, & above all the Equality of our Colored Brethren, shall be maintained; If I get into the Presidential Chair."

This 1857 Currier and Ives cartoon pictures John C. Fremont, first Republican candidate for president, catering to abolitionists, woman's rights advocates, and others who were considered crackpot reformers. The woman's rights advocate wears Bloomer dress and smokes a cigar.

AMELIA BLOOMER

IF, in the late 1840's and early 1850's, Amelia Bloomer had not been living in Seneca Falls, New York—the home of Elizabeth Cady Stanton and the birthplace of the woman's rights movement—it is likely that she would have spent the rest of her life as a conventional church worker and the editor of an innocuous temperance paper appropriately christened *The Lily*. However, since in 1848 Mrs. Stanton needed an outlet for her woman's rights propaganda, she wooed Amelia Bloomer's favor so that she might use the columns of her paper. Soon Mrs. Bloomer was "converted" to woman's rights, and *The Lily* was on the road to becoming a full-fledged woman's rights paper, the first of its kind in the country.

Mrs. Bloomer, born Amelia Jenks in the village of Homer in upstate New York in 1818, was the youngest of a family of six children. A clothier by trade, her father was not well off, and the family had lived in three different towns by the time she was twenty. Her mother, a devout Presbyterian, reared her children in the strictest Puritan manner. Amelia's education was limited to a few terms in district schools, where students were taught the elements of reading, writing, and arithmetic. When she was nineteen, she went to live with a farm family near Waterloo, New York, where she looked after three small children. In 1840, at twenty-two, she married Dexter Bloomer—a tall, quiet-mannered, studious young lawyer who resided in Seneca Falls. Although Bloomer was reared as a Quaker, early in their marriage he and his wife joined the Episcopal Church in which they were both active members for the rest of their lives.[1]

Amelia Bloomer at the time of her marriage was an auburn-haired, unfashionably thin young woman, 5 feet 4 inches tall and weighing 100 pounds. Possessor of a pleasant smile, she nevertheless had little sense of humor with which to temper her serious, intense disposition. The Bloomers, who had no children of their own, often had those of relatives living with them during the days of their Seneca Falls residence. After their move to Iowa in 1855 they became the foster-parents of a brother and sister, two in a family of five English-born Mormon children whose mother had died en route to Utah and whose father was unable to care for them.

Early in their marriage Dexter Bloomer encouraged his wife to widen her horizons through reading. He also urged her to develop her natural talent for writing by composing articles which were printed in the *Seneca Falls Courier* and various temperance papers. These articles were published under pseudonyms, as it was considered unladylike for a woman's name to appear in print.

When the historic first woman's rights convention met in Seneca Falls in July 1848, Mrs. Bloomer attended out of curiosity; but the sentiments expressed were too radical for her basically conservative nature. She not only refused to sign the Declaration of Sentiments but she aroused Mrs. Stanton's ire by her ridicule of the meeting.

That Mrs. Bloomer was not unaffected by the ferment of woman's rights agitation, however, is indicated by her launching of *The Lily* barely six months after the convention. This was an adventurous step into an aspect of the temperance field usually dominated by men. The following summer Mrs. Stanton, who traveled in an elite social circle which did not include Amelia Bloomer, came into Mrs. Bloomer's office—the post office where she served as deputy postmaster for her husband—and proposed to write for *The Lily*. She also invited Mrs. Bloomer to join a conversation club—a group organized to discuss political and social questions—which was led by Mrs. Stanton and met in the homes of its members. Mrs. Bloomer soon succumbed to Mrs. Stanton's blandishments, with the result that *The Lily* became increasingly an organ for woman's rights propaganda.

1. Though Mrs. Bloomer became convinced that the clergy was wrong in interpreting certain passages of the Bible as decreeing woman's subjection, she never broke with the orthodox religious tradition. This was in contrast to Elizabeth Cady Stanton, Susan B. Anthony, and Lucy Stone, all of whom were religious freethinkers. In further contrast to these women, despite her dislike of slavery, Mrs. Bloomer was not an abolitionist, a cause which at one time was looked upon with as much antipathy as communism is today.

THE BLOOMER POLKA.

PORTRAIT OF M^{RS} AMELIA BLOOMER FROM A DAGUERREOTYPE BY FFRENCH

COMPOSED & INSCRIBED TO

M^{RS} COLONEL BLOOMER

BY

J. J. BLOCKLEY.

AUTHOR OF THE BIENON POLKA
& BLOOMER WALTZES

DUFF & HODGSON, 65 OXFORD ST

THE BLOOMER QUADRILLES P.3/
& THE BLOOMER SCHOTTISCHE P./

This polka, published in London and erroneously inscribed to Mrs. Colonel Bloomer instead of Mrs. Dexter Bloomer, is one of a number of musical compositions that were inspired by the Bloomer fad of 1851. (Courtesy of the New York Historical Society, New York City)

❈

The controversial new reform dress received a friendly notice in the July 1851 Harper's Monthly; *in August this same periodical lampooned the new fad.*

TURKISH COSTUME.

There appears to be a decided and growing tendency on the part of our countrywomen, to wear the trowsers. If *properly* done, we certainly can not object. For some time past indications of an invasion, by the ladies, of men's peculiar domain in dress, incited by the strong-minded Miss Webers of the day, have been tangible, but the frowns of Fashion have hitherto kept the revolutionists quiet, and ladies' dresses have every month been increasing in longitude, until train-bearers are becoming necessary. It is conceded by all that the dresses of prevailing immoderate length, sweeping the ground at every step, are among the silliest foibles of Fashion; expensive, inconvenient, and untidy. Recently, in several places, practical reformers, as bold as Joan d'Arc, have discarded the trailing skirts, and adopted the far more convenient, equally chaste, and more elegant dresses of Oriental women. Some ridicule them; others sneer contemptuously or laugh incredulously, and others commend them for their taste and courage. We are disposed to be placed in the latter category; and to show our good will, we present, above, a sketch of ORIENTAL COSTUME, as a model for our fair reformers. What can be more elegant and graceful, particularly for young ladies? The style is based upon good taste, and, if the ladies are in earnest, it must prevail. A crusty cynic at our elbow who never believed in progress in any thing, thinks so too; and has just whispered in our ear of woman, that

"If she will, she will, you may depend on't,
And if she won't, she won't—so there's an end on't."

14

WOMAN'S EMANCIPATION.

(BEING A LETTER ADDRESSED TO MR. PUNCH, WITH A DRAWING, BY A STRONG-MINDED AMERICAN WOMAN.)

IT is quite easy to realize the considerable difficulty that the natives of this old country are like to have in estimating the rapid progress of ideas on all subjects among us, the Anglo-Saxons of the Western World. Mind travels with us on a rail-car, or a high-pressure river-boat. The snags and sawyers of prejudice, which render so dangerous the navigation of Time's almighty river, whose water-power has toppled over these giant-growths of the world, without being able to detach them from the congenial mud from which they draw their nutriment, are dashed aside or run down in the headlong career of the United States mind.

We laugh to scorn the dangers of popular effervescence. Our almighty-browed and cavernous-eyed statesmen sit, heroically, on the safety-valve, and the mighty ark of our vast Empire of the West moves on at a pressure on the square inch which would rend into shivers the rotten boiler-plates of your outworn states of the Old World.

To use a phrase which the refined manners of our ladies have banished from the drawing-room, and the saloon of the boarding-house, *we* go ahead. And our progress is the progress of all—not of high and low, for we have abolished the odious distinction—but of man, woman, and child, each in his or her several sphere.

Our babies are preternaturally sharp, and highly independent from the cradle. The high-souled American boy will not submit to be whipped at school. That punishment is confined to the lower animals.

But it is among *our* sex—among women (for I am a woman, and my name is THEODOSIA EUDOXIA BANG, of Boston, U.S., Principal of the Homeopathic and Collegiate Thomsonian Institute for developing the female mind in that intellectual city) that the stranger may realize, in the most convincing manner, the progressional influences of the democratic institutions it is our privilege to live under.

An American female—for I do not like the term Lady, which suggests the outworn distinctions of feudalism—can travel alone from one end of the States to the other; from the majestic waters of Niagara to the mystic banks of the Yellowstone, or the rolling prairies of Texas. The American female delivers lectures, edits newspapers, and similar organs of opinion, which exert so mighty a leverage on the national mind of our great people, is privileged

to become a martyr to her principles, and to utter her soul from the platform, by the side of the gifted POE or the immortal PEABODY. All this in these old countries is the peculiar privilege of man, as opposed to woman. The female is consigned to the slavish duties of the house. In America the degrading cares of the household are comparatively unknown to our sex. The American wife resides in a boarding-house, and, consigning the petty cares of daily life to the helps of the establishment, enjoys leisure for higher pursuits, and can follow her vast aspirations upward, or in any other direction.

We are emancipating ourselves, among other badges of the slavery of feudalism, from the inconvenient dress of the European female. With man's functions, we have asserted our right to his garb, and especially to that part of it which invests the lower extremities. With this great symbol, we have adopted others—the hat, the cigar, the paletot or round jacket. And it is generally calculated that the dress of the Emancipated American female is quite pretty—as becoming in all points as it is manly and independent. I inclose a drawing made by my gifted fellow-citizen, INCREASEN TARDOX, of Boston, U.S., for the *Free Woman's Banner*, a periodical under my conduct, aided by several gifted women of acknowledged progressive opinions.

I appeal to my sisters of the Old World, with confidence, for their sympathy and their countenance in the struggle in which *we* are engaged, and which will soon be found among them also. For I feel that I have a mission across the broad Atlantic, and the steamers are now running at reduced fares. I hope to rear the standard of Female Emancipation on the roof of the Crystal Palace, in London Hyde Park. Empty wit may sneer at its form, which is bifurcate. And why not? MOHAMMED warred under the Petticoat of his wife KADIGA. The American female Emancipist marches on her holy war under the distinguishing garment of her husband. In the compartment devoted to the United States in your Exposition, my sisters of the old country may see this banner by the side of a uniform of female freedom—such as my drawing represents—the garb of martyrdom for a month; the trappings of triumph for all ages of the future!

THEODOSIA E. BANG, M.A.,
M.C.P., ♦.Δ.K., K.L.M., &c., &c. (of Boston. U.S.)

In 1851 *The Lily*, heretofore a small local paper, was hurtled into national fame when it espoused the new reform dress for women. Woman's rights advocates believed that if women were to be completely emancipated they should throw off the shackles of the currently fashionable mode of dress—the tightly laced, unhealthy corsets; the heavy, burdensome layers of petticoats; and the long skirts which swept up the dirt of the unpaved streets. They advocated a short dress about twelve inches from the shoe top, a loose waist which did not require tightly laced corsets, and pants of the same material as the dress to cover the exposed portions of the legs. (This was an age when even piano legs were draped!) Such a costume, usually called the Turkish dress, had been worn as early as the 1820's in Robert Owen's utopian colony at New Harmony, Indiana, and it was currently in favor at the water cures, or health resorts, which dotted New York State. In the late winter of 1851 Mrs. Stanton shocked the citizens of Seneca Falls by appearing on the village streets in the short dress. To declare her complete emancipation from the demands of fashion, she also cut her hair.

Mrs. Bloomer defended the reform garb in the columns of her paper and within a few weeks she announced that she too was wearing it. (She did not go so far as to cut her hair.) This dress which had already become a national sensation was immediately dubbed the "Bloomer" by the press both in the United States and England, where the costume was also the rage.[2] Crowds flocked to Bloomer balls where the Bloomer polka and the Bloomer quadrille were danced; Bloomer theatricals were popular, and Bloomer-clad lecturers drew overflow audiences.

"Mrs. Bloomer, editor of *The Lily* published at Seneca Falls, New York, has adopted the 'short dress and trowsers' [*sic*]," reported the *Dubuque Tribune* on April 25, 1851, "and says in her paper of this month that 'Those who think we look queer would do well to look back a few years at the time they wore 10 or 15 pounds of petticoat and bustle around the body, and balloons on their arms, then imagine which cut the queerest figure, they or we. We do not say we shall wear this dress and no other, but we shall wear it for a common dress; and we hope it may become so fashionable that we may wear it at all times and in all places without being thought singular.' "

On June 25 the *Dubuque Tribune* announced that the new cos-

---

2. Hannah Tracy Cutler, a woman's rights advocate from Ohio who lectured on woman suffrage in Iowa in 1870, was in London in the summer of 1851 attending a peace conference. Dressed in Bloomer garb she delivered a series of thirteen lectures on woman's rights at Soho Theater.

tume was spreading "like prairie fire." In July the *Dubuque Herald* reported (in a story reprinted in the *Burlington Telegraph* of July 19) that some of the most respectable ladies in town were wearing the new fashion. Several of them had attended a tea party given by Mrs. J. L. Langworthy, Dubuque society leader who had been wearing the reform dress for some time.

In Muscatine, according to the *Muscatine Democrat* of July 3, the new costume was to make its debut at a Fourth of July supper and dance. A large crowd was expected. On July 11 the *Ottumwa Courier* commented that Ottumwa was "waiting with anxious solicitude the appearance in public of the first young lady who would have the moral courage to put on the new apparel." The *Burlington Telegraph* of July 26 reported that some 8 or 10 of the ladies of Farmington, a community on the lower Des Moines River, had made their appearance in the new costume. A Bloomer picnic was planned for the following week. "Now that the new style has the stamp of approval in that community," the *Telegraph* predicted that it would probably "spread like wild fire at least as far up as the forks," location of the village of Fort Des Moines.

As late as October 16, however, the new style had not reached the forks. According to C. Ben Darwin, editor of the *Fort Des Moines Journal* (Darwin's wife Mary was a staunch woman's rights advocate), "the people of this section are eminently practical and while they deplore the pernicious effects of the present female costume, they fail to see any valuable improvement in the Bloomer." By this date, the Bloomer fad had passed its peak and public ridicule was so great (wags even decked out prostitutes in the Bloomer) that most of the women who had tried the reform garb were returning to conventional dress. "I believe I am the only woman in this place who has had the courage to adopt the reformed costume," wrote a Mrs. R. C. of Farmington to the *Water-Cure Journal* in January 1853. "There are some who can see its superiority," this correspondent said, "but yet they dare not adopt it for fear of ridicule."

The Bloomer dress, however, continued to be worn by farm women and women traveling west in wagon trains. For example, a Marshall County history reports that in 1856 "Mrs. Myers, of Washington Township, hired help to do the housework, and with a Bloomer dress made of bedticking, hauled wood, drove a reaper, and was one of the best managers in the county." A letter from Kansas Territory published in the *Dubuque Times,* May 29, 1860, says, "I observe too, that most of the ladies en route for Pikes Peak are dressed in the Bloomer; and this is dictated by wisdom, for it would be difficult, in

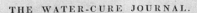

No. 1. THE AMERICAN COSTUME.   No. 2. THE FRENCH COSTUME.

The American and French Fashions Contrasted.

We herewith present our readers with engraved views of the prevailing European and [proposed] American Fashions.

No. 1 represents Mrs. AMELIA BLOOMER, of Seneca Falls, N. Y. It was engraved from a Daguerreotype for the *Cayuga Chief*, an excellent newspaper published in Auburn, N. Y., and kindly loaned to us by Mr. THURLOW W. BROWN, the gentlemanly proprietor.

No. 2 was copied by our own Engraver, from the *Illustrated London News*, and is an *exact* copy of the original, without variation; and is a perfect representation of the FRENCH FASHIONS, as worn in July last. We submit the two styles side by side, for the consideration of AMERICAN WOMEN.

We also append, as an accompaniment, the anatomical views of a *natural* waist and an *artificial* or tight-laced waist, corresponding with Numbers 1 and 2 of the larger figures.

To us these views convey an unanswerable argument, and will need no further comment.

In future numbers we shall present other styles of the AMERICAN COSTUME, with patterns and appropriate descriptions accompanying them.

We should add in this connection, that the friends of Mrs. Bloomer do not regard the above as a *good* likeness of that lady; but as it conveys a *general* idea of the new costume, we consider it well adapted to our present purpose.

NO. 3.—A NATURAL WAIST.

NO. 4.—A TIGHT-LACED WAIST.

In its November 1851 issue, the Water-Cure Journal, *a popular health periodical, contrasts Amelia Bloomer in Bloomer dress with a figure wearing the latest French style. In the lower part of the page, anatomical diagrams illustrate the merits of the natural waist of the reform dress over that of the tightly laced French costume. (Courtesy of the National Library of Medicine, Bethesda, Maryland)* this windswept country, to teach crinoline of even moderate diameter and circumference to observe the rules of good behavior."

Meanwhile, Mrs. Bloomer's notoriety made her a sensation on the lecture platform. In 1853 she was part of a team of Bloomer-clad women, including Miss Anthony, who toured New York State in behalf of temperance. In New York City these women drew a crowd of over 3,000 people, who paid twenty-five cents each to hear them. Mrs. Stanton, Miss Anthony, and Lucy Stone each wore the Bloomer costume for a year or two. Mrs. Bloomer, loath to give up this badge of her fame, continued to wear it for five or six years. *The Lily's* subscription list, meanwhile, jumped from a few hundred into the thousands, and this small paper came to serve as a source of inspiration for woman's rights advocates throughout the country.

Dexter and Amelia Bloomer left Seneca Falls in December 1853, and after a sojourn of a year in Ohio they moved on to Council Bluffs, Iowa, a town of about 2,000 located on the Missouri River in the sparsely settled western section of the state.[3] Since Mrs. Bloomer could not take *The Lily* with her to Iowa, she sold it to a Mrs. Birdsall of Indiana, who continued to publish it through 1855.

When the Bloomers arrived in Council Bluffs on April 15, 1855, after a weary stagecoach journey from St. Joseph, Missouri,[4] curious townspeople noted that Mrs. Bloomer was attired in the reform dress which had gained her worldwide notoriety. Although Mrs. Bloomer knew that Council Bluffs had the reputation for being a lawless community and the wildest town in the West, she was appalled to find conditions even worse than she had expected. Horse races, gambling, and the liquor trade flourished; drunken brawls were a frequent occurrence; and prostitutes comprised a good proportion of the female population. Mrs. Bloomer soon came to the conclusion, she informed *The Lily,* that "the Spirit of Reform" did not dwell in her new hometown.

Undaunted, Mrs. Bloomer began a single-handed but losing moral-reform and woman's rights campaign. In addition to frequent letters advancing various reforms to the *Council Bluffs Chronotype,* she delivered three lectures within a few months after her arrival—on

3. In 1855 Iowa had a population of about 600,000, most of whom lived in the eastern part.

4. Mr. and Mrs. Bloomer went as far as St. Louis by train. They took a Missouri River boat from St. Louis to St. Joseph, Missouri, and completed the journey to Council Bluffs by stagecoach. Although construction had begun on the Rock Island Railroad running west from Davenport, Iowa, the tracks had not yet reached Iowa City. There was no railroad into Council Bluffs until after the Civil War.

temperance, education for women, and woman's right to the elective franchise. She also lectured to the Nebraska territorial legislature which met in the newly founded village of Omaha across the river from Council Bluffs. Here the wags in the House passed a woman-suffrage bill, and the session broke up in near riot when members of the Senate presented General Larimer, the bill's sponsor, with a pair of "unmentionables." Invitations to speak also came to Mrs. Bloomer from as far away as Winterset, Iowa, but because of the difficulties of travel and her lack of physical vitality[5] she confined her efforts to the Council Bluffs area. However, as soon as local curiosity about Mrs. Bloomer was satisfied, Council Bluffs residents lost interest both in her and in her reforms.

Although Mrs. Bloomer was not the first woman to lecture in behalf of her sex in Iowa—Frances Dana Gage, a popular writer and Ohio woman's rights pioneer, had spent three weeks lecturing in the southeast section of the state in the spring of 1854—she was the first woman residing there to speak out on the subject. She also seems to have been the only woman in Iowa to publicly espouse woman's rights in the years before the Civil War, despite the fact that there were a number of other woman's rights advocates residing in the state. With the possible exception of those living in Quaker communities, these women hardly dared admit, even in private, their sympathy with this unpopular and much-ridiculed cause.

5. All her life Mrs. Bloomer suffered from periodic sick headaches and an uniden-tified stomach ailment, possibly partially neurotic.

❧❧

LETTER FOR HOME
This 1863 Winslow Homer lithograph depicts a volunteer hospital aide writing a letter for a Civil War soldier. Hundreds of women served as relief workers and nurses; some, disguised as men, even served in the fighting ranks.

2

1861-1865

❧

THE OUTBREAK of civil war in April 1861 brought the woman's rights movement to an abrupt halt. The annual woman's rights convention scheduled for May was canceled, and there was not another such meeting until 1866.

CIVIL WAR OPENS NEW FIELDS
OF EMPLOYMENT FOR WOMEN

MEANWHILE, despite the hiatus in woman's rights agitation, the Civil War years brought a profound change in the role of women in American society by offering them new opportunities for employment and public service. They served as nurses both on the battlefield and in army hospitals; they worked in factories manufacturing clothing and ammunition for the army; and they were employed in government offices to replace men who had gone to war.

When nineteen-year-old Emily Calkins Stebbins of New Hampton was appointed deputy recorder and treasurer of Chickasaw County in September 1862 to replace H. C. Baldwin who had enlisted with the 38th Iowa Infantry, she became the first woman in Iowa to work in a county courthouse. Miss Stebbins kept the job until 1864 when a man was selected by the voters to fill her position. Miss Stebbins received nationwide publicity in 1866 when Governor Stone appointed her a notary public, thus making her the first woman notary in the United States. Other Iowa women who worked in government offices during the war were Mary Case, who was appointed a deputy clerk of Chickasaw County in 1864; Augusta Mathews (later Mrs. A. E. Foote), who this same year was appointed by Governor Stone (her brother-in-law) to serve as his military secretary; and Linda M. Ramsey (later Mrs. Hartzell), who was employed as a clerk in the office of Adjutant-General Baker.

During the war, newspapers of the country, which had previously maintained that woman's place was in the home, gave unsparing praise to the women working in the fields, factories, and offices of the north. "Any woman who neglects all other duties, and devotes herself to the avocations of warlike times is a heroine forthwith. No eulogy is too glowing, no words of praise are too extravagant to couple with her name," wrote Lizzie Bunnell (later Lizzie Bunnell Read) in the August 1, 1861, issue of the *Mayflower,* a woman's rights paper which she published in Peru, Indiana. "The fact is," Miss Bunnell commented, "men have rather more than got their hands full with this war, and they welcome woman as a powerful and generous ally—the contract being, on our part, that we are to do any work they give us; and on their part, that when they are done with us, they will turn us over to our former occupations and abuse us just as handsomely as ever. We cannot suppose they will consent to wage perpetual war, at the cost of a million dollars daily, just for the purpose of keeping open a proper 'sphere' for women." Miss Bunnell admonished women not to throw away the victory they were now gaining over ancient prejudices. "Men are admitting that there *is* a sphere for woman outside of the domestic circle, and in a path which she had heretofore been forbidden to tread. Let it also be demonstrated that women are capable of *choosing* a path, as well as of accepting that opened to them by the exigencies of the times." Lizzie Bunnell, who married Dr. S. G. A. Read in 1864, moved to Iowa the following year. Here for many years she was an active worker in the woman-suffrage movement.

NORTHWEST SANITARY COMMISSION

As SOON AS the first men marched off to battle, hundreds of women organized soldiers' aid societies throughout the north. At first these societies sent their contributions directly to local regiments; but as the war progressed, they sent them to sanitary commissions—precursors of

Lizzie Bunnell Read, identified as "Pres. Iowa Woman Suffrage Soc'ty., Algona, Kossuth Co." is the only woman pictured in the 1875 Andreas' Illustrated Historical Atlas of Iowa.

THE MAYFLOWER.

DEVOTED TO THE INTERESTS OF WOMAN.

"TEMPERANCE, PURITY, AND HAPPY HOMES."

Volume 2.　　　　　PERU, INDIANA, MARCH 1, 1862.　　　　　Number 5.

THE MAYFLOWER,

A SEMI-MONTHLY QUARTO,

Devoted to Literature and the Elevation of
WOMAN.

PUBLISHED AT PERU, IND., BY

MISS LIZZIE BUNNELL,

EDITOR AND PROPRIETOR.

MARY F. THOMAS, 'M. D.

OF RICHMOND, IND., ASSOCIATE EDITOR.

TERMS—Fifty Cents a Year in advance, or
Eleven copies for Five Dollars.
☞Office at Home Cottage, Peru.
Local subscriptions may be left at the Republican
Office in Peru, where specimen copies may always be
seen.
All communications and remittances should be
addressed to Miss Lizzie Bunnell, Peru, Miami coun-
ty, Indiana.

For the Mayflower.

Is Labor Dishonorable?

That the above question is frequently
answered in the affirmative, either in actions or words, by a large portion of the
American people, is a deplorable fact.—
Such conclusions appear very inconsider-
ate to the reasoning mind, and unprofita-
ble, especially when remembering that
labor is the very foundation of all we have
—that without it we would have nothing.
It is that by which we have all the com-
forts and possessions of life. Nay, even
life itself. And it certainly is one of the
best means of the perfect development of
the entire man or woman. Show me one
on whose cheek sits the glow of health,
and I will show you a worker. Show me
one who enjoys his food, and whose slum-
bers are undisturbed through the night,
who rises early and snuffs the healthful
aromas which float on the breezes of the
morning, and I will show you an active
body, a worker. Show me one who is the
most contented with his lot, seldom heard
to grumble, and whose whole life is agree-
able to himself and those around him, and
I will show you a *willing* worker. And
for another example of a worker, take the
man of learning and research, who bless-
es every circle that may be honored with
his presence. Show me one whose habits
of life are the reverse of all these, and nine
chances in ten they will be found to be
peevish grumblers, around and with whom
there is little or no contentment, and from
whom issues foul and poisonous miasms,
as from the pools of moral and physical
stagnation.

But what is this hateful, unpopular
something which is denominated labor?—
Is it all kinds of work? No! It is certain
kinds of work, with certain outside con-
siderations. It is particularly that kind
of work which *pays* least. It also depends
in some cases upon the manner in which
the pay is received. For instance, the
miner is respectable in his work, especially if he has a "big lead" which pays well,
though the man himself may be daily covered with mud. So many other *dirty* employments are made quite respectable in
the eyes of the world by the amount of
pay they are supposed to yield, even tho'
fraud and dishonesty may lie but partly
hidden beneath its murky folds. Thus it
seems the amount of pay guages the respectability of an employment, rather
than the amount of good the public may
or may not realize from such business.—
Just as though the same labor was not the
same thing with big or little pay, or no
pay at all.

But the nicest distinction between rep-
utable and disreputable labor, is drawn
among poor but otherwise respectable women who engage in the work of general
housekeeping. For instance, a lady may
live in a family as a sister, a sister-in-law
or an adopted daughter, and daily perform all the drudgery that any hired person would be expected to do; but still in
the midst of it all she is respectable, so
long as she does not receive wages per
day, week, or month. But the moment
it is known that she receives pay as wages
for services rendered, her respectability
vanishes, she is then a servant. Here the
scale seems to turn upon the manner in
which the pay is received, or the difference between being provided for as one of
the family, and the simple circumstance
of receiving by agreement a stipulated a-
mount to be used as the individual choos-
es. In one case the laborer and the labor
is respectable, and in the other case the
laborer and the same labor is disreputable. As though the former laborer did
not receive pay as literally as the latter.
Is not a living pay? and is not pay a living? Where then is the difference, that
reputation should depend upon it? It is
true ladies may receive "salaries" in stipulated amounts for services rendered in
certain other of the avocations of life, and
still be respected; but not in house-keep-
ing—not in providing those home com-
forts so highly prized and sought after in

civilized life. Strange it is how hair-split-
ting nice these things are adjusted!
Reader, is this your manner of thinking
and judging? Is it right? Is there profit
in it? Do you claim to be consistent—just
—Christian, perhaps? Know ye not that
all sins committed against ourselves or
neighbors bring upon us a proportionate
amount of punishment as a natural result
in the way of cause and effect?

Let us now candidly look at the effect
of the state of things above referred to,
and see if the oppressed individuals are
the only ones who suffer. Let us enter a
room in which is gathered a company of
mistresses and matrons, and notice if more
than half their conversation is not made
up of complaints of unruly and unman-
ageable "servants."

"Oh," says one, "they literally worry
my life out of me. I cannot have a hired
person about my house who is worth a
cent. It really seems to me there are none
to be had any more. Oh, dear! sometimes
I hardly know what we are to do. It is
enough to drive a body crazy," etc.

Now, what's the matter? Why, nothing is plainer. The good woman and her
associates are reaping of exactly what
they have sown. With but few exceptions
they have united in frowning down all
hired house-help as disreputable, until
they have literally drove out of the arena
of service the very kind of persons who
would be most likely to do good service.
They have frowned out of circulation the
gold coin, and now complain of poor cur-
rency. And how little they think the
troubles they so bitterly complain of are
but the rebound of blows which have by
themselves been inflicted on the heads of
others—nothing but a natural effect of
their own actions.

It is well known by all that our good
ladies never intended to bring on themselves these troubles, but still they have
done it, and the only way to get out of
this dilemma is to retrace their steps, or
in other words, undo what has been done
as far as possible, then "go and sin no
more."

But let us examine this thing a little:
When a lady of good repute is from stern
necessity compelled to become a 'servant'
for a livelihood under the present state of
things they lower in their own estimation.
Their spirits are crushed within them by
the knowledge of a common stigma which
is cast upon them, and they have but lit-

The Mayflower *was a woman's rights paper published in Indiana during the Civil War by Lizzie Bunnell Read. This front-page article was written by S. Y. Bradstreet of Dubuque, whose wife was a leader in organizing the Monticello (Iowa) Woman Suffrage Association in 1869.*

the Red Cross—which acted as distribution agencies. The largest such agency in the Midwest was the Northwest Sanitary Commission in Chicago, headed by Jane Hoge and Mary A. Livermore. Mrs. Livermore, a hard-working organizer and dynamic speaker, traveled extensively in Iowa and other midwestern states, where she encouraged women to support the work of her Commission. She was the leader in organizing a tremendous sanitary fair in Chicago in October 1863, which cleared over $80,000. Here Anna Dickinson, brilliant young lecturer from Philadelphia, made her first Midwest appearance. Many Iowans visited the fair and hundreds more contributed to its success with gifts of food and handiwork. Dubuque women made a unique contribution by cooking hundreds of prairie chickens, wild ducks, and turkeys, which they shipped while still warm via railway express to the fair dining hall. (The railroad at that time extended as far as Dunleith, across the river from Dubuque.) When Mrs. Livermore espoused the cause of woman suffrage in 1869, she gave much-needed prestige to the movement because of her prominence as a war-relief worker.

ANNIE WITTENMYER

Iowa's wartime heroine was Annie Wittenmyer of Keokuk, a well-to-do young widow who had lost three children in infancy; one child survived—a son, Charles Albert. Mrs. Wittenmyer, born in Ohio in 1827, had lived in Iowa since 1850. She was prematurely gray but her physical vitality, clear complexion, and sparkling blue eyes gave her a youthful appearance. Since Keokuk was the point of embarkation for most Iowa troops who went south, Annie Wittenmyer was in a strategic position to observe their needs. During the spring and summer of 1861 she wrote letters to women throughout the state encouraging them to organize soldiers' aid societies. Soon many of these groups were sending supplies to her for distribution and sending money to purchase necessities for the troops. At first she distributed these supplies herself; later she worked in cooperation with the Western Sanitary Commission in St. Louis. So popular was Annie Wittenmyer that when the Iowa legislature met in special session in the fall of 1862, it approved a bill providing that the governor appoint her as one of two sanitary agents for the state. Thus ensconced by law, it was impossible to remove her except by repealing the statute.

During the battle of Shiloh in April 1862, Mrs. Wittenmyer was stationed on a hospital ship (there were 2,500 casualties among Iowa troops alone), where with a surgeon and two other nurses she worked around the clock helping with the wounded who were brought aboard. She was at Vicksburg during the siege of 1863, caring for the wounded and supervising distribution of supplies to Union hospitals. After the fall of the city on July 4, General Grant assigned her a house to use as headquarters.

By this time, powerful political forces in Iowa, eyeing with envy the large amounts of money and materials which were being entrusted to Mrs. Wittenmyer by the local aid societies, had launched a concerted effort to dislodge her from her position. Leader of the opposition was thirty-nine-year-old Ann E. Harlan of Mount Pleasant, wife of Senator James Harlan. A querulous and neurotic woman, Mrs. Harlan had gone to Tennessee from Washington, D.C., after the disastrous battle of Shiloh in 1862. Using her position as the wife of an important United States Senator, she persuaded General Halleck to send wounded men up the river for care in their home states. She developed a violent dislike for volunteer nurses and other civilians working for the comfort of the soldiers—especially Annie Wittenmyer. Mrs. Harlan spent the summer of 1863 in Iowa, where she visited dozens of communities in a campaign to discredit Mrs. Wittenmyer, accusing her of inefficiency in handling sanitary goods and even outright dishonesty.

LADIES STATE SANITARY CONVENTION

MATTERS REACHED A CLIMAX on November 18 and 19, 1863, when a Ladies State Sanitary Convention met in Des Moines. (Despite the name, a number of men participated.) This meeting, called by leaders of the Harlan faction and chaired by Senator Harlan, had the announced purpose of coordinating the sanitary work of the state. The real purpose was to get rid of Annie Wittenmyer. Almost 200 delegates appointed by local aid societies were in attendance, including Mary Livermore of the Northwest Sanitary Commission in Chicago (allied with the Harlan faction), who was admitted as a voting delegate. Amelia Bloomer, appointed a delegate by the Council Bluffs aid society, decided at the last minute that she was not well enough to make the trip to Des Moines (two days by stagecoach). In a letter written on November 16 to Annie Wittenmyer, Mrs. Bloomer said she regretted that there was so much conflicting feeling among the sanitary workers, where all should be harmony. She earnestly hoped that there would be no action at the Des Moines meeting through which the state would be deprived of Mrs. Wittenmyer's services.

Woman's Right to Serve Her Country

"Few if any of the spectators of the Wittenmyer war now raging at Ingham Hall, have failed to observe the indecent manner in which the lady who is the subject of it has been treated by the Harlan faction," commented a correspondent to the *Des Moines Statesman* in a letter written during the first session of the sanitary convention. This writer went on to say that Mr. Harlan himself had been "the most active in a bold and bare-faced species of log-rolling for the purpose of obtaining an organization unfavorable to Mrs. Wittenmyer." Indignant at these tactics as well as the unfair attacks on the personal integrity of Annie Wittenmyer, forty-two-year-old Mary Darwin of Burlington (former Fort Des Moines resident) took the floor at the end of the first afternoon session and stated, "It seems to be questioned here whether woman has a right to risk her life for her country." In an eloquent extemporaneous speech, which made the audience gasp with her audacious advocacy of woman's rights, Mrs. Darwin continued:

> We believe that every created intelligence has the God-given right to seek to perfect itself, to develop all its faculties and powers in any direction it sees fit, so long as it violates no moral obligations, interferes with none of the rights of others. If a man can leave the peaceful pursuits of the farm or the counting room to engage in fierce strife in the political arena, who shall blame me if I demand a voice in the making of those laws by which I am to be governed? If he can gird on his sword and at the call of his country rush to the deadly combat, who shall forbid that I, actuated by the same love of country and her brave defenders, follow him, pick him up wounded and dying from the gory field, and recall him to life by my assiduous care?
> When our fathers, brothers, husbands and sons are falling like autumn leaves on yon battle fields, pining with disease in

the distant hospitals, and we would send the little delicacy, the loving word that is to cheer and sustain them, and receive back the dying message that is to be our life-long solace in our sore bereavement, are we to be told that a woman's hand, a woman's heart is not a fit channel through which to convey them? Who believes it? What woman, who has any proper sense of her mission, will assent to it? Mother, if you cannot go yourself to your dying boy, would you not deem it a rich boon if some woman's soft hand could wipe the death damps from his brow; some gentle, sympathizing heart, catch his last faint whisper, and transmit it to you with a tenderness and delicacy that robs the painful tidings of half of its woe?

The Great Jehovah himself has given his sanction to women's work. Whenever in the great crises of the world's history he has needed some undaunted, unselfish spirit to lead forward the nation in the path of freedom, woman has been the chosen instrument as witness Joan-of-Arc, Charlotte Corday, and may I not name our own Annie Dickinson? For who, that has listened to the magic of her eloquence does not believe her Freedom's inspired Evangel?

When we heard the question asked of one of these noble women, to whose untiring efforts Iowa doubtless owes the life of many of her brave soldiers, why she herself visited the hospital; why she did not leave all to the surgeons, we blushed that the questioner was not a woman; and we thought as well ask the mother why she does not leave her sick child to the sole care of the physician and the servant girl!

We are glad that Iowa has daughters as well as sons in this war; that there is one, at least, whom neither foes abroad, nor detractors at home can drive from the path of duty; who was early in the field; who found our sick at Sedalia on boards and provided comfortable beds; who was the first to present the cup of nutriment to famishing lips from the fields of Shiloh; who has stopped not for summer's heat, or winter's cold; who has braved all the horrors of the hospital and the battle field; whom neither guerillas by the river, nor shells exploding at her feet could daunt. One, in short, who has vindicated by her conduct the right of woman to live, labor, and suffer in her country's cause.

We love our own chosen Iowa. We honor her brave sons who have been foremost in every conflict. We delight in her noble daughters who have not hesitated to leave their quiet peaceful homes for the harrowing scenes and exhausting cares of the hospital. But there is one name among them all we will ever cherish in our heart of hearts—a name deeply engraved on many a suffering soldier's memory; a name that shall become a household word in many a bereaved dwelling; a name whose laurels shall be green when others now verdant with pale honors shall be forgotten; a name which every true woman delights to honor; a name that shall ever live in the heart of a grateful state—the name of ANNIE WITTENMYER!

"At the close of Mrs. Darwin's remarks the house manifested its approval by long, continual applause," reported the *Des Moines Register,* which printed Mrs. Darwin's speech in full. After the convention adjourned the next evening, the two women were serenaded by Hartung's band accompanied by a large group of admiring friends.

The convention voted to establish an Iowa Sanitary Commission with Judge Dillon of Davenport, president. By a vote of 115 to 55 it refused to approve a motion which instructed the commission to send all donations to the Northwest Sanitary Commission in Chicago. This was considered a significant victory for Annie Wittenmyer. However, opposition to Mrs. Wittenmyer continued so strong that she soon abandoned her work in Iowa to join the United States Christian Commission, an evangelistic sanitary organization with headquarters in Pennsylvania. While working for this organization, she made a unique contribution to the war effort by establishing special diet kitchens in army hospitals to prepare suitable foods for the sick and wounded.

In addition to her work for the soldiers, Annie Wittenmyer was instrumental in organizing a home for Civil War orphans in Iowa, which opened at Davenport in July 1864. In 1874 Mrs. Wittenmyer, who moved to Pennsylvania after the war, was elected first national president of the WCTU, a position which she held until 1879. An adamant antisuffragist, she was succeeded by Frances Willard, an advocate of the ballot for women.

The following advertisement for the Talbot Shoe Store, which ran in the *Des Moines Register* for several days after the 1863 sanitary convention in Des Moines, indicates the general interest in Mrs. Darwin's woman's rights speech:

> That ladies have rights it can no longer be denied. Even the most illiberal are bound to acknowledge it. Among other rights they have the right to meet in convention and organize plans for the relief of soldiers. They have the right to stage it 160 miles [the distance by stagecoach from Burlington to Des Moines] and they have the right to stage it back again. Judging from the talk about town, Messrs. Talbot are right not only on Woman's Rights but they are also right on the subject of Boots and Shoes.

Despite such tongue-in-cheek reactions, Mrs. Darwin's talk set the stage for the postwar woman-suffrage campaign in Iowa, a campaign in which she played an active role, serving as chairman of the executive committee of the Iowa Woman Suffrage Association, organized at Mount Pleasant in June 1870 and also as president of the Burlington Woman Suffrage Society, which she helped organize the following month.

LOYAL WOMEN'S LEAGUE

MISS ANTHONY AND MRS. STANTON, temperamentally unsuited to scraping lint (to dress wounds), sewing regimental flags, or nursing the sick and wounded, made their contribution to the war effort by stirring up public sentiment for antislavery legislation. "We have resolved to try and speak the word that shall rouse the women of the North to deeper interest and livelier enthusiasm in the war and to demand that only *freedom* to all shall be the terms of peace," Miss Anthony wrote to Amelia Bloomer on April 10, 1863. This letter, sent from the American Anti-Slavery office in New York, announced a meeting of loyal northern women at Cooper Institute on May 9 and 10. At this meeting, chaired by Lucy Stone, a Loyal Women's League was organized, with Mrs. Stanton as president and Miss Anthony as secretary. The League, under Miss Anthony's direction, launched a mammoth petition campaign asking Congress for legislation emancipating the slaves. Petitions were sent broadside throughout the North and lecturers were dispatched to arouse interest in the project. Touring Iowa in November and December 1863 as an agent of the Loyal Women's League was Hannah Tracy Cutler, pioneer Ohio woman's rights advocate (then a resident of Illinois) who seven years later was to take an active part in the Iowa woman-suffrage campaign. In the course of two years, the Loyal Women's League sent 400,000 signatures to Congress— 6,000 from Iowa. It was Mrs. Stanton's and Miss Anthony's hope that after the Negro was given his freedom, the abolitionists would join forces with the women in a combined drive to secure the ballot for women and black men.

THE WIFE AND MOTHER AT A PRIMARY,

THE FATHER STAYS AT HOME, ATTENDING TO THE CHILDREN.

An illustration from an antiwoman-suffrage book published by L. P. Brockett in 1870 depicts the evils of women voting. "In the rural areas the corruption and villainy are not so open but in the cities, the primaries which must be placated if a nomination is to be obtained, are nests of unclean birds, festering pit holes of all iniquity. Is it possible to touch pitch and not be defiled?"

3

1866

❧

T HE REPUBLICAN PARTY had already begun to turn its
attention to the problems of Negro suffrage when the
Civil War ended in April 1865. The Thirteenth
Amendment abolishing slavery, which was submitted to
the states in February, became the law of the land in
December. Meanwhile, Radicals (Republicans who
opposed President Andrew Johnson's moderate reconstruction policy) had begun a drive for enfranchisement
of the newly freed slaves, despite the fact that only six
northern states permitted any of their colored residents
to vote.[1] Motives behind the campaign to force Negro
suffrage on the South were a mixture of genuine concern for the welfare of the colored man and a desire to
establish a Negro-based Republican stronghold in the
rebel states. The task of drawing up a constitutional
amendment to accomplish this purpose was entrusted

1. Maine, New Hampshire, Vermont, Massachusetts, Rhode Island,
and New York. New York required that Negroes own property worth
$250 over all encumbrances; Rhode Island, that they own $130 in real
estate; the other four states had literacy tests for all voters.

to a joint Committee on Reconstruction, appointed by the Thirty-ninth Congress, which convened in December 1866.

Not until April was the committee able to find a formula for a Fourteenth Amendment which Congress was willing to approve. This amendment, submitted to the states for ratification in mid-June, was designed to force Negro suffrage on the South by reducing representation in Congress in proportion to the number of *male* citizens denied the right to vote in each state. All persons born or naturalized in the United States were declared to be citizens and entitled to equal protection of the law.

WOMAN SUFFRAGE ENTERS THE POLITICAL ARENA

WOMAN'S RIGHTS LEADERS were alarmed that the word *male* was about to be inserted into the United States Constitution. Heretofore suffrage had been a matter for state regulation, and these women had taken satisfaction in the fact that there was nothing in the federal Constitution to prevent their enfranchisement. Now they were faced with losing even this negative advantage.

For many months women in the vanguard of the woman's rights movement had been watching the course of events with both hope and dismay—hope that women could be enfranchised at the same time as the Negro and dismay that almost no Republican would help them advance their cause. The women were warned not to impede the drive for Negro suffrage with demands for their own enfranchisement. "This is the Negro's hour," they were told. "The Negro once safe, woman comes next," was the catch phrase of the moment.

Elizabeth Cady Stanton, by then residing in New York City, refused to be convinced of the merits of this argument. "Woman's cause is in deep water," she wrote in August 1865 to Susan B. Anthony, who was currently in Kansas. "Come back and help," Mrs. Stanton pleaded. "I seem to stand alone." Alarmed by events in the East, Miss Anthony returned to New York in October and together the two women launched the woman-suffrage campaign.

The opening gun was fired by Mrs. Stanton in a letter dated December 26, 1865, and published in the *Anti-Slavery Standard*. "The representative women of the nation have done their uttermost for the last thirty years to secure freedom for the Negro, and so long as he was lowest in the scale of being we were willing to press *his* claims," Mrs. Stanton told the women of America, "but now as the celestial gate to civil rights is slowly moving on its hinges, it becomes a serious question whether we had better stand aside and see 'Sambo' walk into the Kingdom first."

"Are we sure that the Negro, once entrenched in all his inalienable rights may not be an added power to hold us at bay?" Mrs. Stanton asked. "Have not 'black male citizens' been heard to say they doubted the wisdom of extending the right of suffrage to women? Why should the African prove more just and generous than his Saxon compeers?"

Women were not demanding anything unreasonable, Mrs. Stanton said. "The same logic and justice that secures suffrage to one class gives it to all." She urged women to avail themselves of the present opportunity to secure their rights and, if unsuccessful, to "begin with renewed earnestness to educate the people into the idea of universal suffrage."

During the fall Mrs. Stanton and Miss Anthony had prepared petitions addressed to Congress asking that no person be disenfranchised because of either race or sex. They were unable, however, to raise funds to pay for circulation, since none of their Republican friends, including Mrs. Stanton's husband, wanted to burden the drive for Negro suffrage with the odium of woman's demand for the ballot. Lacking any other benefactor, Mrs. Stanton and Miss Anthony accepted the offer of help from James Brooks of New York, the Democratic leader in Congress. Brooks, as head of a party opposed to the extension of civil rights to Negroes, was pleased to embarrass his Republican opponents by mailing out under his frank thousands of these woman-suffrage petitions broadside over the North.

Further difficulty for the women arose when the Republicans in Congress failed to present the signed petitions which were sent them. Mrs. Stanton and Miss Anthony once more turned to Brooks for help. Sending him a copy of their own petition (signed by just eleven women), which the chairman of the Committee on Reconstruction had pocketed, they requested him to present it at his earliest convenience. "Although the Democrats are in a minority," Miss Anthony wrote Brooks on January 20, 1866, "they can drive the Republicans to do good works—not merely to hold the rebel States in check until Negro men shall be guaranteed their right to a voice in their government, but to hold the party to a logical consistency that shall give every responsible citizen in every State an equal right to the ballot."

On January 23, while a proposal for a Fourteenth Amendment was being discussed in the House, Brooks rose to ask why no consideration was given to extending the franchise to women, "the fairest, brightest portion of creation." It cannot be said that women do not want to vote, Brooks declared. To prove his point, he had the clerk read both Miss Anthony's letter and the accompanying woman-suffrage petition—the first request for woman suffrage ever presented in Congress. When asked if he were in favor of woman suffrage, Brooks responded that he was if Negroes were permitted to vote, as he "preferred his own color and white women above the Negro."

Although Republican papers ignored this and similar incidents in Congress, Democratic papers over the country reported them with relish. Soon Republicans in Congress decided it was better to present the woman-suffrage petitions themselves rather than have them presented by Democrats, who accompanied their presentations with extravagant, tongue-in-cheek speeches on the merits of woman's demands.

Mrs. Stanton's and Miss Anthony's friends were horrified at their defection to the enemy camp. "The Democrats are hypocrites, not believing in the extension of suffrage to either women or Negroes," they told the two women. "If the Democrats advocate a grand measure of public policy in which they do not believe, they occupy a much higher ground than Republicans who refuse to press the same measure which they claim to believe," Mrs. Stanton retorted. In any event, Mrs. Stanton said, the hypocrisy of the Democrats was serving the woman's cause better than the treachery of the Republicans.

In April 1866 Mrs. Stanton and Miss Anthony sent out a call for a meeting of the American Woman's Rights Association to be held in New York on May 9. A note to Amelia Bloomer (then residing in Council Bluffs, Iowa), which Mrs. Stanton enclosed with a copy of the call, is no doubt typical of dozens of others that went to old associates scattered over the country. "If possible we should be glad to see you at our coming convention," Mrs. Stanton told Mrs. Bloomer. "If not, send a letter [to be read to the meeting]. With so many joint resolutions before Congress to introduce the word 'male' into the Constitution, we cannot be silent in justice to ourselves." Mrs. Bloomer did not attend this meeting, but she carefully saved the letter, which is now on display in the Historical Building in Des Moines.

The May convention in New York was the first meeting of the American Woman's Rights Association since 1860. The delegates—any interested person was welcome—adopted a platform denouncing the Fourteenth Amendment as a "cruel injustice to women" and demanding "equal suffrage for all, regardless of race or sex." They also changed the name of their organization from American Woman's Rights Association to the American Equal Rights Association. "As women we can no longer claim for ourselves what we do not for others," Miss Anthony said in support of this change of name, "nor can we work in two separate movements to get the ballot for the two disfranchised classes, Negroes and women, since to do so must be double cost of time, energy, and money."

Congress submitted the Fourteenth Amendment to the states for ratification on June 16, five weeks after this convention adjourned. The following October Mrs. Stanton created a sensation by announcing herself as an independent candidate for Congress. Although she could not endorse the platform of either party, she said in her announcement, she desired election "to rebuke the dominant [Republican] party for its retrogressive legislation in so amending the constitution as to make invidious distinctions on the grounds of sex." At the election held in November she received 23 votes, the first ever cast for a woman congressional candidate.

WOMAN SUFFRAGE AND POLITICS IN IOWA

SINCE THE REPUBLICANS could not force Negro suffrage on the South without leaving themselves open to charges of gross hypocrisy for not enfranchising the Negroes in their home states, in 1865 the Radicals bent every effort to remove from northern state constitutions all barriers to the Negro's voting. Thus despite the fact that there were only 3,600 Negroes out of a total population of almost 760,000 in Iowa, the question of enfranchising the colored man was the paramount issue in the 1865 election campaign.

At the Republican convention in Des Moines in June the resolutions committee proposed the following equivocal suffrage plank: "That with proper safeguards to the purity of the ballot box, the elective franchise should be based upon loyalty to the Constitution and Union, recognizing and affirming the equality of all men before the law."

After a bitter floor fight Radicals succeeded in amending the plank by adding the following statement: "Therefor, we are in favor of amending the Constitution [of Iowa] by striking out the word 'white' from the article on suffrage." This plank as amended was so unpopular that it split the Republican party in the state and put a conservative Republican, anti-Negro–suffrage ticket in the field.

During the campaign the Radicals soft-pedaled the Negro-suffrage issue, pointing out that any constitutional amendment must be approved by two successive sessions of the General Assembly followed by a vote of the people. "The question is not whether the Negroes are prepared for it . . . but whether we are willing that the people *three years hence* may determine for *themselves* . . . as to giving the right of suffrage," declared C. C. Cole, a justice of the Iowa Supreme Court. Cole said that even if he were opposed to a Negro-suffrage amendment, he would nevertheless vote for its submission.

The Democrats in Iowa joined forces with conservative Republicans in supporting a coalition ticket which vigorously opposed Negro suffrage and the "equality of the white and black races." Democratic papers were outspoken on the Negro question.

"We do not want to hold out inducements for Negroes to settle in Iowa," said the *Council Bluffs Bugle,* a paper bitterly opposed to "Nigger voting."

"The people are in favor of preserving the government founded by white men for the use of white men, and will not consent that an inferior race shall be permitted to control its administration," commented the *Dubuque Herald.*

The Iowa City State Press—edited by John Irish, a future champion of woman suffrage in the Iowa General Assembly—called the Republican platform "an attempt of political fanatics to wipe out a decree of Nature and Nature's God." He called the Negro "low and vile."

Irish who argued the folly of granting ignorant Negroes a privilege denied intelligent white women was one of a number of Democratic editors who suggested that it would be more sensible to extend the franchise to white women rather than to black men. "Humbly begging its lady readers pardon for bringing their names into the controversy," the *Cedar Falls Gazette* noted that "women have high moral and intelligent minds, nearly equal to those of men, and if anybody is accorded the right to vote, other than white men, women should receive it."

The fall elections in Iowa resulted in a substantial victory for the Radicals, so that when the legislature convened in January 1866 they were faced with the task of fashioning a palatable Negro-suffrage amendment. This was not the first time that an effort had been made to enfranchise the Negro in Iowa.

When Iowa became a separate territory in 1838, no one questioned the exclusive right of white males to the elective franchise. Nor was there any question of extending the franchise in 1846 when the first state constitution was adopted. However in 1857, when the present constitution was under consideration, Negro suffrage became a political issue in the state. The 1857 constitutional convention, narrowly controlled by the newly organized Republican party, was faced with the problem of satisfying the demands for Negro suffrage made by a vocal minority of dedicated abolitionists. After much debate a compromise was finally agreed upon, whereby a separate proposition would be submitted at the same time as the constitution on the question of whether or not to delete the word "white" from the section setting forth the qualifications for voting. Although not even its proponents thought this option had a chance of success, they argued that since Negro suffrage was right in principle no harm would be done in submitting it to a vote of the people. To make sure the Negro-suffrage option would not pass, the convention provided that to carry it must receive an affirmative vote equal to a majority of all the votes cast on the adoption of the constitution itself.

Only a few Republican papers in Iowa supported Negro suffrage in 1857. One was the *Anamosa Eureka,* which was also a pioneer in advocating woman suffrage. The rest, despite the goading of the Democrats, kept silent on the issue or took the position that it was a matter for the voters to decide.

On the other hand Democratic papers denounced the proposed constitution as a "Nigger Republican" document and vigorously attacked the option for Negro suffrage. "Had the Republicans proposed to strike the word 'male' instead of 'white' in the right of suffrage," said the *Keosauqua Mirror,* "they would have shown more respect for the female portion of the country, than by the course they have adopted." The *Mirror* accused the Republicans of seeking "to place the Negro upon a level with the white electors of the State, but above the white female population." White women, this paper asserted, were willing to "surrender unto their *white male* protectors certain political rights, but not to the African race."

The 1857 referendum on the new constitution resulted in its adoption by a narrow margin, with 40,316 votes in its favor and 38,856 opposed. The Negro-suffrage option was overwhelmingly defeated, with 8,489 votes in the affirmative and 49,387 in the negative. In other words, of the more than 79,000 men voting in the election, less than 8,500 favored Negro suffrage.

Now, only nine years later the Republicans of Iowa were seriously seeking to enfranchise the Negro. In contrast to 1857, there was also in 1866 a serious demand on the part of a small number of Republicans for the enfranchisement of women. While Republican leaders could ignore the tongue-in-cheek demands for woman suffrage made by the Democrats, it was more difficult to ignore the demands for woman suffrage which came from within their own ranks. Because almost all the women asking for the right to vote were the wives, daughters, or sisters of loyal Republicans, their request required some kind of an answer.

"The time has not yet come for a thorough ventilation of the subject," declared the *Dubuque Times* on January 25 in reporting the circulation of woman-suffrage petitions in Kansas. (If similar petitions were circulating in Iowa, the *Times* did not mention them.) "What political rights shall be accorded to loyal black men and disloyal white is just now pressing for settlement," the *Times* asserted. Although the two questions seemed to be related, they were really distinct issues "not to be decided upon the same principles," this paper said. The *Times* conceded that it was not strange or even ill-timed to petition for woman suffrage, "but it is idle to expect any immediate action upon the matter either in state or nation." An immense amount of work needed to be done, the *Times* asserted, before public sentiment would be prepared to take action upon a subject of such magnitude about which there was so much real ignorance.

Despite the desire of Republican leaders to avoid the woman-suffrage issue, they were not completely successful in keeping it off the floor in the Eleventh General Assembly. Just ten days before the *Times* statement appeared, a bill containing a woman-suffrage provision had been presented in the Senate by James Crookham of Oskaloosa, a pioneer Mahaska County lawyer who had introduced a bill in the previous General Assembly to enfranchise all soldiers, black and white.[2] The current bill, authored by Crookham, proposed to enfranchise the following classes of persons:

1. All white female citizens of 21.
2. All soldiers honorably discharged who are under the age of 21.
3. All male citizens of foreign birth, 21 years of age, who volunteered in the service and have been honorably discharged.
4. All male citizens of African descent, 21 years old, provided they have served in the forces of the United States and have been honorably discharged.
5. All male citizens of the age of 21, of African descent, who are worth $250 of taxable property and have paid the taxes on the same and are of good moral character and can read and write.

2. Stiles in his *Recollections and Sketches of Early Lawyers and Public Men of Iowa* says of Crookham: "I served with him as a fellow member of the State Senate in 1866. He was par excellence the eccentric member. He was plain and homely in dress and appearance, and delighted to represent the common people. . . . He was not felicitous in speech, was very absent-minded, and perpetually perpetrating bulls at which, however, he never laughed himself, because he apparently never noticed them."

Crookham and others in the Iowa legislature believed it was unnecessary to amend the constitution to enlarge the franchise. He reasoned as follows: The Iowa constitution granted the right of suffrage to "white, male citizens of the United States." The only persons specifically denied the right to vote by the Iowa constitution were idiots, insane persons, and persons convicted of infamous crimes. Inasmuch as Negroes, women, war veterans, noncitizens, or other classes affected by his bill were not specifically excluded by the constitution from the privilege of voting, the legislature was not barred from conferring the elective franchise upon them by statute.

Crookham's bill must have caused a great stir in the legislature; but since legislative debates were not published and the subject of woman suffrage was generally ignored by the Republican press, one can only guess at its impact. The *Des Moines Register* tersely commented in its legislative summary that the bill "created quite a sensation." In a separate story the *Register* stated that Crookham supported the suffrage plank in the Republican platform but that he preferred to enfranchise the Negro by statute rather than by the slow process of constitutional amendment. The *Register* completely ignored the fact that Crookham's bill also called for woman suffrage. The *Burlington Hawkeye,* edited by staunch woman's rights advocate Charles Beardsley, stood almost alone among the Republican papers in reporting the Crookham bill in full. The *Hawkeye* took the position that Negro suffrage should be "a straight issue," separate from all other suffrage questions.

Democratic papers had a good time twitting the Republicans about the Crookham bill. "It may be accepted as indubitable evidence of the spirit of progress which characterizes the present General Assembly," said the *Des Moines Statesman.* "What a glorious time we will have when boys and women, black and white, get to fighting over the ballot and carousing around saloons." The *Dubuque Herald,* correctly assuming that woman suffrage would not receive serious consideration by the legislature, remarked that "the free men of Iowa will have the satisfaction of knowing that suffrage will be granted to 'skillet headed samboes' while it is withheld from their intelligent, enlightened, and competent 'better halves'."

Sending a copy of his bill and a long letter of explanation to the *Oskaloosa Herald,* Crookham defended his woman-suffrage proposal at some length. "Do you want all grogshops, gambling houses, and corrupt houses of ill-fame banished from the State?" he asked. "If so, let women vote. They will elect men who will execute the laws, and legislators who will enact laws. They will knock lager beer out of the

Republican platform and bring whiskey out of the Democratic platform. It will cause them to read more and make them more learned
and intelligent and it will make our election days as sober and quiet
as a school meeting or a church meeting on a week day. The army has
destroyed slavery and the day the people let the women vote, King
Whiskey and all his auxiliaries of vice will be driven like chaff before
the wind, from society." If woman suffrage were not a success, Crookham said, the legislature could always repeal the bill.

Crookham's bill, which died in committee, was the first proposal
for woman suffrage to be introduced in the Iowa legislature. Legislative leaders took pains to see that it was the last for the duration of the
Eleventh General Assembly.

Although no further bills for woman suffrage were introduced, a
resolution asking that the Committee on Constitutional Amendments
"be instructed to inquire into the expediency of striking the word
'male' where it occurs in the constitution in relation to the franchise"
was introduced in the House by George M. Maxwell, a Republican
from Story County. According to the *Des Moines Register* he assured
the House that he was in earnest in this matter and hoped the subject
would receive careful consideration. Maxwell's resolution was referred to the Committee on Constitutional Amendments, where it
seems to have died a quiet death.

Records of the Eleventh General Assembly reveal that one petition for woman suffrage was presented during the session by Benjamin
Palmer, a member of the House from Clinton County. This petition
was signed by Mrs. E. W. Weston and twenty-six other women living
in the vicinity of Low Moor. No doubt Palmer's wife, an ardent
woman-suffrage advocate, was one of the signers.

Woman suffrage, of course, was only a side issue in the 1866
legislature. The main interest centered on the enfranchisement of the
Iowa Negro. Republican leaders were extremely dubious about the
ultimate success of this measure. During the fall Negro-suffrage referendums had failed in Connecticut, Wisconsin, and Minnesota; and
in Colorado a constitution had been adopted which excluded the
colored man from the right of the franchise. Radicals in Iowa, therefore, were looking for ways to make the Negro-suffrage amendment
palatable to the voters.

Many Negro-suffrage advocates in the legislature wanted to limit
voting rights to those men—black or white—who could read and write
English. The *Dubuque Times* and the *Des Moines Register,* the leading Republican papers in the state, supported this position. The
Register pointed out that in New England the system of suffrage based

on ability to read had worked well. However, an educational qualification for the right of franchise was not likely to be popular, especially with voters who might be disqualified by such a provision; and it was therefore soon discarded.

The drive to enfranchise the Negro without restriction was led by C. Ben Darwin of Burlington, graduate of Oberlin College and the Radical leader in the House. Darwin, a brilliant and tempestuous lawyer, whose wife Mary had defended Annie Wittenmyer at the 1863 Sanitary Convention, argued that the ballot should belong to "every mature, sane man, not be restricted by poverty or ignorance, or color, but based on *manhood.*"

On January 30 Darwin introduced a joint resolution to amend the constitution by deleting the word "white" from the qualifications for voting and for service in the Iowa militia. When the Committee on Constitutional Amendments reported this resolution favorably on March 2, it qualified its endorsement by stating that since a respectable minority of the electors of the state seemed to desire a change in the constitution, "it would be magnanimous as well as eminently proper and right that the majority should grant them the privilege of expressing their views on the subject."

The Negro-suffrage amendment was approved by both houses of the General Assembly in late March. The five Democrats in the Senate and the ten in the House were united in voting against the measure.

The initiation of this Negro-suffrage amendment by the 1866 General Assembly was a clear indication to woman's rights advocates that they would have to wait until this measure had completed its course through another session of the legislature and was submitted in a popular referendum before their claims to the ballot would be seriously considered. Nonetheless, they did not cease to agitate for their cause.

When the state Republican convention in June 1866 adopted a platform which declared that "the first and highest duty of our government is to secure to all citizens, regardless of race, religion or color, equality before the law, . . . and to all who have proved their loyalty by their acts, an equal voice in making it," woman's rights advocates saw a loophole for woman suffrage.

"Now as the distinction of sex is not mentioned, we presume it was not intended," said "Kate" in a letter to the *Register*. "If women are citizens, and if they, by their acts of devotion to the cause of the Union, proved their loyalty, then according to the Republican platform, they should have a right to an equal voice in making the laws," she argued. "Women, as a general thing," Kate pointed out, "would be on the side of moral and political reform." To prove her point, she noted that "every liquor dealer and every Democrat" is opposed to women having the elective franchise.

"Of course the Republican platform was not made with reference to any controversy on the subject of female suffrage," replied the *Register*. Although the subject was not currently an issue, the paper did concede that "many Republicans have committed themselves in favor of the right of women to vote." The paper facetiously suggested that it might be proper for Iowa women to vote, but "those insolent women of Dixie, who spat on Yankee prisoners and cursed them, should have no more moral right to the franchise than other full-grown rebels, North or South."

PROLONGED WOMAN-SUFFRAGE DEBATE IN DES MOINES

ALTHOUGH the woman-suffrage issue was suppressed in the legislature during the 1866 session, it was the subject of lively discussion at a series of meetings of the Farmer's Legislative Club, a group of lawmakers which met informally one evening a week during the session. Grape culture, grasses most profitable to raise in Iowa, cattle and hog raising, and a dog-control law comprised some of the programs during the winter. Early in February George Maxwell of Story County, who had asked the House to look into the expediency of woman suffrage, suggested that the club devote a meeting to this subject. When some members suggested this was not germane since it did not pertain to agriculture, Maxwell retorted that a good housewife was of more importance than a dog law.

Whatever their reasons for doing so, the club members did agree to discuss woman suffrage at their February 27 meeting. Although the daily papers failed to give this meeting more than passing notice, the *Iowa Homestead,* which routinely reported the proceedings of the Farmer's Legislative Club, carried a full stenographic report. The hall of the House of Representatives where the meeting was held was filled with visitors, both men and women. Obviously, the subject to be discussed was one of great interest to many people in Des Moines.

Maxwell, the first speaker for the proponents, said he had once hoped that he would soon see the day when women could vote but was now beginning to doubt that this dream would come true. While most people granted that suffrage for women, in theory at least, was as correct as suffrage for Negroes, they were not willing to work for both causes at the same time. These people contended Negro suffrage was timely and expedient; woman suffrage was not. Maxwell himself believed that woman suffrage was not only right but that it was expedient. He quoted the Declaration of Independence that "all men are created equal" and pointed out that he considered the word "men" could well mean "persons." He presumed that his opponents would not take the position that their mothers, wives, and daughters were not persons, even though many of them would deny that "the sable sons of Africa have either souls or persons."

Maxwell went on to say that he did not know what objections the opponents of woman suffrage would make, "but we who take this side of the question do not think that if we should give females the right of franchise that it must necessarily follow that they must put on jack boots and beat the bass drum. As to what is to become of the babies and little ones, while the mother is stumping for the Legislature, or pleading law, we will divide the labor with them; as to making rails and driving the hogs to market, we will try and not let them trespass quite that far; as to their patronizing the doggeries, drinking and carousing, I will say that we of this side have no such female relatives." Maxwell predicted that if women could vote, "all intoxicating drinks will have to get out of Iowa in double quick time."

Wilberforce P. Gaylord, Republican member of the House from Floyd County, was one of the principal speakers for the opposition. A native of Connecticut and father of eight children, Gaylord was a lawyer who had come to Iowa in 1854. He said he was an advocate of "woman's rights" and "would not wrong them by placing the ballot in their hands." He admired women who were "virtuous, modest, and retiring." Women like pioneer feminist Lucy Stone and Anna Dickinson, who had recently risen to fame as an orator for the Republican party, are "admired only for their stamina, their intellectual power, *and not for their womanly virtues.*" Such women, Gaylord said, were straining to be men and must have a "screw loose" somewhere. Men who proposed to make women voters, candidates for office, and politicians, were condemning them to "the cussedest life outside of purgatory—a life which causes men to neglect honorable occupations, depletes the pocket, deranges the nerves, and drags in its odious train a thousand and one disasters. Feminine nerves," he said, "are not always in condition to accept the intense excitement which precedes a political victory or follows a political defeat. Nero could fiddle while Rome was burning, but Nero was not a woman."

Gaylord said he would not want to see the day when his wife would give him orders "what to do, and when and how to do it." Nor would he want her to "leave his home in charge of the *hired gal* to ramble around the country on an election tour, *perhaps* to call on his friend Maxwell and other Legislators 'to have a little confidential talk' and then to return home at a late hour at night to order him out of bed *'to take care of the team.'* " And "the *hired gal* out of ———! ———! ———! to get her supper." (These remarks were considered too vulgar to be printed in full.) Gaylord added that he would regret to see the day when his wife would be sent to the legislature "perhaps to board at the same hotel with these same kind friends whose good natures might be much annoyed and often aroused by the *midnight cry*—a cry for a re-dress—of little grievances." If a legislator supported a bill sponsored by a woman, "would it not look as though———?" (Here again vulgarity was omitted by the reporter.) "No politician," Gaylord said, "escapes the scorching of the slanderous barbed tongue."

Gaylord argued that exposure to politics would degrade woman and teach her all the bad habits of men. He denied the contention that just because a woman might have an intellect superior to her husband she ought to be allowed to vote. Children often were smarter than their parents, he said, and they were not permitted to go to the polls. Finally, he argued that "those who make laws should, if necessary, be compelled to defend them, not only by their prayers and their votes, but by 'force of arms.' " There may even be times, he joked, when the ladies' "force of arms" could be confined to the "breast works" much nearer home.

"Whenever I see a woman uneasy to be a man," Gaylord concluded, "I despise her, and in doing so I am not obliged to despise any lady with a well-balanced mind, for no sensible woman would ever really desire to vote."

Benjamin Palmer, who presented the woman-suffrage petition in the House, said he was educated in the Society of Friends where women were equal in all matters of religion and had an equal voice in all matters of government. Hence it was easy for him to recognize woman's political equality and demand for her the right of suffrage.

Senator Wharton of Cedar County, another Republican, made some comments in the vein of low humor which seemed to dominate the discussion of the opponents of woman suffrage. He thought that women ought to be given the right to propose marriage and that a farmer's club was the legitimate place for the discussion of the woman question as it was "purely an agricultural proposition!" But seriously, he said, the proposition to give woman the vote was premature—"Not one in ten of the women desire this and if submitted to them they would vote it down by an overwhelming majority." To grant woman suffrage during the nineteenth century, he said, "would be utterly impracticable."

The evening ended with Representative Tisdale, a Republican from Chickasaw County, answering Gaylord's contention that if women were permitted to vote they should also be expected to take up arms in defense of their country. Tisdale objected to this kind of reasoning. "Because one man votes, should he therefore follow the same occupation as his neighbor?" Tisdale asked. "I say that a man is an animal and a hog is an animal; but it will not do to say, therefore, that a man is a hog, and a hog is a man, though one of these conclusions might sometimes be true."

Woman suffrage proved to be a topic of such lively interest that the Farmer's Legislative Club devoted three more meetings to the subject. The first was devoted to general debate; the second to an address by C. Ben Darwin; and the third to an essay written by Phoebe Palmer, wife of Benjamin Palmer. The *Iowa Homestead,* which apparently felt that it had done its duty in reporting the initial meeting on woman suffrage, ignored the subsequent three meetings on the subject. The topic, however, was of sufficient interest for the *Des Moines Register* to publish Mrs. Palmer's essay in full.

Mrs. Palmer thanked the club members for asking women to speak for themselves. Since it was impossible for her to address them in person, she explained, she was setting forth her views in writing. Mrs. Palmer's failure to come to Des Moines to address the legislators in person may have been due in great measure to the fact that at this time there was no railroad running into the city. Although the Northwestern Railroad had been completed from Clinton to Boone, it was necessary to make the forty-five-mile journey from Boone to Des Moines by stagecoach.

Any conjectures about PHOEBE PALMER, however, are based upon the most meager information. Nowhere is she mentioned by Iowa historians, and only a few facts about her have been gleaned from the Iowa census and contemporary newspapers. Thirty-six years old and the mother of three children ranging in age from thirteen to eight, Mrs. Palmer had migrated to Iowa from New York State with her husband and youngest child in 1855, the same year Amelia Bloomer had come to Council Bluffs. The Palmers setled on a farm near the village of Low Moor in Eden Township, one of the richest farming districts in Clinton County located on the eastern border of the state.

They were members of the Eden Meeting of Progressive Friends, organized in 1857. Progressive Friends, sometimes known as Congregational Friends or Friends of Human Progress, were Quakers who had seceded from the Hicksites in a struggle over the right to speak in meeting on social reform questions, especially the subject of slavery. The Progressive Friends Meeting—first organized at Waterloo, New York, in 1848—was the first religious organization to admit men and women on equal terms as well as the first to advocate woman's rights. These Friends played an important part in the first woman's rights convention at Seneca Falls in July 1848; and it is entirely possible that Phoebe Palmer, then a girl of eighteen, was living in the area at this time.

The Quakers in Eden Township are mentioned in Clinton County histories for their hospitality to fugitive slaves. E. W. Weston, whose wife headed the list of signers on the woman-suffrage petition presented to the 1866 legislature, was the leader of the underground railroad in Low Moor in the 1850's; and Benjamin Palmer was a prominent associate.

Reports of the Low Moor Farmer's Club (where women were active participants), which were published in the *DeWitt Observer* in 1863 and 1864, give a glimpse of Phoebe Palmer's liberal views and wide range of interests. At one meeting she presented a paper on healthful dress for women; at another, she described her ideas of an ideal farm home—one with an efficient kitchen, a special room for the children to play, and a bay window for plants. She was vitally interested in the progress of education in Iowa and argued that the proposed Agricultural College should be located at Iowa City, the site of the State University, rather than elsewhere in the state.[3]

Mrs. Palmer's essay, which was read to the Farmer's Legislative Club, was an able and comprehensive argument for woman suffrage, treating point by point all the current objections to woman's enfranchisement. These objections, which varied little during the whole course of the campaign for woman suffrage, and a summary of Mrs. Palmer's answers follow.

The majority of women do not want the right to vote but say that they have all the rights they want. Mrs. Palmer contended that this

---

3. The Agricultural College, chartered by the legislature in 1858, did not open until 1869. It was situated on land near Ames in Story County. The State University, chartered by the legislature in 1847, held its first classes in 1855. Both institutions were coeducational from the beginning.

argument only proved that "habits of submission make women, as well as men, servile-minded." Granted that there were many women who were not in favor of woman suffrage, she said, still there were others who might secretly believe in it but would not admit it for fear of being considered unfeminine. In circulating petitions, she also had found many women who said they might be willing to sign if they thought it would do any good but considered the cause so hopeless they were unwilling to commit themselves. And finally, Mrs. Palmer said, there was at that time not a small class of women which was already asking for the franchise. She would not concede that women did not want to vote.

Woman, because of her physical inferiority, should not be allowed to vote. Mrs. Palmer felt that this argument carried too little weight to occupy much time. Men were not barred by age or weakness from the right of suffrage, so why should women be disfranchised for these reasons?

If woman could vote, she should also be subject to military duty. "Do you think that Iowa women sacrificed no less during the War than did their men?" Mrs. Palmer asked. Women not only worked on the farms while the men were away but they also acted as nurses in army hospitals and on the field of battle. Certainly women shared equally in defending their country.

WOMEN IN THE ARMY—THE DRESS PARADE
L. P. Brockett's antiwoman-suffrage book argued that if women were permitted to vote, they should also be required to serve in the army.

Woman's want of knowledge in the affairs of government disqualifies her from voting. This objection might be admitted to some extent, Mrs. Palmer said. If women were permitted to vote, they would have the impetus to be better informed about political matters and would make as intelligent voters as men. She also noted that a majority of male voters knew very little about the issues involved at any election.

Politics is not woman's sphere. "What right have you men to prescribe the sphere of any human being?" Mrs. Palmer asked. "Did God give woman faculties which she must not use, powers which she must not possess, rights which she must not exercise?"

"In the agitation of moral questions women often assume a full share of the campaign," Mrs. Palmer pointed out. She went on to say that women had been workers in the antislavery campaign despite insults and mobs. They had canvassed the state in behalf of temperance, speaking daily to large audiences and exhorting men to vote in favor of morality. The noted lecturer Anna Dickinson, whose perfect womanliness had never been questioned, was credited with having saved the state of Connecticut for the Republican party. Yet Miss Dickinson was not permitted to vote because the exercise of the franchise was not considered to be woman's sphere. Mrs. Palmer believed that woman "should do whatever she desires so long as it is not in conflict with moral law."

If woman voted, she would neglect her household duties. "Do not your wives go to church or attend to even less important matters away from home, leaving their infants for a period as long as it would be necessary to deposit a ballot?" she asked.

There would be discord in the family if women had the franchise. Such an argument was very weak, Mrs. Palmer said. It implied that men and women could not have an honest difference of opinion without contention, and that they had no respect for each other's opinions.

If woman could vote, her fine, womanly nature would be destroyed. This same argument formerly had prohibited women from entering into many activities in which they were now engaged. She could not agree that politics was not woman's sphere.

In conclusion Mrs. Palmer thanked the men for their protection in the past but asked for the ballot, so women could protect themselves in the future.

"Mrs. Palmer deserves the thanks of all women, and I am sure she has those of all earnest, thinking ones," wrote a correspondent, too timid to sign her name, in a letter published in the *Des Moines Register* on March 17. This woman wished "a God-speed to Mrs. Palmer and to all others in such noble work."

By March 20 the suffrage debate around Des Moines had become so heated that Ed H. Wright, Speaker of the House, published a letter in the *Register* in an apparent attempt to cool the tempers of opposing forces. Although Wright, a Quaker, was personally sympathetic to woman suffrage,[4] his words could hardly have been very reassuring to the woman's rights advocates.

"The subject of the extension of the elective franchise to ladies is being pretty fully discussed in the Farmer's Club, and somewhat in social circles," he wrote. He did not know whether the women desired an extension of their rights and, if so, in what direction they would have them extended. Women would certainly not desire additional privileges which would increase their burdens. He could see no evidence of an unfriendly feeling toward the ladies in the opposition to their enfranchisement, nor wild fanaticism in its advocacy. Both the friends and the enemies of woman suffrage, he was sure, were equally sincere and earnest in seeking the truth.

The only objection Wright could see to giving woman the elective franchise was that she already possessed "irresistible and almost unlimited power." She did not need this additional privilege to make her equal to those now exercising this right. However, even this objection he was willing to waive.

The day after Wright's letter appeared in the *Register,* this paper published a facetious editorial on the question of woman suffrage. Finding much difficulty in proving a negative stand to the question, it had chosen to take the affirmative. All the good which the country possessed was attributable to woman, the *Register* quipped. "No man but a misogynist and a fool would doubt the truthfulness of this declaration." Women would not, as often charged, vote in accordance with the opinions of their husbands. "No such thing! Women are independent thinkers—inclined to have their own way or send the fragments of domestic establishments crashing through the kitchen window!" If a spade or a mattock from the bogs of Ireland were permitted to vote against its adopted country in time of war, the *Register* thought the mothers (if living) of generals Grant, Sheridan, and Sherman must be equally trusted with the dignities of the ballot box.

4. When the Polk County Woman Suffrage Association was organized in 1870, Mrs. Wright was a charter member.

"Fellow-sisters in great suffering, if not in suffrage," concluded the paper, "our opinon is that you ought to vote."

WOMAN'S RIGHTS UNDER IOWA LAW

WOMAN SUFFRAGE was also a lively subject of debate among Des Moines lawyers in 1866. Their discussions centered on the legal disabilities of the married woman and the question of whether or not she needed the ballot to emancipate herself from oppressive laws.

One prospective lawyer, Captain M. C. Wright, a Civil War veteran and member of the first graduating class of the Des Moines Law School, delivered an oration on "Woman's Rights at Common Law" before a large audience gathered at the courthouse on the occasion of his graduation on December 5, 1866. According to the report in the *Des Moines Register,* Wright "didn't believe much in what is called 'Woman's Rights.' "[5] He thought the progress of the law in regard to her rights was in perfect consonance with the spirit of the age. Nowhere else had woman risen so high. Wright held that even though woman had wielded the scepter of power both nobly and wisely (e.g., Queen Victoria), the arena of politics could not be argued to be her legitimate domain.

One enchanted Des Moines girl, who heard Captain Wright that evening, recorded in her diary, "He electrified his audience. I thought the old Court House would fall, they cheered him so." However, the *Register* noted that there were probably a few women present who did not agree with all his arguments.

What was the "progress of the law" that Wright could claim it to be in "perfect consonance with the spirit of the age?"

When Iowa became a territory in 1838, its legal system was based on the English common-law rule which held that husband and wife were one, and that one was the husband. The wife was considered to be civilly dead—a legal concept which in practice meant that the wife's person, her earnings, her children, and her personal property (including her clothing) belonged to her husband. During marriage he had sole control of any real property she might have acquired before marriage and could dispose of it as he wished. Such property was liable for his debts. No married woman could make a will without her husband's consent.

When the wife died, the husband was entitled to a life interest

5. Wright's father, James Wright—a former Secretary of State—helped organize the Polk County Woman Suffrage Association in 1870.

in all her real estate if a child had been born alive. On the other hand, the wife at the death of the husband was entitled to only a life interest in one-third of his real property, which at her death went to the husband's heirs.

The woman's rights movement was a direct outgrowth of agitation in the early 1840's for amelioration of the legal disabilities of married women. In Iowa the first substantial modification of the common-law rule relating to the property of the married woman was adopted by the Eighth Territorial Assembly in 1846. It enacted a law giving a married woman the right to any real estate which she might have acquired by bequest, gift, or purchase, as long as she did not acquire it from her husband or purchase it with funds supplied by him. Such property was free from liability from the husband's debts; but the husband still had complete control, including the right to the income therefrom. S. Clinton Hastings, thirty-one-year-old Muscatine lawyer who sponsored this law, later settled in California where the Hastings School of Law of the University of California bears his name in appreciation of the $100,000 which he donated for its establishment.

The Iowa Code of 1851, adopted by the Third General Assembly, embodied a chapter on "Husband and Wife" which substantially liberalized the rights of married women and gave the state some of the most progressive laws in the country relating to women. It provided that personal property of the wife did not vest at once in the husband but if left under his control would presume to have been transferred. This could be prevented if the wife filed a notice with the county recorder stating the amount in value of such property and that she had a claim therefrom out of the estate of her husband. Specific items of personal property could be owned by the wife exempt from the husband's debts if a notice of ownership was filed with the county recorder prior to the claim of any creditor.

The wife was not liable for the separate debts of the husband, except for family expenses, nor was the husband liable for the separate debts of the wife. Married women abandoned by their husbands could obtain authority from the district court to transact business as though unmarried. Heretofore, it had been necessary for a married woman to go to the legislature for such authority. The husband could not remove his wife nor their children from their homestead without her consent; and if he abandoned her, she was entitled to the custody of their minor children.

Husband and wife alike were each entitled to one-third outright interest in the estate of the other. However, the legislature repealed this provision three years later, going back to the common-law rule which allowed the wife only a life interest in one-third of the husband's estate. During the Civil War—probably in consideration of the numerous war widows in the state—the law was again changed to permit the wife outright ownership of her one-third share of the husband's property.

The chapter on "Husband and Wife" in the 1851 Code was not enacted without a great battle in the General Assembly. At one point the House voted to strike the whole chapter, "the majority believing that it had a tendency to diminish the happiness enjoyed in the domestic circle, and would eventually lead to separations and vastly increase the application for divorces." While the debate was in progress, a crowd of spectators, most of them women, attended the legislative sessions in the capitol at Iowa City.

The rights of the married woman were further enlarged in the Code revision of 1860 in a law permitting her to sue and be sued without the husband joining with her when the action concerned her separate property or was founded on her own contract. An explanatory note in the Code, written by C. Ben Darwin of Burlington, states that the right of property "to be of any value, must be accompanied by adjective rights which will secure their enjoyment. The right to sue follows necessarily from the right of property."

Iowa Supreme Court rulings during the 1860's indicate a strict interpretation of the laws concerning the property rights of married women. In 1861 the court ruled that a married woman could not convey her separate real estate unless her husband joined in the deed. In June 1864 the court ruled that "the services of the wife and the products of her labor belong as much to the husband, under Iowa statute, as at common law."

In December 1864 the court declared that a married woman had no power to make contracts (except in regard to her own separate property), sign notes, or engage in business generally. "In this very inability to thus contract," the court said, "consists her best and surest protection. Her disability is thus wisely converted into a security more certain and effective, perhaps, than any which, if the disability were removed, could be thrown around her by the most carefully constructed and elaborate legislative defenses." The court did suggest that the legislature might "guardedly modify" the common-law rule which vested in the husband during marriage the money or property of the wife and made it liable for his debts.

The Eleventh General Assembly, meeting in 1866, acted on the court's suggestion by passing two laws enlarging the property rights of married women. One law provided that "any married woman may in her own name and for her own separate use and benefit conduct and carry on any trade, business, or profession; and the wages, and profits arising therefrom shall be her own separate property exempt from her husband's debts." The law provided, however, that the wife must, "at or before entering upon such trade, business, or profession, obtain the consent of her husband in writing . . . which consent must be filed for record in the county where the business is to be carried on."

The second law, designed to protect wives of improvident husbands, stated that "the separate earnings of any married woman, whose husband, through idleness, intemperance, mental or bodily infirmity, imprisonment or involuntary absence, does not support and provide for the family, or who has deserted his wife, shall be held by her, in her own right, exempt from liability for the debts of her husband."

Thomas S. Wilson of Dubuque—a former judge who sponsored this bill in the Senate—said on January 25 that he had only recently read "of a milliner who was broken up four times by a spendthrift husband who waited every time until she amassed a little property and then swooped down and carried it off." He also knew of a case in one county of "a poor woman who had a family of helpless children and a drunken husband. After years of labor in washing clothes by the day, she saved up $150, by small sums, consisting sometimes of a few cents, and placed it in the hands of a friend for safekeeping. Yet this money was attached and taken to pay a debt of the husband."

"The common-law rule under which such evils result ought to be changed," Wilson declared. "It is inconsistent with the progress of the age and is a relic of barbarism. Now that African slavery is abolished," quipped Wilson, a Democrat, "let us look to those who are worse than slaves."

Judging from the rapid enlargement of the rights of married women in Iowa during the twenty-eight years of the state's existence, Captain Wright doubtless made an impressive argument for his thesis that "the progress of the law in regard to the rights of woman was in perfect consonance with the spirit of the age."

Woman's rights advocates, on the other hand, could cite many laws which still unjustly discriminated against women. As a general rule, the services of the wife and the products of her labor still belonged to her husband. Unless she filed the written consent of her husband to permit her to engage in business or was married to a man whom she could prove incompetent or improvident, a married woman could not by her own labor and industry acquire property which was absolutely her own, free from her husband's creditors. Unless she filed a certified inventory of her personal property, a married woman could not claim title even to those articles purchased with her own earnings. Although a woman might spend a lifetime working with her husband to build up an estate, she was entitled to only a dower right of one-third of her husband's property and perhaps a life estate in the homestead. In justice to the wife, woman's rights advocates asserted, at least one-half of the husband's property should belong to his widow. The husband was still the sole guardian of the children, whereas the wife should have equal responsibility as a co-guardian. Finally, woman as a property holder could not vote and therefore had no voice in the taxes she must pay.

ANNA DICKINSON LECTURES IN IOWA

ANNA DICKINSON, brilliant young orator cited by both Phoebe Palmer and Mary Darwin, was so well known in Iowa that the *Davenport Democrat*, in announcing Miss Dickinson's lecture on February 22, 1866, felt no need to identify her other than to say that her name was a household word. All of Davenport, the *Democrat* said, was "on tiptoe as to the celebrated lady's looks, manners, and style of speaking."

Despite the fact that it was raining the evening of Miss Dickinson's appearance in Davenport and the streets were in "a deplorably muddy condition," Metropolitan Hall, the town's largest auditorium, was jammed with spectators anxious to see and hear this famous woman. The reporter for the *Democrat* found her to be somewhat smaller than the medium female in size, rather round-shouldered with short black hair worn in loose curls and with flashing eyes and a remarkably clear and pleasing voice. She spoke from notes inscribed upon some half-dozen slips of paper which she held in her hand; and when not requiring their aid, both hands were crossed behind her. "It was evident," this reporter said, "that the greater part of Miss Dickinson's lecture had been committed to memory and that her occasional outbursts of eloquence were not spontaneous outpourings of soul feeling, but carefully studied mechanisms to move her auditors."

Anna Dickinson's lecture, entitled "Flood Tide," was an impassioned appeal for Negro rights. As was to be expected, the reporter for a Democratic paper had no liking for the sentiments she expressed. "She spoke exactly as we would expect a woman to speak," he said. "The Negro was her theme, and the rousing of *sympathy* and *passion* her aim. In her estimation the ship of state has been stranded. The flood tide that will bear it to fame and honor is getting seaward. Place

Anna Dickinson's receipt for payment of $100 for a special train to take her from Des Moines to Mount Pleasant was found among her papers in the Library of Congress.

District Court.

S a'e vs G B Brown. The arguments in this case closed yesterday about 3 o'clock, D O Finch making the closing argument for the prosecution, which is said to have been a brilliant effort. The case is now with the jury.

ANNA DICKINSON ON AN ENGINE!—Miss Dickinson was ten minutes too late for the morning train of the Valley Road yesterday, and in order to keep her promise true and meet her engagement at Mt. Pleasant last night, hired a special train to take her through, paying the round little sum of one hundred dollars therefor. This was doing no more than any lecturer who gets $200 a night ought to do, but it was more than any other lecturer has ever done in Iowa, and shines most beautifully in contrast with the actions of Tilton, Sumner, Taylor, and half a dozen other great big men who didn't come to Des Moines when they had positively engaged to be here. The plucky Anna's special train left at 11 o'clock, with the brave girl occupying a seat in the engine—a seat she preferred to take rather than the ones of velvet and plush in the coach. We wish every man in the lecture business had the grit of Anna Dickinson !

PRESERVE ALL LAND MARKS !—The attention of the public is invited to the following extract from section 4323 of chapter 170 of the Revision of 1860:

"If any person maliciously

Anna Dickinson

Front-page story about Anna Dickinson's special train in the Des Moines Register, *March 11, 1859.*

the Negro at the masthead and the old bark will glide onward in safety and glory."

That she had truly aroused the ire of the Democrats is indicated by other commentators in the *Democrat*. One called her "the crino-lined crowing little hen in pantalets" and took her to task for cackling at the Democrats for supporting President Andrew Johnson in his fight with the Radicals in Congress.

"Miss Dickinson can well afford to howl for the nigger. She is well paid for it," sneered another correspondent. "To what are we drifting?" he asked. "A petticoat government with Miss Dickinson and some 'American citizens of African descent' at the helm?" He was perfectly willing to trust the ship of state to Andy Johnson's guiding hand.

While all the Republicans at Metropolitan Hall may not have been in sympathy with Anna Dickinson's ardent plea for justice for the Negro, many would certainly have applauded her eloquent argu-ments in behalf of Negro suffrage—an issue for which the Radicals were currently fighting both in Congress and in the state legislature. Even those Republicans who loved the Negro less than Anna Dickin-son and thought it improper for a lady to appear on a public plat-form grudgingly admired her for her service to their party as well as her meteoric rise to fame.

Anna Dickinson, born in Philadephia in 1842, lost her father when she was an infant and was reared by her Quaker mother, who eked out an existence by teaching and taking in boarders. A bril-liant, moody, and sensitive child, Anna was deeply affected by the discussions of social injustice which she heard among Quaker reform leaders during her girlhood.

When she was fifteen, she began teaching school at $16 a month. That same year she made her first public speech at a meeting of Progressive Friends—rebel Quakers like those in Eden Township, Clinton County, Iowa—who were dedicated to fighting "Negro chattel slavery, slavery of women to men, Demon Rum, war, capital punish-ment, and the use of tobacco." When a man at the Friends' meeting spoke against woman's rights, Anna Dickinson rose to the defense of her sex and is said to have sent him skulking from the hall.

Her debut as a lyceum lecturer was made in February 1861 at the age of seventeen, when she delivered a two-hour oration on the "Rights and Wrongs of Woman" before an audience of 800 at Concert Hall in Philadelphia. She was introduced on this occasion by Lucretia Mott, the Quaker who thirteen years before had helped Elizabeth Cady Stanton organize the first woman's rights convention at Seneca Falls.

In 1863 Anna Dickinson shattered the tradition of all-male political campaigns when she stumped New Hampshire and Connecticut as a paid speaker for the Republican party. In the fall of that year she was invited to come to Chicago to appear at the mammoth Northwest Sanitary Fair. Here she was paid $600 for two lectures which were so successful that they earned over $1,000 for the fair's sponsors, with tickets probably selling at the usual price of 25 and 50 cents each. Since the fair attracted thousands of visitors from neighboring states, there were doubtless many Iowans who heard Miss Dickinson at this time.

In January 1864 Anna Dickinson was invited to Washington, D.C., where she spoke in the House of Representatives. Even Abraham Lincoln came to hear her. She donated the proceeds of this lecture—over $1,000—to the Freedman's Relief Society. Miss Dickinson continued to espouse the northern cause until the end of the war, speaking free of charge in army camps and hospitals, while elsewhere she regularly earned $100 for each lecture appearance.

A Washington correspondent writing to the *Des Moines Register* in May 1864 described Anna Dickinson as "rather better looking than most strong-minded women." Although this writer did not like orators in crinoline generally, he was willing to bet "his bottom dollar that Miss Dickinson could make an audience laugh, cry, or hold its breath better than any man in America."

With the close of the Civil War there was no necessity for Anna Dickinson to return to teaching at less than $4 a week or to earn a bare subsistence as a milliner, a trade which she had once briefly followed. Instead, she could continue to earn her living as a well-paid lyceum lecturer, a profession whose doors she had almost single-handedly opened wide for her sex.

The lyceum, or lecture course, which had flourished throughout the country in the 1850's, reached a height of popularity in the United States in the postwar decade. In those days before television, radio, the moving picture, or even the telephone the public in every hamlet and city turned out to attend local lyceums for entertainment, education, or simply to see and hear famous public figures.

Iowa, which possessed only 800 miles of railroads at the close of the Civil War, attracted an increasing number of lecturers each season as travel was facilitated by the rapid construction of railroads across the state. Young Men's Associations (sometimes called Young Men's Christian Associations or Young Men's Library Associations) sprang up in almost every community for the purpose of sponsoring lecture courses. Proceeds, if any, were used to establish local libraries. By 1866 forty of these groups in Iowa and neighboring states had banded together into an Association of Western Literary Societies, with headquarters in Chicago. So sought after was the lecturer that this association booked tours at no cost to the speaker.

The lecture season, which regularly ran from November 1 to March 15 each year, attracted many well-known public figures to Iowa in the immediate postwar years. Among the prominent speakers who appeared in the state during the 1866 and 1867 seasons were Horace Greeley, editor of the *New York Tribune* (the leading Republican paper in the country); Theodore Tilton, editor of the *Independent* (a popular religious journal); Wendell Phillips, president of the American Anti-Slavery Society; George Thompson, noted English abolitionist and orator; Frederick Douglass, a former slave and champion of his race; Ralph Waldo Emerson, writer and philosopher; John Gough, noted temperance orator; P. T. Barnum of circus fame; Clara Barton, the Civil War nurse; and Grace Greenwood, a popular writer. With the exception of Gough, Anna Dickinson outdistanced all these in her consistent ability to draw a packed house wherever she went.

During the 1865–1866 lecture season Anna Dickinson's Iowa engagements were limited to Davenport and perhaps a few other towns on the eastern border of the state. The following season she booked a more extended tour in Iowa. Her most popular lecture during this season, titled "Something to Do," was an impassioned appeal for greater economic opportunities for women and for wages adequate enough to ensure self-respect. Inability to earn a decent living, she pointed out, was forcing thousands of women into lives of prostitution.

In Mount Pleasant, where Miss Dickinson "filled the hall to the utmost capacity," Frank Hatton—the Republican editor of the *Mount Pleasant Journal*—found her talk "weak in argument and weak in denunciation." He accused her of betraying a "soured disposition at the fates which made her a woman." Hatton did not think "any intelligent person would deny that woman is equal and far superior to man," but he thought it did not necessarily follow that she "can enter the prize ring, run a locomotive on the railroad, drive a stagecoach, and go as a soldier." There were a number of young ladies in Mount Pleasant, he asserted, who could have delivered a better lecture at a much lower price.

Pursuant to this review, Hatton had about "six or eight talented ladies into his editorial wool with their steel pens." One young woman, signing herself "Ada," took him to task for his "nauseous flattery." She thought it only revealed his stupidity in supposing for a moment that the daughters of the "Athens of Iowa" (a popular name for Mount Pleasant) could be wheedled with such vulgar bait.

During Anna Dickinson's stay in Mount Pleasant she was the guest of old Philadelphia friends, John and Mary Dugdale. Many of the town's leading citizens came to call on her at their home. She also spent the day prior to her lecture—a Sunday—with Dugdale's parents, Ruth and Joseph Dugdale, in their farm home ten miles from town. Joseph Dugdale, a prime mover in organizing the Progressive Friends in 1848, was a dedicated woman's rights advocate destined to play an important role in inaugurating the woman-suffrage movement in Iowa.

Miss Dickinson's Burlington lecture was preceded by a storm of controversy concerning the propriety of a woman lecturing in public. One young woman was quoted as saying that she "did not go to see the wild men and didn't attend Menageries and would not go to hear Miss Dickinson."

The *Burlington Hawkeye* thought "Miss Dickinson (if every *woman* does not have it) has fairly earned the right to speak in public and to be heard, by that unfailing test, success." The ladies "wouldn't object to hearing Jenny Lind sing or Charlotte Cushman in some of her powerful impersonations," said the *Hawkeye*. Why would it be more "unwomanly or more unlady-like to speak one's own thoughts than to sing or recite the composition of another"? The *Hawkeye* suggested that the ladies of Burlington overlook their scruples against women speaking in public and go to hear Miss Dickinson *"just this once."* The paper assured them they would hear one of the most fascinating speakers of the day.

Despite threats of the lecture being boycotted, Anna Dickinson was greeted in Burlington by an audience which completely filled Mozart Hall. At the conclusion of her lecture she was the recipient of "a diminutive shower of bouquets" as she retired from the platform.

A letter from an anonymous gentleman, published in the *Hawkeye* the day after Anna Dickinson's appearance, called her lecture "an incoherent, whining tirade" by an "unwomanly female making outrageous demands for her sex."

An ardent female admirer, "Y.H.M.," on the other hand, castigated those Burlington women who criticized Anna Dickinson. No doubt they were the women, she said, who had never had to earn their own living. This writer hoped the men of Burlington would respond to Anna Dickinson's plea for better wages and working conditions for women, and she even went so far as to suggest that they might employ women as clerks and bookkeepers "not only in the stores but in the post office and better still in the office of the *Hawkeye*."

Stirred by Anna Dickinson's lecture, this letter writer even dared take the Young Men's Literary Association to task for having no women as members. If women were permitted to join, she was sure the club would soon have books on its shelves and become a literary association in more than name only.

Another feminine disciple of Anna Dickinson's, in a letter to the *Hawkeye*, wished a "God speed to her and to all other women who *dare* to be free."

The price of her freedom was not only criticism and vilification but also physical exhaustion caused by a grueling schedule of lecture engagements six nights a week, with only Sundays for rest. Adding to the rigors of her profession were the unventilated and overheated lecture halls which she found in almost every community. In early December 1866, shortly after her Burlington appearance, Miss Dickinson was stricken with a case of "typhoid pneumonia" which forced her to cancel her western engagements for the rest of the season. "She has been as near death as she possibly ever can be and live," wrote Anna Dickinson's sister to the secretary of the Dubuque Lecture Association. She reported that Miss Dickinson had been told by her physician that she might return to her home in Philadelphia before Christmas if she used the Palace Sleeping Car but must never again attempt a winter lecture tour in the West.

Hardly more than a year had elapsed, however, before Anna Dickinson was again lecturing to Iowa audiences.

Some popular lecturers as caricatured by Harper's Weekly. *Figures in the middle row from left to right are: Louis Agassiz, John B. Gough, Henry Ward Beecher, Theodore Tilton, Elizabeth Cady Stanton, William Lloyd Garrison, and Susan B. Anthony (in male costume).*

4

1867

❧

W HEN THE SECOND SESSION of the Thirty-ninth Congress convened in December 1866, congressional friends of Negro suffrage, encouraged by the overwhelming victory of the Radicals in the fall elections, took further steps to enfranchise the Negro. Still lacking strength to secure a direct federal guarantee of Negro suffrage by constitutional amendment, they pressed for suffrage for the colored man wherever it was clearly within congressional power.

PROGRESS OF NEGRO SUFFRAGE AND WOMAN SUFFRAGE IN CONGRESS

IN MID-DECEMBER 1866 Congress approved a bill to enfranchise male Negroes in the District of Columbia despite the fact that in a referendum the previous year the voters had defeated a Negro-suffrage proposition by 7,342 to 36. This bill was promptly vetoed by President Andrew Johnson, who observed acidly that those congressmen who supported Negro suffrage for the District were from states which denied the black man the franchise. The bill was passed over Johnson's veto in early January 1867.

In January the Thirty-ninth Congress also extended

the franchise to Negroes in all federal territories by prohibiting the denial of suffrage in these areas to any citizen because of race, color, or previous condition of servitude and by requiring Negro suffrage in Nebraska as a condition of statehood. On March 2, the day of adjournment, a Reconstruction Act was passed which included a section requiring Negro suffrage as a condition for readmitting the former Confederate states to the Union and to Congress.

A week later, as soon as the Fortieth Congress had convened, Senator Henderson, a Missouri Republican, submitted a constitutional amendment to prohibit the denial of suffrage to any citizen because of race, color, or previous condition. This proposal, which was to become the basis of the Fifteenth Amendment, did not receive serious consideration until December 1868 when the third session of the Fortieth Congress convened.

With the enfranchisement of male Negroes in the District of Columbia and in the territories in January 1867, woman-suffrage advocates hoped for early congressional action to enfranchise women in these areas. A woman-suffrage association was organized in the District in the summer of 1867; and by early 1868 petitions were circulating throughout the country, asking Congress for legislation giving women equal voting privileges with men in the District. The petition campaign for woman suffrage in the territories failed to gain much momentum, since these areas were too remote and too sparsely populated to be of great interest to women in the East.

Meanwhile, opponents of Negro suffrage in Congress—both Democrats and administration Republicans—continued to taunt the Radicals with charges of inconsistency in enfranchising large numbers of ignorant Negroes while at the same time denying the ballot to educated white women. In December 1866 when the District of Columbia franchise bill was under consideration in the Senate, Edgar Cowan, administration Republican from Pennsylvania, caused a furor when he offered an amendment to the bill striking the word "male" from the qualifications for voting. He not only precipitated three full days of debate on the question of woman suffrage but managed to bring his amendment to a vote. It was defeated by a count of 37 to 9. This was the first vote to be taken in Congress on the question of enfranchising women and was widely publicized by newspapers throughout the country. The fact that nine United States senators were willing to vote for woman suffrage was generally regarded by its advocates as an omen of early success for their cause. The *Dubuque Herald,* a Democratic paper, deplored this "latest phase of radical legislation" which it said presented the country "with something novel in the history of politics—something too preposterous to be thought of by men of common sense." The *Herald* had "all along suspected that Negro suffrage would be but the prelude to something more absurd," and the events that were now transpiring in Congress confirmed its suspicions.

BARREN HARVEST IN KANSAS

WOMAN-SUFFRAGE ADVOCATES throughout the country were further elated in March 1867 when the Republican-dominated Kansas legislature approved submission at the coming November elections of two separate amendments to the state constitution—one to delete the word "white" and the other to delete the word "male" from the article on voting. This action meant that woman suffrage would be tested in a popular referendum for the first time.

The sponsor of the woman-suffrage proposition in the Kansas legislature was Colonel Sam Wood, Republican senator from Cottonwood Falls and well-known as an opponent of Negro suffrage. Although the Radicals in the Kansas legislature regarded Wood's championship of woman suffrage with suspicion, woman-suffrage leaders in the East to whom Wood appealed for help had implicit faith in his sincerity. In answer to Wood's request Lucy Stone agreed to go to Kansas immediately to help launch the woman-suffrage campaign; and Miss Anthony and Mrs. Stanton, currently busy with a campaign in New York State, made plans to go to Kansas in late summer.

Accompanied by her husband Henry Blackwell, Lucy Stone arrived in Topeka on April 2 in time to help with the organization of a Kansas Equal Rights Association. From this time until late May she stumped Kansas, speaking in forty of the state's forty-four counties. Traveling by stagecoach, carriage, open wagons, and oxcarts over this rough frontier country, she drew large crowds wherever she spoke. Mistaking popular curiosity about her as a person for agreement with the cause she represented, Lucy Stone was elated by her reception in Kansas. "Impartial suffrage without regard to color and sex will succeed by overwhelming majorities," wired Lucy Stone from Atchison on May 10 to the annual convention of the American Equal Rights Association then meeting in New York City.

Woman's rights advocates the country over were delighted with this and similar encouraging reports from Kansas. In Iowa John L. Loomis of Independence, editor of the *Buchanan County Bulletin*, noted on May 31 that "the course of womanhood suffrage in Kansas is represented as prospering beyond the most sanguine anticipations of those who originally embarked on it." Plans for a fall campaign were being completed, Loomis reported, in which a "large and distinguished force of the leading suffrage advocates from the East" would participate.

Despite this optimism the prospect for equal rights in Kansas was actually anything but hopeful. By summer it was obvious to Radical leaders in the state that the Negro-suffrage amendment was in serious danger and to have permitted a woman-suffrage amendment to be submitted at the same time was a serious error. In August firm action was taken to silence Colonel Wood, leader of the woman-suffrage forces; this resulted in his retirement to Cottonwood Falls, where he remained incommunicado until after the election. Some Republicans went so far as to stump the state in opposition to woman suffrage, hoping in this way to save Negro suffrage from the increasing prospect of certain defeat.

When Miss Anthony and Mrs. Stanton arrived in Kansas in early September,[1] they found the woman-suffrage forces completely demoralized. Undaunted, they determined to bend every effort to turn the tide of public opinion. Mrs. Stanton went on tour with Charles Robinson (first free-state governor of Kansas and a relative of Lucy Stone's), who volunteered to take her in his own carriage and to pay all expenses. For almost two months she toured the state speaking two and three times each day on a trip so strenuous that it killed both a pair of mules and a pair of Indian ponies. Mrs. Stanton, being of hardier stuff, weathered the journey without permanent injury.

Meanwhile, Miss Anthony stayed in Lawrence with her brother Daniel and his family, waiting for a man willing to help her with the difficulties of Kansas travel. "A Mrs. Brinkerhoff and her husband are making a tour of the State with their own team," she wrote to Anna Dickinson on September 23. (Mrs. Brinkerhoff made an extensive tour in Iowa during the winter of 1868–1869.) Miss Anthony said she was expecting to go with some "honorable" the following week, "the dignitary not yet fixed." Unfortunately this dignitary never materialized.

In early October Miss Anthony received word from Omaha that a Democrat, George Francis Train, was willing to come to Kansas at his own expense and win every Irish vote in the state for women. After consultation with Mrs. Stanton she accepted Train's offer of help. Thirty-eight years old and tall, handsome, and charming, Train was famous as a world traveler and successful entrepreneur. He was a

---

1. In early August 1867 a constitutional convention in New York State had defeated a proposal for woman suffrage by a vote of 125 to 19.

brilliant and entertaining person but an eccentric who loved the lime-light. He was a champion of the Irish, an opponent of the Negro, and a self-nominated candidate for president of the United States. Miss Anthony, to the horror of her antislavery friends, went on tour with Train, goading him on when the difficulties of Kansas travel proved more than he cared to endure.

At the election in November, Negro suffrage in Kansas was de-feated by a vote of 19,420 to 10,483, and woman suffrage by a vote of 19,857 to 9,070. The women, however, took satisfaction in the fact that over 9,000 men were willing to cast their ballots in favor of woman's enfranchisement.

Much ill will was left in the wake of the Kansas campaign. Miss Anthony and Mrs. Stanton felt victory could have been theirs if they had had the support of the Radicals. These men, on the other hand, were angry with the two women for their alliance with the Democrats. Their Republican friends were further enraged when they accepted an offer from Train to finance a speaking tour which took them to sixteen cities, beginning in Omaha on November 19 and ending in New York City on December 14. Train, who accompanied Miss Anthony and Mrs. Stanton as manager and chief barker, appeared with them at each meeting advancing his own candidacy for the office of president of the United States.

When Lucy Stone heard that Miss Anthony and Mrs. Stanton were traveling with George Francis Train, she thought the story must be a monstrous rumor spread by the enemies of woman suffrage. When she found that the rumor was true, she published a notice in New York papers disavowing any responsibility on the part of the American Equal Rights Association for the actions of these two women.[2] This was the first public indication of a rift between Lucy Stone and the Susan B. Anthony–Elizabeth Cady Stanton team, which was to widen into an unbridgeable gulf during the course of the next two years.

PROGRESS OF WOMAN SUFFRAGE IN IOWA

WHILE THE ATTENTION and energy of the woman-suffrage leaders of the country was directed toward Kansas in 1867, there was sufficient

2. Forty years later Miss Anthony made the following note on a printed collection of Train's Kansas speeches: "With all of Mr. Train's oddities, he would make speeches on woman's *wrongs* that could be equalled only by John B. Gough [a popular temperance orator]. Whether my doing so meets the approval of future generations or not, let them remember that no other man except Parker Pillsbury and Robert Purvis stood with us through this fearfully alone period for Mrs. Stanton and myself."

Theodore Tilton as portrayed in the 1868 edition of Brockett's Men of Our Day. *However, the 1872 edition does not carry Tilton's picture nor his biography, a good indication of the abrupt decline of his popularity.*

sentiment for woman suffrage in Iowa for Theodore Tilton—a Brooklyn, New York, resident lecturing in Iowa during December 1866 and January 1867—to predict that "Iowa would be the first state in the Union to achieve the political equality of the sexes." Thirty-two-year-old reformer and editor of the *Independent,* a widely read religious weekly, Tilton was making the first of four successful annual tours in Iowa. He was deeply impressed by the "spirit of equality which strikingly pervades not only western men but western women." In a report published in the *Independent* on February 7, Tilton went on to say that everywhere he went in the state he found "a fruit-promising thoughtfulness on the question of the political rights of women." If any man supposed that the discussion of woman's rights was confined to a few writers and speakers, he did not discern the signs of the times. The claims of women, Tilton asserted, were eliciting the attention of nearly all the intellectual women whom he had met in the West. "Of course," he added, "fastidiousness, prejudice, and fashion still deter many excellent and well-meaning ladies from giving serious thought to the question and many persons continue to treat this subject with an unpardonable levity."

An exuberant, romantic-looking young man and one of the most sought-after speakers in the country, Tilton was a close friend of Elizabeth Cady Stanton's and Susan B. Anthony's. In 1866 he had encouraged these women to reorganize the American Woman's Rights Association into the American Equal Rights Association, and he was currently serving as a vice-president of this organization. Wherever Tilton went in Iowa he reenforced the convictions of the woman's rights advocates whom he met with his own enthusiasm for the cause.[3]

In early January 1867 Tilton lectured in Independence, a town of about 2,000 in Buchanan County. Here he found a warm and admiring friend in twenty-nine-year-old John L. Loomis, crusading editor of the *Buchanan County Bulletin*. The following June a group of Independence residents, meeting in the home of Loomis, organized the "American Equal Rights Association of Independence, Iowa," the first association in the state to advocate the twin reforms of Negro suffrage and woman suffrage.

In announcing the organization of the association in the June 7 issue of the *Bulletin,* Loomis called attention to the fact that "this is the initiatory movement for the State of Iowa. If the success with which it is meeting here is any criterion of its prospective success throughout the State," he said, "we may well predict an almost universal acceptation of the great fundamental principle of government— *equal rights to all citizens, irrespective of race, color, or sex."* This principle, he asserted, should be made a part of the platform to be adopted at the coming Republican State Convention.

Loomis, then a bachelor (he was married December 10, 1867), was born in Madison County in upstate New York and migrated to Iowa with his parents in 1856. A teacher at the time of the Civil War, he enlisted in the summer of 1861 and served with the 42nd Illinois Infantry until he was mustered out in March 1865. Upon his return to civilian life he purchased the *Bulletin.* Loomis was the first editor in postwar Iowa to endorse woman suffrage, and the *Bulletin* under his ownership (1865–1869) was the most ardent advocate of the cause in the state.

The list of officers of the Independence Equal Rights Association indicates that Loomis had the support of some of the most respected and substantial citizens in the community in launching this first association in the state. The president—fifty-year-old Captain D. S. Lee— was a handsome, affable, and popular lawyer currently serving his second term as mayor of the town. A native of upstate New York, Lee came to Independence in 1852 and was the first man in Buchanan

3. Although Tilton privately endorsed the principle of equal suffrage, his lecture during the 1866–1867 season was devoted to the advancement of Negro suffrage which he felt was a necessity, while woman suffrage, although desirable, was at present a political impossibility.

County to volunteer in the Civil War. Members of the executive committee included Captain E. C. Little, postmaster of Independence (a young man crippled by wounds he had received in the Battle of Vicksburg), and Colonel Jed Lake, a native of Courtland County, New York, and a Civil War veteran. Lake, a lawyer, was one of the wealthiest men in the community, and his daughter Harriet, born February 7, 1870, was for many years a prominent woman-suffrage advocate in the state. Four women—Mrs. N. O. Lawton, Miss Carrie Hancock, Mrs. E. B. Older, and Mrs. Creerey—are also listed as officers of this pioneer Equal Rights Association; but as usual with their sex, their identity has been lost in the mists of history.

Encouraged by the reception of the Equal Rights Association in Independence, Loomis went to the state Republican Convention in Des Moines on June 19 prepared to do battle for woman suffrage. When the convention adopted a plank proclaiming "the rights of the ballot . . . the protection of the law and equal justice to all men,[4] irrespective of color, race, or religion," he made a motion to substitute the following statement: "That we affirm as a cardinal principle of the Republican party of Iowa, the natural political equality of all mankind, and that we favor the adoption of such amendments to the constitution of the State of Iowa as will secure equal rights, equal privilege, and equal protection of all citizens, irrespective of race, color, or sex." Loomis's motion, made despite the strenuous efforts of the chairman to silence him, was earnestly supported by about a dozen men amidst raucous laughter on the part of most delegates. No vote was taken on the motion and it was tabled as quickly as possible.

The *Des Moines Register,* in publishing the proceedings of the convention, gave only passing mention to Loomis's efforts in behalf of woman suffrage, noting that he made a motion to "guarantee equal rights to all persons regardless of sex." Loomis indignantly took the *Register* to task for its summary treatment of a serious subject, claiming that it had suppressed his resolution. As the leading Republican paper in the state, which printed the official proceedings of the convention, the *Register* should have published his resolution in full. In the *Bulletin* of June 28, Loomis called upon all Republican papers of the state to publish his equal rights resolution exactly as he had offered it. "Let it go upon the record as a matter of history," Loomis declared, "that an Iowa Republican convention in the year 1867

4. The 1866 Iowa Republican platform had endorsed suffrage for all "citizens" regardless of race, religion, or color. Since women were claiming the rights of citizens it was deemed desirable in 1867 to substitute the word "men" for "citizens."

voted to lay on the table a resolution in favor of granting to all citizens, equal rights, equal privileges, and equal protection. It is already upon the record that the same convention unanimously and enthusiastically voted that these blessings of liberty ought to be secured to male Negroes. It is a curious phase of civilization which virtually declares that the Negro must have accorded to him the exercise of rights and privileges which we absolutely deny to the most intelligent and high-minded woman."

"Our usually courteous friend, Loomis, has allowed a most trivial matter to upset his editorial equanimity," replied the *Register*. The only reason that the resolution had not been published, the paper said, was the simple fact that it could not be procured; the paper had received nothing from the secretary of the convention. The only difference between its own abstract of the motion, the *Register* said, and the original as submitted by Loomis, was that one was "written in the faultless syntax of the author" while the other was told "in the bungling language of the reporter."

Loomis's woman-suffrage resolution was the first to be presented to an Iowa Republican Convention. Similar resolutions were offered almost annually thereafter until in 1874 the Iowa Republican party, although still avoiding endorsement of woman suffrage, went on record favoring submission of a woman-suffrage amendment to the voters of Iowa.

WOMAN'S RIGHTS AND WOMAN'S WORK

A LETTER from Burlington, Iowa, signed "M. E. S.," which appeared in the *Independent* on January 24, 1867, sustained Tilton's report to this paper that educated women in Iowa wanted political rights for their sex.

M. E. S. were the initials of Miss Mary E. Shelton, a twenty-six-year-old teacher in the Burlington High School. She was the daughter of an itinerant Methodist minister who came to Iowa in 1852. In 1861 she graduated from Iowa Wesleyan College—a coeducational Methodist institution in Mount Pleasant, which was chartered as an academy in 1844 and became a college in 1854. Miss Shelton's letter, published while Tilton was lecturing in Iowa, was in response to a series of articles entitled "Household Suffrage" which were currently running in the *Independent*. These articles, written by a Professor Dio Lewis, advanced the argument that since the household was the unit of society, a man as head of the household voted not only for himself but also for the members of his family. To change this system, Professor Lewis maintained, would result not only in the disruption of the family but also in the disintegration of society.

Miss Shelton could not help but regret that "some of our profound thinkers think to so little purpose" on the subject of woman suffrage. "It has been the fashion for a long time to tell us that we are angels, and that all contact with the rough outer world will destroy that femininity. What a pity," she lamented, "that we cannot, like angels, be free from care of providing what we shall eat, what we shall drink, and where withall we shall be clothed!"

Miss Shelton pointed out that a great number of women in all the western towns depended entirely on their own labor to support themselves. "They cannot teach, because for every vacancy that occurs in the schools there are fifty applicants; and they are compelled to do the only work they can obtain, and that is to sew from dawn to dark, and receive in compensation $4 a week." To clothe themselves from this meager amount, sewing women must live in the cheapest boarding houses, where they must pay a minimum of $3 a week, Miss Shelton said. Here they are "brought into contact with people of low habits." It was no wonder that after long weary months of ill-paid labor hundreds of these women turned to prostitution and were "lost to all purity and goodness."

Nor was there much incentive for women to become educated, Miss Shelton continued. In Burlington there were "five large, flourishing public schools." In charge of four of them were "gentlemen, each with a good common school education." Of the sixteen lady teachers in the community, "a number have graduated from colleges where gentlemen and ladies take the same course of study, and could read a page of Latin, Greek, or Hebrew as readily as Professor Lewis himself. . . . Yet, because they are women they receive less than one-half the wages that the gentlemen do."

Miss Shelton, in what may have been a biographical note,[5] went on to tell of "a brother and sister who toiled side by side through college. After graduation, the brother immediately obtained a teaching position in which he received a salary of $800 a year, while the sister after long and patient effort was considered remarkably fortunate when she secured a position at $250 a year."

Miss Shelton knew of another girl—a college graduate—who did not want to go into teaching. "By the most pinching economy," she

5. Miss Shelton's brother, Ortus C., also graduated from Iowa Wesleyan in 1861. He was in charge of Elliott Seminary, Burlington, when he enlisted in the army. He died in service in October 1864.

managed to pay for a commercial course and subsequently secured a
position as a bookkeeper in a state institution at a salary of $20 a
month. She soon found that it was impossible to live on this amount
and was "obliged to take a school in a country village" where she
could earn more money.

"These women desire and confidently hope ere long to have the
ballot," Miss Shelton said in concluding her letter, "and then and
not till then do they look for the dawning of better days. All our
reading, thinking women are on one side of this great question." To
the brave, true women of the Equal Rights Association in the East
she sent kindly greetings from "the sisterhood of Iowa."

Although she did not say so, Miss Shelton could justly claim the
right to vote as a reward for her service to her country in time of war.[6]
In 1863, two years after her graduation from college, she enlisted in
the ranks of volunteer war workers as secretary to Annie Wittenmyer,
Iowa's hard-working Sanitary Agent. She accompanied Mrs. Wittenmyer on a trip south during the summer of 1863, visiting sick and
wounded troops in the vicinity of Vicksburg. In the fall she returned
to Iowa to help defend Mrs. Wittenmyer against political forces
which were seeking to oust her from her position as Sanitary Agent
for the state. During 1864 and until the war ended in 1865, Miss
Shelton was constantly in the field, working part of the time as Mrs.
Wittenmyer's secretary and at other times taking charge of special diet
kitchens in army hospitals in the Nashville and Wilmington areas.
In these hospitals one of her co-workers was her younger sister
Amanda, also an Iowa Wesleyan graduate.

After the war Miss Shelton taught in the Burlington High School
until her marriage in December 1869 to Emory S. Huston, a young
attorney and Civil War veteran. Mary Shelton Huston helped organize the Burlington Woman Suffrage Association in July 1870 and
served as its first secretary. A note in Susan B. Anthony's diary reveals
that when she lectured in Burlington in March 1871, Mr. Huston's
carriage was dispatched to the hotel to take her to an evening reception to meet Burlington woman-suffrage advocates. By this time, the
esteem in which Miss Anthony once was held had diminished substantially because of her association with Victoria Woodhull, a woman
of decidedly unsavory reputation, but the "sisterhood" in Burlington
was still willing to give her a welcome.

6. See Frank Moore, *Women of the War,* (Hartford, Conn., 1866) pp. 213–37.

Portrait of Annie Savery by Napoleon Sarony, New York painter and photographer. Mrs. Savery, brilliant, cultured, intellectual, liberal, and socially concerned Des Moines citizen was the outstanding woman-suffrage leader in Iowa from 1870 to 1872.

5

1868

❧

As the campaign for Negro suffrage progressed after the Civil War, woman-suffrage advocates found themselves without a publication for the dissemination of their propaganda. William Lloyd Garrison's *Liberator,* a longtime friend of woman's rights, had ceased publication at the end of 1865; and the *Anti-Slavery Standard,* organ of the American Anti-Slavery Society—also a friend of woman's rights—refused to add the burden of woman suffrage to its campaign for the ballot for the Negro. As Wendell Phillips, president of the society explained, the two causes "were not equally ripe."

In the fall of 1866 Lucy Stone and Henry Blackwell sent out a prospectus to their Republican friends asking for support for a publication to be titled *Universal Suffrage,* which they hoped would begin publication January 1, 1867. According to the prospectus, the leading object was "to effect the enfranchisement and complete recognition of the industrial and social and political equality of women and Negroes." Despite strenuous efforts Lucy Stone and her husband were unable to secure financing for this paper.

THE REVOLUTION BEGINS

NOT UNTIL JANUARY 8, 1868, did the woman's rights movement in the United States acquire a much-needed national publication—a sixteen-page weekly christened *The Revolution* by its founders, Elizabeth Cady Stanton and Susan B. Anthony. This paper, whose slogan was MEN—Their Rights and Nothing More; WOMEN—Their Rights and Nothing Less, was launched by Miss Anthony and Mrs. Stanton with the financial assistance of George Francis Train and David Meliss, a Democratic cohort of Train's. The editors of the publication were Mrs. Stanton and Parker Pillsbury, a maverick abolitionist who believed that women should be enfranchised at the same time as Negroes. Miss Anthony had charge of the business end of the paper, which included such matters as selling advertisements, securing subscribers, and running the office. Ten thousand copies of the first issue of *The Revolution* were sent to all parts of the country under the frank of James Brooks, the Democratic leader in Congress.

The Revolution was a lively and controversial paper and claimed to be the Organ of the National Party of the New America. Miss Anthony and Mrs. Stanton believed the new National party would soon rise from the ashes of the Republican party which was so corrupt and degenerate that it was about to expire. "With the moral chaos that surrounds us . . . the corruption in the State, the dissensions in the church, the jealousies in the home, what thinking mind does not feel that we need something new and revolutionary in every department of life?" Mrs. Stanton asked in her salutatory editorial.

The Revolution—"hatched out of Democratic eggs," as the *Mount Pleasant* (Iowa) *Journal* expressed it—was promptly disowned by Lucy Stone and other moderate woman's rights advocates who feared a paper under the domination of women as aggressive and radical as Miss Anthony and Mrs. Stanton. These moderates looked with particular disfavor on the association of these two women with Democrats, which they considered tantamount to betraying all liberal principles. Women should put their trust in the Republican party, the moderates maintained, since this was the party of true reform. Mrs. Stanton and Miss Anthony, for their part, looked upon the moderates as completely subservient to Republican men and a perfect example of the depth of degradation to which the women of the nation had fallen—that they would "be willing to stand aside, silent and indifferent spectators while all the lower stratas of mankind" were permitted to legislate in their interests. During the preceding four years, Mrs.

Stanton pointed out, the only help the woman-suffrage cause had received had come from the Democratic party.

Besides a "financial department" under the control of Meliss and Train, *The Revolution* had three main areas of interest—economic, social, and political. In the economic field (Miss Anthony's special concern) the paper stressed the need for working women to unionize to achieve better wages and working conditions. News of working women's societies, which Miss Anthony helped organize in New York City in 1868, was reported at great length in its columns.

The social area (Mrs. Stanton's particular interest) covered a variety of issues concerned with woman's sexual status. Discussion of such taboo subjects as abortion, prostitution, and birth control further distressed the moderates, who shuddered at adding fuel to the charges of free love under which the woman's rights movement had labored since its inception. *The Revolution* was outspoken in its opposition to a bill in the New York legislature to license prostitutes—a proposal which the paper claimed was designed to "legalize the profession for the safety and convenience of men." *The Revolution* argued for the right of divorce because marriage in many cases was only "legalized prostitution, a mere outward tie, impelled by custom, interest, necessity; founded not even in friendship to say nothing of love." The prevalence of abortion was deplored; this practice, the paper said, was the result of "forced maternity, not out of marriage but within it. Women keep silence upon many points, not breathing their thoughts to their dearest friends because of their inner reticence. . . . Most of this crime of abortion lies at the door of the male sex. . . . So deeply implanted is the sin of self-gratification that consequences are not considered." *The Revolution* also deplored the plethora of advertisements in nearly all the newspapers of the day touting "female medicines" which in thinly veiled terms guaranteed their abortive powers.[1] In addition the paper kept up a constant attack on the double standard of morals, a standard which permitted a man to shoot his wife's paramour with impunity but condemned to death by hanging a poor servant girl found alone in a cold attic with her newborn, illegitimate baby lying dead beside her.

1. The following advertisement for "Velpau Pills" in the *Bellevue* (Iowa) *Journal*, October 15, 1868, is typical: "These pills, so celebrated many years ago in Paris for the relief of female irregularities, and afterwards so notorious for their criminal employment in the practice of abortion, are now offered for sale for the first time in America. . . . In overcoming female obstructions they seem to be truly omnipotent bursting open the flood gates from whatever cause may have stopped them but they are offered to the public only for legitimate uses. . . . Agents are forbid to sell them when it is understood that the object is unlawful."

This advertisement for a popular "female medicine" in the Cedar Rapids Times of April 27, 1865, boasts of its abortive powers in thinly veiled terms. Similar advertisements were not uncommon in the 1860's and 1870's.

Miss Anthony and Mrs. Stanton believed that all the ills of society, both economic and social, would be cured as soon as women
obtained their political rights—rights which would automatically bring
dignity and self-respect to their sex. *The Revolution,* however, did
not advocate suffrage for all men and women but only those who
could meet certain (undefined) educational standards. With educated
suffrage, Mrs. Stanton argued, the lower orders of mankind—ignorant
and degraded former slaves and uneducated and venal foreigners who
were crowding into the country—would be denied the ballot while
virtuous, educated, Anglo-Saxon men and women could use their
power to purify the politics of the nation.

Communications from Iowa indicate that *The Revolution* met a
warm response from many friends of woman suffrage in the state.
Amelia Bloomer sent a letter of greeting saying that she was residing
with her husband in Council Bluffs—leading a quiet, retired life—and
was not to be confused with a Mrs. Bloomer who had been reported
as currently lecturing to the Mormons in Utah. Catherine S. Goff, an
elderly farm woman, wrote from her home near Cedar Rapids that
she was so pleased with the way in which *The Revolution* was being
conducted she felt prompted to express her gratitude "though it may
not be any great matter to you as I am but one of the obscure ones.
. . ." Mrs. Goff said she had been a woman's rights advocate ever
since she was "old enough to reflect on the subject" and was quite out
of patience with the way in which the abolitionists were treating the
woman suffragists. Mary Coppoc Ralley, sixty-four-year-old Quaker
resident of Springdale, welcomed *The Revolution* since it was "a
bloodless one and just such a one as I have been wanting for years."
She sent two dollars for a year's subscription with the expectation of
at last reading something that would not insult her dignity as a
woman. (Mrs. Ralley was the mother of Edwin and Barclay Coppoc,
the two Iowa boys who were with John Brown at Harper's Ferry.)[2]
Mattie Griffith, a twenty-six-year-old school teacher in Mount Pleasant,
wrote to *The Revolution* that "the existence of this paper is a cause
of great rejoicing. Let us batter away with cannons, guns, pistols, and
clubs—everyone can wield some weapon—and soon the old fortification
of prejudice and foggyism will crumble beneath our united efforts."[3]

---

2. Edwin Coppoc was hanged at Harper's Ferry in 1859. Barclay, who escaped, enlisted in the Union army in 1861 and was killed while in service.

3. In 1940 Olive Cole Smith, a Mount Pleasant resident, wrote to Mary Hunter,
Des Moines woman-suffrage historian: "Mattie Griffith was the militant type who
offended rather than won votes. That may account for the long delay in granting
suffrage—there were too many *militants.*"

Miss Griffith, the paper reported, had visited every house in Mount Pleasant and vicinity and had secured 460 signatures on petitions for woman suffrage in the District of Columbia.

The Revolution for the first two years of its existence was the unchallenged spokesman for the woman's rights movement in the United States. Meanwhile, the moderates led by Lucy Stone raised $10,000 to launch the *Woman's Journal,* a weekly woman's rights paper which began publication in Boston on January 1, 1870. *The Revolution,* never a paying proposition, was unable to compete with this new publication; and within six months Miss Anthony was forced to turn over her paper to new owners who continued to publish it for another year and a half. The *Woman's Journal* and its successor, the *Woman Citizen,* continued regular publication until the enfranchisement of women by the Nineteenth Amendment in 1920.

PROGRESS OF NEGRO SUFFRAGE
AND WOMAN SUFFRAGE IN IOWA

BECAUSE the extension of suffrage to the Negro in the North continued to be an unpopular issue during 1867,[4] Radicals in the Twelfth Iowa General Assembly, which convened in Des Moines in January 1868, were in no hurry to take action on the Negro-suffrage amendment which had been approved by the Eleventh General Assembly in 1866 and needed further approval by the current session before it could be submitted in a popular referendum. There was even some talk of abandoning the proposed amendment because of legal technicalities. Seeing a good opportunity to embarrass the Republicans, Democrat W. W. Cones of Davenport seized the initiative on January 17 by introducing the Negro-suffrage amendment in the Iowa Senate. Although Cones was opposed to Negro suffrage, the *Dubuque Herald* pointed out, he took the position that since the Radicals had chosen to make it an issue in Iowa the question should be submitted to a vote of the people. This amendment was kept in committee until late in the session when it was approved with a minimum of debate by the General Assembly for submission at the November 3 election.

Contrary to expectations Iowa voters on November 3, 1868 (the date General Grant was elected President), approved the Negro-suffrage amendment by a substantial majority. This vote marked Iowa as a leader in liberal legislation; along with Minnesota it shared the

4. In 1867 popular referendums on Negro suffrage were defeated in Ohio, Kansas, Wisconsin, and Minnesota. The Wisconsin and Minnesota referendums were the second for each state within a period of two years.

honor of being one of only two states ever to enfranchise the Negro in a popular referendum.[5]

Because there is little mention of woman suffrage either in the newspapers or in legislative records during the Twelfth General Assembly, it is difficult to piece together even a faint reflection of the woman-suffrage picture during this session. There are indications, however, that woman-suffrage advocates were more vocal than contemporary records would indicate. The journals of the House and the Senate, for example, do not record one instance of a woman-suffrage petition being submitted during the session; yet two years later, in arguing for woman suffrage in the Thirteenth General Assembly, John Irish recalled that during the previous session "he saw memorial after memorial presented from thousands of ladies all over the State asking that there be some legislation upon the woman suffrage question." These petitions, Irish said, "were made a matter of merriment and laughter . . . and were referred to a committee which brought in reports that would have been witty had it not been for their vulgarity." (The Committee on Domestic Manufactures was the favorite repository for all matters relating to women which the legislators wished to treat as a bawdy joke.) It is possible that Irish may have exaggerated the number of petitioners, but the fact that no one challenged his statement leads one to assume that it was essentially correct.

The question of extending the ballot to women was brought up in the House on January 23 when Republican Benjamin F. Murray of Winterset, a true friend of woman suffrage, made a motion to amend a resolution offered by Republican John Stone of Glenwood, endorsing suffrage for "all men in the State of Iowa irrespective of race or color" by striking the word "men" and substituting the words "all persons of the age of 21 and upwards." Stone opposed Murray's motion to amend his resolution. While he had a proper respect for ladies of all races, he did not think the time for allowing them to vote had come. Women were as faithfully represented in the legislature as were persons of the opposite sex, Stone said. When a second amendment was offered to Stone's resolution proposing to limit the endorsement of the extension of suffrage to those who could read and write, majority leader John Kasson of Des Moines called a halt to the debate by pointing out the necessity for Republican unity on the question of suffrage. To put the resolution to a vote, Kasson said, would only emphasize differences of opinion among the Repub-

5. The question of Negro suffrage was submitted twice in Minnesota before it was approved in 1868. It was estimated that 178 Negroes were eligible to vote in Iowa; 42 in Minnesota.

licans. He therefore made a motion, which was carried, to refer it to the Committee on Constitutional Amendments. "But for this timely move," reported the correspondent for the *Burlington Hawkeye*, "the Republicans of the House would certainly have given strong grounds to their enemies to gloat over their divisions." To avoid further embarrassment, the House agreed that in the future all resolutions relating to suffrage would be read and referred without debate.

On February 27 the Committee on Domestic Manufactures made a facetious report on the request of a Mrs. Kilburne of Adair County for use of the hall of the House of Representatives to deliver what the committee termed a discourse on "Woman's Wrongs." This committee reported that it had examined a copy of Mrs. Kilburne's proposed speech and recommended that both the speech and the request to present it be tabled. The committee believed "that no permanent good could result to women in their moral or political position among men by the reading of this discourse and that in the 'new era' that is to open . . . the lawmakers will then as now, be willing to give women all they ask, that is legally in their power to do so." Mrs. Kilburne (although identified in the House *Journal* as Mrs. S. A. Kilburne) was most probably thirty-year-old Jennie A. Kilburne—wife of Galen F. Kilburne, a leading Adair County citizen who represented Adair, Cass, and Montgomery counties in the 1868 General Assembly. Jennie Kilburne, referred to by the *Davenport Democrat* as "a female Captain in the reform army of the 'upper plane'" whose request to the legislature was "couched in such language as spirits use in the flowing communications made through the chosen mediums . . ." was evidently a spiritualist, a popular cult in the mid-nineteenth century.

In addition to belief in the possibility of communication with the dead, spiritualism stressed a practical humanitarianism as a substitute for ritualistic religion—a humanitarianism which gave women equal status with men in all aspects of life.[6] "From the frequent

6. In 1894 Susan B. Anthony paid the following tribute to the spiritualists for their contributions to the woman's rights cause: "If instead of Spiritualists, this great body of people had been Baptists, Presbyterians, Methodists, or Catholics, their praises for the firm stand they have taken for the enfranchisement of half the people of this country, would have been everywhere sung in song and told in story. But the suffrage women of America always have been afraid to give voice to the 'thank you' in their hearts, for Spiritualism has been fully as unpopular as woman suffrage; and they feared if they displayed too much gratitude for this endorsement the public would at once pronounce them Spiritualists and they would be doubly damned. . . . There are still a few of us brave enough to publicly express our thanks therefor, notwithstanding the denunciation of orthodox religionists and orthodox politicians." Ida Husted Harper, *The Life and Work of Susan B. Anthony,* vol. 2 (Indianapolis, 1898), pp. 773–74.

notices that have appeared in your paper concerning the movement of spiritual lecturers," wrote Anna M. Middlebrook, a spiritualist, in a letter published in *The Revolution,* March 19, 1868, "I judge that you must be aware that of the ten or eleven million of the spiritualists in the country, and their 50,000 mediums, the majority sympathize with and work for the advancement of the cause of Female Suffrage." In December 1868 Henry C. Wright, a respected New England Garrisonian abolitionist, arrived in Des Moines where he delivered a series of lectures to the Spiritual Society, including one on woman suffrage. Under Wright's encouragement, the society sent a resolution to the *Des Moines Register* stating that it is a "self-evident truth that all men and women are created equal in natural rights."

On March 31, after the Negro-suffrage amendment was finally approved by the General Assembly, William G. Wilson of Davis County, a Civil War veteran and the youngest member of the House, offered a woman-suffrage resolution based on the rhetoric of the Declaration of Independence. Declaring that the word "men" in this document "refers to the whole human race, regardless of nationality or sex," Wilson's resolution went on to say that it is "the sense of this House that steps should be taken looking towards a change in the constitution of this State so as to allow women the right of franchise, for the proper use of which her quick perception, strong intellect, and above all, her high sense of right and justice have proven her so well qualified." Wilson's resolution was referred to the Committee on Constitutional Amendments, which reported on April 4 that a majority of its members recommended adoption. However, it was not put to a vote in the House.

Immediately after the November 3 elections, when the voters of Iowa approved the deletion of the word "white" from the article setting forth voting qualifications in the state constitution, Republican editors friendly to woman suffrage began a campaign to delete the word "male" from this same section. "It is not greatly to our credit that Negroes have been enfranchised before the same privilege has been accorded to our wives, mothers, and sisters," said Benjamin F. Gue, editor of the *Fort Dodge North West.*[7] "We have taken one step in the right direction at the recent election but we have only partial suffrage. Let Iowa be the first state to make it impartial."

7. Gue, born in western New York in 1828, heard Elizabeth Cady Stanton deliver one of her first lectures on woman suffrage at a meeting of Progressive Friends at Farmington, N.Y., on October 6, 1848. On that date he noted in his diary that he had signed a petition which Mrs. Stanton was circulating "praying the Legislature to allow women of legal age to exercise the right of *Elective Franchise.*"

The *DeWitt Observer,* edited by S. H. Shoemaker, hoped that woman suffrage would receive bipartisan support. "The Democrats who opposed Negro suffrage cannot now do better than join in this movement and enfranchise their wives and daughters, and thus enable them to offset the colored vote which they would more than balance. Don't drag this thing in as a party question," Shoemaker advised, "but let both parties unite and press it to a successful termination."

"During the past four years the *Register* has been repeatedly questioned to ascertain its opinion of female suffrage," said Frank Mills, editor of the *Des Moines Register,* in early December 1868. "Its reply has been that it was and is in favor of woman having the ballot whenever she expressed the wish for it and now that she is pretty generally expressing the wish, it takes a pleasure in falling in line with her for the contest." In this connection Mills called the attention of his readers to a recent woman's rights convention in Boston, at which the moderates had banded together into a New England Woman Suffrage Association under the leadership of Julia Ward Howe. Mrs. Howe, author of "Battle Hymn of the Republic," was a recent convert to woman suffrage who lent great prestige to the New England association. (Lucy Stone, prime mover in organizing the New England group, preferred the less conspicuous office of chairman of the executive committee.) *"The Revolution* [i.e., Miss Anthony and Mrs. Stanton] had no voice or mention in the deliberations of this meeting," Mills pointed out. Noting Mrs. Howe's recent conversion to woman suffrage, he went on to say, "The enfranchisement of the slave and the quick reception of the foreigner has convinced her that the day is almost here for the voice and counsel of the good women to be heard in the councils of politics." Ten years before he had never expected to see the day when women would vote, but now he expected to march to the ballot box with his female neighbors before Time grayed his hair.

Only a few Republican papers, however, were genuinely in favor of woman suffrage. The rest merely gave lip service to the cause. The *Council Bluffs Nonpareil* said that "as a matter of principle" it was forced to maintain the justice of woman suffrage, yet it confessed "to much hesitation in the determination of the question and the need for much further investigation and education." The *Marshalltown Times* declared, "The tendencies of the present time are toward universal suffrage and in our opinion it is coming along sometime. . . . You cannot stop the march of events even though you don't like the way they are marching." In any event, "you are an old fogy if you get in their way." Since it was doubtful if women really wanted to vote,

Julia Ward Howe, author of the "Battle Hymn of the Republic," gave prestige to the New England Woman Suffrage Association when she consented to take the office of president at the time of its organization in 1868.

and it would not be right to "impose a weighty obligation upon them unasked," the *Times* proposed that the next legislature provide a special referendum, so that women could express themselves on the subject. The *Mount Pleasant Journal* announced that it was in favor of female suffrage "after the questions growing out of the late war have been permanently settled and the great questions of National Finances solved." It warned the women, however, that they would "have to choose other leaders than the female blatherskite [Mrs. Stanton] who sits in the editorial chair of the New York *Revolution*."

WOMEN SPEAK FOR THEMSELVES

DESPITE the efforts of Republican editors and politicians in Iowa to silence spokesmen for woman suffrage before the 1868 November elections, a number of women who refused to be intimidated by these men made tours in the state, speaking in behalf of woman's rights. Among them were Iowa residents, novices on the platform, who were anxious to start the ball rolling for woman suffrage; reformers from other states; and Anna Dickinson, the professional lyceum speaker, who included a lecture on woman's rights in her repertoire each season.

ANNA DICKINSON, who made her third Iowa tour in January 1868, was the star attraction on a lyceum circuit which included some of the leading men of the country. Wherever she went, she spoke to standing-room-only houses;

and despite the fact that she was now charging $200 for each appearance, she was invariably a money-maker for local lecture associations, often saving them from unprofitable seasons.[8]

In "Women and Idiots," Miss Dickinson's woman's rights lecture in 1868, she pointed out that women were classed with paupers, criminals, and idiots in being denied the right of property and suffrage and argued that they deserved a better fate. A correspondent who heard her deliver this lecture in Waterloo reported to the *Dubuque Herald* that "no greater humbug ever plumed her wings than this human monstrosity. She is a disgrace to the female sex and an insult to man." The *Herald,* on the occasion of her third annual lecture in Dubuque in 1870, dubbed Anna Dickinson "an enemy to the homes of America." Miss Dickinson "is a smart, glib, pleasant talker," said the *Herald,* "who sows broadcast false doctrines that will sooner or later ruin many families that are now contented and happy. . . . Women go to hear her who during 364 days in the year thought they had pleasant homes and good husbands and enjoyed all the mental and moral culture that their circumstances in life afford. But on the 365th day along comes Anna Dickinson with her twaddle, and they discover all at once that they are very much abused."

In March ELIZABETH A. KINGSBURY of Vineland, New Jersey—a peripatetic abolitionist and woman's rights pioneer—toured Iowa speaking on woman suffrage. Mrs. Kingsbury, fifty-one-year-old daughter of a Connecticut minister, began her lecture career in 1856. In 1857 she traveled as far as Indiana, Ohio, Michigan, and Illinois speaking on woman's rights. During the Civil War Mrs. Kingbsury was employed by the New England Freedman's Aid Society as a lecturer and fund raiser. Her 1868 trip— which took her to Ohio, Illinois, Iowa, and Wisconsin— was undertaken on her own initiative. She spoke for lyceums when she could obtain engagements and used the money she earned from this source to help defray the ex-

8. In Des Moines, for example, where Anna Dickinson attracted the largest audience of the season for three successive years, the profit of $231.70 from her 1868 appearance helped offset losses of $40.50 incurred by Clara Barton, the Civil War nurse, and $21.45 by Ralph Waldo Emerson, the writer. Because of Miss Dickinson the Lecture Association in Des Moines was able to wind up the 1867–1868 season with a small profit.

penses of the free lectures which she gave in other communities. The only notices which have come to light of her presence in Iowa are found in *The Revolution* which in 1868 listed her as its Iowa agent. It reported on March 19 that an Iowa correspondent had written that, although Iowa newspapers generally were opposed to the woman's rights movement and maintained a dignified silence on the subject, Mrs. Kingsbury was receiving "much appreciation orally and by writing. One notice of her says, 'clear logical, eloquent speaker.' Another, 'pleads simple justice for her sex in a manner that commands the attention of all.'" The editors of *The Revolution* heartily endorsed Mrs. Kingsbury and wished her well wherever she went.[9]

On January 23, 1868, ANNIE SAVERY of Des Moines delivered a lecture at the courthouse entitled "Angels and Politicians." This lecture, given for the benefit of the Library Association, marked the first time that a Des Moines woman dared admit in public that she wanted to vote. Although Annie Savery was to become the most able and influential exponent of the cause of woman suffrage in the state, her reception in 1868 gave little indication of her future prominence in the Iowa woman-suffrage movement. The *Des Moines Register* gave no synopsis of the content of Mrs. Savery's speech and merely reported that a "large and intelligent audience" had listened to her "unanswerable plea for governmental franchises for woman." An anonymous reader, "V. C. T."—in a letter published a few days after this review—accused the *Register* of slighting Mrs. Savery's speech because it was delivered by a woman. Had it been given by a man, the writer said, it would have been reviewed exhaustively. He (or she) went on to say that Mrs. Savery was under the burden of presenting an unpopular subject—"a task far more onerous than floating with the tide of universal assent." This writer could not but regret that such a well-digested argument for the rights of women could not have been listened to by a larger number of ladies. "As it was, its inculcations fell upon the stoney ground of the minds of a dissident majority. At all events the question is up for discussion. The revolution is begun."

9. In Mrs. Stanton's and Miss Anthony's three-volume *History of Woman Suffrage* there is no mention of Mrs. Kingsbury. Doubtless they were displeased because in February 1869 she became a lecturer for the New England Woman Suffrage Association, a society organized in the fall of 1868 by moderates who disapproved of *The Revolution's* radical views. The *Woman's Journal* of April 18, 1896, carries a letter telling of Mrs. Kingsbury's work for woman suffrage.

In Iowa City, where Mrs. Savery delivered this same lecture on February 18, the Democratic *State Press* said she was "listened to by such an audience as usually greets the lecturer not famous for literary honors gained by long practice on lyceum stages." Her speech, the *Press* said, "embraced more points of aggression than the efforts of the Philadelphia scoldress [Anna Dickinson] and was enunciated with less vituperation, more lady-like expressiveness. . . . Notwithstanding its literary merit, it was marred by a want of familiarity with the rostrum and a lack of confidence in herself by the lecturer." The *Press* predicted that the "female Elysium whose advent she portrayed on the granting of the ballot to women was far in the future."

Mrs. Savery, a plump woman of medium height with a pleasant expression and a great zest for life, was born in London, England, in 1831 and came with her parents to the United States when she was still an infant. Nothing is known of her childhood except that she had only a few years of common school education. In January 1854 she was married to James C. Savery at Saratoga, New York, and the young couple settled in Des Moines the following spring. Savery, a genial gentleman and an inveterate speculator whose fortunes fluctuated widely during the course of his life, was riding the wave of prosperity in the 1860's. The Hotel Savery in Des Moines, which he had promoted, was the meeting place for all Iowa; and the American Emigrant Company of which he was a partner was a prosperous organization whose business was to bring immigrants to America to settle the vast tracts of land which the company owned in the Midwest. Savery, in connection with his work for the American Emigrant Company, spent several months each winter in New York and Washington. In addition he made occasional trips to Europe. Since the Saverys had no children, Annie Savery was free to accompany her husband on these journeys.

A woman with a keen and inquiring mind, Mrs. Savery was largely self-educated.[10] She spoke French fluently, had broad knowledge of literature and history, and al-

---

10. Frank M. Mills, owner of the *Des Moines Register* from 1866 to 1870 and co-owner of a job printing shop and bookstore in Des Moines from 1856 to 1886, refers to Mrs. Savery in his *Autobiographical Reminiscences* as the "wonder wife" of James Savery "who starting with scarcely the advantages of a primary school education, made herself probably the best educated woman in Iowa, . . . beginning by ordering through our bookstore text books of all the grade schools and through all the courses, bringing a governess [tutor] to coach her through the higher branches and topping it off by extensive travelling all over the world."

though a religious freethinker was a lifelong student of religious thought. The library in her elegant home on Greenwood (now Grand) Avenue was said to be the finest in Iowa. In her reform interests Mrs. Savery went far beyond the personal charity and temperance work which were considered proper activity for a woman of her time. In addition to her support of woman suffrage in 1868 Mrs. Savery, during that year, also evidenced her concern for the advancement of women by endowing a twenty-year scholarship for girls at Grinnell College. She was an ardent advocate of a strong public-school system for Des Moines and one of two women (along with seventy-seven men) to contribute $50 for a life membership in the Des Moines Library Association after its organization in 1866. In 1867 Mrs. Savery initiated a campaign to better living conditions for prisoners confined in the dank, smelly, and unventilated county jail located in the basement of the courthouse.

Mrs. Savery, who was presented to Emperor Louis Napoleon at the Tuileries Palace in Paris during a trip to Europe in 1866,[11] made her first platform appearance in Des Moines in January 1867 with a lecture titled, "From the Tuileries to the Forum." The lecture—given for the benefit of J. M. Dixon, a local newspaperman who was losing his sight—brought a net profit of $155. This success led Mrs. Savery to repeat the lecture in February for the benefit of the poor of Des Moines. She subsequently delivered it in several other Iowa communities.[12] Although Des Moines society would tolerate one of its woman members on the platform if she confined herself to cultural topics; the attitude of the community changed sharply when she took up the subject of the franchise for women. In 1870, when the legislature had made the cause respectable

11. The *Des Moines Register* reported on February 14, 1866, that Mrs. Savery was among twenty-four American ladies and gentlemen presented to Louis Napoleon (emperor of France from 1852 to 1870) at the Tuileries Palace in Paris.

12. Dixon in his book *The Valley and the Shadow,* published 1868, says: "I am glad that Mrs. J. C. Savery has given her consent to appear occasionally in the capacity of a lecturer. To those persons who know this lady, it is not necessary to say that she possesses an original aptitude for literary acquisitions. Her mind is clear and vigorous, giving her those elements of thought which are defined as readiness of perception and great power of abstract reflection. Her mental versatility takes in such a range of endowment as to assure success, with but little comparative toil, in any department of literature or science. . . . She excels in conversation, possessing a fine command of language, a well-stored mind, and abundant vivacity. She has studied much and travelled extensively, both in the United States and Europe, and it must be evident that her native and acquired qualifications are such as to give her a high position among the female lecturers of our country."

by approving a woman-suffrage amendment and women were willing to jump on the bandwagon, Mrs. Savery recalled in a letter to Amelia Bloomer the bitter denunciation which she had experienced at the time of her lecture on woman suffrage two years before.

In the last issue of *The Revolution* for 1868 Mrs. Savery received the thanks of Susan B. Anthony for her help in rolling up a long list of subscribers during the year. Mrs. Savery spent most of 1869 in Europe and upon her return home in the fall suffered an attack of diphtheria. Hence it was not until December 1869 that she responded to a letter from Amelia Bloomer, written the previous spring, soliciting her help in organizing the woman-suffrage movement in Iowa. This was the beginning of a close friendship between the two women. Mrs. Savery was elected corresponding secretary of the Iowa Woman Suffrage Association when it was organized at Mount Pleasant in June 1870, and upon her return from this meeting she was instrumental in calling the first meeting of woman-suffrage advocates in Des Moines.

Another Iowa woman-suffrage advocate to mount the platform in 1868 was MATTIE GRIFFITH, the twenty-six-year-old Mount Pleasant schoolteacher whose work for woman suffrage was noted by *The Revolution*. Miss Griffith, who made her home with her widowed mother, was born in Pennsylvania in 1842 and spent most of her girlhood in Ohio, where she attended Hopedale Academy. She came to Iowa in 1862. In late March 1868 Miss Griffith embarked on a tour of southern and central Iowa communities with a lecture titled "Shall Women Vote?" A slender, pretty, young woman with a pleasant voice, Miss Griffith was sufficiently at ease on the platform to be able to speak without a manuscript. The *Mount Pleasant Journal* thought she had the "vim and get up" to make her popular; and the *Des Moines Register,* in announcing her appearance at the courthouse on April 4, praised her as a speaker with a "Dickinson-like vim" and predicted that her lecture would equal "Women and Idiots." Despite this advance notice the *Register* did not bother to review Miss Griffith's speech. During the next three years she made several tours in various sections of the state speaking on temperance and woman suffrage. Following her marriage to Francis M. Davenport on May 30, 1870, she moved to Oskaloosa, where she was elected secretary of the Oskaloosa Woman Suffrage Association when it was organized in June of that year.

Mattie Griffith was the first of several Mount Pleasant women who lectured on woman suffrage during the next few years. MRS. MARY A. BEAVERS, a young woman who had served as a nurse in the Civil War, became well known throughout the state for her lectures on temperance and woman's rights. BELLE MANSFIELD, who was to become the first woman lawyer in the United States in 1869, lectured on woman's rights in communities in the Mount Pleasant area; and ALICE BIRD, an 1869 graduate of Iowa Wesleyan College, began lecturing on woman suffrage in 1870. Miss Bird (who in 1873 married Belle Mansfield's brother Washington I. Babb) served as the first president of the P.E.O. Sisterhood, a sorority which she and five other Iowa Wesleyan students founded in the spring of 1869. "It is said that Miss Allie Bird, the new lecturer that Mount Pleasant has just turned out of her orator-mill, is a real duck of a girl—plump as well as profound, of good looks as well as good speech," said the *Des Moines Register* in March 1870. "On her lips is the carmine as well as the eloquence of the living coals. But can it be that these woman-suffrage folks are going to make ducks out of Birds?" the *Register* asked.

By April 8, 1868, so many women had lectured in Iowa that the *Des Moines Register* deplored "The Female Lecture Mania." "The Anna Dickinsons, the Mattie Griffiths, and the other females and so-forths, having swept through the State in elocutionary flashes, the public's eyes and ears have become nearly sated, and would now be willing to rest awhile. But we are sorry to inform you, dear public," said the *Register*, "that you are not through with the show yet. A female colored lady from Boston has invaded the State, and was posted for a speech at Mount Pleasant last night and is to come to Des Moines next week." About this same time the *Boone County Advocate* announced another woman lecturer, a Mrs. C. A. Jacobs of Anamosa. Women on the lecture platform, observed the *Advocate*, "are becoming thick as hops."

In October 1868 NETTIE SANFORD—a tart-tongued, thirty-eight-year-old Marshalltown resident—began speaking on woman's rights in a tour which took her to several communities in central Iowa. Mrs. Sanford, born in Ohio, came to Iowa with her parents in 1856. A teacher prior to her marriage to Daniel Sanford in 1863, Mrs. Sanford was the mother of an eight-month-old daughter Mary and author of a history of Marshall County, a work not highly regarded for its accuracy. Mrs. Sanford's lecture in 1868 was titled "Mary Queen of Scots." According to the *Jasper County Republican,* a Newton paper, Mrs. Sanford "appealed to her sex to adopt a more exalted aim than that which now seems to be the height of her ambition—to prepare themselves for the responsibilities which the grand march of events seem to indicate will soon devolve upon them." When the Marshall County Woman Suffrage Association was organized in May 1870, Mrs. Sanford was elected president. She was also named a vice-president of the Iowa Woman Suffrage Association when it was organized at Mount Pleasant a few weeks later. In 1871 Mrs. Sanford emerged as the leading spokeswoman for the anti-free-love faction in the Iowa Woman Suffrage Association.

MARY DARWIN of Burlington, who defended Annie Wittenmyer in Des Moines in 1863, had by 1868 established herself as one of the most able speakers among the women in Iowa. The *Henry County Press,* in announcing a lecture by Mrs. Darwin at Mount Pleasant in December 1868, called her "Iowa's most popular lecturer." This same month Mrs. Darwin and Mary E. Shelton, whose letter about the economic plight of women was published in Theodore Tilton's *Independent,* were announced as speakers for the Burlington Lecture Association series for the 1868–1869 season.

In late October 1868 MARTHA H. BRINKERHOFF of Missouri, the young woman who had stumped Kansas in 1867, began a tour of northeast and north central Iowa which lasted until sometime in March. Since her tour for the most part was made after the question of Negro suffrage was settled in the November 3 referendum, Republican editors in the communities she visited were willing to publicize her appearances and even to give her friendly reviews.

Following Mrs. Brinkerhoff's lecture in Fort Dodge on February 3, 1869, Benjamin F. Gue reported in the *Fort Dodge North West* that although she was young and with barely two years experience she was rapidly acquiring a reputation that would soon place her "side by side with the ablest and most popular lecturers of the day. Her style is easy and graceful and womanly—her arguments clear, logical and pointed—and there is a calm earnest eloquence in her address that carries conviction to the hearer." Mrs. Brinkerhoff's Fort Dodge address was the first on woman suffrage ever delivered in the community and Gue said it "awakened among our citizens for several days a general discussion on its merits."

A correspondent for the *Dubuque Times* who heard Mrs. Brinkerhoff lecture in Osage reported that he found her "an able and fluent speaker and close reasoner and thoroughly acquainted with the cause in which she is interested." Here too she "set the community to thinking and talking about woman suffrage."

Even the *Dubuque Herald* had a good word to say for Mrs. Brinkerhoff after her lecture at the Universalist Church in Dubuque on March 9. "The lady has been giving free lectures throughout Iowa and at the close has taken up a contribution to pay her expenses," the *Herald* told its readers. "She collected [in Dubuque] $26 whereas Anna Dickinson received $200. If women were in the habit of carrying purses or having one of their own, the receipts would have been larger." The *Herald* found Martha Brinkerhoff and Anna Dickinson "both alike in wearing short hair and black dresses, but that is all. Mrs. Brinkerhoff is a wife and a mother. Miss Dickinson's discourse was so rambling and disconnected that it would have sounded as well to have commenced in the middle and gone either way. Mrs. Brinkerhoff's was logical, not sensational but earnest and truthful. What she says will be remembered when an extravagant scold leaves only an unpleasant impression but never brings conviction."

Mrs. Brinkerhoff, in addition to lecturing during her Iowa tour, acted as an agent for *The Revolution,* selling subscriptions wherever she went. She also managed to organize a few equal rights associations. In Mount Vernon—the home of Cornell College—where Mrs. Brinkerhoff delivered two lectures in early December 1868, Charles W. Rollins—young Civil War veteran and student at the college—reported to *The Revolution* that a Mount Vernon Equal Rights Association was organized during the course of Mrs. Brinkerhoff's visit. The Reverend Mr. Stevens, pastor of the Methodist Church, was president; Mrs. King, wife of the Cornell College president, was secretary. The members agreed to "make every exertion to obtain such an amendment to our state and national constitutions as shall confer the right of Suffrage upon woman."

In a report to the annual meeting of the American Equal Rights Association held in New York on May 12 and 13, 1869, Mrs. Brinkerhoff gave a resume of her work in Iowa. She entered the state at Clinton and spoke in nearly all the towns on the North Western Railroad as far as Boone. From Boone she went north by stagecoach to Fort Dodge, working her way east again on the Dubuque and Sioux City Railroad (the present Illinois Central). In Lowden, Clarence, Mechanicsville, Mount Vernon, and other towns (all communities of a few hundred population) on and off the railroad she "succeeded in effecting organizations and in every case the leading men and women were made officers and each Association contributed a certain sum of money to buy speeches upon the subject to distribute among the people. In Blairstown, friends sent a sum sufficient to have a copy [of *The Revolution*] sent to every family in town. . . . In Cedar Rapids, with only one day's notice, the largest hall in the city was filled with the first people of the place. At the close of the meeting, the many warm shakes of the hand and the liberality with which they responded, when asked to subscribe for *The Revolution,* plainly indicated that the cause of Woman's Enfranchisement had taken deep root in the minds of the people. . . . In Independence, a notice of the same length effected the same result. . . . Small, lukewarm audiences were definitely the exception." The greatest difficulty, Mrs. Brinkerhoff said, was that she did not have time enough to enable her to accept half the invitations to lecture which she received from every quarter.

"The reputation that Iowa has of being one of the most liberal and progressive States in the country, she richly merits," Mrs. Brinkerhoff reported. "The proposition to strike the word 'white' from the State Constitution was carried by a majority of many thousands," and she believed that "after one canvass of the State upon the Woman question its voters would as readily dispose of the word 'male.'" A few efficient workers were all that were needed "to entirely prepare the people for the issue."[13]

13. Despite the favorable reception which Mrs. Brinkerhoff received in Iowa and other states at this time, she is almost completely ignored by woman-suffrage historians of the period. The reason is revealed in a letter, written in 1880 by Mary Newbury Adams of Dubuque to Amelia Bloomer, in which she gives a history of woman-suffrage work in the Dubuque area. In a "private" appended note Mrs. Adams says: "I did not mention our having Mrs. Brinkerhoff because she so hurt our cause here. After I had opened my house to her and Mr. Adams got several places for her to speak in northern Iowa—off in Michigan she left her husband and created a scandal by taking another. I thought I would not serve the matter by her name. Yet she spoke well and the Universalist Church was crowded to hear her. It is better to tell too little than too much."

❊

THE AGE OF BRASS.
or the triumphs of Woman's rights

Susan B. Anthony (second from right) is depicted as a man-tamer in this 1869 Currier and Ives print.

6

1869

❋

AFTER THE NOVEMBER 1868 presidential elections the Republicans were ready to act on a Fifteenth Amendment which would guarantee Negro suffrage in both the North and the South. Although Ulysses S. Grant had won an overwhelming electoral vote, his popular majority—only 300,000—was less than the number of Negroes voting. Hence the practical politicians were willing to join the abolitionists in the Republican party in framing an amendment which would not only ensure continued Negro suffrage in the South but would also enfranchise Negroes in the North and increase Republican strength in large cities where the Democrats predominated.

The following Fifteenth Amendment was approved by the final session of the Fortieth Congress—meeting from December 1868 to March 1869—and submitted to the states for ratification on February 27, 1869: "The right of citizens of the United States to vote shall not be denied or abridged by the United States or by any State on account of race, color, or previous condition of servitude."

PROGRESS OF WOMAN SUFFRAGE:
THE UNITED STATES CONSTITUTION,
THE DISTRICT OF COLUMBIA, THE TERRITORIES

WHILE the Fifteenth Amendment was under consideration in Congress during the winter of 1868–1869, there were two proposals for constitutional amendments designed to give women as well as Negroes the right to vote. The first—introduced in the House by an ardent woman-suffrage advocate, Republican George W. Julian of Indiana—guaranteed suffrage to all citizens "without distinction or discrimination whatever founded on race, color, or sex." The second—introduced in the Senate by Republican Samuel C. Pomeroy of Kansas—made U.S. citizenship as defined in the Fourteenth Amendment the basis of suffrage. It gave "all native or naturalized citizens . . . the same rights and privileges of the elective franchise." Pomeroy, who professed to be a true friend of woman suffrage, argued that because women as well as men were citizens they should have an equal opportunity to vote. Since Pomeroy's proposal did not carry a specific guarantee of suffrage for either women or Negroes, there is good rea-

THE AGE OF IRON.

The fate of man at the hands of strong-minded women is depicted in the Currier and Ives companion piece to the opening illustration of this chapter.

son to doubt the sincerity of his arguments. Soon after the Forty-first Congress convened in March 1869, Julian introduced a Sixteenth Amendment for woman suffrage which prohibited the denial of suffrage to any citizen because of sex. This marked the beginning of the long campaign for a separate woman-suffrage amendment, which did not end until 1920 when the Nineteenth Amendment was ratified.

In addition to these attempts to secure a constitutional guarantee of woman suffrage, bills also were introduced in both the last session of the Fortieth Congress and the first session of the Forty-first Congress to enfranchise women in the District of Columbia and the territories, where Negroes were already enfranchised by congressional action. However, there was no serious interest in Congress in extending the franchise to women, either by constitutional amendment or by statute; and all proposals to do so died in committee.

Meanwhile, woman-suffrage advocates throughout the North were busy circulating petitions asking Congress for the right to vote. Most of the petitions which circulated during 1868 asked for woman suffrage in the District of Columbia and the territories. After the November elections, when there was an increasing certainty that the next session of Congress would submit a Fifteenth Amendment, the petitions requested "that in any change or amendment of the Constitution you may propose to extend or regulate suffrage, there shall be no distinction made between men and women." Three petitions from Iowa were among hundreds presented in Congress during the winter of 1868–1869.

In January 1869 Miss Anthony and Mrs. Stanton, who had come to Washington to lead the first woman-suffrage convention to be held in the city, chalked up another record for woman suffrage by securing a hearing before the Senate Committee on the District of Columbia. This hearing—the first for woman suffrage held by a committee of Congress—attracted nationwide publicity. The following year Miss Anthony and Mrs. Stanton were again granted a hearing by the District of Columbia Committee, but despite repeated requests both in 1869 and in 1870 they were refused a hearing by the judiciary committees of the House and the Senate—the committees responsible for framing constitutional amendments.

Woman suffrage for the District of Columbia ceased to be an issue in 1871 when Congress disfranchised all the residents by abolishing local self-government and placing the District under direct congressional control.

Meanwhile, in the territory of Wyoming the cause of woman suffrage won an unexpected victory in December 1869 when the predominantly Irish, solidly Democratic legislature passed, during its first session, a woman-suffrage bill in protest of congressional imposition of Negro suffrage on the territory. The wags in the Wyoming legislature who promoted this bill fully expected that the Republican governor appointed by the President would veto the measure. The governor, however, called the legislature's bluff and signed the bill.[1]

"As I have always predicted," Mrs. Stanton commented in *The Revolution*, "this right [suffrage] has been first conferred on us by a Democratic Legislature."

LUCY STONE LEADS A REVOLT

FRICTION between Mrs. Stanton and Miss Anthony and the moderates in the woman-suffrage movement, who had banded together in the fall of 1868 under the banner of the New England Woman Suffrage Association, continued to increase during 1869. Although Julia Ward Howe was the president of the New England association, Lucy Stone, chairman of the executive committee, was the de facto leader and the most active in trying to counter the extremism of Miss Anthony and Mrs. Stanton.

In January 1869, when Miss Anthony and Mrs. Stanton organized a national woman-suffrage convention in Washington to oppose any Fifteenth Amendment which did not enfranchise women along with the Negro, the meeting was not only boycotted by the moderates but Lucy Stone came to Washington to tell congressional leaders that women would be willing to wait for their own enfranchisement in a separate Sixteenth Amendment. While there, Lucy Stone also lobbied for women suffrage in the District of Columbia.

Miss Anthony and Mrs. Stanton caused further consternation among the moderates—especially those who had been closely associated with the abolitionist movement—by their stubborn refusal to endorse the Fifteenth Amendment even after its approval by Congress. Their attitude caused a heated debate at the third (and last) annual meeting of the American Equal Rights Association in New York in May 1869, when former slave Frederick Douglass proposed a resolution gratefully welcoming the pending Fifteenth Amendment and earnestly soliciting the state legislatures to approve it without delay. Mrs. Stanton retorted that she did not rejoice in the passage of an amendment which placed every type of ignorant manhood over her. To do so was "requiring

---

1. In February 1870 the legislature of the territory of Utah followed suit, passing a woman-suffrage bill in protest against antipolygamy bills pending in Congress. This law remained in effect until 1887 when Congress disfranchised the women of Utah in a move against polygamists.

more than God-like generosity of the intelligent, cultivated women of America." Miss Anthony, who also opposed the Douglass resolution, argued that the Fifteenth Amendment was not equal rights. "It put two million [Negro] men in the position of tyrants over two million [Negro] women who had until now been the equal of the men at their sides." Lucy Stone, on the other hand, said she must rejoice in any legislation which would enfranchise any oppressed class.

Although the Fifteenth Amendment provided the moderates with a respectable issue to use in an open battle with Miss Anthony and Mrs. Stanton, they were actually far more disturbed by Mrs. Stanton's outspoken and radical views on prostitution, abortion, birth control, and divorce. Despite the fact that such subjects were too delicate for public discussion, the undercurrent of criticism was so strong and the charges of free love so prevalent that Mrs. Stanton, in *The Revolution* of April 8, 1869, felt obliged to reply to "many letters asking if *The Revolution* was opposed to marriage." Her answer provided little solace to those who were looking for reassurance. She was not opposed to marriage per se, she said, only to the *present system* which "is in no way viewed as an equal partnership. Nearly every man feels that his wife is his property, whose first duty, under all circumstances, is to gratify his passions, without the least reference to her own health and happiness, or to the welfare of their offspring. . . . Until men and women are wise enough to apply the same laws of science to themselves that have already so greatly improved the lower animals," she said, "we shall have infanticide, prostitution, and divorce."

When the American Equal Rights Association met in early May 1869, Mary Livermore of Chicago, a recent convert to woman suffrage, introduced a resolution putting the association on record as "abhorrently repudiating free-loveism as horrible and mischievous to society and disowning any sympathy with it." Mrs. Livermore said the idea had become so prevalent in the West that free love was associated with the woman's rights movement that she wanted a strong statement so that the "world would understand beyond doubt that women were for the ballot and against free love in any and every phase."

Longtime workers in the woman's rights movement vigorously objected to Mrs. Livermore's antifree-love resolution, not because they disagreed with its principles, but because they thought it unwise to deny false accusations. Women might as well deny they were thieves, burglars, or prostitutes argued Ernestine Rose, a close friend of Elizabeth Cady Stanton's and Susan B. Anthony's. A compromise resolution, proposed by Henry Blackwell (Lucy Stone's husband), was finally adopted by the convention; it stated that the woman-suffrage movement was not seeking to undermine marriage but rather to ennoble it by removing the legal disabilities which oppressed married women.

MARY LIVERMORE—a forty-eight-year-old, Boston-born Universalist who had introduced the antifree-love resolution at the May convention—was the most prominent addition to the woman-suffrage ranks during 1869. Well known throughout the Midwest for her work for the Northwest Sanitary Commission during the Civil War, Mrs. Livermore had a wide acquaintance in Iowa, where she stumped the state in behalf of the Sanitary Commission.

"Before visiting the hospitals, she would have deemed it something terrible, horrible for a woman to come before the public and talk," she told a Dubuque audience in the spring of 1864, "but since she had seen the misery and suffering of the soldiers she could not, would not be still. . . . Some would say that women ought to keep quiet and not put themselves before the public so prominently, and be around begging for money all the time," Mrs. Livermore said apologetically. "Well, when the jubilant bells shall ring in the return of peace . . . then we are going to quit begging, and be quiet, and sew, and embroider nice little ornaments, and let the men be lords of Creation, and we will be the ladies of Creation."

But with the return of peace Mrs. Livermore was not satisfied to be quiet and to sew. She missed the challenge and excitement of her soldiers' relief work and was soon attracted to the woman-suffrage movement. In early 1869 she organized the first woman-suffrage convention ever held in Chicago which met in Library Hall on February 11 and

12.[2] This convention, which Mrs. Livermore chaired with great dignity and ability, was a spectacular success. Mrs. Stanton and Miss Anthony, who came west for the meeting, were the star attractions. Even Anna Dickinson, who rarely came to a woman's rights meeting, participated in the program one afternoon. Thousands of curious people packed Library Hall during the convention. Newspapers of the city gave the meeting full coverage, and enthusiastic reports appeared in papers in neighboring states.

A correspondent of the *Burlington* (Iowa) *Hawkeye,* wrote from Chicago, "The meeting has created a great sensation. It is the theme of conversation and comment everywhere." This writer described Mary Livermore as "a lady combining all the traits of womanly kindness and courtesy, yet firm and decisive in executive duties, ready in emergency, never thrown off her guard—she is eminently a successful leader. Beside her there is not a woman in the Northwest (I doubt if there be in the country) who has more emphatically demonstrated the ability of woman to achieve where she has the liberty than has Mrs. Livermore. The millions of dollars raised through her exertions for our soldiers, beside active service rendered in hospital and on the field have endeared her to all the loyal hearts of America. Under her charge the meeting was managed with consummate tact."

On March 13 Mrs. Livermore, an experienced writer, launched *The Agitator,* a woman's rights weekly. Soon she began to consider herself a Joan of Arc who was to lead the women of America to the land of the ballot. But her efforts to direct suffrage affairs, combined with her conservative attitudes, soon piqued Mrs. Stanton and Miss Anthony, and their friendly relations were of short duration. By late September 1869 Mrs. Livermore had teamed up with Lucy Stone and the New England moderates in a bid for control of the woman-suffrage movement.

The first open break in the suffrage ranks came in May

2. The Library Hall convention was countered with a meeting in Music Hall in Chicago, on these same days, organized by a group of spiritualist woman-suffrage advocates with whom Mrs. Livermore refused to be associated. Leader of the spiritualist faction was Cynthia Leonard (a former Clinton, Iowa, resident), who in late 1868 launched *Sorosis,* the first woman-suffrage paper in Chicago. (Mrs. Leonard's eight-year-old daughter Helen Louise later became the famous actress Lillian Russel.) The spiritualist convention was chaired by a Mr. W. Perkins, whom the *Chicago Tribune* identified as "Judge Perkins" of Ottawa, Illinois. However, in April— two months after this meeting—Perkins wrote to the *Marshalltown* (Iowa) *Times,* indicating that he was a resident of Marshall County and suggesting that a woman-suffrage convention be held in Marshalltown.

1869 immediately following the annual convention of the American Equal Rights Association in New York. This convention, noteworthy for the number of delegates from the Midwest, including Amelia Bloomer (this was the first woman's rights meeting she had attended since coming to Iowa in 1855), resolved itself into a combination of New Englanders and midwesterners who opposed Mrs. Stanton and her faction. As a result, Miss Anthony and Mrs. Stanton called together some of their followers (Mrs. Bloomer was not invited) in an impromptu gathering shortly after the close of the convention and organized a National Woman Suffrage Association with Mrs. Stanton as president. This association, more national in name than in fact, was primarily a front for the activities of Mrs. Stanton and Miss Anthony and replaced a so-called Woman Suffrage Association of America under which these women had been operating during the past year.

Within a few weeks Lucy Stone was leading a drive to organize an American Woman Suffrage Association to counter Miss Anthony's and Mrs. Stanton's group. She hoped to make the American Association a haven of respectability for woman's rights advocates and a grassroots organization with branches in every state. On August 19 Lucy Stone sent a circular to Amelia Bloomer in Council Bluffs—one of hundreds which were sent throughout the country—giving notice of the intention to call a convention to organize an American Woman Suffrage Association and asking her endorsement. "Without depreciating the value of Associations already existing," the circular stated, "it is yet deemed that an organization at once more comprehensive and more widely representative than any of these is urgently called for." Only accredited delegates, the circular said, would be admitted to the meeting. This was a move both to minimize the influence of the Radicals in the movement and to control the type of women representing the cause, such as Dr. Mary Walker, a dress reform fanatic who embarrassed the women by appearing in her short dress and pants at many conventions. Heretofore, the platform of woman's rights meetings had always been open to anyone who had anything to say remotely related to the subject.

In a personal note written on the back of this circular, Lucy Stone explained that nearly all the antislavery people were repelled by Miss Anthony and Mrs. Stanton because of their attack on the Fifteenth Amendment, and a still larger number were repelled by their association with George Francis Train and Olive Logan. (Train was the fi-

The Agitator: Chicago
Saturday, October 23, 1869.

LETTER FROM
MRS. AMELIA BLOOMER

COUNCIL BLUFFS, IOWA, Oct. 3, 1869

*Unlike most woman's rights advo-
cates who donned the reform dress
in the 1850's, Dr. Mary E. Walker
continued to wear it for the rest of
her life. Amelia Bloomer in* The
Agitator, *a woman's rights paper published by Mary Livermore, defended
Dr. Walker's right to wear the reform dress at woman suffrage conventions; at the same time she advised her that such dress "in the present state of public opinion" was a
detriment to the cause.*

I have just read the proceedings of
the Cincinnati Convention, as published in the *Enquirer.* Dr. Mary
Walker seems to have been the only
disturbing element. Pity she had not
the good sense to withdraw from the
platform when she found herself an
object of annoyance; and yet I do not
learn that she said or did anything
that was wrong, or calculated to cause
alarm, or ill feeling. . . .

To me Dr. Walker is an entire
stranger, personally, and I know little of her peculiarities, or the style of
her clothes, but if her independence
in dress is her only fault, then she
needs that every true woman should
stand by her, when occasion requires.
I believe, indeed I know, that a woman may be just as good, just as true,
just as much of a lady, in a short
skirt and pants, as in a trailing skirt
of the most fashionable length. . . .

It would be well, in the present
state of public opinion, if Dr. Walker
could conform to the fashionable
style, or else make herself less conspicuous. . . . If a dress, everyway desirable to ourselves, causes another to
stumble, and reject the great truths
we bring before them, then let us sacrifice our own comfort and preference
for the sake of the great cause in
which we labor. So would I counsel
Dr. Walker, while defending her right
to choose her own costume. . . .

Yours truly, AMELIA BLOOMER.

nancial backer of *The Revolution;* Olive Logan was a flamboyant,
witty former actress invited by Miss Anthony to speak at the May
Equal Rights Association convention.) "People who cannot work
with Susan can work with the new organization which will make no
war or quarrel with Mrs. Stanton and Susan, but will furnish a field
where all can work who differ from them," Lucy Stone told Mrs.
Bloomer.

A more revealing statement of the reasons for organizing the
American Woman Suffrage Association is contained in a letter dated

May 16, 1870, from Lucy Stone to Amelia Bloomer. In recapitulating the conflicts of the previous years, Lucy wrote: "Mrs. Stanton's attitude toward the Fifteenth Amendment had repelled a great many Republicans and the discussions held in the meetings in New York City in the name of the National Society as to *what was the reason why women do not have more babies, etc., etc., etc.,* [emphasis added] disgusted so many people who would work in a different society but could not with them, that it seemed necessary to have another. . . . There was no use in seeming to be ignorant of what everybody knew—that the way the work had been carried on was such that many excellent people would not join it."

In late October 1869 a call was issued by Lucy Stone and her cohorts for a convention in Cleveland on November 24 and 25 to organize the American Woman Suffrage Association. The names of eleven Iowans appear on the call, including Amelia Bloomer; Benjamin F. Gue, editor of the *Fort Dodge North West;* Frank Mills, editor of the *Des Moines Register;* and Mattie Griffith of Mount Pleasant. Other Iowans signing the call for the Cleveland meeting were: Mrs. Benjamin Gue, Mary Adams and Edna Snell of Dubuque, John and Belle Mansfield of Mount Pleasant, and Mr. and Mrs. Charles Pomeroy of Fort Dodge. However, it was easier to find Iowa sponsors for the meeting than to locate anyone in the state willing to attend the convention.

On November 8 Lucy Stone wrote Mattie Griffith urging her to be present, but Miss Griffith replied that much as she would like to "represent our noble State" it would be impossible for her to attend.

In a letter to Mr. and Mrs. Gue written on November 13, Lucy Stone said, "In view of the importance of the object and the necessity of an American organization worthy of the cause—so broad that it cannot be controlled by any individual, clique, newspaper, or locality —so impartial that it cannot be perverted to assail, or advocate side issues ['side issue' was a euphemism for prostitution, abortion, birth control, and divorce] I hope that you will both make the necessary sacrifice of time and convenience and give us the benefit of your presence in Cleveland."

Two days later Mary Livermore, who had thrown herself into organizing this new association with all the enthusiasm of a neophyte, wrote to Amelia Bloomer: *"You must come to Cleveland. It is of the greatest importance that you should be there,* for if you are not, Iowa will have no representation. I beseech of you, do not fail to be at that convention. . . . *One* delegate from Iowa will be sufficient and I hope you will be there no matter what the circumstances. . . . There has never been a time since our Woman Movement was started, when your presence was so important as at this convention. There never has been so important a movement. And if you will only come now, we can excuse you from attending any half dozen conventions. . . . If by writing a dozen pages, tired and busy as I am, I should send them. *Do come."*

Despite these urgent letters, there was no representative from Iowa at the Cleveland convention when it opened on November 24. However, the following day Judson N. Cross of Lyons, Iowa, arrived on the scene. Cross, a thirty-one-year-old lawyer who had studied at Oberlin College, was a Civil War veteran who settled in Lyons (now a part of Clinton) in 1866. He had not signed the call for the Cleveland meeting nor does his name appear in connection with future suffrage activities in the state.[3] Nonetheless, he must have been a most welcome sight to Lucy Stone and Mary Livermore. One more state was represented at the birth of the American Woman Suffrage Association, making twenty-one in all.

Henry Ward Beecher—the popular Brooklyn, New York, minister —was elected president of the American Woman Suffrage Association; but he did little more than lend his name and prestige to the organization. Lucy Stone, chairman of the executive committee, assumed the burden of organizational work. Mary Livermore, a vice-president-at-large, gave up her foundering paper, *The Agitator,* and became the editor of the *Woman's Journal,* the paper which began publication January 1, 1870, as the organ of the American Woman Suffrage Association. Since the headquarters of the association and the editorial offices of the *Journal* were located in Boston, both Mrs. Livermore and Lucy Stone and their families moved to the Boston area.

Although it was the stated intention of Lucy Stone not to make war on the National Association, the very fact that she organized a rival suffrage group was an act of the greatest hostility. Miss Anthony and Mrs. Stanton, deeply resentful of their ostracism by the Boston Brahmins, felt they were being unjustly persecuted. It was inevitable that a bitter rivalry would follow in the wake of this break in the suffrage movement and the emerging state organizations, such as the one in Iowa, would be sadly affected by the feuds in the East despite their desire to remain neutral.

3. Judson N. Cross moved to Minneapolis in 1875, where he became a prominent civic leader. He was city attorney for several years and a member of the first Minneapolis Park Board. As a member of the State Forestry Commission he helped lay the foundations for the Minnesota forestry system.

NORTHERN IOWA
WOMAN SUFFRAGE ASSOCIATION

FOLLOWING the woman-suffrage convention at Library Hall in Chicago in February 1869 Miss Anthony and Mrs. Stanton spent about a month touring the Midwest. On March 3, shortly before their return East, they were the star attractions at a woman-suffrage convention at Galena, Illinois, modeled on the Chicago meeting. Since Galena was only about twenty miles from Dubuque, Iowa, with direct rail connections, that convention was attended by several Dubuque residents. The *Dubuque Times,* which covered the meeting with a long front-page story, reported that nine Dubuque citizens were at the meeting. The *Dubuque Herald* noted that there were four "estimable and wide awake ladies" from Dubuque in the audience. Mary Newbury Adams of Dubuque recalled eleven years later that the six Dubuque women who signed the call for the first woman-suffrage meeting in the city in mid-April 1869 all had attended the Galena convention. Regardless of the exact number, they were so inspired by Mrs. Stanton that they returned home determined to initiate a woman-suffrage organization in Iowa.

To help accomplish their purpose, the Dubuque women enlisted the help of Martha Brinkerhoff, who had been touring northern Iowa in behalf of woman suffrage during the past winter but whom they met for the first time at the Galena meeting. Mary Adams invited Mrs. Brinkerhoff to stay in her home, and arrangements were made for her to speak at the Universalist Church in Dubuque on March 9.

On March 19 the *Des Moines Register* reported that it had received letters from some parties in Dubuque stating that the friends of woman suffrage had decided to hold a state convention at Des Moines in April. Mrs. Brinkerhoff would be one of the speakers; and among the noted women expected to attend were Anna Dickinson, Susan B. Anthony, Elizabeth Cady Stanton, and Mary Livermore. The convention to be held in Des Moines was planned as one of a series throughout the state before the May convention of the National Equal Rights Association in New York. "It is deemed advisable to have Iowa thoroughly waked up from border to border that a large delegation from this state may attend the general convention," the *Register* said. (Nevertheless, Amelia Bloomer of Council Bluffs was the only Iowa woman to attend the New York convention.) The "parties" in Dubuque who had written the *Register* (it is indicative of the unpopularity of the cause that they wished to remain anonymous) had requested that if any persons in Des Moines would be willing to make arrangements for a woman-suffrage convention they should contact Mrs. Brinkerhoff at Dubuque.

On April 2 the *Register,* in connection with an announcement of the Equal Rights Association convention in New York, remarked that it had heard nothing further concerning the convention in Iowa. "It looks rather as though the women of Iowa are not coming as yet," the paper said.

Two weeks later "a Mother" from Rising Sun, Iowa, wrote to the *Register* taunting the woman suffragists for their reluctance to act. "The middle of April is here and I hear no more about the proposed state convention. Why don't they come, that we may know the true causes of why women want to vote? Is not *this* the reason they do not come—because they are not assured of the $200 an evening?" she asked.

Failing to find anyone in Des Moines willing to sponsor a woman-suffrage convention, the Dubuque women gathered their courage and announced a woman-suffrage meeting at the home of Henrietta Wilson of Dubuque on Saturday afternoon, April 17. (By this time, Mrs. Brinkerhoff was lecturing in Wisconsin.) The call for the meeting was signed by Henrietta E. Wilson, Mary Newbury Adams, Laura G. Robinson, Lucy C. Graves, Rowena Guthrie Large, and Edna Snell. With the exception of Miss Snell, a teacher in the high school, the women who signed the call for the Dubuque meeting were all wives of well-to-do and socially prominent Dubuque businessmen.

HENRIETTA WILSON, thirty-six years old, was a native of Erie, Pennsylvania; and her husband, David S. Wilson, was one of the leading lawyers of the city. Wilson, a war Democrat who settled in Dubuque in 1841, had served several terms in the state legislature. He was the brother of Judge Thomas Wilson, who introduced the bill in the 1866 General Assembly giving married women the right to their own earnings under certain conditions.

MARY NEWBURY ADAMS, thirty-two years old, was married to Austin Adams, a Dartmouth College graduate and a Harvard-trained lawyer, who since his arrival in Dubuque

Home of Lucy Graves. According to a county history, this was "one of the most pleasant, attractive homes in Dubuque, situated on the bluff commanding the finest view of the Mississippi from St. Paul to St. Louis."

in 1854 had been a civic leader in the community. Adams, one of the founders of the Republican party in Dubuque, was an ardent woman's rights advocate. Mrs. Adams' father, Samuel Newbury—an educator and Presbyterian minister— settled in Dubuque in the early 1850's. Prior to this time he had lived in Michigan and Ohio, where Mary Adams spent most of her girlhood. In 1856 Mary Adams was sent East to study for a year at Emma Willard's Troy Female Seminary in New York State, where she graduated with the class of 1857. She and Austin Adams were married this same year.

In 1868 Mary Adams was instrumental in organizing a study club for Dubuque women—a radical innovation at a time when women were not supposed to have serious intellectual interests. This same year she was invited by the ladies' literary society of Grinnell College to speak during commencement-week exercises, but when the members of the Grinnell faculty learned of the invitation, they sent an emissary to Mr. Adams requesting that Mrs. Adams not come, as they considered it unsuitable for a woman to lecture from a college platform. In 1870 Bronson Alcott, New

England Transcendentalist and father of Louisa May Alcott of *Little Women* fame, delivered a series of parlor conversations in the Adams' home; and a year later writer and philosopher Ralph Waldo Emerson read a paper to about thirty guests assembled in Mr. and Mrs. Adams' parlor and library.

LAURA G. ROBINSON, thirty-seven years old and a native of Vermont, was married in 1857 to Frank M. Robinson, a Dartmouth College graduate who had come to Dubuque the previous year. Robinson, a Republican, was a law partner of Austin Adams.

LUCY C. GRAVES, twenty-seven years old, was born in Salem, Massachusetts, and spent her girlhood in Michigan. In 1869 she married J. K. Graves, a banker with widespread financial interests in the Dubuque area. Despite the fact that Graves was a Protestant and a Republican in a predominantly Catholic and Democratic community, he was elected mayor of Dubuque in 1867. The Graves lived in an elegant home on the bluff above Dubuque with a broad view over the Mississippi River.

ROWENA GUTHRIE LARGE, forty-seven years old and a native of Morgan County, Ohio, was the wife of William P. Large. Married in Ohio in 1844, Mr. and Mrs. Large settled in Dubuque in 1856. Large, a staunch Republican, was a successful wholesale dealer in boots and shoes. Their imposing home was known for its fine view of the city and the river.

EDNA SNELL—the only unmarried woman to sign the call for the Dubuque woman-suffrage meeting—was a bright, attractive young woman about twenty-two years old, whose parents were devout Quakers. Miss Snell, whose home was in New Sharon, Iowa, was a Progressive Friend and graduated in 1867 from the Ladies Course[4] at Grinnell College. For three years following her graduation from Grinnell she was the assistant principal of the Dubuque High School, which had a faculty consisting of the principal, the assistant principal, and a teacher of German. In 1871 Miss Snell was elected superintendent of schools in Mahaska County and in later years (then Edna Snell Paulson) she conducted the Snell Seminary in Berkeley, California.

The meeting in Dubuque on April 17 at the home of Henrietta Wilson resulted in the organization of the Northern Iowa Woman Suffrage Association with Mrs. Wilson, president; Mrs. Large, vice-president; Mrs. Adams, corresponding secretary; and Mrs. J. L. Mc-Creery, wife of the local editor of the *Dubuque Times,* secretary. Women throughout Iowa in sympathy with the woman-suffrage movement were asked to take the lead in organizing woman-suffrage associations in their communities and also to write to Mrs. Adams, so that suffrage advocates throughout the state could become known to each other. The Dubuque women chose the name Northern Iowa Woman Suffrage Association because they hoped that it would soon outgrow its local character and become a delegate body for woman-suffrage associations which would be organized throughout the northern part of the state.

Although equal rights associations in Iowa—all headed by men—seem to have been accepted with relative complaisance, the emergence of an organization headed by women to work for suffrage for women raised a storm of excitement. "The ladies of Dubuque are extremely radical; they are free thinkers and have dared step over the door-sill of domestic matters and explore the outside world. They have a woman suffrage association joined by the best women here. . . ." reported a visitor from Illinois to the *Chicago Tribune.* "The masculine element in Dubuque" this writer said, was "in a flutter on account of these goings on."

A humorous but revealing account of the reception of the Northern Iowa Woman Suffrage Association by the citizens of Dubuque is contained in a letter from J. L. McCreery—thirty-two-year-old city editor of the *Dubuque Times* and husband of the recording secretary—to J. L. Loomis of Independence, editor of the *Buchanan County Bul-*

4. Women were not admitted to the Collegiate Course at Grinnell College until after the Civil War. Mary Snell, sister of Edna Snell who graduated in 1869, was the first woman to take the full four-year Collegiate Course at the college.

letin. This letter which was published on April 23, pointed out that "Iowa has of late been somewhat agitated on the subject of woman's rights by Anna Dickinson, Mrs. Brinkerhoff, and one or two other speakers." McCreery, an enthusiastic woman-suffrage advocate, went on to say:

> Agitation is the first step in reform; the second is organization. This step, also, has been taken in Iowa; and our much maligned Dubuque city has the honor of being the first in this State to organize a "Woman Suffrage Association." And this has been accomplished under the most happy and promising circumstances.
>
> Not for years has so tempting a theme been offered as a mark for the coarse wit and contemptuous derision of the brainless buffoons and brutes of our city, as when it became known that a woman's suffrage meeting was in contemplation. It was accepted as a matter of course, by these generous and sympathizing souls that nobody would be connected with anything of this sort except a lot of "scrawny old maids," a few nimble-tongued Xantippes, vixens at home and gossips abroad, with a sprinkling of dissatisfied wives, grass-widows, half-insane she-fanatics, and perhaps females of a more doubtful character.
>
> Friday morning last a call appeared in the morning papers for a meeting of all women in the city in favor of woman suffrage. This call was a surprise and a sudden damper to the hilarity of these jocular individuals. For to the call were signed the names of a number of ladies occupying the very highest social position in the city; leaders in literary and fashionable circles, concerning whom no man or fiend dare breathe a disrespectful word. Then it was prophesied that the project would certainly prove a failure; that as a few of the "aristocracy" were "running the thing," and that their interest in the matter would last as long, perhaps, as the velocipede mania, or till a new style of spring bonnets arrived to create a fresh "sensation."
>
> The meeting was held on Saturday afternoon. Its projectors, unable to help feeling a little anxious and uncertain as to the result, made up their minds that if a dozen were present they would not call the affair a failure. Twice that number were present; besides which, numerous letters of sympathy and hearty cheer were read from those whom business or illness prevented from attending. There were unlooked-for meetings there, of persons who never had suspected each other of any sympathy with this hitherto "unpopular" movement.
>
> But the best and most promising feature of the affair was the character of those who took part in it. Here were representatives of every respectable class in society; the wives of our leading lawyers; our largest bankers; our heaviest merchants; our best known business men; our army officers; and our city

officers. Nor was the least taint of "caste" anywhere perceptible. Rich and poor, school-teacher and seamstress, the wife of the millionaire and the wife of the mechanic, mingled on equal footing as sisters and co-laborers in a common cause.

There was a sudden end to the sneers of the sphere-prescribing "lords of creation" who had all along been asserting that no pure woman ever wanted to vote, and no virtuous woman would ever ask it. These were precisely the women who, it had been all along declared, would not "unsex themselves" and outrage decency by touching that unholy thing— the ballot. The woman's suffrage movement leaped at a bound from disgrace and scorn to respectability and popularity.

That woman suffrage was not as respectable and popular among Dubuque residents as McCreery reported in his letter to Loomis is indicated in an editorial which he wrote for the *Dubuque Times.* "We may call the advocates of this reform 'strong minded,' " McCreery told his readers. "We may laugh at their rhapsodical philosophy and sentimental policies—we may point to the fact that the great body of mothers and sisters in the land keep aloof from the movement—yet the fact remains that there are many women, intelligent to a marked degree, who are dissatisfied with the condition of their sex. We may say that the reformation proposed is a tremendous innovation. . . . It is not more so than the abolition of slavery, nor so likely to breed hatred, confusion, and bloodshed. . . . We may ridicule the insignificant numbers who champion the new theory. Yet they are far more numerous than were the radical abolition agitators twenty years ago, and equally energetic. Nor is it unreasonable to suppose that they have a great body of silent adherents whose sensitive natures restrain them from bearing the heat and burden of the conflict."

Members of the Dubuque woman-suffrage association carried on a variety of activities during the summer of 1869. Acting on Mrs. Stanton's suggestion in *The Revolution* that women should speak for their independence on the Fourth of July, Edna Snell read the Declaration of Independence and delivered a speech on woman's rights at the celebration in the village of Sand Spring, Delaware County. According to the *Times* twelve men and women from nearby Monticello attended the celebration "having been induced to go through curiosity to hear the oration delivered by a young lady." Two other Iowa women delivered Fourth of July orations in 1869—Mattie Griffith in Mount Pleasant and Caroline Ingham in Algona.

On July 16 the Northern Iowa Woman Suffrage Association sponsored a lecture by Phoebe Couzins of St. Louis, an attractive twenty-seven-year-old law student at Washington University. Miss Couzins, famous as the first woman in the United States to be admitted to a law school, spoke on "The Law and the Ballot for Women." Judging from the "disheartening array of empty benches" which faced Miss Couzins, the *Times* concluded "that the woman's rights movement was yet in its infancy" in the city.

Meanwhile, a number of women responded to the appeal of the Northern Iowa Woman Suffrage Association to contact Mary Adams, and a correspondence was commenced with women in Iowa and other states, which Mrs. Adams carried on for several years.

On September 9 and 10 Mrs. Adams attended a woman-suffrage convention in Chicago, organized by Mary Livermore for the purpose of forming a Western Woman Suffrage Association. Both Susan B. Anthony and Lucy Stone were present at this meeting. Mrs. Adams, described by the *Chicago Tribune* as a "pleasant, modest-looking lady," gave a sanguine report of the status of woman's rights in Iowa.[5] "Women in the State had been working quietly and there had been no opposition to them," she said. The Legislature was so willing to repeal obnoxious laws and grant new ones protecting every woman from tyranny that there was little to strive for. Mrs. Adams felt that the time had now come for women to petition for the right to vote but that the work must be done quietly. "It is owing to the indifference of the women themselves in Iowa that they do not have the ballot, and they are indifferent because they are so well cared for," she told the delegates.

The hope expressed by the Dubuque women in April that woman-suffrage associations would soon be organized in many Iowa communities was slow to be realized. The first fruits of their endeavors ripened in early October when the women of Monticello, a village in Jones County about thirty miles southeast of Dubuque, organized a woman-suffrage association. This group had an auspicious beginning, with over thirty women in this community of 1,200 joining, and was headed by Maria Hill Bradstreet—wife of S. Y. Bradstreet, the town's wealthiest citizen. Bradstreet, an avowed spiritualist and dedicated woman's rights advocate, was elected mayor of Monticello when the town was incorporated in 1867. The Monticello women hoped to hold a North

5. Two other Iowa women, Marianne Thompson of Mount Pleasant and Matilda Fletcher of Council Bluffs, attended the Chicago convention. Miss Thompson, who was ordained a Universalist minister in 1870, gave the invocation. Subsequently married to A. P. Folsom of Marshalltown, Miss Thompson was for many years an active suffrage worker both in Iowa and other states. In 1885 she inaugurated the first woman-suffrage campaign in Texas. Matilda Fletcher, married to an impecunious schoolteacher, began her career as a professional lyceum lecturer in the fall of 1869.

Iowa Woman Suffrage Convention if Mrs. Stanton, who was scheduled to lecture in Dubuque in early December, could be secured as a speaker. Mrs. Stanton, however, had more invitations to speak than she could possibly accept and the proposed North Iowa Convention at Monticello did not materialize.

The only other woman-suffrage association established in Iowa in 1869 was the Equal Rights Association organized on December 11 in Algona, a village in sparsely settled Kossuth County in northwest Iowa. Leaders in the Algona association were Caroline Ingham, wife of William Ingham, Kossuth County pioneer and one of its leading citizens; and Lizzie Bunnell Read, wife of S. G. A. Read, an Oberlin-educated physician.

CAROLINE INGHAM, thirty-eight years old, was educated in New York State and came to Kossuth County as a bride in 1857. Her oldest son Harvey was born the following year in the log cabin in which Mrs. Ingham set up housekeeping. Harvey Ingham, who became editor of the *Des Moines Register* in 1902, was a staunch champion of woman suffrage and one of the great liberal editors of the state.

LIZZIE BUNNELL READ, thirty-five years old, was known to woman suffrage advocates over the country through *The Mayflower,* the woman's rights paper which she published in Indiana during the Civil War. When Mrs. Read—an experienced printer—came to Algona in 1865, she established the *Upper Des Moines,* a weekly county newspaper which she published for about a year. "Circumstances"—ill health, lack of finances, or perhaps both—forced her to sell this paper.

ELIZABETH CADY STANTON
LECTURES IN IOWA

IN MID-NOVEMBER 1869 Elizabeth Cady Stanton, succumbing to the lure of the lyceum and the substantial financial rewards which it offered, embarked on a lecture tour of the Midwest which took her first to Michigan and then to Wisconsin and Minnesota. From St. Paul she went to Dubuque, where she delivered her first Iowa lecture on December 3. Letters which Mrs. Stanton regularly wrote for *The Revolution* give a lively account of the people she met during her tour and also of the difficulties of travel—long waits for trains in cold and dismal hotel lobbies; trips part way by train, part way by stagecoach; all-night journeys with two and three changes of train; and arrival at a lonely station in the middle of the night to find the station locked and no one to meet her.

In Dubuque Mrs. Stanton stayed with Mr. and Mrs. Myron Beach, former Seneca Falls residents. She was sorry to report that Mrs. Beach was not in favor of woman suffrage. In Burlington she was the guest of Dr. McClaren with whom she had competed for a Greek prize in her Johnstown, New York, school days. Her Burlington visit coincided with a Methodist fair organized by the ladies aid society to raise funds to furnish new church parlors. Mrs. Stanton thought women should secure equal rights in administering church affairs before they spent their time and energy in raising money for these institutions. At Mount Vernon Mrs. Stanton was entertained at dinner in the home of Dr. King, president of Cornell College. She was pleased to find Mrs. King an enthusiastic woman-suffrage advocate. She reported that at both Cornell and at Iowa Wesleyan College in Mount Pleasant the coeducational system was working most successfully.

Mrs. Stanton had "a splendid audience" at the Opera House in Dubuque where she delivered her lecture, "Our Young Girls." "Brought many white male sinners to repentance, and stirred up some lethargic *femme coverts* to a state of rebellion against the existing order of things," she reported to *The Revolution*. This lecture, which Mrs. Stanton also delivered at Mount Vernon, was an argument for an independent and healthy life for every girl—sensible dress, adequate exercise, education that would enable her to be self-supporting, equal opportunities in business and the professions, and the right to vote.

The *Dubuque Times,* which reviewed Mrs. Stanton's lecture at length, thought it "contained much good practical common sense. Mrs. Stanton has her peculiar ideas of course, but these ideas are more than half right."

The *Dubuque Herald* thought the fashionable and select audience which crowded the hall to hear Mrs. Stanton was "prompted in no small degree to hear a lady speaker." This paper did "not doubt Mrs. Stanton's sincerity . . . but to be reminded how pants should be worn, suspenders adjusted," was to its way of thinking somewhat unnecessary. "What affinity braced suspenders and other etceteras have to do with tight lacing [for girls] and dresses worn above the ankles," the paper was at a loss to discern. The *Herald* was willing to give Mrs. Stanton credit "for condemning the use of artificial means to beautify" as well as her advocacy of "loose clothing, regularity of diet, an occasional five-mile walk and plenty of sleep." Nonetheless, the *Herald* thought that "women should do their lecturing at home."

In Mount Pleasant, Burlington, and Keokuk where Mrs. Stanton lectured in late December, she delivered an argument for woman suffrage titled, "Open the Door." This was essentially the same speech which she delivered in Washington, D.C., in January and later in Chicago and Galena. The *Keokuk Constitution,* a Democratic paper, found Mrs. Stanton "a well preserved woman of about 50 with a benevolent expression indicative of great intellectual power. She has a fine command of language and in style is earnest and impressive. While a proper regard is paid to logic and argument, her language is not destitute of the garb of poetry."

According to the *Constitution* Mrs. Stanton predicted that within five years every woman in the United States would be a voter. She rebuked the Republican party for introducing the word "male" into the United States Constitution and "boldly asserted that thus far woman suffragists had received little or no favor from the Republican party. Democrats had treated them much better. . . . The Republican party now has their last opportunity to secure equal rights to all by bringing forward and adopting the Sixteenth Amendment. Having no distinguishing principle to give it life, without some such living, vital issue the party will fall in pieces. Woman suffrage may be as good a card as General Grant has. The Republicans took him up for president, not because they thought him the best man for the office but because they found that if they did not nominate him the Democrats would. If the Republicans do not now take hold of woman suffrage, the Democrats may, and will be sure to win."

Following Mrs. Stanton's speech in Mount Pleasant Frank Hatton —editor of the *Journal,* a Republican paper—commented that *"The Revolution* of which Mrs. Stanton is the editor was hatched forth from Democratic eggs and it is but natural that she should cackle accordingly." Aside from Mrs. Stanton's abuse of the Republican party,

Hatton thought her lecture the best plea for woman suffrage which he had heard.

Mrs. Stanton received a friendly review in the *Burlington Hawk-eye*—edited by Charles Beardsley, an ardent woman-suffrage advocate recently elected to the Iowa Senate. Beardsley commented that "Mrs. Stanton *talks* to her listeners like one who has something to say and is not afraid to say it because she is a woman. . . . She has left a good impression on Burlington and we doubt not that her desire that Iowa shall be one of the first states to give women the ballot will be speedily gratified."

Mrs. Stanton's own letters from the West, glowingly eloquent as they are, convey but a faint idea of the enthusiasm with which she is everywhere received," reported *The Revolution* on January 13, 1870. "The papers in all the large cities she visits give long reports of her lectures and tell of the breathless attention with which she is heard even in her most radical demands for woman's enfranchisement. Most emphatically is this woman's hour, and nobly is she seizing its opportunity, and meeting its responsibility."

❧❧

Joseph and Ruth Dugdale. Dugdale issued the call for the Mount Pleasant woman-suffrage convention. He holds a gold-headed walking stick given him by his friend Lucretia Mott.

7

1870

✄

T HE THIRTEENTH GENERAL ASSEMBLY meeting in Des Moines from January to April 1870 gave ample evidence to woman's rights advocates that the woman's hour had indeed struck in Iowa.[1]

THE WOMAN'S HOUR

The 1870 legislative session opened with the hiring of a woman, Mary E. Spencer of Clinton County, as engrossing clerk in the House of Representatives. Miss Spencer was the first woman to work for the legislature, and her appointment was hailed throughout the state as a sign of great progress for women. She was even paid the same salary set for a man in the same position, the Des Moines correspondent to the *Chicago Journal* noted.[2]

1. A stenographic report of these proceedings was published in the *Des Moines Bulletin*. This is the only time in the history of the Iowa legislature that its debates were printed in full. Thus it is possible to follow the course of the woman's rights discussion during this session in more detail than during others when the subject received scant attention in the newspapers.

2. An examination of the Iowa census for 1870 reveals that in Des Moines, a city of 12,704, there were no women employed as clerks in stores or as office workers. There were 381 working women employed as follows:

When Mary Spencer's appointment as engrossing clerk was voted on by the House of Representatives on January 11, the Democrats (who held only 14 of the 100 seats in the House)—to show they were equally as gallant as their Republican adversaries—also cast their votes for Miss Spencer, thus making her election a matter of unanimous consent. In return, however, the waggish minority leader John Irish asked the Republicans to give a young woman of his party's choice the position of assistant postmaster in the House. Irish hoped that the gallantry of the Republicans and the progress of the state would not stop short by the failure to appoint a second lady to office. One dour Republican questioned whether or not the election of any lady was a progressive step. In any event, he said, his fealty to party exceeded his gallantry. He proposed to vote for the man chosen by the Republican caucus, at the risk of being considered a slight obstacle in the way of progress. After further repartee concerning voting for any woman sight unseen, the Republican majority proceeded to give the assistant postmastership to their own male nominee.

MARY SPENCER—the daughter of Benjamin Spencer, Representative from Clinton County—was a pretty, demure young woman who was the belle of the ball at social functions in Des Moines during the legislative session. Miss Spencer, the *Des Moines Register* said "was the queen of hearts," monopolizing the attention of three of the bachelor members of the House at the B. F. Allen's reception for members of the legislature. "Her dress was simplicity; white alpaca, neatly trimmed with snowy satin. Over it she wore a black lace overdress." At General Tuttle's reception, Miss Spencer, "the representative of the progress of the age in the Iowa Legislature, wore a magnificent black velvet dress trimmed with sable satin and lace."

A former schoolteacher, Miss Spencer had studied for a year at Cornell College, graduating with the class of 1865. Contemporary newspapers, however, noted only that Miss

---

Servants in homes, boarding-house keepers, and other housekeeping related occupations 313
Seamstresses, dressmakers, milliners 42
Teachers (including music) 14
Hairdresser 1
Circus rider 1
Librarian 1
Nuns 9
Women in Des Moines earning their living as keepers of houses of ill fame or as prostitutes were not, as in Council Bluffs, listed by name and occupation.

Spencer had a good education. (In 1870 a college diploma was not a badge of honor for a woman.) An excellent pen-woman and efficient in her work, Mary Spencer was the pet of the Thirteenth General Assembly. On March 8, on the occasion of her first appearance in the Senate to report a bill passed by the House, the senators stood while she read her message and applauded enthusiastically when she finished. "The world moves and no part of it moves faster in the pathway of progress than our Iowa," commented the *Des Moines Register* in reporting this "first official act performed by a woman in the Iowa Senate."

At the concluding ceremonies of that session, members of the House presented Miss Spencer with a twenty-piece silver service (purchased at Plumb Brothers, net cost $130), which included a five-piece tea set, card basket, pickle glass, molasses cup, and six butter dishes, inscribed "M. E. S., Eng. Clerk, from the members of Iowa H. R., April 1870." In accepting this gift, Miss Spencer confessed that she had taken the office of engrossing clerk with almost doubting heart, thinking there might be a mutual unfitness with a lady as incumbent. Her fears were soon dispelled, she said, and she would treasure the memories of her experience in the legislature as among the happiest of her life.

Miss Spencer returned to Des Moines at the opening of the 1872 session, believing that as the pioneer in opening the way for women to obtain positions in the legislature, she deserved reelection. However, Miss Mattie Locke (later Mrs. J. K. Macomber), a student at the Agricultural College at Ames, secured the position of engrossing clerk in the House, defeating Miss Spencer by a vote of 45 to 14 with 14 other votes divided between three additional candidates.[3] Miss Locke was one of six clerks employed by the Fourteenth General Assembly.

On the evening of January 21 young and attractive Matilda Fletcher of Council Bluffs, who had recently embarked on a career as a professional lyceum lecturer, delivered a plea for woman suffrage in the hall of the House of Representatives at the invitation of forty legislators and state officials. Mrs. Fletcher, described in extravagant

3. Miss Spencer was principal of Tremont School in Cleveland, Ohio, from 1875 to 1882. She taught in Yonkers, New York, from 1882 to 1890; and was the proprietor of a private school for girls in Cleveland from 1890 to 1920. She died in Washington, D.C., in 1934.

terms by the Des Moines correspondent of the *Dubuque Times* as a woman "with a charmingly rounded, well developed figure, clear complexion, blue eyes, slightly retroussé nose, light hair that falls about her brow in a wreath of natural curls, a hand and arm that look as though they had been sculptured in Parian marble, and a voice musical as a bell," delivered her argument in the form of a one and one-half hour poem titled "Unclose the Door." (Elizabeth Cady Stanton was already using the title "Open the Door.") When she finished, Attorney General Henry O'Connor made a short speech warmly endorsing Mrs. Fletcher's views.

When Theodore Tilton lectured in Des Moines on January 29, he paid tribute to the Iowa Senate for its action the previous day in unanimously approving a bill permitting the mother of a deceased child, if she were the surviving parent, to inherit the property of such child outright, rather than merely having the right to a life income therefrom. This bill, giving the mother the right to inherit property on the same terms as the father, passed the House on February 1. Although it was in fact noncontroversial, *The Revolution* credited its enactment to the "blandishments of the woman's rights advocates."

Even more significant was the action of the General Assembly in early March amending the code to permit women to practice law in Iowa. Credit for initiating this action goes to a Democrat in the Senate who, to ridicule a House bill removing the word "white" from the qualifications for lawyers, moved to amend the bill to remove the word "male" also. This amendment was accepted by both Houses without significant protest on the part of the Republican majority. According to the *Chicago Legal News*—edited by Myra Bradwell, an aspirant to the legal profession in Illinois—this law made Iowa the first state to provide for the admission of women to the bar by express statute.[4] "The word 'MALE' going!" exclaimed the *Des Moines Register* in reporting this bill. "The woman of Iowa soon can be a lawyer if she cannot be a voter. And the sign is now seen in the sky that the good day is coming fast when she will vote."

The *Register*'s optimism about woman suffrage was confirmed when a joint resolution to amend the Iowa Constitution to delete the word "male" from the sections specifying the qualifications for voting and membership in the General Assembly was approved by the House on March 29 and by the Senate the following day.

4. When the circuit court admitted Belle Mansfield of Mount Pleasant to the Iowa bar in June 1869, it ruled that the affirmative declaration that male persons may be admitted to the bar is not an implied denial of the right of women to practice law in the state.

Once again, woman's rights advocates could thank the Democrats for spurring the Republican majority to grant their demands. On January 19, when ratification of the Fifteenth Amendment to the United States Constitution was expected to be the first order of business in the House, minority leader John Irish managed to get a motion on the floor asking for the appointment of a Committee on Constitutional Amendments, with instructions to report "a joint resolution amending the Constitution so as to confer on women the right to vote and hold office in Iowa."

John Kasson, the majority leader, accused Irish of trying to supersede the main question by that of woman's rights. He thought all men should have the right to vote before they voted to give it away. Kasson moved to amend Irish's resolution to instruct the committee to "inquire into the expediency of woman suffrage" in lieu of instructions to report a constitutional amendment to grant women the right to vote.

Irish objected to Kasson's amendment to his motion. "If it is adopted," he said, "the committee will use the same tactics which have been employed in the past—it will bring in a report which will indulge in all the fine and fanciful phrases complimentary to the ladies . . . but at the same time it will recommend that such an amendment be not adopted or proposed." He said he had seen this done at the previous session and wanted no such treatment of the subject at this time.

William Mills, Irish's Democratic cohort from Dubuque, saw no reason to sidestep the woman-suffrage question. "We have up for consideration the Fifteenth Amendment which proposes to embrace the pigtails of China, the kinky heads of Africa, and all the rest of mankind." Why should Republicans "stop so suddenly in their onward march of reform? Why all the rest of the world and the ladies excluded?" Mills asked. The Democrats were few in number, he said, but they would always be sound on the question of the ladies.

Kasson's amendment to limit Irish's motion to an inquiry into the expediency of woman suffrage was adopted by a large majority. A few Republicans, sincere advocates of woman suffrage, joined the Democrats in voting against it. The motion as amended then passed the House, and this body proceeded with its regular order of business—the ratification of the Fifteenth Amendment.

On March 22, when the Committee on Constitutional Amendments reported to the House on woman suffrage, the majority report, as Irish had predicted, stated that it was "inexpedient to take any steps toward a change in the constitution so as to allow women the right of suffrage." A minority report, however, offered a joint resolution to amend the Iowa Constitution to delete the word "male" from the sections relating to qualifications for voting, membership in the General Assembly, and service in the militia. On the motion of Marcellus Cutts—Republican from Oskaloosa and a member of the committee who had signed the majority report—action on the woman-suffrage question was postponed until Tuesday afternoon, March 29. "Whatever is worth considering at all, should be done above board," Cutts commented.

When the House convened at 2 P.M. on March 29, the spectator's gallery and the narrow public lobby behind the members' desks in the old capitol were jammed with a standing-room-only crowd in which women predominated. On only one other occasion during the session—the day the bill for an appropriation for a new statehouse was voted on—had so many people assembled at the legislature. Prominent among the out-of-town visitors was Amelia Bloomer of Council Bluffs, making her first visit to Des Moines as the guest of Annie Savery.

On the motion of Republican John Green from Davenport, chairman of the Committee on Constitutional Amendments, the House voted to substitute the minority report proposing a woman-suffrage amendment for the majority report which pronounced woman suffrage inexpedient. Green, a sincere friend of woman suffrage, led off the debate with a long and eloquent argument in favor of the extension of the franchise to women. He said he was well aware that the subject afforded abundant opportunities for the caricatures of the press and the sarcasm of the orators of the opposition, but he was also aware "that all efficient reforms have had to contend with the same facetious opposition." He argued that the ballot was woman's best weapon in combating legal discrimination and cited many instances in which women were unjustly treated under the Iowa law. He concluded with a plea to abolish old customs and prejudices which acted as barriers to woman's progress. "It is a day of advancement in act and idea, why not in government?" he asked. "Give to woman the ballot and Iowa will crown her loyalty by proclaiming in the truest and broadest sense, 'Liberty throughout the land and to all the people thereof.' "

Next on the floor was John Stone, a Republican from Glenwood who had opposed woman suffrage in the Twelfth General Assembly. A member of the Committee on Constitutional Amendments who signed the minority report favorable to woman suffrage, Stone explained that he had done so because he felt that when a right was

widely demanded it was the duty of a republican government to submit the question to the people for decision. He had taken the same
stand in regard to Negro suffrage, he said.

John Russell, Republican from Jones County, made a motion to
delete the section requiring service in the militia from the proposed
amendment. "There are men enough to perform the duties of soldier,"
he said. "Women can be useful in time of war in other ways."

Stone hoped the motion would not prevail. He did not "think it
proper for the friends of the measure to deprive woman of one of her
most essential rights—the opportunity of serving her country in time
of war."

John Irish, who had remained silent up to this point, rose to say
that he was willing that the requirement to serve in the militia be
dropped. "Friends of the measure do not believe that women should
fight," he said. "It is to be expected that I, as the member who introduced the resolution out of which the joint resolution is moved, should
say something on the question," Irish said during the course of the
debate. "Gentlemen who may object to the passage of this joint resolution cannot object thereto because it has not been demanded by the
class proposed to be affected by it. The best and the most talented
women of our land have organized movements all over the land in
favor of the thing which we contemplate today." In contrast, he said,
"but a very insignificant portion of the Negroes and the inferior races
of the Union asked that the privilege of the franchise be conferred
upon them. . . . Are we now to make such base use of the power conferred upon us as lawmakers by the people as to deny another and more
important class—the women of the land—the privilege for which they
plead?"

Speaking for the Republicans, John Traer of Benton County said
he felt like welcoming Irish "into the party of progress and progressive ideas." He did not propose that Irish, "at this late day, when the
great battle for human rights had been won, should come in and steal
Republican thunder." Traer was happy to have the privilege of casting his vote to submit the question of woman suffrage to the people.

After further banter and some serious argument, the question
was called and a division ordered. The motion to delete the requirement that women serve in the militia carried by only one vote. The
joint resolution as amended—for a constitutional amendment to permit women to vote and hold office in Iowa—carried by a vote of 52
to 33. When the tally was announced, the crowd of spectators applauded and cheered.

The following day a large crowd from town packed the small

Senate chamber to observe the action there on the woman-suffrage amendment. In addition, many members of the House crowded into the entryway to observe the proceedings. The occasion was dramatized by Miss Spencer, who was sent to report the House action on woman suffrage to the Senate. The Senators greeted her with a standing ovation; they remained on their feet while she read her message, and they applauded when she finished. "The fine looking Miss returned to the House as happy as a princess," reported the Des Moines correspondent to the *Keokuk Gate City*. The rules were suspended and the Senate took immediate action on the suffrage amendment. All attempts at debate were choked off and the measure was approved on a roll-call vote of 32 to 11. Once again the audience cheered and applauded.

Woman's right advocates were delighted with the legislature's approval of the woman-suffrage amendment. Without any campaigning on their part, the legislators had recognized that the woman's hour had at last arrived, now that the Negro was finally enfranchised. There was no question in the minds of the women that the 1872 General Assembly would give the proposed woman-suffrage amendment the required second approval and that it would then be submitted to a vote of the people. The job ahead was to create a favorable public sentiment so that the amendment would be ratified by the voters of the state when submitted for their approval three years hence.

"The referendum seems a long way off," Amelia Bloomer wrote to the *Woman's Journal* on April 11, shortly after her return to Council Bluffs from Des Moines, "yet it is probably better so, as it will be more sure of success than if acted on sooner. Public sentiment is rapidly growing in favor of Woman Suffrage, and, I trust, will in that time be ripe for action in the right direction, and by overwhelming majorities. Meantime, we have much to do to enlighten the people, and prepare them for the great change to be effected by woman's emancipation." Mrs. Bloomer called on long-time workers in the cause to come to Iowa to help with the campaign. "No other field is now more inviting—no other gives greater promise of success," Mrs. Bloomer said. She greatly regretted that poor health prevented her from doing much besides "what she could do with pen or in a quiet way" despite the fact that many were looking to her for leadership.

A letter dated April 12 from Annie Savery to Amelia Bloomer indicates that, while in Des Moines, Mrs. Bloomer spent an afternoon with a group of women at the home of Mrs. Thomas Withrow, wife of a prominent young lawyer. Now that the legislature had made woman suffrage respectable, these women, who previously had been unwilling to commit themselves, seemed enthusiastic about forming a woman-suffrage society. This sudden change of heart—especially that of her sister-in-law, Mrs. Chester Savery—brought the following reaction from Annie Savery: "I am not much surprised at what you say in regard to the ladies who met at Mrs. Withrow's that afternoon and yet it made me smile to think what a sudden change has been wrought in them since the enfranchisement of woman has become a popular idea. Could you have heard the denunciatory and *bitter* words spoken to *me* by Mrs. Chester Savery after I delivered my lecture on Female Suffrage [in 1868] you too would smile now. In the words of Homer in regard to a friend's action, 'Oh, Testorides, do you not know that of the many things hidden from the knowledge of man there is nothing so incomprehensible as the human heart?' I never mingle in society and see the mental somersaults which many make without thinking of poor but wise Homer."

Mrs. Savery told Mrs. Bloomer that she would probably hear more of this new movement, as she was the first woman in Des Moines to publicly proclaim her opinion and thought these women would not do much without her. "As soon as we have straightened out our place a little and put the plants in a condition to grow," Mrs. Savery wrote, "I mean to turn my attention to the subject of which we have talked so much. I shall change my former lecture on the woman question and write another in regard to governments and people in general." The proceeds from these lectures, she said, would go "for the benefit of some *woman's society.*"

THE IOWA WOMAN SUFFRAGE ASSOCIATION

ALTHOUGH Mrs. Bloomer and Mrs. Savery were anxious to hold an Iowa woman-suffrage convention in Des Moines as soon as possible, their plans did not materialize before Joseph Dugdale of Mount Pleasant issued a call for a convention to meet in his community on June 16 and 17. This call, signed by fifty men and women the majority of whom lived in southeast Iowa, stated that the meeting was being called "with the view to the organization of a State Association at that time if deemed best, or so as our only desire is the good of the cause, at some subsequent period at the Capitol, that the united force of the movement may be concentrated as to secure its final triumph." Dugdale also issued a call for a peace convention to meet in Mount Pleasant on June 18, the day after the woman-suffrage meeting. However, because peace was not a subject of general public interest, that meeting was both poorly attended and generally ignored by the press of the state.

JOSEPH DUGDALE was a sixty-year-old, peripatetic Quaker minister who was born in Pennsylvania, lived in Ohio as a young man, returned to Pennsylvania in 1851, and settled in Iowa in 1862. A quiet, gentle man who dressed in Quaker drab, Dugdale was an earnest and fearless champion of the downtrodden—the insane, the Indian, the Negro, and woman. His wife Ruth, ten years his senior, was also a devout Quaker who shared his reform interests. In 1848 (the year the first woman-suffrage convention met at Seneca Falls) Dugdale seceded from the Green Plain Meeting of Hicksite Friends in Clark County, Ohio—to be free of a clerical rule which frowned on his abolitionist and woman's rights views—and organized a Progressive Friends Meeting founded on the congregational principle. This group gave men and women an equal voice in its management. The following year Dugdale attended the Progressive Friends Meeting at Waterloo, New York, which issued an Address to Reformers that included a strong endorsement of woman's rights. In 1853 Dugdale was a leader in organizing the Longwood Meeting of Progressive Friends in Chester County, Pennsylvania, a group which for many years fostered reform activities in that state. The Longwood Meeting House is preserved on the Pierre S. Du Pont estate near Kennett Square, Pennsylvania.

Dugdale's name appears as a member of the central committee appointed in 1850 by the first National Woman Suffrage Convention at Worcester, Massachusetts, along with the names of Lucy Stone, Lucretia Mott, Elizabeth Cady Stanton, and other suffrage pioneers. In 1852 Dugdale was one of a group of Quakers, including his good friend Lucretia Mott, who organized a woman's rights convention in West Chester, Pennsylvania, the first such meeting held in that state. The following year Dugdale was one of the speakers in New York City at the national woman's rights meeting known as the mob convention because it was broken up by a crowd of unruly hecklers.

When Dugdale and his wife came to Iowa in 1862, they settled on a farm near Mount Pleasant, where they associated with the Prairie Grove Meeting of Hicksite Friends. In 1868 they sold their farm and moved into town to be near their only surviving child John and his family. Here they often had the pleasure of entertaining old friends from the East when they came to Mount Pleasant to lecture, prominent among whom were Anna Dickinson and Theodore Tilton.

Not all suffrage advocates in Iowa were pleased with Dugdale's plans for a convention. On April 26 after receiving a letter from him about the proposed meeting, John L. Loomis of Independence—organizer of the first Equal Rights Association in the state—wrote to Amelia Bloomer, "It seems clear that unity cannot be secured by holding a convention in one corner of the State." Loomis said he had written Dugdale that the friends of woman suffrage in Buchanan County would no doubt unite in a call for a convention to be held in Des Moines but would find it impossible to spend the time or the money necessary to reach Mount Pleasant. Loomis thought a state convention should be held at a point equally convenient to north, south, east, and west. He suggested to Mrs. Bloomer that she write Dugdale asking him to delay action "until a more general understanding is had among the friends in the State."

When it became evident that Dugdale was not willing to delay the convention, Loomis agreed to sign the call. "Although I find it impossible to be present," he wrote to Dugdale on June 14, "I still wish to express my hearty concurrence with every proper effort toward the organization of the friends of equal rights in our state." He hoped the convention would not attempt more than a local or district organization. To have an effective state organization, he said, there should first be a suffrage society in every county. He warned that it was particularly important to keep all the Iowa organizations entirely independent of conflicting interests in the East.

Mrs. Bloomer was even more perturbed than Loomis by Dugdale's plan to call a convention in Mount Pleasant. For over a year she had been writing to woman-suffrage advocates throughout the state, trying to find someone willing to organize a convention in Des Moines. Finally, in late 1869 she found a willing helper in Annie Savery, who wrote Mrs. Bloomer on December 11: "On my return from Europe a few weeks ago I found your letter of last April. Since than I have been suffering from a severe attack of Diphtheria combined with inflammation of the bowels. I am still confined to my room and quite weak. . . . You are quite right in supposing that I am in full sympathy with the Woman's Rights Movement. I am deeply interested and anxious for its success, and intend to do all in my power to bring about that result. . . ."

During the early months of 1870 these two women corresponded frequently, both with each other and with suffrage leaders in the East, hoping to organize a convention while the legislature was in session. Mrs. Savery, although anxious to help with such a meeting, lacked experience in organizational work and looked to Mrs. Bloomer for guidance. "You may not have the health, but you certainly have the experience and ability to organize this or any other Association," Annie Savery wrote on January 25. "Hence, if you can not do it, because of your health, if you will come to me and teach me, I will agree to be a willing pupil. Will you not name some day next week when you can come?" she asked Mrs. Bloomer. But Mrs. Bloomer, overwhelmed at the thought of coming to Des Moines to visit the wealthy and urbane Mrs. Savery, kept finding excuses for postponing the trip.

Furthermore, Amelia Bloomer hesitated to call a convention unless assured that one of the well-known woman-suffrage leaders from the East—preferably Lucy Stone or Elizabeth Cady Stanton—would be the featured speaker. Neither of these women, however, could come to Des Moines while the legislature was in session. Although booked for lectures in eastern Iowa during this time, Mrs. Stanton was not available for a Des Moines appearance. Lucy Stone, busy launching the *Woman's Journal* and campaigning in Vermont where a constitutional convention was scheduled in June, wrote to Amelia Bloomer on February 13 suggesting that the Iowa convention be postponed until fall. The American Woman Suffrage Association was planning to hold its annual meeting in Cleveland in November, Lucy Stone said, and she could come to Iowa immediately after this. Other speakers, too, might come to Iowa from Cleveland not only to attend an Iowa convention but also to canvass the state. "We will cooperate with you, dear Mrs. Bloomer, in every way we can," Lucy Stone said. "*Now*, Vermont is to be canvassed, conventions and meetings to be held all over the State.[5] We have just had one convention in New Jersey. All this, in addition to the paper. I am so overworked that with all my strength I feel ready to give out half the time. But the *work* goes bravely on and we are sure to win."

Both Lucy Stone and her husband Henry Blackwell urged Mrs. Bloomer to make her Iowa society auxiliary to the American Woman

5. In Vermont, which was staked out as the exclusive stumping ground of the American Association, a campaign was inaugurated in February to secure the election of delegates to a constitutional convention who would be favorable to woman suffrage. Lucy Stone, Henry Blackwell, Mary Livermore, Julia Ward Howe, and William Lloyd Garrison all came into the state to speak. Despite an all-out campaign by the proponents of woman suffrage, the convention, meeting in June, turned down the women-suffrage article by a vote of 231 to 1. "Iowa Shaming Vermont" boasted Tilton's *Independent* on June 23 in the headline of the story reporting the Mount Pleasant convention.

Suffrage Association. "It is not with my wife or myself or any of us a personal matter," Blackwell wrote Mrs. Bloomer on February 8, "but one of principle—one object being to distribute the real power and responsibility among the State Societies and not to allow it to be concentrated in New York or anywhere else." Blackwell warned Mrs. Bloomer, "Of course, if you enlist the aid of Mrs. Stanton and Miss Anthony, they will oppose your allying yourselves with the American Society and urge your joining theirs, as their wish is to force a combination under their personal leadership." Lucy Stone, in her letter of February 13, reminded Amelia Bloomer of her part in launching the American Woman Suffrage Association and asked her if she did not see the propriety of making the Iowa society auxiliary to the organization she had helped create.

By February 10 Annie Savery had concluded that perhaps it would be best not to call a convention in Des Moines during the current legislative session. "Unless we could get good speakers such as Lucy Stone or Mrs. Stanton, I fear the results would not be satisfactory," she wrote Mrs. Bloomer. The legislature was already in midsession recess, and when it reconvened there would be such a pressure of business she feared the woman question would go begging for hearers. "As Lucy Stone says, it seems rather late in the season to do much now," Mrs. Savery remarked. "Late for some things," she added, "and yet perhaps too early to submit this question to the people."

Mrs. Savery repeatedly invited Mrs. Bloomer to come to Des Moines so they could discuss their plans in person. She also hoped that Mrs. Bloomer would deliver a lecture in Des Moines while the legislature was in session. But Mrs. Bloomer, using her health and the expense of the trip as excuses, remained at home.[6] Finally on March 24, accompanied by her husband who had business in Council Bluffs, Annie Savery went to see Amelia Bloomer. A few days later Mrs. Bloomer arrived in Des Moines to return the visit and to attend the March 29 and 30 sessions of the legislature when the woman-suffrage amendment was approved. During her stay in the city Mrs. Bloomer conferred with Mrs. Savery and others about holding a suffrage convention in Des Moines in the fall.

6. A character analysis of Amelia Bloomer made in 1853 by Orson Fowler, the famed phrenologist of his day, says: "She has two classes of faculty existing in nearly equal power. . . . One impels her forward to do and dare everything that she thinks is right; the other leads her to shrink from rough encounter with the world, to dread criticism and censure. . . . The one tells her she *can* do if she will, the other that she cannot. . . . And as these mental conditions alternately gain the mastery, her character is differently estimated." *American Phrenological Journal,* Vol. 17, No. 3 (March 1853), p. 50.

A few weeks later when Mrs. Bloomer heard from Joseph Dugdale that he was planning to call a convention in Mount Pleasant in June she was thoroughly displeased. Although she signed the call, she at first declined to go to the meeting. The distance from Council Bluffs and the expense of the trip would prevent her from coming, she wrote Dugdale on May 7. "There will be enough without me," she said, "and I shall not be missed. I have hardly strength for much speaking, or active participation in the work, so I readily yield to others, both in matters of work and judgement." Nonetheless, when the convention opened on June 16, Mrs. Bloomer was in Mount Pleasant prepared to deliver a full-scale woman-suffrage lecture and to carry out instructions from Lucy Stone to "prevent the friends at Mt. Pleasant from organizing auxiliary to the Union." Let the Iowa society be independent or friendly to both the national associations, Lucy Stone advised.

The Union Woman Suffrage Association to which Lucy Stone referred was the National Woman Suffrage Association marching under a new banner. The name Union had been adopted at the annual convention of the National Association meeting in New York on May 9 and 10 at the insistence of Theodore Tilton, who hoped to make himself a hero by uniting the two suffrage factions into a Union Association under his leadership. Mrs. Stanton was persuaded to step aside as president and Tilton was elected in her place. Tilton's friend Edwin Studwell of Brooklyn, a thirty-three-year-old Quaker, was made chairman of the executive committee.

The Union Woman Suffrage Association was represented at the Mount Pleasant convention by Studwell, who in 1869 had published a small volume of commentary on the writings of Margaret Fuller in conjunction with Mrs. R. Anna Canby of Mount Pleasant. Although announced as a speaker, Susan B. Anthony did not get to the Mount Pleasant meeting. On May 19 (the day after she was forced to turn her *Revolution* over to new owners) she wrote Dugdale in response to a letter from him, "I am now hoping to be at your state convention—ready to work the coming summer for the *Union* of our *grand army* of *women*. . . . The battle seems so nearly over that I feel like redoubling my work that it may be over. . . . I am not officially invited," she told Dugdale, "but take it for granted you want me." Word that she had a change of plans (Miss Anthony spent the week of June 16 campaigning in Indiana) never reached Mount Pleasant, and she was momentarily expected throughout the meeting.

Lucy Stone's American Woman Suffrage Association was represented at Mount Pleasant by fifty-five-year-old Hannah Tracy Cutler, pioneer Ohio woman's rights advocate who in November 1870 was

*Hannah Tracy Cutler, second president of
the American Woman Suffrage Association,
was a graduate of the Women's Homeopathic
College of Medicine in Cleveland. She attended her first woman's rights convention
in 1851, and this same year she created a sensation in London by lecturing in Bloomer
costume.*

to succeed Henry Ward Beecher as president of the American Association. Mrs. Cutler—a tall, dignified woman, thoroughly at ease on
the platform—had toured the state in behalf of the Loyal Woman's
League during the Civil War. After the Mount Pleasant convention,
Mrs. Cutler spent the summer in Iowa speaking on woman suffrage,
promoting the *Woman's Journal,* and organizing woman-suffrage societies in several communities.

The Mount Pleasant convention was a sensation in southeast
Iowa, attracting a tremendous audience of curious spectators. Saunders
Hall, where the meeting was held (a room 71 x 44 feet, with a balcony
on three sides) was variously estimated to seat from 800 to 1,200 persons and was filled to capacity at all sessions. There is no way of knowing how many woman-suffrage advocates were in the audience, as no
list of delegates was published. William R. Cole of Mount Pleasant,
partner in a lucrative lightning rod business and a Harvard-trained
Unitarian minister, opened the meeting with prayer. Joseph Dugdale
acted as temporary chairman, and Belle Mansfield served as permanent
chairman. Speakers were Mary N. Adams, Charles Beardsley, Mary
Darwin, Mary A. Beavers, Amelia Bloomer, Austin P. Lowry, Henry
O'Connor, and Annie Savery.

Despite the fact that Amelia Bloomer and others were anxious
to postpone the organization of an Iowa Woman Suffrage Association
until a later meeting in Des Moines, the Mount Pleasant convention
formed a state association with a membership open to all, regardless of
race, color, or sex and announced that a second convention would be
held in Des Moines in the fall. The following officers were elected:

PRESIDENT .... Henry O'Connor—*Muscatine,*
Attorney General of Iowa

VICE-PRESIDENTS .... Amelia Bloomer—*Council Bluffs*
Joseph Dugdale—*Mt. Pleasant*
John P. Irish—*Iowa City*
John L. Loomis—*Independence*
J. L. McCreery—*Dubuque*
Mrs. Frank Palmer—*Des Moines*
Nettie Sanford—*Marshalltown*

RECORDING SECRETARY .... Belle Mansfield—*Mt. Pleasant*

CORRESPONDING SECRETARY ..... Annie Savery—*Des Moines*

EXECUTIVE COMMITTEE .... Charles Beardsley—*Burlington,*
Chairman
Mary Darwin—*Burlington*
Augusta Chapin—*Iowa City*
Mattie Griffith Davenport—
Oskaloosa
Mrs. J. L. McCreery—*Dubuque*
Mrs. Albert West—*Council Bluffs*

HENRY O'CONNOR, forty years old, was a small, wiry, Irish-born Catholic who had left the Church by the time he settled in Iowa in 1849. A Civil War veteran and a lawyer of ability, O'Connor was an impulsive, genial, warm-hearted man and was one of the most eloquent temperance and political orators in the state.[7] O'Connor, who served as Attorney General of Iowa from 1868 to 1872, created a sensation in December 1869 when, in a ringing declaration

7. A hopeless alcoholic in later life, O'Connor died in the Soldier's Home in Marshalltown in 1900.

of woman's rights, he ruled that Miss Julia Addington, a young woman recently elected superintendent of schools in Mitchell County, was eligible to hold this position. Miss Addington was the first woman elected to public office in Iowa, and O'Connor's ruling was the first in the United States declaring women eligible for such a position. O'Connor lectured on woman suffrage in Dubuque in October 1870 and introduced Lucy Stone when she spoke in Des Moines the following month.

However, by the spring of 1871 Henry O'Connor was having second thoughts about his association with the suffragists. Victoria Woodhull, a notorious woman of unsavory reputation, had become prominently identified with the movement in the East; and critics throughout the country were smearing all suffragists with free-love epithets. Men such as O'Connor, who depended on politics for their livelihood, found it expedient to quietly fade out of the suffrage picture. When Susan B. Anthony and Elizabeth Cady Stanton visited in Des Moines in June 1871, Miss Anthony noted in her diary that she had met Henry O'Connor at Mrs. Savery's home but that he "cares as do the *men* champions much more for his and Republican party success than for Woman Suffrage."

Amelia Bloomer stayed on in Mount Pleasant after the suffrage convention, attending Dugdale's peace meeting and traveling with Mrs. Cutler as far as Des Moines. The two women campaigned for woman suffrage en route, visiting Ottumwa, Pella, and Oskaloosa. In the latter community they succeeded in organizing a suffrage society. In Des Moines, where they were guests of Annie Savery, they delivered temperance addresses (larded with woman's rights arguments) on Sunday, June 26, at a meeting presided over by Governor Samuel Merrill.[8] This meeting, held on the shaded square in front of the old capitol—a favorite place for outings on hot summer days—drew a crowd of 2,000, according to Mrs. Cutler's report to the *Woman's Journal*. The following evening, June 27, the two women lectured on woman suffrage at a meeting held in the Baptist Church, at which Mrs. Savery presided—the first woman-suffrage meeting held in Des Moines. Exhausted by her campaigning in the torrid heat of the Iowa summer, Mrs. Bloomer returned to Council Bluffs on June 28.[9] In early September 1870 Mrs. Bloomer (with the help of Mrs. Cutler who

8. It was considered sacrilegious to lecture on woman suffrage on Sunday.

9. Entry in Dexter Bloomer's diary, Tuesday, June 21, 1870: "Letter from Mrs. Bloomer. She is on the war path again and nearly sick."

spent a week in Council Bluffs as a guest in the Bloomer home) organized a Council Bluffs Woman Suffrage Society with herself as president.

During 1870 and 1871 Amelia Bloomer became well known to the citizens of Iowa through her spirited defense of woman suffrage in the columns of the *Council Bluffs Nonpareil* and the *Des Moines Register*, which carried a number of communications from her during this period. Mrs. Bloomer presided at the first annual convention of the Iowa Woman Suffrage Association held in Des Moines in October 1871 in place of Henry O'Connor who was "necessarily absent," and she was elected to succeed him as president.

Handsome and witty JOHN P. IRISH—twenty-seven-year-old editor of the *Iowa City State Press* and the champion of woman suffrage in the Thirteenth General Assembly—did not attend the Mount Pleasant convention. Although many people were skeptical of Irish's sincerity in his advocacy of woman suffrage, the suffragists had good reason for believing in his support of their cause. Of Quaker ancestry, Irish was a member of the liberal Universalist Church in Iowa City whose minister, Augusta Chapin, was one of the leading suffrage advocates in Iowa. For a few months in 1871, newspapers of the state linked Irish's name romantically with that of Miss Chapin, who was five years his senior. However, in 1875 Irish married Miss Anna Fletcher of Iowa City, and in 1882 they moved to California, where for four years Irish edited the *Oakland Times*. In 1894 he was appointed Naval Officer of Customs in San Francisco, a position which he held until 1910. In 1911 Irish became a professional antiwoman-suffrage campaigner, returning to Iowa in 1916 to help defeat the only referendum on woman suffrage ever held there. Happily for the woman suffragists of the 1870's they did not have a crystal ball with which to read the future.

J. L. McCREERY, city editor of the *Dubuque Times* was described by J. M. Dixon as "one of the most gifted local editors in the state. He is somewhat awkward and un-gainly in manner and figure," Dixon said in his book *The Valley and the Shadow,* "but decidedly a genius who has suffered the pains and perils of persecution and poverty." McCreery published a paper at Delhi in Delaware County from 1859 to 1864 which, according to Dixon, "died of starvation." He went to work for the *Dubuque Times* in 1866. McCreery's thirty-six-year-old wife Loretta, who was three years his senior, was recording secretary of the North-ern Iowa Woman Suffrage Society. The McCreery's had two daughters, ages 11 and 2.

Little is known of MRS. FRANK PALMER. Her husband (often called Francis) was born in Indiana in 1827 and came to Iowa in 1858, where he purchased an interest in the *Dubuque Times.* From 1860 to 1866 Palmer edited the *Des Moines Register.* He was described by F. M. Mills, who purchased the paper from him, as "a radical of radicals." Palmer, elected to the House of Representatives in 1868, served two terms in Congress. After leaving Congress, the Palmers settled in Chicago where Palmer edited the *Inter-ocean* for a number of years. Although there are a number of biographical sketches about Frank Palmer, not one mentions his wife. The author has been unable to find the Palmers in the Iowa census, usually a last, sure resort for biographical data.

Forty-year-old NETTIE SANFORD was also president of the Marshall County Woman Suffrage Society organized in late May 1870. Mrs. Sanford did not attend the Mount Pleasant convention but was suggested for office by Austin P. Lowry, a young Marshalltown attorney who had spear-headed the organization of the Marshall County group.

BELLE MANSFIELD of Mount Pleasant was a twenty-four-year-old Methodist, born in Des Moines County in south-east Iowa. The only girl in a class of four members, she graduated as class valedictorian from Iowa Wesleyan Col-lege at Mount Pleasant in 1866. She taught at Simpson College in Indianola during the 1866–1867 school year, re-

Arabella (Belle) Mansfield

turning to Mount Pleasant in 1867, where she began the study of law in the office of her brother, Washington Irving Babb. In June 1868 she married John M. Mansfield, twenty-seven-year-old Iowa Wesleyan graduate and a teacher of chemistry and natural history at the college. A year later Mrs. Mansfield, along with her husband (who seems never to have practiced law), was admitted to the Iowa bar, despite the fact that the Iowa code restricted the practice of law to white males only. The examining committee, which consisted of two Mount Pleasant attorneys imbued with woman's rights fervor, in announcing their decision stated that they took unusual pleasure in recommending the admission of Mrs. Mansfield to the Iowa bar not only because she was the first lady who had applied for this authority in Iowa but because in her examination she had given the very best rebuke possible to the imputation that ladies could not qualify for the practice of law. This action made her the first recognized woman lawyer in the United States, a distinction which brought her nationwide publicity. However, her law career (if indeed she ever practiced) was of short duration. In 1872 she went to Europe with her husband; and upon her return the following year she went back to teaching, a career which she followed for the rest of her life.

Thirty-nine-year-old ANNIE SAVERY did much more than carry on a perfunctory correspondence for the society. A writer of unusual ability, her defense of woman suffrage in the columns of the *Des Moines Register* soon made her its leading exponent in Iowa.

In early 1871 Mrs. Savery lectured in Muscatine, Council Bluffs, and Glenwood as well as in Des Moines, where on February 24 she was drafted by the suffrage advocates of the city to refute the antiwoman-suffrage arguments of Lillian Edgarton, an alluring young blond who had recently lectured under the auspices of the Library Association. So successful was Mrs. Savery's Des Moines speech that the *Register* advised the friends of woman suffrage in Iowa that they could "do no better than to keep such an able champion in the field as Mrs. Savery." On March 1, 1871, Annie Savery wrote to Amelia Bloomer: "My efforts at Muscatine and here have been perfect successes. The papers have praised me so much that I feel a little ashamed. But it is because I am an Iowa woman. Had a fine hall full here and a good deal of applause."

While Mrs. Cutler was in Des Moines following the Mount Pleasant convention, Mrs. Savery called a meeting at Moore's Hall for the purpose of organizing a Polk County Woman Suffrage Society; and in the summer of 1871, when the Iowa Woman Suffrage Association was about to disintegrate for lack of leadership, Annie Savery rallied the forces and took the lead in organizing the first annual meeting of the Iowa Association, which was held in Des Moines in October.

CHARLES BEARDSLEY, forty-year old editor of the *Burlington Hawkeye,* was a member of the Congregational Church, like his good friend Theodore Tilton. Born in Knox County, Ohio, and graduated from the Ohio Medical College in Cincinnati, Beardsley came to Iowa in 1855, where he practiced medicine, first in Muscatine and then in Oskaloosa. In 1861 he became editor of the weekly *Oskaloosa Herald,* and in 1865 he moved to Burlington where he edited the *Hawkeye* until 1874. Beardsley, described as "the gentlest man that ever actively engaged in politics," was a member of the Iowa Senate in the Thirteenth and Fourteenth general assemblies. In cooperation with Mary Darwin, he was instrumental in organizing the Burlington Woman Suffrage Society in July 1870, an accomplishment which led the *Burlington Argus* to refer to him as "that eminent old female" and to publish the following poem in his honor:

SISTER BEARDSLEY

One summer's morn when earth was gay
And sunshine lit the balmy air
She laid her petticoats away,
Her hoops and pads and hair,

> And other things of various styles
> That women love to don
> And then intent on wicked wiles
> She pulled a pair of breeches on.

Loyal to woman suffrage despite such defamation, Beardsley was the leading spokesman for the cause in the 1872 General Assembly.

MARY DARWIN of the executive committee (by the summer of 1871 she had succeeded Beardsley as chairman) was the woman who so eloquently defended Annie Wittenmyer at the 1863 Sanitary Convention in Des Moines. Mrs. Darwin, forty-nine years old and a member of the Congregational Church, was appointed professor of logic, rhetoric, and English literature at Burlington University in the winter of 1870. Born Mary Abigail Platt in Milford, Connecticut, she was educated at Oberlin College, where she was graduated from the classical department in 1845—two years before Lucy Stone received her degree from this same school. The following year she married Charles Ben Darwin, an Oberlin classmate. The Darwins went to Paris, Tennessee, where two years later their first child, Charles Carlyle Darwin, was born and where Mary Darwin taught in a select (private) school. During their residence in Tennessee, Darwin made an extended trip to Mexico.

In 1851 the Darwins came to the outpost community of Fort Des Moines, Iowa, but after a few months they settled in Burlington, where Mary Darwin continued teaching to supplement the family income. A letter in the Grinnell College Library—dated March 28, 1894, and written by William Salter, pioneer Burlington minister—recalls that Ben Darwin was the first principal of the Burlington High School at $40 a month. "His wife, who was a much superior person, taught a select school for girls, and afterwards at Burlington University in which she was principal of the Ladies Department. . . . She was a woman of ripe culture, eminent in moral excellence and for skill and tact in awakening the attention of her pupils and helping them in knowledge and goodness. She was a successful teacher and is remembered with affection and honor."

Darwin—a brilliant, egotistical, and hot-tempered lawyer—went to Washington Territory in 1866, where he had received an appointment as federal judge. His departure for the West seems to have marked an end to his marriage and his association with his three children, the oldest of whom was graduated from Oberlin College in 1868. The outspoken *Revolution,* however, was the only contemporary paper to mention Mary Darwin's marital status, referring to her in February 1870 as "the former wife of C. Ben Darwin." Mary Darwin was elected president of the Burlington Woman Suffrage Society when it was organized in July 1870, and in late August she went on a week's tour across southern Iowa speaking on woman suffrage and promoting *The Revolution.* Her trip ended on August 29 in Council Bluffs, where she stayed with Amelia Bloomer; she departed only a few hours before Mrs. Cutler, agent for the *Woman's Journal,* arrived to be a guest in the Bloomer home.

AUGUSTA CHAPIN, thirty-four years old, was one of the pioneer women ministers in the United States. She preached her first sermon in 1859 while a resident of Michigan and was formally ordained in December 1863. Miss Chapin was minister of the Universalist Church in Mount Pleasant in 1868, going from there to Milwaukee, Wisconsin, where she served for about a year. From January 1870 to mid-1873 she was minister of the Universalist Church in Iowa City where John Irish was chairman of the committee to build a new edifice. Miss Chapin lectured on "The Coming Woman" in Des Moines in January 1870 and in Council Bluffs in January 1871. Doubtless she gave the same lecture in other Iowa communities in the intervening period.

MATTIE GRIFFITH DAVENPORT, married May 1, 1870, to Francis M. Davenport of Oskaloosa, was the Mount Pleasant girl who began lecturing on woman suffrage in 1868. In her letter of May 7, 1870, to Joseph Dugdale,

Amelia Bloomer added the following postscript about Mrs. Davenport, "The papers announce the marriage of our lecturer Mattie Griffith. She has changed the field of her labors sooner than I anticipated when she was here. Hope she is the gainer by the change."

KATE WEST, thirty-seven-year old wife of Council Bluffs banker Albert West, was elected to the executive committee of the Council Bluffs Woman Suffrage Society when it was organized in September 1870. A native of Indiana, Mrs. West came to Iowa in the 1850's. She was the mother of five children ranging in age from 14 to 5.

The *Mount Pleasant Journal* seems to have been the only paper in Iowa which carried a complete report of the June Iowa woman-suffrage convention, but unfortunately there is no extant copy for the week of the meeting. The *Woman's Journal* carried several informal letters from Hannah Tracy Cutler, written during the course of the meeting; and *The Revolution,* in which the most complete account of the convention can be found, carried two snide stories (probably based on a stenographic report) which attempted to prove that the Iowa society was tied to the Union Woman Suffrage Association. (See Appendix B.)

The *Woman's Journal* at first maintained a dignified silence about the malicious accounts of the Iowa convention in *The Revolution,* but when this paper refused to retract its "outrageously false reports" the *Journal* on August 13 published a letter from an Iowa woman indignantly denouncing the actions of the Union partisans. It was evident from the outset that the Union association was trying to manipulate the convention, this writer said; but for the sake of harmony these maneuvers were not exposed, and little did anyone think that the Union wire pullers would publicly boast of their meanness. The question of making the Iowa association auxiliary to either the American or Union association was not broached in the convention, but as far as any feeling was expressed it was decidedly for independent action, this writer asserted.

"So far as the speaking on the question of Woman Suffrage, and the attendance was concerned, the Convention was a success; but the business part of it was very irregularly and badly managed, and out of all order, by men from whom we expected better things," the letter continued. "It was felt at the time, and is proved now that the 'Union' faction was the cause of it all. This mismanagement was much regretted by the honest workers, but they have kept silent and smothered their indignation, willing that the public should believe that all was well done, and hoping the wrong might be corrected by future action. . . . Many of the friends are disheartened over this commencement, and the recklessly setting aside the cause to promote the selfish ends of a party; and if this course is persisted in and the affairs of the Association hereafter conducted after the manner of the convention that formed it, they will withdraw from the connection and move for a new organization," this writer, who signed herself "Justice," concluded.

On October 30 the *Des Moines Register* carried a notice that the Iowa Woman Suffrage Association would meet in Des Moines on November 17. However, a week later Annie Savery announced that the meeting had been canceled. "Upon consultation with the Executive Committee of the Iowa Woman Suffrage Association, it is considered that as the season is too far advanced and the notice too short to hold the proposed convention at Des Moines on the 17th, it has therefore been determined to postpone the convention to the anniversary of the Society's formation—June 1871." The convention, however, did not materialize until October of that year.

THE POLK COUNTY WOMAN SUFFRAGE SOCIETY

ON SUNDAY, OCTOBER 30, the *Des Moines Register* announced that five days previously a Polk County Woman Suffrage Society had been organized at a meeting held in the YMCA rooms on Fourth Street. A constitution was adopted and the following slate of officers elected:

PRESIDENT . . . . .Mrs. B. F. Allen

TREASURER . . . . .Mrs. James Callanan

CORRESPONDING SECRETARY . . . . .Mrs. Martha Brown Haven

EXECUTIVE COMMITTEE . . . . .Mrs. C. J. Pitman, Chairman
Mrs. J. M. Coggeshall
Mrs. Jonathan Cattell
Mrs. Mary Work
Mrs. C. C. Nourse

"The attendance was not large," the *Register* reported, "but the meeting was composed of the leading and most influential ladies of the city." The society, the first community-wide woman's club to be organized in Des Moines, was to meet again at the call of the president.

KITTY ALLEN, the thirty-four-year-old wife of millionaire banker B. F. Allen, was the social leader of Des Moines.
Her husband, reputedly the wealthiest man in the state,
served as senator from Polk County in the Thirteenth General Assembly, where he voted to approve the woman-suffrage amendment. Mr. and Mrs. Allen, members of the
socially elite Central Presbyterian Church, lived in Terrace
Hill—a mansion costing over $200,000, completed in 1868
and still standing on Grand Avenue on a plot of ground
considerably smaller than the forty acres of elaborately land-
scaped lawns and gardens which comprised its setting in
1870. The Allen's mansion, staffed by eight servants, and
their extravagant receptions, catered by chefs from Chicago,
made them famous throughout the state. "Any reader of a
Des Moines paper for the past two years has been stared in
the face every week or day with the name of B. F. Allen—
Allen's mansion—Allen's public spirit—Allen's benevolence
—Allen's parties—Allen's cookery—until Allen has become
a newspaper nuisance," quipped the *Lyons Mirror* in early
February 1870, following a rash of stories about the elegant
reception given by Senator and Mrs. Allen for the members
of the legislature and their families on January 29, the date
of their sixteenth wedding anniversary. The women who
organized the Polk County Woman Suffrage Society could
find no one with more social prestige to head their group
than Kitty Allen, and they elected her president despite the
fact that she was not at the meeting.

MARTHA COONLEY CALLANAN was the forty-four-year-
old wife of James C. Callanan, hard-headed Des Moines
financier, reformer, and philanthropist who moved to Des
Moines from Albany, New York, in 1863 to look after his

Home of Martha Callanan at 28th and Woodland, Des Moines, built in 1876. Here Mrs. Callanan entertained many suffrage workers, including the board of the National Woman Suffrage Association at the time of the national convention in Des Moines in 1897.

extensive real estate holdings in Iowa. Mrs. Callanan, born on a farm near Albany, was a Quaker who associated with the Congregational Church after coming to Des Moines. The Callanans, who had no children, lived comfortably but unostentatiously in a home on Ninth Street, a mile north of town. In 1876 the Callanans built an elegant brick home complete with mansard roof and tower on spacious grounds at the corner of 28th and High streets, which until Mrs. Callanan's death in 1901 served as unofficial headquarters for the suffragists of Iowa. Mrs. Callanan was a longtime woman's rights advocate whose name appears on the subscription lists of Amelia Bloomer's *Lily* and Lizzie Bunnell Read's *Mayflower*.

A humorless woman of indomitable will and steadfast purpose who had substantial property in her own name, Mrs. Callanan was one of the few women in Iowa with money of her own to use in furthering suffrage work in the state. Although in later years Mrs. Callanan was president of both the Polk County society and the Iowa association, in 1870 she preferred to work quietly behind the scenes, where she soon became the de facto leader of the Polk County group.

MARTHA BROWN HAVEN, forty-year-old native of Vermont, had lived in Indiana and Ohio before coming to

Des Moines in the fall of 1869. Her husband, Oscar D. Haven, ran a home-furnishings store which sold such typically Victorian items as Nottingham lace curtains, lambrequins, chromos, and lithographs (perhaps by Currier and Ives). In early March 1870 Mrs. Haven wrote to Amelia Bloomer inquiring about the possibility of organizing a woman-suffrage society in Iowa. "I have been identified with this cause, I may say, always," Mrs. Haven told Mrs. Bloomer. She said that when she was teaching in Richmond, Indiana, she had helped Mary Birdsall (who succeeded Mrs. Bloomer as editor of *The Lily*) by reporting for this paper and assisting in other ways with its publication. She had not yet met any other woman-suffrage advocates in Des Moines. Mrs. Haven, a radical in her woman's rights views, served as corresponding secretary of the Polk County society from the time of its establishment in October 1870 until August 1871, when she resigned in the wake of the free-love controversy which was then shaking the organization.

MARIA GRAY PITMAN, forty-three years old, was a member of the Methodist Church. Born Maria Freeman in Massachusetts, she came to Des Moines in 1855 with her husband John H. Gray, a lawyer who was a district judge at the time of his death in 1865. Mrs. Pitman opened a select school in Des Moines in 1866, which she operated until shortly before her marriage in 1869 to C. J. Pitman, owner of a building-supply business. Mrs. Pitman, a lifelong woman-suffrage advocate, was active in suffrage work in San Francisco in the 1890's. At this time she was using the name Maria Freeman Gray, an indication that in the intervening years she was divorced from Mr. Pitman.

Mary Jane and John Coggeshall

Thirty-four-year-old MARY JANE COGGESHALL came to Des Moines in 1865 from Indiana in a covered wagon with her husband, John Milton Coggeshall, and their three children.[10] Mr. Coggeshall, partner in a successful pottery business, was to acquire substantial real estate in the city. His wife, a Quaker who associated with the Unitarian Church after coming to Des Moines, was a dedicated woman's rights advocate from the time of her girlhood in Indiana when she was influenced by the writings of Hannah Tracy Cutler and Frances Dana Gage in the *Ohio Cultivator*. A modest, gentle woman, who came to be noted for her brilliant repartee and sharp wit, Mrs. Coggeshall gave steadfast devotion to the woman-suffrage cause from the date of the organization of the Polk County society in 1870 to the time of her death in 1908. Mrs. Coggeshall never forgot her lonely days during her first years in Des Moines, when "a few women unknown to each other walked their daily rounds of domestic duties with the thought in the mind of each, that 'I alone of all women in this young city *believe* in the equality of women with men.' " These women first became known to each other, Mrs. Coggeshall said, when the "active, educated, and many-sided" Annie Savery invited Mrs. Bloomer and Mrs. Cutler to Des Moines following the Mount Pleasant convention in June.

DEBORAH CATTELL, fifty-four-year-old Quaker, was born in Ohio where she married Jonathan Cattell in 1842. Four years later they came to Iowa, settling in the Quaker com-

10. The Iowa census reveals that by 1870 two of these children had died. Mrs. Coggeshall had seven children, only three of whom lived to adulthood.

munity of Springdale in Cedar County. In 1856 Cattell was elected state auditor, a position which he held for three terms. The Cattells moved to Des Moines in 1858. Well informed about public affairs, Mrs. Cattell was interested in all the reform movements of her day. During the Civil War she was chairman of the Sixth Ward sanitary board and in 1872 she served as treasurer of the Union Relief Society, the first community-wide organization to aid the poor. She was a dedicated temperance worker and a life-long suffragist. Because of her interest in prison reform Governor Carpenter appointed her in 1874 to a commission to investigate alleged cruelty in the state reform school at Eldora. Jonathan Cattell is remembered for his successful fight to secure admission of Negro children to an east-side school in 1858. In 1866 he was instrumental in organizing the east-side board of education and served as its first president. Cattell, who never acquired great wealth, was esteemed for his Roman simplicity, Spartan courage, and inflexible honesty.

MARY WORK, forty-four-year-old wife of Henry D. Work, was born in Connecticut. Married when young, she and her husband taught in North Carolina and Kentucky, before settling in Polk County in 1853. "My interest in the woman question dated from the organization of the Polk County Society, previous to which I knew nothing of the work or workers," Mrs. Work wrote to Amelia Bloomer in December 1880. This same year Mrs. Work was elected a director of School District 6 in Delaware Township and soon was made president of the board, a position which she held until her death in 1885.

REBECCA NOURSE, forty-one years old, was born in Kentucky. In 1853 she married Charles C. Nourse and settled in Keosauqua, Iowa, where Nourse had opened a law office two years before. The Nourses moved to Des Moines in 1858. Charles Nourse, a founder of the Republican party in Iowa, had served as attorney general, member of the supreme court, and judge of the district court. Both Mr. and Mrs. Nourse were ardent Methodists and uncompromising prohibitionists who sent their only son to the Agricultural College at Ames because they felt he would not be exposed to as much drinking as at the state university at Iowa City. Rebecca Nourse, according to her obituary in the *Des Moines Capital* (November 11, 1909) "was of a quiet, reserved nature, deeply loved in the family circle and by many friends. She has been intimately acquainted with the best things and people in the city."

The meeting which Annie Savery called for the purpose of organizing a Polk County Woman Suffrage Society was held at Moore's Hall on June 30, while Mrs. Cutler was still in Des Moines. (Mrs. Bloomer, exhausted by the heat, had returned to her home in Council Bluffs two days before.) Only a few people attended this meeting. The hot weather kept many away, the *Des Moines Register* said, and the Episcopal Fair was also held the same evening. The truth of the matter was that despite the large number of people who had turned out earlier in the week to hear Mrs. Bloomer and Mrs. Cutler, only a very few Des Moines residents were interested in consummating a woman-suffrage society. Mrs. Savery opened the meeting, and on her motion Corydon E. Fuller, a partner in Mr. Coggeshall's pottery business, was elected chairman. Mrs. Cutler made a few remarks, and Mrs. Savery then read a proposed constitution for a Polk County society.

The meeting, however, was apparently unwilling to go ahead with organization. Again, on a motion of Mrs. Savery, a committee of five on permanent organization was appointed, with Mrs. Coggeshall as chairman. Other members of the committee were Mrs. Savery, Mrs. Callanan, Mrs. Cattell, and Mrs. Ed Wright.[11] The meeting adjourned after Mrs. Savery and Mrs. Coggeshall had passed through the audience taking up a collection to pay for the hall.

This committee on permanent organization called the meeting at the YMCA rooms on October 25 where the Polk County society was finally organized—as announced in the *Register*.

On Friday, November 4, however, the society lost its first president when the following letter from Mrs. B. F. Allen appeared in the *Register*: "Ed. of the Register: I see by your Sunday issue, that, at a meeting of the Polk County Woman Suffrage Association, held some days since in this city, my name appears as President of the same. Please allow me to state through your columns that I was elected without my knowledge or consent; and I beg leave to decline the position, on the sufficient grounds that I am not in sympathy with the Woman Suffrage movement." News of this letter traveled as far as New York City, where on November 17 the *World* commented on the discomfiture of the Polk County society.

11. Ed Wright was Speaker of the House in the 1866 General Assembly.

However, the doughty ladies of this group, once their association had been set in motion, refused to be overwhelmed by this embarrassment; and at their second regular meeting on November 25 Mrs. Susan Sharman, a fifty-five-year-old self-supporting widow, was elected president. Mrs. Sharman, a Protestant born in Ireland, came to Des Moines in 1856. Her husband died soon after and to support herself and her three children she opened a private school for girls. She subsequently became a music teacher and for many years operated a music store where she sold organs and pianos. The society also added two men to its board of directors—Corydon E. Fuller and Dr. James Wright,[12] who were elected vice-presidents.

The Polk County society held its monthly meetings at the courthouse during the winter of 1870–1871, at which opponents as well as friends of woman suffrage were invited to air their views. The unflagging persistence of the Polk County women in advancing the woman-suffrage cause, soon made their society the strongest and most durable in the state. With only one exception (December 1876, when a member's son was killed in a railway accident), it held regular monthly meetings from the date of its founding in 1870 to 1920 when all suffrage work in the nation came to an end with the ratification of the Nineteenth Amendment.

In December Hungarian-born Louis Rutkay—a newcomer to Des Moines and a nephew of the famed Hungarian patriot Louis Kossuth— lectured to the society, and his speech was subsequently printed for distribution as a suffrage tract. At the regular meeting in January 1871 Corydon E. Fuller was the principal speaker. On January 25, C. R. Pomeroy, minister of the Methodist Church, delivered a lecture at the courthouse in reply to the argument that the Bible forbids women to vote. Mrs. Haven read a paper at the February meeting; and a week later, on February 13, Susan B. Anthony, in her first appearance in the city, spoke under the auspices of the society. At the March meeting Mrs. Coggeshall read a paper; and on April 19 Mary Livermore, editor of the *Woman's Journal*, was sponsored by the Polk County society in her first Des Moines appearance.

The Polk County group was also busy in other ways during the

12. Corydon E. Fuller, a member of the Christian Church, was one of the founders of Drake University in 1881. Dr. James Wright, a former Secretary of State, was an agent for the Washington Life Insurance Company. His son, Captain M. C. Wright, delivered the address "Woman's Rights at Common Law" at the graduation of the first law class in Des Moines in 1866. Mrs. Coggeshall in later years commented: "There were a few giant men in those days such as Dr. James Wright and Corydon E. Fuller, who stood by us at the beginning and with their better knowledge of the workings of organized bodies were an invaluable help until the society had gained courage and experience to stand alone."

winter, 1870–1871. The *Woman's Journal* on February 4 commended the society for "doing a great work in distributing woman suffrage tracts and newspapers, for which they send repeated orders to our office." Petitions for a Sixteenth Amendment were sent to Congress,[13] and a committee was appointed to prepare a memorial to be presented to the Fourteenth General Assembly. In March Mrs. Haven and Mrs. Pitman organized a society in Mitchellville at a meeting held in the Universalist Church—a building which is still a landmark in that community.

Four prominent members of the Polk County Woman Suffrage Society—Mrs. Pitman and Mrs. Haven on the west side and Mrs. Cattell and Mrs. Rankin (wife of the state treasurer) on the east side—were candidates in the March 13, 1871, school elections for two vacancies on the independent boards in each district. Mrs. Haven and Mrs. Pitman, although they ran at the bottom of the list of five candidates on the west side, drew enough votes so that only one contestant received a majority. On the east side Mrs. Cattell and Mrs. Rankin each received 95 votes, one less than the top candidate. "Thus it will be seen that woman's first entry into elections in this city has had the effect of at least making another election necessary as but one director has been elected in each district, and the upshot of this matter will be that some ladies will be found on our school boards for the ensuing year," commented the *Des Moines Register* on March 14.

The women, however, were to be cheated out of their victories. The west-side board (after consultation with C. C. Nourse, a former judge whose wife was a member of the executive committee of the Polk County society) decided that a majority was not necessary for election, and the candidate with the second highest number of votes was declared the winner. The east-side board (which also consulted Mr. Nourse) declared that a tie could not be decided by lot, and therefore there was no election of a second trustee. Instead of calling a runoff, the board decided that Wesley Redhead, an incumbent who had received ten votes less than either of the women, would be a holdover candidate.[14]

13. A petition asking for a Sixteenth Amendment for woman suffrage—signed by 207 Polk County residents and presented to Congress by Senator Harlan of Iowa (who was not an advocate of woman suffrage) on February 1, 1871—is still in Congressional Archives. This petition carried the signatures of all the first officers of the Polk County Woman Suffrage Society (Mrs. B. F. Allen excepted).

14. In 1912 Miss Flora Dunlap became the first successful woman candidate for the Des Moines School Board. Miss Dunlap, director of Roadside Settlement, was president of the Iowa Equal Suffrage Association, 1913–1915, and first president of the Iowa League of Women Voters, 1919–1921.

At the first annual meeting of the Polk County Woman Suffrage Society held at the courthouse on May 4, 1871, Mrs. Pitman succeeded Mrs. Sharman as president; Mrs. Coggeshall assumed the position of recording secretary; and Mrs. Callanan continued as treasurer.

Elected a vice-president was twenty-seven-year-old, attractive and vivacious ELIZABETH BOYNTON HARBERT, a former resident of Crawfordsville, Indiana, who had come to Des Moines in the fall of 1870 at the time of her marriage to W. S. Harbert, Des Moines lawyer and Civil War veteran. Mrs. Harbert, well known throughout the country as a writer and lecturer on woman suffrage, was a valuable addition to the Iowa woman-suffrage ranks. She worked enthusiastically for woman suffrage in the state until she moved to Illinois in 1874.

In view of Annie Savery's leadership in spearheading the woman-suffrage movement in Des Moines, one wonders why she was not an officer of the Polk County society—either when it was organized in October 1870 or at its first annual meeting the following March—and also why she is not mentioned as having participated in the meetings of the society during this time. Lacking any evidence to the contrary, one can only assume that Mrs. Savery, as an officer of the Iowa Woman Suffrage Association, chose to concentrate her energies on strengthening the state organization.

LUCY STONE, SUSAN B. ANTHONY, AND MARY LIVERMORE LECTURE IN IOWA

THE 1870–1871 LECTURE SEASON brought into Iowa three prominent woman's rights advocates who had not lectured there previously. Lucy

Stone made her promised visit to Iowa in November; Susan B. Anthony toured the state in February; and Mary Livermore came in April, giving her last lecture of the season in Dubuque on April 24.

LUCY STONE, who had been lecturing in behalf of women since shortly after her graduation from Oberlin College in 1847, had a nationwide reputation as a woman's rights spokesman. When she appeared in Des Moines on November 30 (this was probably her first lecture in Iowa) she drew the largest audience that had ever assembled at Moore's Hall—an upstairs auditorium, 44 x 92 feet, with a balcony at one end—which was said to seat 850 people. "Every seat had an occupant, aisles and standing places were supplied with chairs, and every inch of the Hall put to use," reported the *Des Moines Register*. This crowd had bought tickets costing 25 or 50 cents each, depending on whether or not the seats were reserved, to see and hear this notorious woman who used her maiden name though married and had refused to pay her taxes because she was not a voter. "She looked just like nineteen out of twenty people didn't expect she would," reported the *Register*. Her stout figure, plain hairdress, and sober black dress made her a "farmer's wife-looking woman, very much resembling your aunt," the *Register said*. "Her appearance made the audience her friends and her lecture most of them her admirers."

Lucy Stone—introduced by Henry O'Connor, Attorney General of Iowa and president of the Iowa Woman Suffrage Association—spoke without notes in a conversational tone, giving all the time-honored arguments for woman suffrage. In addition, she cited the recent election in Wyoming, where women voting for the first time had disproved the assertion that women were faithless to principle. "It was the Democratic party that had been most instrumental in giving them the ballot, and it was supposed that out of pure gratitude the ladies would repay the debt at the first election. But it so happened that the Republican candidates were the best men and the women voted for them." The result, Lucy Stone predicted, would be that at the next election the Democrats would nominate better men. She admonished the women in her audience "not to be trapped into saying they didn't want to vote. If your husband says he don't want you to vote, ring it in his ears that you want to and shall. When he says good morning, tell him you want to vote; when he asks what you are going to have for dinner, tell him you want to vote; and whatever he asks from the time you rise up in the morning until you lie down at night, tell him you want to vote." While in Des Moines, Lucy Stone was a guest in the home of Annie Savery.

SUSAN B. ANTHONY, the workhorse of the woman's rights movement, felt stiff and ill at ease on the platform and had always left the oratory to her partner, Mrs. Stanton. However, when Mrs. Stanton became ill during her lecture tour in the spring of 1870, Miss Anthony filled her engagements with enough success to give her the courage to strike out on her own the following season. What she lacked in grace of style and rhetorical ability, she compensated for by the logic of her arguments and the fervor of her conviction. While some of Miss Anthony's lectures were booked through an agent, many times she made her own schedules and was happy to take the net proceeds of the evening however small they might be. The money she earned in this way went toward reducing the debt of $10,000 which she had incurred as manager of *The Revolution*—a debt which Mrs. Stanton, who was well off financially, never helped her to pay.

Miss Anthony's first Iowa lecture was given at Council Bluffs on February 7, 1871. During the next few weeks she spoke in eight other Iowa communities—Cedar Rapids, Toledo, Des Moines, Mount Pleasant, Ottumwa, Burlington, Davenport, and Clinton. In her lecture Miss Anthony argued for woman's right to vote by virtue of the Fourteenth Amendment, but newspapers wherever she went were too busy lampooning her as the perfect caricature of the woman's right advocate to report what she had to say.

In Council Bluffs, where she was introduced by her hostess Amelia Bloomer, the *Nonpareil* said of Miss Anthony: "She is dreadfully in earnest and ably and vehemently clamors for her rights, but at 50 cents a head, the people of Council Bluffs were not very strong on her side last night. It is not worthwhile for anyone to talk to us for pay unless they have some plan whereby we can turn an honest penny."

An unidentified Cedar Rapids paper (in a story reprinted both in the *Des Moines Register* and in the *Sioux City Journal*) gave the following review of Miss Anthony's Cedar Rapids lecture: "Miss Anthony appeared at the hall which was filled, about 15 minutes after time. She paused at the door, took a shawl from her head, adjusted her spectacles,[15] pushed her arm through the arm of the president of the Association, leaned very heavily upon it and walked very hitchingly to the platform. It was the hall of some church society [Universalist] and right above her head appeared in bold relief the suggestive words 'God is love!' [a jibe at suffragists who were accused of being free-love advocates]. The theme was the ballot and she began by saying she had been engaged in *the* cause for twenty years, and then looked over the top of her spectacles as if she believed that the young men, not believing her to be so old, would rise to dispute the assertion. But nobody got up and Susan went on. . . ." When she finished speaking, "Susan put her shawl over her head again, got upon the president's arm and hobbled to Brown's Hotel, where she took her spectacles off, scoured them with her pocket handkerchief, put them on again, counted the money over carefully and then allowed the self-sacrificing head of the Association to go home to his wife and babies."

In Des Moines, where Miss Anthony was the guest of Annie Savery, the *Register* had this to say of her lecture: "We desire to enter our protest against the manner in which this great moral movement is being carried forward. The prime movers appear to be grasping money with an avaricious and unsatisfied appetite. . . . In what age of the world heretofore have reformers gone forth retailing their sentiments at 25 or 50 cents per dose? . . . It is true that those who travel and labor should be paid their expenses, and a reasonable consideration. . . . It is true we are willing to pay a liberal sum for the exhibition of such noble specimens of female humanity as Miss Logan [an alluring former actress] or Miss Edgarton [a blond beauty currently lecturing against woman suffrage] but when they possess none of these divine pulchritudes which man loves to see and adore, the show ceases to be interesting and the money is spent for little use. . . . In Miss Anthony's case there is no particular beauty of form or face to divert the attention from the great truths she illustrates."

The *Register*'s remarks which were reprinted in the *Council Bluffs Nonpareil* brought an indignant reply from Amelia Bloomer. "The spite against Miss Anthony," Mrs.

15. "The entire world has grown tipsy with laughter at Susan B. Anthony's spectacles. . . . Future generations will discover that the world made a sorry spectacle of itself in refusing to see through Miss Anthony's far-seeing lenses." Elizabeth Boynton Harbert, *Out of Her Sphere* (Des Moines: Mills Publishing Company, 1871), p. 182.

Bloomer wrote to the *Nonpareil*, "is not the cause she advocates . . . but that she is neither young nor handsome.
Let old, ugly women take warning, and foot all the bills
out of their own pockets. I know not why women or the
woman suffrage movement should be expected to labor
without assistance any more than men and their enterprises can be sustained without help. Give us justice; we
ask no more."

In Des Moines Martha Brown Haven replied to the
Register's comments on Miss Anthony in a letter published
in the *Des Moines Review*: "Now if such language had
been used in discussing the fine points of a thoroughbred
on the famous Grundy County farm [owned by Ret Clarkson, editor of the *Register*] there might not have been anything coarse or sensual in it; but that a living truth, a
great principle of right or a moral reform should be judged
by the external appearance of the person giving utterance
to it is a sad commentary on the moral and intellectual
degeneracy of those who use the argument." Mrs. Haven
said that every lady who read the *Register*'s criticism felt
personally insulted.

Miss Anthony's line-a-day diary for 1871, now in the
Library of Congress, is of interest for its indication of her
complete disregard of all this vilification by the press.
"Splendid audience," she noted after her Des Moines
speech, "and Mr. Savery said it was the happiest circumstance for me that I had followed Lucy Stone—that she
was so much less than people had anticipated and I so
much stronger than he had expected."

It is also of interest to note that Miss Anthony, who was
lampooned by the press in her younger years as a doddering
old maid, became in later years the venerable and respected
symbol of the woman-suffrage movement. In January 1897
when Miss Anthony, then seventy-seven years old, came to
Des Moines to preside over the first national woman-suffrage
convention held west of the Mississippi, the *Des Moines
Register* (still under Clarkson management) said of Miss
Anthony, "Time has, indeed, passed lightly over her and
though her hair is silvery, she still retains all the vigor and
enthusiasm and loving interest in humanity which has distinguished her years of leadership in the cause."

In contrast to Susan B. Anthony, who was lampooned
by the press wherever she went in 1871, MARY LIVERMORE,
the conservative editor of the *Woman's Journal* who lectured in Iowa in April of that year, found a tolerant ac-

ceptance if not outright praise in the newspaper reviews of her lectures. The *Register* asserted that "the friends of woman suffrage have an advocate in Mrs. Livermore of whom they can feel proud." The *Dubuque Herald,* which seldom had a good word to say for a woman's rights advocate, said of Mrs. Livermore, "If she can't convince, she at least commands respect."

In Des Moines, where Mrs. Livermore spoke at the courthouse on April 20, her lecture was not well attended. Probably by the time of Mrs. Livermore's appearance, which was late in the season, Des Moines citizens were tired of lectures by women, having already heard Lucy Stone, Susan B. Anthony, Lillian Edgarton, Olive Logan, Augusta Chapin, Matilda Fletcher, and Annie Savery. From Des Moines Mrs. Livermore went to Grinnell, Iowa City, and Dubuque. In Dubuque, where she had delivered her first public address[16] to a "promiscuous" audience (mixed audience of men and women) in behalf of the Sanitary Commission in 1864, Mrs. Livermore had many old friends from Civil War days who helped fill the lecture hall to capacity. Here she spoke under the auspices of the Northern Iowa Woman Suffrage Society and was introduced by Henry O'Connor, president of the Iowa Woman Suffrage Association. This occasion, as far as is known, marks O'Connor's last public appearance in connection with woman suffrage.

While on tour Mrs. Livermore wrote regular reports for the *Woman's Journal,* giving interesting glimpses of the people she met along the way. In Des Moines, where she was the guest of her old friend Elizabeth Boynton Harbert, she met for the first time "Mrs. Annie N. Savery a lady of talent, education, and culture, enlarged by travel at home and abroad, a woman of wealth, influence, and position, all of which she has consecrated to the cause of woman. She is a power throughout the State," Mrs. Livermore wrote, "and will never cease her efforts till women are enfranchised."

In Iowa City Mrs. Livermore was the guest of her fellow Universalist, the Reverend Augusta Chapin. Here she had an opportunity to have several visits with another old friend, John Irish, "who introduced and carried triumphantly through the last Iowa Legislature the bill to amend the Constitution so that women may vote. It is often asserted that this measure was commenced by Mr. Irish in

16. For Mrs. Livermore's account of this event see her book, *My Story of the War.*

jest," Mrs. Livermore wrote, "but this is not true." Irish, she asserted, was "a noble man, of unusual intelligence, far-seeing, very executive, and respected even by his political opponents. . . . He has always believed in Woman Suffrage, the well-known action of his past life has been in that direction, and he undertook the measure honestly." However, Mrs. Livermore's faith in Irish's honesty is belied by the disingenuous story he told her of how he succeeded in getting the amendment approved by the General Assembly. "Watching his opportunity all through the session," Mrs. Livermore told her readers, "he brought it forward at a time when there was an intense excitement concerning an appropriation for the building of a State House. Just at the right moment, when the attention of the whole State was fastened on the Legislature, when its leading political men of both parties were in attendance, and when those who were opposed to it, *per se,* consented to its introduction because the discussion would retard the passage of the appropriation for the proposed new Capitol, he threw the constitutional amendment into the arena. . . . Immediately the discussion began; it grew in interest and excitement; the Capitol appropriation was forgotten; and when it was put to vote, the amendment was approved by a handsome majority."

Mrs. Livermore reported that Mr. Irish was confident that the amendment would receive the endorsement of the next legislature and then would come "the tug of war" in a popular referendum. She was almost certain that the woman-suffrage reform would be carried first in Iowa, where the women as a whole were "superior to the women of any other State."

Victoria Woodhull before the House Judiciary Committee presenting her argument in favor of woman's voting on the basis of the Fourteenth and Fifteenth Amendments, as pictured in Frank Leslie's Illustrated Newspaper, *February 4, 1871.*

8

1871

Bᴇʟᴏᴡ is a letter by a lady among the most prominent of the champions of woman suffrage in Iowa, written to a gentleman who has asked her if she was in favor
of the movement to compel Congress to declare that the
Fourteenth and Fifteenth Amendments made a woman
a citizen and a voter," said the *Des Moines Register* on
January 18, 1871, in a foreword to a statement by Annie
Savery concerning a woman-suffrage memorial presented to Congress the previous month. This memorial
presented in the name of Victoria Woodhull of New
York but generally conceded to have been written by
her friend General Benjamin Butler, a well-known
member of Congress from Massachusetts, asked for a
law declaring women enfranchised by virtue of the
Fourteenth and Fifteenth Amendments. It argued that
because the Fifteenth Amendment declares that "the
right of citizens of the United States to vote shall not be
denied or abridged . . ." and because the Fourteenth
Amendment declares that "all persons born or naturalized in the United States . . . are citizens . . . and are
entitled to an equal protection of the laws, . . ." therefore all citizens regardless of sex have a constitutional
right to vote.

"It must be admitted by the friends of the movement that those who framed the amendments as well as those who voted for them never intended that they should apply to women. Therefore it was not so intended," Mrs. Savery stated in her letter published in the *Register*. She cared not a straw what Congress might declare to be the legal effect of the mere phraseology used. A high sense of honor and self-respect should make women scorn the ballot through a mere technicality. "If our claim for the ballot is not founded upon justice, or cannot stand upon its own merits, then let it fall," Mrs. Savery said. As for herself, she would "rather don man's apparel and take her place in the line of voters and boldly deposit her ballot" rather than reach for the right to vote "by entering a back door which had been left ajar by accident. . . . If the zealous friends of the cause, now at Washington will bide their time, there will soon be no necessity to seek indirectly that which will soon be offered to them," Mrs. Savery concluded.[1]

WOMEN CLAIM ENFRANCHISEMENT UNDER THE FOURTEENTH AND FIFTEENTH AMENDMENTS

THE ARGUMENT that women were enfranchised under the Fourteenth Amendment was first expounded in October 1869 in a series of resolutions presented by Virginia Minor, president of the Missouri Woman Suffrage Association, at the first woman-suffrage convention held in that state.[2] The Minor resolutions—written by Mrs. Minor's husband Francis, a prominent St. Louis lawyer—were endorsed by the Missouri convention as well as by the second national woman-suffrage convention meeting in Washington in January 1870. Mrs. Minor said it was her intention to try to register and to vote in the next federal election and, if refused, to carry her case to the courts, as far as the Supreme Court if necessary.

1. Martha Brown Haven did not agree with Annie Savery. In a letter published in the *Des Moines Register*, January 22, 1871, Mrs. Haven said, "Is it not meet that we go through the same door hand in hand with the colored man, thus making the triumph of the late war complete? If any bars in the constitutional fence have been left down, or any gate unfastened, whether by accident or design; if there are any back doors unguarded, I wish to go in at once, and take possession of my inheritance as an American citizen."

2. The Fifteenth Amendment was not ratified until March 30, 1870, hence it was not cited in the Minor resolutions.
    Although the Woodhull memorial claimed woman's right to vote by virtue of both the Fourteenth and Fifteenth Amendments, woman's rights advocates relied principally on the equal-protection clause of the Fourteenth Amendment in arguing for their rights under the constitution.

The route to the ballot via the courts seemed a slow and dubious process to most woman-suffrage advocates who looked to a Sixteenth Amendment to the federal Constitution and removal of barriers to their voting in the various state constitutions as surer and quicker methods. The Woodhull memorial, however, which argued that women need not wait for court decisions but could gain the ballot by a simple declaration of Congress, made the argument that women already had a constitutional right to vote seem more attractive.

In early January 1871 it was announced that the House judiciary committee of which Butler was a member would hold a hearing on January 11 at which Mrs. Woodhull would present her appeal for a declaratory act. This was the same day the third annual woman-suffrage convention was to convene in Washington; and Miss Anthony and her cohort Isabella Beecher Hooker,[3] who were in the city making arrangements for the meeting, were in a dilemma as to whether or not to appear at this hearing. They were eager to do so because this was the first woman-suffrage hearing held by a judiciary committee of Congress, a privilege vainly sought by Mrs. Stanton and Miss Anthony at the time of the previous two national conventions in Washington. Nevertheless, Miss Anthony and Mrs. Hooker disliked appearing with Mrs. Woodhull, a woman whose reputation was decidedly unsavory.

(Courtesy New York Historical Society)

VICTORIA WOODHULL, born in a shack on the wrong side of the tracks in Homer, Ohio, in 1838, was the daughter of Buck Claflin, a pettifogging character, and Roxanna

---

3. Mrs. Hooker (half sister of Henry Ward Beecher and Harriet Beecher Stowe) had assumed the responsibility for the Washington convention in 1871, hoping to keep the meeting free of extraneous "side issues" and to attract delegates who had been alienated by Mrs. Stanton and Miss Anthony. Mrs. Hooker soon found her task more difficult than she had anticipated and sent for Miss Anthony to help her.

Claflin, a slovenly woman with a fiery personality who raised a fiercely loyal brood of seven children despite their constant quarreling. The Claflins left Homer in the late 1840's to wander throughout the Midwest as a cure-all outfit with Tennessee, Victoria's fair-haired younger sister, the feature attraction as a clairvoyant physician. Wherever the Claflins settled for any length of time, they were usually accused of selling love as well as bogus cures.

In 1853 when she was fifteen, Victoria married Canning Woodhull by whom she had two children. An incompetent alcoholic and quack cure-all physician with headquarters in Chicago, Woodhull advertised his miraculous healing powers in newspapers as far away as Muscatine, Iowa. In 1864 Victoria divorced Woodhull, and two years later she teamed up with Colonel James Harvey Blood of St. Louis—married and the father of two children. Blood, better known at that time as Dr. J. A. Harvey, was a clairvoyant physician who also advertised his healing powers in Iowa journals. During a tour of the Midwest in 1867 Colonel Blood and Victoria, traveling as Dr. and Mrs. Harvey, spent some time in Des Moines where they set up shop in the Des Moines House, a second-rate hotel. They skipped town without paying their bills.[4]

In the summer of 1868 Victoria Woodhull, a spiritualist, went to New York pursuant to a message from her favorite spirit, Demosthenes. Somehow the whole Claflin tribe as well as Colonel Blood and Canning Woodhull seemed to have received the same message, as they all gathered there before long. Within a few months Victoria and her sister, who now called herself "Tennie C.," had amassed a small fortune by means of tips on the stock market given them by seventy-four-year-old Commodore Vanderbilt, a man well-known for his fondness for young women.

With the acquisition of wealth Victoria Woodhull, who hungered for social acceptance, sought to use the woman-suffrage movement to climb to a more respectable rung on the social ladder. She attended the first woman-suffrage convention in Washington in January 1869, at which time the *Washington Star,* in an article titled

---

4. In 1874 when Victoria Woodhull, accompanied by Blood, lectured for the first time in Des Moines, the couple was recognized as the Dr. and Mrs. Harvey who had come to town in 1867 and who had left owing money to the *Des Moines Register* for advertising and printing and to a Mrs. Benedict who had done sewing for Victoria.

"The Coming Woman," described her as a person of "commanding intellect, refinement, and remarkable executive ability" who planned to stay on in Washington during the current session of Congress in the interest of equal suffrage, elevated railways, the pneumatic dispatch, and other enterprises.

A year later (January 1870) Victoria Woodhull and Tennie C. created a sensation by opening an elaborate brokerage office in the Wall Street district under the aegis of Commodore Vanderbilt. Crowds of curious spectators thronged about this establishment to catch a glimpse of the notorious lady brokers, and the newspapers carried daily reports about them for several weeks. *The Revolution* was alone among the journals of the day in defending Mrs. Woodhull's right to earn her living on Wall Street and in castigating those who sneered at her as a woman of ill repute.

On April 2, 1870, Mrs. Woodhull announced herself as a candidate for President of the United States. The following month she and Tennie C. launched *Woodhull and Claflin's Weekly,* a journal which, in addition to backing Mrs. Woodhull for President, advocated a variety of reforms including woman suffrage, Marxian socialism, licensing of prostitutes, and sexual freedom. Stephen Pearl Andrews, a brilliant eccentric who did much of the writing for *Woodhull and Claflin's Weekly,* was a free-love advocate who had been dogging the woman's rights movement since its inception in the 1850's.

In the summer of 1870 Mrs. Woodhull rented an elegant four-story brownstone mansion at 15 East 38th Street in the fashionable Murray Hill district of New York, which she furnished in a lavish fashion and offered to the New York suffragists as a ladies' clubhouse for "thinkers and reformers." But the ladies of New York (Miss Anthony included) would have nothing to do with this mansion furnished more like a sumptuous house of assignation than a clubhouse for respectable reformers. The 38th Street residence was soon housing most of the Claflin clan as well as Colonel Blood, Victoria's husband of the moment; Canning Woodhull, her former husband; and Stephen Pearl Andrews, the writer and reformer.

In December 1870 Mrs. Woodhull had come to Washington with her memorial for which she found sponsors in both houses of

Congress. In early January 1871 the House judiciary committee announced that on January 11 it would hold a hearing at which Mrs. Woodhull would appear in support of this memorial. It was doubtless no accident that this was scheduled for the same day the woman-suffrage convention was to open in Washington. After a good deal of hesitation about whether or not to appear with Mrs. Woodhull, Miss Anthony and Mrs. Hooker finally decided to do so. They therefore postponed the opening of their convention until the afternoon of January 11 and arranged to speak at the hearing in support of the Woodhull memorial. Mrs. Stanton, who had been the leading spokesman for woman suffrage at hearings before the District of Columbia Committee in 1869 and 1870, did not come to Washington in 1871. Angered because she had been asked by Mrs. Hooker to refrain from discussing her pet social theories at the Washington convention, she had refused to have anything to do with the meeting.

The judiciary committee hearing on January 11 with the notorious Mrs. Woodhull as the star attraction was a national sensation. *Frank Leslie's Weekly* depicted the scene in a full-page woodcut, and papers throughout the country carried news of the event.[5] Iowans were particularly interested in the fact that William Loughridge of Oskaloosa, representative from Iowa's Sixth District, was the only committee member to join with Butler in supporting Mrs. Woodhull's memorial.

Despite the qualms of Miss Anthony and Mrs. Hooker concerning their appearance with Mrs. Woodhull, they were so impressed with her refinement, her beauty, her sincerity, her logical arguments, and the respect with which she was listened to by the members of the judiciary committee that they invited her to sit on the platform at the suffrage convention when it convened the afternoon of January 11 and to present her morning's speech to the assembled delegates. The convention, equally impressed with Mrs. Woodhull and the success with which she was pressing her claim for suffrage, decided to drop agitation for a Sixteenth Amendment and to concentrate on a campaign for congressional recognition of their right to vote by virtue of the Fourteenth and Fifteenth Amendments. The convention also urged women to attempt to register and to vote and if refused, to apply to the courts for judicial recognition of their right to the ballot.

5. Newspapers in 1871 were not illustrated. Probably this is the reason that Des Moines residents did not recognize Mrs. Woodhull as having been in the city in 1867 under the name of Mrs. Blood until she appeared there in person again in 1874.

A National Woman Suffrage and Education Committee[6] was named by the convention to lobby for a declaratory act and to carry on an educational campaign among the women of the country. Mrs. Woodhull, a member of the committee, headed a list of contributors with the astronomical sum of $10,000.[7] Ben Butler permitted the women to use his frank in flooding the country with copies of the Woodhull memorial and other tracts setting forth arguments for woman's constitutional right to the ballot. Embarking on an extended lecture tour immediately after the Washington convention, Miss Anthony carried the good news to her audiences in Iowa and other midwestern states that women were already enfranchised by virtue of the Fourteenth and Fifteenth Amendments. Within a few months the national committee was able to present Congress with petitions carrying 80,000 signatures asking for a declaratory act.

Meanwhile, in late January the judiciary committee reported to the House on the Woodhull memorial. The majority of the committee held that suffrage was a matter for state regulation and therefore Congress had no power to act. Butler and Loughridge, however, in a minority report not only presented an exhaustive argument for woman's right to vote by virtue of the Fourteenth and Fifteenth Amendments but also declared that Congress had both the right and the duty to decide who the voters should be. This report was hailed as a great victory by the National Woman Suffrage Committee.

"Bravo! *My dear Woodhull*," wrote Miss Anthony on February 4 from Kansas City, Missouri, after receiving word from Mrs. Woodhull about the favorable minority report. "Everybody here chimes in with the conclusion that we are free already." Miss Anthony was now sure "that Mr. Train's prophecy three years ago in the Kansas campaign, that the women would vote for the next President" was about to be realized. "Go ahead! bright, glorious, young and strong spirit," Miss Anthony told Mrs. Woodhull, "and

6. The women wanted to avoid using the name Union Woman Suffrage Association; hence they chose a name which would identify them with the former National Association. Tilton resigned the presidency of the Union Association in March 1871, and at the annual convention in May Mrs. Stanton was reelected to her former position as president. Another National Committee, of which Annie Savery was a member, was appointed by the May convention to carry on the work for the ensuing year.

7. The total annual income for the American Equal Rights Association announced at its convention in May 1866 was $257.50. By 1869 annual income had risen to $1,745.94.

believe in the best love and hope and faith of Susan B. Anthony." This letter, which Mrs. Woodhull published in *Woodhull and Claflin's Weekly,* was reprinted in the *Dubuque Times* of February 21 under the heading "Characteristic Letter from Susan B. Anthony."

Also encouraged by events in Washington, Mrs. Stanton wrote to Victoria Woodhull on February 20 that she was glad the national committee had pitched their tents with her. At first Mrs. Stanton had questioned the wisdom of seeking enfranchisement under the Fourteenth and Fifteenth Amendments, fearing it might be "a mere Republican dodge to get rid of a Sixteenth Amendment and Congressional action by sending us to the courts, where we would hang by the eyelids for a quarter of a century." But her mind had been set at rest by the able minority report of Loughridge and Butler. Mrs. Stanton's letter was also published in *Woodhull and Claflin's Weekly* and subsequently widely quoted in other papers throughout the country.

Miss Anthony's and Mrs. Stanton's enthusiasm about Mrs. Woodhull's campaign for a declaratory act was not universally shared by woman-suffrage advocates, many of whom hesitated to jump on the Woodhull bandwagon. The *Woman's Journal,* which regarded Mrs. Woodhull with undisguised holy horror, advised women to stick to the slower and surer process of education leading to the adoption of a Sixteenth Amendment rather than to seek any shortcut to the ballot. Even *The Revolution,* generally friendly to Miss Anthony and Mrs. Stanton, avoided involvement with the campaign for a declaratory act.

Despite the hesitancy of many women about seeking enfranchisement under the Fourteenth and Fifteenth Amendments, a number of women attempted to register and to vote in the spring of 1871. In Michigan one woman succeeded in casting her ballot and having it counted; in Washington, D.C., where thirty women marched in a body to the polls and were turned away, a suit was brought against the election officials.[8] Although no Iowa women attempted to vote in the spring elections, the Clarinda registry board in jest added the names of all women over twenty-one to the rolls of registered voters. According to the *Des Moines Register* of March 15, "Several gentlemen 'got on their ear' about it and erased their wives' names. Several ladies got their precious backs up also and

8. The Supreme Court of the District ruled in October 1871 that while women may be voters by virtue of the Fourteenth Amendment, it makes no bestowal of the right of suffrage and that a special act of Congress would be necessary to grant women the ballot.

erased their own names. None but the sons of Adam, however, offered to vote and Clarinda is now as peaceable as Mary's little lamb."

The action of the Clarinda registry board in adding the names of all women over twenty-one to the list of eligible voters could well have been a practical joke aimed at the ninety-two citizens of Clarinda (county seat of Page County) and nearby Taylor County who had sent a petition to Congress the previous year asking for woman suffrage. In October 1871 one of the young women who had signed this petition, Miss Kizzie (pet name for Keziah) Anderson of Taylor County astonished her fellow Iowans by actually casting

Keziah Anderson (Mrs. Walter Dorrance)

her vote. Miss Anderson, a twenty-seven-year-old teacher, rode to the polls with her younger brother who was about to vote for the first time. The election judges were Kizzie's father, William Anderson, and Edwin Henshaw, a close friend whose name also appears on the woman-suffrage petition. When Henshaw dared Kizzie to vote, she accepted his challenge, casting a Republican ballot which the friendly judges accepted and counted. According to a widely quoted story from the *Bedford South West* (a Taylor County paper) the election judges decided Miss Anderson had a legal right to vote by virtue of the Fourteenth Amendment. The *Clarinda Republican* reported that the incident had caused considerable rejoicing by the strong-minded of that section of the state. "Who would have guessed that the first woman to vote in Iowa would be named Kizzie?"[9] this paper asked.

9. On October 3, 1872, Miss Anderson married Wallace F. Dorrance of Page County. The couple settled in Paonia, Colorado, in 1897, where Mrs. Dorrance died in May 1927.

During 1871 and 1872 a number of women appealed to the courts in tests of their right to vote under the Fourteenth Amendment. In the presidential election of November 1872, Susan B. Anthony succeeded in leading a group of fourteen women in Rochester, New York, in registering and then in voting. Miss Anthony had planned to bring suit against the election officials for denying her rights under the Fourteenth Amendment if, as she had anticipated, they refused to let her vote. Instead she found herself under arrest for having violated an 1870 federal law (aimed at Southern rebels) which stipulated that anyone voting knowingly without having the lawful right to vote was guilty of a crime and on conviction would be punished by a fine not exceeding $500 or by imprisonment not exceeding three years. Miss Anthony challenged the lawlessness of her arrest but nonetheless was convicted and ordered to pay a fine (which she refused to do) in a trial notable for its lack of fair procedure.

Virginia Minor of St. Louis, former president of the Missouri Woman Suffrage Association, also tried to vote in the 1872 presidential election. When she was not permitted to register, she brought suit against the registrar for denying her constitutional right to the ballot. Mrs. Minor's suit eventually reached the United States Supreme Court which, in a unanimous decision delivered in

※ *Victoria Woodhull at the polls in New York City unsuccessfully asserting her constitutional right to vote, as pictured in* Harper's Weekly, *November 25, 1871.*

March 1875, held in substance that the Constitution did not confer the right of suffrage on those who were citizens at the time it was adopted, and that suffrage was not coextensive with citizenship.

Meanwhile during the summer of 1871 the *Woman's Journal* reported that the Iowa Supreme Court might rule favorably "on the Fourteenth and Fifteenth Amendments and thus enfranchise by a word from the bench the women of that State." This wasn't likely, replied an Iowa correspondent who wished it might be so; but as three of the judges were known opponents of the cause and the fourth was "just where his own interest calls him," there was not much hope of success through this tribunal. This writer said that the women in Iowa proposed to work with the legislature by all legal means in their power. Although "the Woodhull and Claflin movement" had injured the cause, she was sure that eventually the "fearful ones will see that free-love and woman suffrage are not so closely related as those women assert."

FREE LOVE

VICTORIA WOODHULL's emergence as a leader in the National Woman Suffrage Committee marked the first time that a so-called "free lover" had been granted a position of honor in the woman-suffrage movement. Not only was Mrs. Woodhull by general reputation a practicing free lover but her mentor, fifty-nine-year-old Stephen Pearl Andrews, was a philosophical anarchist, widely known as the leading free-love advocate in the country.

Free-love votaries dreamed of a utopia of sexual innocence, where coition would occur only between willing partners and the state would have no jurisdiction over the wedding rite. They argued that women could never achieve their full equality without sexual freedom. "You talk of woman's rights," declared a Mrs. Branch at a much publicized general reform convention in Rutland, Vermont, in 1858, "but do you say anything about her right to love whom she will, where she will and when she will?" This same year Stephen Pearl Andrews at the Eighth National Woman's Rights Convention in New York City (chaired by Susan B. Anthony) argued that woman's first right was to maternity under the best circumstances, and that she had a right to ascertain by experiment the best condition of serving the generation to come. Andrews, who said he had attended woman's rights conventions for the past seven or eight years but had not spoken, stated that he was aware his opinions were more radical than those held by the convention and wished to absolve it from responsibility for what he said. Newspapers, however, screamed "free love" in reporting the meeting.

Both Andrews and Mrs. Woodhull were spiritualists—a cult which dwelt on the idea of a mystical kind of spiritual affinity and therefore attracted free-love advocates who preached that the only true marriage was a union of congenial spirits. While most spiritualists were people of conventional morality,[10] it is also true that free lovers were invariably spiritualists. This, combined with the fact that spiritualists were pioneers in supporting the woman's rights movement, served to support the popular argument that woman's rights, spiritualism, and free love were synonymous.[11] Mrs. Woodhull, who represented all three, was the perfect target for the enemies of woman suffrage and a decided embarrassment to the friends of the cause.

In mid-May 1871 Miss Anthony and Mrs. Stanton, who had maintained that Mrs. Woodhull was a pure woman despite her reputation as a free lover, were faced with a crisis when gossip about her private life was confirmed in New York City at a police court hearing in which Annie Claflin accused Colonel Blood of taking all her daughter's money. At this hearing, widely publicized in Iowa papers, Victoria Woodhull readily admitted that she was sharing the 38th Street mansion with Canning Woodhull and Colonel Blood as well as Stephen Pearl Andrews and numerous members of the Claflin clan. According to a report of the hearing

10. In "Notes on the History of Pottawattamie County," *Annals of Iowa* (July 1874) Dexter Bloomer states that in 1872 "modern spiritualism found many followers in the county, among them some of the best and most substantial citizens. They held regular meetings and numerous lectures were delivered by its advocates. In September they organized themselves into a permanent society."

11. Two of the many spiritualist lecturers who toured Iowa in the post Civil War years—Mrs. Lois Waisbrooker and Mrs. Addie L. Ballou—can be associated with both woman's rights and sexual freedom.

Mrs. Waisbrooker addressed the Iowa Spiritualist convention in Des Moines in October 1869. A month later a correspondent to the *Marshalltown Times* indicated that Mrs. Waisbrooker had lectured on woman suffrage in that community. The *Times* did not review the speech. In 1875 Mrs. Waisbrooker participated in a social-freedom convention led by Moses Hull, editor of a spiritualist, free-love publication. In 1896 she published "My Century Plant," which advocated self-ownership for women, including limitation of offspring. In the early 1900's she was living in Home Colony, Washington, a utopian community which was deprived of its post office when the colonists claimed the right to bathe in the nude.

Mrs. Ballou, who lived in Minnesota in the 1860's and early 1870's, was listed in the *Banner of Light*, a spiritualist paper, as state missionary for Iowa in 1869. She addressed the Minnesota Legislature in behalf of woman suffrage in 1869, and in 1871 she was named a vice-president for Minnesota in the National Woman Suffrage Association. At the Washington woman-suffrage convention in 1872 Mrs. Ballou nominated Mrs. Woodhull for President of the United States against Miss Anthony's wishes.

Advertisement placed by Canning Woodhull, Victoria Woodhull's first husband, in the Muscatine (Iowa) Journal, *December 25, 1863, and one placed in the* Mount Pleasant Home Journal, *June 9, 1865, by Colonel Blood, alias J. A. Harvey, her second husband. Both doctors claimed sure cures for cancer as well as "happy results" for all female difficulties.*

in the *Dubuque Times* Mrs. Claflin testified that she did not know whether or not Blood was married to her daughter. She called Stephen Pearl Andrews "that old free-lover—the worst man that ever lived." Mary Sparr, a sister of Victoria's, testified that she did not "know what relation Mr. Blood now bears to Mrs. Woodhull" but she did know "that they were married twice in six months." Colonel Blood testified that his right name was James Harvey Blood but that he had "been advertising at times as Dr. James Harvey."

A storm of outraged denunciation of Victoria Woodhull, joined by the entire press of the country, followed the police court hearing. Mrs. Stanton and Miss Anthony, who had seen too many women sacrificed to sentimental, hypocritical prating about purity, refused to be shaken in their loyalty to Mrs. Woodhull. "The present howl is an old trick to divert public thought from the main question," Susan B. Anthony warned the readers of *The Revolution* in a letter written from her home in Rochester, New York, on May 27. Miss Anthony deplored the double standard of morals which demanded that women be immaculate by birth, family, and fame and made them outcasts for the slighest deviation from the narrow path, while men were permitted the greatest latitude in sexual conduct. She urged women to "Stand by the Course" in the face of the current storm. "We are falling on strange times but there is no way but to live with them," Miss Anthony wrote to her friend Martha Wright a few days later.

On May 31 Miss Anthony went to Ohio to meet Mrs. Stanton, and the two women embarked on a summer-long journey to the Pacific coast. They traveled by slow stages stopping en route for lectures and visits with fellow suffragists. In Des Moines, where they arrived on June 9 for a three-day stay, Mrs. Stanton lectured twice at the courthouse, once on woman suffrage and once to an audience of women only on the delicate subject of "Marriage and Maternity." While in Des Moines Miss Anthony and Mrs. Stanton were widely entertained by the suffrage leaders of the community, including Annie Savery, Martha Callanan, Elizabeth Boynton Harbert, and Maria Gray Pitman (president of the Polk County society) who held an evening reception for them in her home across the street from the courthouse.

After leaving Des Moines, Miss Anthony went to northwest Iowa where she delivered lectures at Sioux City, Cherokee, Fort Dodge, and Missouri Valley. In Fort Dodge Miss Anthony stayed at the newly opened Iowa House. "Splendid audience," she noted in her diary, "but oh the bedbuggy room."

From Des Moines Mrs. Stanton went to Council Bluffs, where she was the guest of Amelia Bloomer. Here she delivered the same two lectures she had given in Des Moines and, as usual wherever she went, she charmed people with her gracious, lively manner, her sense of humor, and her brilliant conversation. "People all greatly pleased with her" Dexter Bloomer noted in his diary on June 14, following an evening reception in his home in Mrs. Stanton's honor.

"I wish you could see how Susan and I are treated and feted all along the route," Mrs. Stanton wrote from Omaha to her friend Martha Wright on June 19. "I mention this as evidence of the growing popularity of our cause as well as proof that Boston [Lucy Stone's faction] has not killed us yet. We are entertained by the first people who give us letters of introduction to everybody worth knowing and free fares on the railroads," Mrs. Stanton said.

Despite their favorable reception as they crossed the country during the summer of 1871, Miss Anthony and Mrs. Stanton found a profound disquiet about Mrs. Woodhull wherever they went. "Why did you make a leader of her?" they were invariably asked. "Now we don't make leaders, they make themselves," Miss Anthony responded. "If anyone can accomplish a more brilliant effort than Victoria Woodhull, let him or her go ahead and they will be leaders. Mrs. Woodhull came to Washington from Wall Street with a powerful argument and lots of cash behind her and cash is a big thing with Congress," Miss Anthony said. "If it takes youth, beauty, and money to capture Congress, Victoria Woodhull is the woman we are after." Miss Anthony, too honest to uphold the morality of Mrs. Woodhull, told her critics that she cared no more about the "antecedents" of Mrs. Woodhull than she did about those of any member of Congress. She would gladly welcome the help of any prostitute who was willing to work for woman suffrage.

Mrs. Stanton went even further than Miss Anthony in her defense of Mrs. Woodhull. In speeches in Des Moines and Council Bluffs she stoutly defended Victoria's morality and declared that she was a much maligned and unjustly persecuted woman. There was no reason not to call her a woman of good repute, Mrs. Stanton said. If the men who troubled themselves so much about the virtue of women would only make one moral code for both sexes, the world would be much better off, Mrs. Stanton asserted.

To special confidantes Mrs. Stanton related the facts of a suppressed but juicy scandal which was currently being whispered about in New York circles—a scandal which served to underscore her indignation about the double standard of morals. This was the story of Henry Ward Beecher's extramarital relations with Theodore Tilton's wife Elizabeth.[12] Beecher, America's most sacrosanct minister and former president of the American Woman Suffrage Association (the Boston faction), had first seduced Mrs. Tilton, an admiring parishioner, while Tilton was lecturing in the Midwest in the fall of 1868. Mrs. Tilton had confessed her unfaithfulness to her husband in July 1870, and soon after, Tilton told Mrs. Stanton about his marital troubles. Mrs. Stanton whispered to her Iowa friends that Mrs. Woodhull knew all about the affair and had threatened to make it public during the outcry about her living in the same house with two husbands, following the police court hearing the previous month.

Meanwhile Mrs. Stanton was adding her own fuel to the free-love flames during the summer of 1871 with her lecture on "Marriage and Maternity," in which she dwelt on the taboo subject of birth control. "Wherever we stay in a town two days I talk one afternoon to the women alone from three to six and they linger still," Mrs. Stanton wrote to Martha Wright in her letter of June 19. "The new gospel of fewer children and a healthy, happy maternity is gladly received." Although no Des Moines or Council Bluffs paper reported Mrs. Stanton's lecture to women during her stay in Iowa (talks to women alone were considered private affairs) the *Des Moines Register* on July 29 created a sensation by reprinting a verbatim account of the "Marriage and Maternity" lecture as it was delivered in San Francisco by Mrs. Stanton. The *Register* published the *San Francisco Chronicle* story without editorial comment other than the following sensational headline:

12. In November 1872 when the Beecher-Tilton scandal was exposed in *Woodhull and Claflin's Weekly,* Mrs. Bloomer in a letter to the *Council Bluffs Nonpareil* stated that she was sure Victoria Woodhull had not invented the story for the purpose of blackmail. According to the *Nonpareil* (November 23, 1872), "One year and a half ago this scandal was whispered in the ears of Mrs. Bloomer by one of the parties given as authority by the Woodhull [Mrs. Stanton] and the one so whispering gave Mr. Tilton himself as her authority. She further said that the Woodhull knew all about it and threatened its publication. Mrs. Bloomer has kept this scandal to herself and never would have revealed her knowledge of it if it had not come so fully before the public."

FOR WOMEN ONLY

**Mrs. Elizabeth Cady Stanton Discourses on
Marriage and Maternity—That Secret Lecture—
Peculiar Ideas on Matrimony, Divorces and
Babies—Important Questions and Answers**

Other papers gave no indication to their readers that Mrs. Stanton's talk was for women only. According to the *DeWitt Observer* of August 4, 1871: "The extracts from Mrs. Stanton's speech made lately in San Francisco that some editors have characterized as too indelicate to communicate to a miscellaneous audience of men and women and adduced by them as evidence she was a coarse, unrefined woman, prove to have been made to "Women Only" and was so advertised, and apparently women only attended. But nevertheless the speech was reported *verbatim,* either by a male reporter in female garments, or by some woman who understood the business; and men, or rather male sneaks, gave it to the types, knowing it was strictly a private lecture, and circulated it without stating facts as evidence that Mrs. Stanton is not as refined in her public expressions as she ought to be. *That is mean."*

The following are a few of Mrs. Stanton's "peculiar ideas" as published in the *Des Moines Register.*

The Bible says that maternity is a curse—most women accept this doctrine as true; it is simply horrible; IT IS A MONSTROUS LIE. The Bible has been translated BY MEN AND FOR MEN. . . . We must educate our daughters that motherhood is grand, and that God never cursed it.

I want to teach women that the begetting of a child by a drunken or a licentious father is a sin—is a crime; and I hold that the law which binds a woman to such a man IS IN ITSELF A CRIME. It is the woman's duty to break such obligations. I honor the woman who sunders such a tie.

It is of more importance what kind of a child we raise than how many. It is better to produce ONE LION than twelve jackasses. We have got jackasses enough; LET US GO INTO THE LION BUSINESS.

A number of questions were asked. One lady inquired: "How can we follow your advice and keep from having children?"

> Mrs. Stanton announced that all truths run in parallel lines, and woman's perfect independence is the answer to that question. Woman must at all times be THE SOVEREIGN OF HER OWN PERSON.
>
> Another lady anxiously inquired: "What are we to do when men don't agree with us about this matter?" Mrs. Stanton replied that the men must be educated up to the higher civilization as well as the women. That the same powerful force that governs the masculine passions can be controlled and directed into the brain force, and made to result in great deeds.
>
> One lady asked a question which hinted at prevention by other than legitimate means and Mrs. Stanton promptly replied that such views of the matter were too degrading and disgusting to touch upon, and must be classed in the category of crime alongside of infanticide.
>
> A lady asked what a devout Roman Catholic should do in a case where she ought to obtain a divorce which her church forbade? Mrs. Stanton answered that she thought her whole lecture was an answer to that query.

Mrs. Stanton dared go no further in her public lectures than to advocate sexual abstinence as a means of family limitation. The following letter, now in the Seneca Falls Historical Society, written by Mrs. Stanton in about 1880 gives her candid opinion concerning birth control: "My dear [name obliterated]: I think the Doctor to whom you refer is Mrs. Sarah Chace. I think you probably know as much as she does as you will readily ascertain at one interview. I never saw her, but she has made it a speciality to teach women how to avoid a too generous perpetuation of the race, which I consider a commendable kind of knowledge to hand down to our overburdened mothers. When women have a voice in the laws, that kind of knowledge will not be tabooed. . . ."

"The whole movement of woman's rights is progress in a terrible form," wrote "R. W. T.," an anonymous critic in Four-Mile Township, in a letter printed in the *Register* on August 10. "Twenty or thirty years ago if a woman had used such language or conveyed such obscene meanings in language before the public as Mrs. Stanton did in Des Moines . . . they would have been shunned by all respectable citizens and classed with courtesans." R. W. T. found the whole tone of *The Revolution* and the *Woman's Journal* "to comprise the same substance as *Woodhull and Claflin's Weekly*—the paper which demonstrates the *free-love* picture of woman's rights." R. W. T. recommended *The True Woman,* an antiwoman-suffrage paper breathing of purity and love and published in Baltimore under the auspices of Mrs. General Sherman.

The free-love situation was further complicated during the summer of 1871 by Theodore Tilton who, in one of the most bizarre aspects of the Beecher-Tilton affair, undertook to placate Mrs. Woodhull to keep her from exposing Beecher's relations with his wife. Soon Tilton was completely under Mrs. Woodhull's spell (she later claimed he was her lover for six months). Suffrage advocates in Iowa read in the *Golden Age,*[13] that Mrs. Woodhull was "one of the most remarkable women of her time . . . a person of true nobility of character, the Joan of Arc of the woman movement and among the whitest and purest of her sex."

"We are informed that Mrs. Woodhull actually has not a few women in Iowa talking in her favor—some of them ladies whose actions lie close to their consciences," said the *Des Moines Register* on August 13 in commenting on a circular "from the female herself" asking for this paper's support of her candidacy for President of the United States. "The trouble is that most of these women take Mrs. Woodhull as Mr. Tilton paints her instead of taking her as she is portrayed in the colors of her own life," the *Register* said. In order that those women who supported Mrs. Woodhull could have no excuse for ignorance about "whom it is and what it is that they support," the *Register* printed the following quotations from *Woodhull and Claflin's Weekly:*

> The time is approaching when public sentiment will accord to women the complete protectorship of their own persons, with the right to choose the fathers of their children, and hold their relations with whom their hearts may be inclined.—August 27, 1870.

> When boundless love prevails, to conceive and bring forth a child will not be a censurable act. . . . The merit or demerit of maternity will not then be influenced in any degree by considerations of the permanent or temporary relations of the parents. . . . When woman attains this position she will consider superior offspring a necessity and be apt to procreate only with superior men. Her intercourse with others will be limited

13. Tilton was fired as editor of the *Independent* in December 1870 after publishing an article commenting on the agonies of couples who are unhappily married and suggesting that divorce was the only way out. Shortly after this he was made editor of the *Golden Age,* a paper which began publication in March 1871.

and the proper means taken to make it unprolific.—October 15, 1870.

One of the first needs of society is to be able to do openly what is already done secretly. . . . With the full assurance and approval of their own consciences everybody should become their own law-givers.—October 15, 1871.[14]

"If the good women who are talking Woodhull in their politics would have more of the most noted of their candidate's utterances with which to electioneer," said the *Des Moines Register,* it would "be glad to furnish any quantity on demand."

In early September Tilton published a laudatory and highly fictitious biography of Mrs. Woodhull *(Golden Age Pamphlet,* 36 pages, 10 cents) which circulated widely throughout the country. "Great as has been Mrs. Woodhull's success in other respects, the Tilton biography is her master triumph," commented the *Davenport Gazette.* "Here is the virtuous and orthodox Tilton—orator, lecturer, and man of genius generally—eulogizing the mountebank adventuress, chronicling her miraculous raising of the dead and gravely proving, as something to her credit, that she is possessed by, and the chosen 'medium' of the spirit of the great Demosthenes!" In commenting on Tilton's biography of Mrs. Woodhull, the *Des Moines Register* quoted Horace Greeley, editor of the *New York Tribune,* who acidly observed "that if apples are wormy this year and duck's eggs addle it may all be ascribed to the unhallowed influence of this newly-born book." Tilton knows Mrs. Woodhull "not wisely but too well," Greeley asserted.

By midsummer most Iowans were convinced that woman-suffrage advocates were nothing more than a crowd of free lovers, despite their earnest protestations to the contrary. On February 4, 1871, the Henry County Woman Suffrage Society, on the motion of Joseph Dugdale, adopted the following resolution: "In presenting the claims for women we recognize the doctrine and sentiment in regard to marriage and all other subjects as set forth in the teachings of Jesus Christ." On July 6, 1871, the Polk County Society adopted a resolution stating, "As Christian women . . . we do not believe that liberty means license, and that we have no sympathy with any sentiments taught by any of the champions of woman suffrage which have a tendency to loosen the bonds of Christian people which we believe to actuate the vast majority of the women of America."

14. These are typical of quotations from *Woodhull and Claflin's Weekly* which appeared in Iowa papers all during the summer and fall of 1871; for example, the *Mount Pleasant Journal,* May 31; the *Des Moines Register,* August 10 and August 20; and the *DeWitt Observer,* August 18.

"It is not all pleasant to be ridiculed or have the cold shoulder turned to us because we advocate unpopular justice" wrote Rowena Guthrie Large of Dubuque to *The Revolution* in mid-August. "Still harder is it to have motives of every degree of baseness imputed to us, as is done by the more intolerant and malignant of our opponents," she said.

Under these circumstances it is not surprising that many erstwhile woman-suffrage advocates fled before the free-love storm. "Too many of our friends lack *moral courage,*" John L. Loomis of Independence wrote to Amelia Bloomer on October 14, "the first sneering cry of 'Free Love' puts them to flight—they almost believe the charges true themselves." Loomis thought that "the unfortunate course of Mrs. Stanton and Theodore Tilton and the seemingly *disreputable* position of others in New York," had done more than would be admitted to cloud the prospect of success for woman suffrage in Iowa during the coming year. In his letter written in reply to an invitation to attend a convention of the Iowa Woman Suffrage Association in Des Moines on October 19, Loomis stated that although he had neither the time nor the means to attend the meeting he was still heartily in favor of woman suffrage—his belief in the justice and rectitude of the cause growing stronger with every assault from unscrupulous foes.

TEMPEST IN A TEAPOT

THE OCTOBER CONVENTION of the Iowa Woman Suffrage Association in Des Moines, the first since the Mount Pleasant meeting in June 1870, had been announced in a call issued in late September by Henry O'Connor, president of the association, and Mary Darwin, chairman of the executive committee. However, O'Connor, politically embarrassed by his connection with the suffrage movement, did nothing more than let his name be used as president of the Iowa association until his successor was elected at the October meeting. Meanwhile Annie Savery stepped into the breach and served as spokesman for the woman's cause. Accompanying the call for the convention was a message to the women of Iowa signed by Mrs. Savery, which she had prepared at the request of the executive committee but for which she assumed personal responsibility.

"The noble men of Iowa who have stood by us complain of our faltering and inactivity while our enemies vanquished in argument have descended to personal scandal for the purpose of poisoning the public judgment against us and are seeking to make the suffrage party responsible for the opinions of fanatical adventurers who always attach themselves to a great reform," wrote Mrs. Savery. She went on to declare that the woman-suffrage party of Iowa was neither responsible for the individual opinions of those who in other states were exciting the public mind upon the so-called doctrine of free love nor was it connected in any way with any other organizations, state or national, leaders or followers, who were seeking to incorporate into the platform of the woman-suffrage party the principle of what was interpreted by the public as free love.

"The woman suffrage party of Iowa is made up of the mothers, wives, and daughters who believe that the marriage bond is to the social what the Constitution is to the political Union," Mrs. Savery asserted. "The individual examples of the women of this State who are identified with the suffrage cause should be sufficient guarantee of their integrity of purpose and the estimate they place upon a well-defined moral standard of social life. In this respect," Mrs. Savery said, "they challenge comparison with other political organizations."

Mrs. Savery urged every county to send representatives to the coming convention. "Let the friends of Woman Suffrage organize and rally for one combined effort and victory will be ours," she asserted.

By stating their position on free love ahead of time, the officers of the state association hoped to avoid time-consuming wrangling over this question at the convention; and by using only Iowa speakers, they hoped to avoid the injection of out-of-state factional disputes such as those which marred the Mount Pleasant meeting. The proceedings of the convention as reported in the *Des Moines Register* of October 20 indicate that the meeting did proceed peaceably—with the exception of a difference of opinion over the one question which the officers hoped to avoid—that of free love and Mrs. Woodhull's association with the woman-suffrage movement.

Presiding at the meeting in the place of Henry O'Connor, the president who (according to the *Des Moines Register*) was "necessarily absent," was Amelia Bloomer, elegantly dressed in grosgrain silk with sweeping drapery. Other out-of-town delegates included Belle Mansfield and William R. Cole of Mount Pleasant, Nettie Sanford of Marshalltown, Will R. Shoemaker of Council Bluffs,[15] and Mary Darwin of Burlington. There were also four delegates from Oskaloosa, two from Mitchellville, and one from Springvale (Humboldt). Joseph

---

15. Will Shoemaker, a lawyer, was corresponding secretary of the Council Bluffs Woman Suffrage Society. Letters from him published in the *Religio-Philosophical Journal* reveal that he was a dedicated spiritualist.

Dugdale, prime mover in organizing the Mount Pleasant meeting in June 1870, did not attend the Des Moines convention.

At the morning session Mrs. Bloomer reported on the status of woman's rights in Iowa, proudly noting that four women had recently been elected county superintendents of schools. A series of resolutions was adopted, offering help to the women of Chicago made destitute by the recent great fire in that city. Louis Rutkay of Des Moines delivered a long address and Nettie Sanford of Marshalltown made "a few remarks concerning the steps which should be taken before and during the coming Legislative session."

First order of business at the afternoon session was the consideration of seven resolutions presented by the resolutions committee, all but one of which were unanimously adopted without debate. These included a statement declaring that women as citizens were entitled to vote by virtue of the Fourteenth Amendment; a request to the Iowa legislature for submission of a woman-suffrage amendment to the state constitution; and a message of thanks to editorial friends in Iowa who had "so nobly advocated the great principle of equal rights." The seventh (and controversial) resolution, after lengthy debate, was finally adopted in the following form: "Resolved, that the object for which the Iowa Woman's Suffrage Society is organized is to secure the ballot for woman, and that it expressly disavows any responsibility for the opinions or utterances of any party upon questions foreign to this, believing as we do that the ballot is a power to be used only in the interest of virtue and morality." This resolution, according to the *Register,* was "enthusiastically discussed" by Mrs. Savery, Mrs. Bloomer, and others—"the unanimous desire of those present evidently being to declare themselves in no sympathy whatever with those who attach themselves to ideas and practices perversive of good order and the morals of society, without passing a wholesale denunciation upon all other organizations."

The next order of business was the election of officers. Mrs. Bloomer was chosen president for the coming year; twelve vice-presidents were named, including Henry O'Connor, Joseph Dugdale, John Irish, Lizzie B. Read of Algona, Lizzie Boynton Harbert of Des Moines, and Dr. Maria W. Porter of Davenport.[16] In addition an

16. Mrs. Porter came to Iowa after graduating from the Woman's Medical College in Philadelphia in 1859. She is the first trained woman physician known to have practiced in the state, but because of prejudice against her sex her professional career was short. She became president of the Iowa Woman Suffrage Association in 1876.

executive committee of nine members was elected, one of whom was Nettie Sanford. However, at the evening session this committee was scaled down to five members, Mrs. Sanford being among those eliminated. The constitution of the association as adopted at Mount Pleasant was passed around for the delegates to sign, and a finance committee headed by Mrs. Callanan of Des Moines proposed that a permanent fund be raised for the work of the association. William R. Cole and Annie Savery each offered to contribute $100 toward a goal of $1,000. They hoped that eight others would do the same. However, no other donors rose to meet this challenge. A collection taken up in the audience amounted to $31.75. When all this business was completed, no time was left for scheduled speeches and they were added to the already crowded evening agenda.

By the time the evening session convened at a little after seven, the courtroom was packed with one of the largest audiences ever to gather there, the *Register* reported. The program for the evening included addresses by William R. Cole of Mount Pleasant, Mary Darwin of Burlington, and C. E. Fuller and Annie Savery of Des Moines. The audience was particularly anxious to hear Annie Savery, who had let it be known that she planned to talk about Victoria Woodhull.

However, before the speaking could begin, Nettie Sanford—who had tried unsuccessfully to get a resolution adopted at the afternoon session bitterly denouncing the "Woodhull-Claflin clique"—got the floor and proposed the following resolution: "That this Association denounce the doctrine of free-love, believing that marriage is sacred and binding on all good men and women of Iowa and that the Bible is the Palladium of our liberties." According to the *Register*, "Mrs. Savery thought it was letting down the dignity of the Association to denounce a thing which nobody suspects its members of believing in. The president—Mrs. Bloomer—said she had a few words to say on this question. She felt it was an insult to the convention to bring up this question, for the Association was not organized to debate such a question." To cut off a time-consuming debate over divorce and free love and get on with the speaking, Mrs. Bloomer suggested that the resolution be tabled. A motion to do so was adopted, and the convention then proceeded to hear the four scheduled speakers.

Mrs. Savery, the sensation of the evening, told her audience that although Victoria Woodhull had specifically stated that though she had never attempted to saddle the suffrage party with her own peculiar views,[17] "yet her enemies throughout the length and breadth of

17. Mrs. Savery read to the audience a long letter written to her by Victoria Woodhull in answer to a request from Mrs. Savery to state her position on this point.

the land had descended to this malicious trick to poison the public judgment against the woman suffrage cause."

But the timid need not quake, Mrs. Savery said, the cry of free love was nothing new: "From the day that Mrs. Branch in the 1858 Rutland convention proclaimed what has since been interpreted by the public as free-love, the Woman Suffrage party has been charged with endorsing the individual opinions of every fanatical adventurer, that has chosen to follow in the wake of this great reform. . . . The press of the country catch up the words of these self-appointed leaders, and ask us to be responsible for their pernicious teachings. The husband reads to his wife the false doctrines of such fanatics as Stephen Pearl Andrews and with great complacency looks over his specs and says, 'There! Don't you see what the woman's rights party want to do with the ballot?' And the poor woman who has been in the habit of taking all her mental as well as physical food from this Solomon, just as birds in a nest open their bills and take in the worm, so she swallows this insult to her womanhood and tells her next neighbor woman that if that's the way women are going to act, become free lovers and all that sort of thing, she hopes they'll never get the ballot. . . ." In this way the public judgment has been poisoned, said Mrs. Savery, and—instead of meeting this unjust charge in the spirit it deserved—women have permitted these idle vaporings to go unrebuked and have allowed the great question at issue to be smothered and pushed to the wall. "Our 'on to Richmond' has been checked. Not from any lack of faith in the great principle, or any loss of numbers, but for lack of moral courage to face these Quaker guns. . . ."

"Victoria Woodhull has given to the cause of woman suffrage the devotion of a master mind," Mrs. Savery declared. Of her private life she was neither her accuser nor defender, nor did she care to learn what it was from those who regarded the acts of women as any more criminal than those of men.

Mrs. Savery reminded her audience that Mrs. Woodhull had "at one time contributed ten thousand dollars to the National Suffrage Society, and many thousands besides." If it were true that she had come by her money dishonestly, she certainly could never have used it for a better purpose. Neither the Republican nor the Democratic party, Mrs. Savory pointed out, had been too immaculate to accept "some of the fruits of the grand larcenies" handed over to them by the infamous New York City politicians, Boss Tweed and Collector Murphy. Nor did she believe that any of the Christian churches which had received money from both these men had sought "to restore to the rightful owners any of these criminal gains."

Mrs. Savery said she mentioned these facts only to show how un-just and uncharitable are the accusations of the opponents of woman suffrage, many of whose private lives were far from unblemished. She stated that the women of Iowa regarded the discussions of many questions which had been raised in other states "as unwise, impolitic, and premature" and reaffirmed the independence of the Iowa Woman Suffrage Association, declaring it had "no sympathy with or responsi-bility for the opinions of any friends in other states, beyond the one question of granting woman the ballot."

"We have never seen a convention conducted with more decorum, or a greater degree of intelligent accord in the routine proceedings," the *Register* commented the day after the meeting. "A majority of the members were women. They took up the convention work with-out being awkward, and conducted discussions in a manner which many conventions of men might well pattern from. Of course, "there were hotspurs and rash persons among them but they were few and in a majority men. . . . The convention strengthened the workers in whose names it met," said the *Register*, "not only among themselves but with the public." This latter point proved to be the grossest mis-statement of the year.

The opening gun in a barrage of criticism which deliberately distorted the aims of the convention was fired by "R. W. T." of Four-Mile Township in a letter written two days after the meeting and published in the *Register* on October 26. R. W. T. (who claimed to be a woman although her identity was never established) said that although she was sure there were many pure and high-minded women at the meeting, she was also convinced that they were only subserving the purpose of the radicals (i.e., Mrs. Savery and Mrs. Bloomer) whose will was law. These radicals, she said, wanted to ignore "all Stantonian and other side issues such as 'free-love,' 'marriage on trial,' 'one lion in a family,' 'divorce made easy,' 'the Bible all bosh,' etc., etc., feeling sure that the ballot in the hands of woman would set all these things right. The radicals fought the adoption of a strong resolution de-nouncing Mrs. Woodhull and permitted a watered-down version to be adopted 'for the sake of policy.' " This, said R. W. T. was only "finely gilded bait for the voters of Iowa—a seeming fly to hide the sharpness of the hook."

That R. W. T. was not above using a little bait herself is re-vealed by the following portion of her letter: "While I sat there in the court-room, in conversation with one of the members of the Con-vention, I held in my hand 'Tilton's Title Deed to Women's Suffrage.' She, being one of the more conservative members, said, 'Oh! Tilton;

we have nothing to do with him,' and when I asked, 'What about Mrs. Stanton and her lecture here in Des Moines?' she said, 'We in Iowa want nothing to do with Mrs. Stanton or Miss Anthony, or any of those fanatics. We are a separate organization.' " Yet, said R. W. T., while this woman was making these denials, Mrs. Bloomer "congratulated the Assembly on the noble array of persons who were working for the great cause of suffrage, naming Beecher and Tilton, and those noble and self-sacrificing persons, Mrs. Stanton and Miss Anthony!"

To clinch her argument that the Iowa Woman Suffrage Association was nothing but a tool of the free-love ring, R. W. T. pointed out that the convention had unanimously adopted a resolution declaring women enfranchised by virtue of the Fourteenth Amendment. This, she said, smacks of having something to do with Mrs. Victoria C. Woodhull, for who but she was the author of the idea? Only the previous winter, when Annie Savery—the acknowledged leader of this movement in Iowa—had been requested to give her opinion concerning the enfranchisement of women under the Fourteenth Amendment, she had said she was not willing to go in at the back door. What a letting down of dignity for Mrs. Savery to accept this amendment after all, R. W. T declared.

Four days later Annie Savery replied to R. W. T. in a long letter published in the *Register*. "As to my views upon the Fourteenth and Fifteenth Amendments," Mrs. Savery said, "I entertain no opinions whatever upon this or any question of public importance that I am not willing to state over my own signature." She regretted that R. W. T. showed such a want of confidence in *her* opinions as to screen herself from identification. Mrs. Savery assured her anonymous critic that she still believed that "woman should compel a recognition of her rights upon the immutable principle of justice" and that she was willing to bide her time. However, "others believe that woman is justified in seizing her rights, as man has done, either by diplomacy, strategy, or scaling battlements at the point of the bayonet." Since she found herself greatly in the minority at the meeting and, "as Woman Suffragists claim to be democrats in the true sense of the word," Mrs. Savery had, for the sake of unanimity, voted for the resolution claiming enfranchisement under the Fourteenth Amendment. "I would escape bondage though the worst criminal on earth should point the way," Mrs. Savery said, "but I would *prefer* to have my liberty decreed by a tribunal of justice."

"Our anonymous critic occupies but little space on the important question of woman's voting," Mrs. Savery continued, "but takes a whole column to unburden her brain of the free-love pressure. It is free-love in her first, and free-love in her last paragraph, with Wood-hull and Tilton sandwiched between. . . . This is all that the opposition have left to talk about," Mrs. Savery asserted, "and 'R. W. T.' has made it quite evident that this was the intention which took her to the convention."

In a postscript to her letter Mrs. Savery asked the many papers in Iowa that had commented on R. W. T's letter and made such free use of her name to please do her the justice of copying her answer.

R. W. T. did not attend the evening session of the convention and seems to have been unaware at the time she wrote her letter of Mrs. Sanford's resolution declaring against free love and for the Bible as the palladium of woman's liberties. However, it was the action of the convention in tabling this so-called "palladium resolution" which proved to be the most convenient tool for the enemies of woman suffrage to use in discrediting the movement. "The action of the convention in voting down the resolution means that the Woman Suffragists desire the ballot that they may by legal enactment carry out the views of the marriage relation advocated by Tilton, Woodhull and Co., declared the *Council Bluffs Nonpareil* in response to several letters from Mrs. Bloomer explaining the action of the convention. "The members of the Convention may quarrel with this statement—may waste columns upon columns of words in pronouncing it a flagitious misrepresentation—but they can no more convince the people that it is devoid of solid foundation, than they can prove that the moon is made of green cheese." The *Cedar Rapids Times* thought the proceedings looked very much like "an attempt to compromise between Claflin-Tilton free-loveism and the good opinion of the Iowa public." Since "the female suffragists of Des Moines evinced great anxiety to have the public believe there were no free-lovers among them, why was the resolution tabled?" this paper asked.

An amusing secondary battle between the *Des Moines Register* and the *Marshalltown Times*[18] arose in the wake of the convention. According to the *Times* Mrs. Sanford claimed that the *Register*'s report of the convention was made "entirely in the interest of the free-love ring, in order to make it appear that the great body of woman-women sympathized with the 'lovers' in their endeavor to make the marriage knot a tie upon a rope of sand." Goodson, city editor of the *Register*, was said to be "completely under the thumb of the ring and that a dish of oysters, a smile from painted lips, or an ogle of the eye from a bedizened beauty of three score years would secure his service."

18. Mrs. Sanford, widowed in 1873, married E. H. Chapin, editor of the *Marshall-town Times*, in 1886. Chapin was popularly known as "old grizzly."

The *Register* retorted that it had reported the proceedings literally as it "had no interest in the quarrel between the two factions, if factions there were, unless it could be said that Mrs. Sanford was to be called a faction and all the rest of the members of the convention another." Only one person asked to have the report garbled, said the *Register,* and that was Mrs. Sanford herself.

As the free-love storm raged, local woman-suffrage societies rushed to disassociate themselves from the action of the state convention. On November 2 the Polk County society adopted the following widely circulated resolutions:

> Whereas, we hear it openly charged by the opponents of this cause, through the press, the pulpit, upon the highways of travel, and in private circles that we endorse the doctrines of "free-love" as advocated by *Woodhull and Claflin's Weekly* and
>
> Whereas, we feel that longer silence on the subject would be detrimental to the interests we have at heart . . . it is as much a duty to deny that of which we are falsely accused as a privilege to demand a right of which we are unjustly deprived,
>
> Resolved: That we emphatically declare our condemnation of the so-called "free-love" doctrine as taught by *Woodhull and Claflin's Weekly* that we consider it in the highest degree, degrading alike to man and woman.
>
> Resolved: That we believe the ballot in the hands of woman will not affect the sanctity of the marriage relation and that we do not believe in divorce except for good scriptural reasons.[19]

A few days later the Marshall County society, spurred on by its irate founder, Austin P. Lowry, not only endorsed the sentiments of the Polk County society but also demanded the immediate resignation of all the officers of the state association who "favored free-love and free lust." This society called for a new state convention to meet before January 3 to reconsider the actions of the October meeting. Lowry said it was his opinion that women were entitled to the franchise by virtue of the Fourteenth and Fifteenth Amendments "but

19. A copy of these resolutions published as a tract is preserved in the woman-suffrage collection at the Iowa State Historical Building. On the margin is the following notation written about 1935 by Mary Ankeny Hunter, Iowa woman-suffrage historian: "Miss Susan B. Anthony came to Iowa for the first time in 1871. Victoria Woodhull accompanied her on at least one speaking tour in Iowa according to the oldest anti-suffrage stories. This may be true." Miss Anthony, in fact, never toured with Mrs. Woodhull. This is a good example of the persistence of the Woodhull legend.

under existing facts, 'Free-love,' etc., he would consider the courts justified in withholding from them the use of that right. No legislature or body of sensible men, although in a free land, would use their influence, or cast their vote, to enfranchise a free-love community."

"I brand all, whether open foes or pretended friends as *base liars* and *slanderers* who dare charge that the Iowa Woman Suffrage Association or its leaders are 'in favor of free-love and free lust!'" Mrs. Bloomer wrote to the *Marshalltown Times* in angry response to the action of the Marshall County society. "From the enemies of the cause we may expect such things," Mrs. Bloomer said, "but in this case it comes not so much from enemies as from those who claim to be with us." In view of this fact, she was led to exclaim, "Good Lord deliver us from our friends."

For weeks after the convention Annie Savery was deluged with letters from friends in Iowa and other states inquiring about the action of the state convention in tabling Mrs. Sanford's resolution. In reply to both friends and foes Mrs. Savery wrote a long letter of explanation published in the *Des Moines Register* on November 19 under the heading "A Final Word on the 'Palladium Resolution.'" Mrs. Savery said she had decided to state the facts in an open letter so that all might fully understand what a trifling incident had been seized upon by the opposition press to create this "Tempest in a Teapot."

"If an unequivocal endorsement of the marriage bond, as expressed in the call; a distinct disavowal of responsibility for the opinions of any party upon questions foreign to the enfranchisement of woman; and a plain declaration that 'the ballot is a power which should be used only in the interests of virtue and morality'—if these sentences can possibly be construed into a desire on our part for *vice* and *immorality,* then, either the English language has lost its power to convey ideas, or it is owing to the stupidity of those who interpret it," Mrs. Savery said.

Mrs. Savery called Mrs. Sanford's palladium resolution the apple of discord which had "thrown the *immaculate chivalry* of the State into such spasms of virtuous indignation, and frightened some of the county societies into suing for pardon by passing long preambles and resolutions declaring that they were not free-lovers."

"In view of the resolutions already passed by the convention," Mrs. Savery said, "had this 'palladium resolution' been introduced by some enemy intent upon burlesquing the entire proceedings, the newspaper press would have regarded it as a good thing, and would have no doubt drawn from some portions of the Bible such a 'palladium of our liberties' as would have put even the 'Woodhull-Claflin clique' to shame."[20]

"But when we consider that intelligent men—and women too— who *ought to know better* allowed themselves to be caught by this verbiage, and frightened by the pointless and malicious ridicule of the enemy into doing just what the opposition would have them do, then we are compelled to treat it—not as it deserves—but in all seriousness."

"Can any of our friends be made to believe that if we had passed the 'Palladium Resolution' that we should have received any praise or support from those who now denounce us?" Mrs. Savery asked. "Yet, one would think to hear them discourse upon the sanctity of the marriage tie that they were ready to embrace our cause just as soon as they could be assured that *their spotless purity* would not be tarnished."

"As sure as political governments exist, just so sure will woman's political equality be recognized," Mrs. Savery declared. "If we are to get the ballot by act of Congress," she said, "the time might be near at hand. But if we must wait for state legislation, the time will depend entirely upon the harmony of our friends, and if, from this cause, we must wait, then we may inscribe upon our banner the words of Cassius: 'The fault, dear Brutus, is not in our stars but in *ourselves* that we are underlings.' "

In the contest for the ballot Mrs. Savery said she would cooperate with all who were loyal to the principle of political equality, irrespective of any opinion they might have upon any other question. But whenever a convention of which she was a member was assembled for the purpose of discussing woman's right to the ballot would so far "let down its dignity" and self respect as to descend to personal abuse or interpose the Bible as a condition precedent to membership, she would always be found opposing it.

"We have little to fear from the common enemy, and the woman suffrage cause because of its inherent justice can well afford the company of Victoria Woodhull," Mrs. Savery said in conclusion. "But from carping friends who in the name of Christianity offer us a menace with their friendship, we shall hope to be delivered. Such friends of woman's cause have yet to learn the first rudiments of Christian charity before they can comprehend the fact that domestic fidelity, like all other womanly virtues is a life and not a manifesto."

20. Mrs. Savery referred her readers to Gen., Chapter 4; Deut., Chapters 22, 23, 24; 1 Kings, Chapter 11.

Get thee behind me (Mrs.) Satan!
Wife (with heavy burden): I'd rather travel the hardest paths
of matrimony than follow your footsteps.

Full-page cartoon in Harper's Weekly, *February 17, 1872, lambasting Victoria Woodhull at the time of the debate on woman suffrage in the Iowa General Assembly.*

9

1872

❧

Although Republican leaders knew that the woman-suffrage amendment had little if any chance of success in the Fourteenth General Assembly, they assured the women that the 1872 legislature would be willing to give the measure its required second approval if they still wished it to do so. However, they advised the suffragists that in view of the current free-love storm it would be advisable to postpone putting the suffrage amendment to a vote of the people.

HALT IN PROGRESS
OF WOMAN SUFFRAGE

The *Des Moines Register* said there was nothing to be gained by pushing the woman-suffrage proposition to certain slaughter. "It is clear to all observing minds," the *Register* said, "that the progress of women toward the ballot in Iowa is stopping in halt, if indeed the march is not backwards." The *Register* recognized how unjust it was to "hundreds of thousands of honest men and pure women earnestly in favor of the reform to say that they were following at the leadstring of the notorious female, Mrs. Woodhull and her gushing lover and eulogist, Theodore Tilton, yet five out of six of the people think so, and cannot be led to think anything else." The *Register* thought it best to rescue the suffrage cause from the slough into which the Woodhull-Tilton clan had plunged it before venturing to place it on final trial before the voters of Iowa. However, the final decision was up to the women, this paper said. "If the managers of the movement in Iowa think now is the hour, it is for them to choose."

When John Irish's *Iowa City State Press* accused the *Des Moines Register* of going back on woman suffrage, the *Register* retorted that so far as it could see the *Press* had committed itself in only a few straightforward articles advocating woman suffrage while "we are now, as we have always been, since we voted to enfranchise the Negroes—(which was long before the editor of the *Press* had said he thought women ought to vote . . .)—we have always said that to women, on many grounds belongs the right to vote."[1]

The *Register* then proceeded to give the reasons it believed women should *not* have the ballot; first, "because women, while they could use the ballot in bringing war on, could not and would not use the sword after war had come," and second, because "very few women, married and raising families, could meet the duties of office and the duties of maternity."

The *Register*'s attack on woman suffrage brought an immediate response from Annie Savery who, in a long letter published in the *Register* on January 25, pointed out that everyone—even the *Register* —admitted that women have the abstract right to vote. "Now then if woman has the right to vote, why should she be compelled to discharge all the duties for which men are fitted . . . any more than a man is compelled to discharge all the duties for which women are fitted because he is a voter?" Mrs. Savery asked. If laws compelled all who vote to perform what is voted for, voting would soon be at a discount "and all who now claim that special privilege would avoid the polls, as they did the draft office during the war!"

Women need not necessarily be soldiers, Mrs. Savery said. In time of war they could serve their country in a variety of ways—as nurses and relief workers as well as carrying on at the home front— but if men would not exempt women voters from army duty, there doubtless could be found one woman in a thousand (the ratio of men needed to defend their country) who would not only be *qualified* but

---

1. F. M. Mills, a sincere advocate of woman suffrage, sold the *Register* in late 1870 to J. S. Clarkson who owned the paper until 1902. Clarkson never gave woman suffrage more than tongue-in-cheek support.

willing to carry the musket and even, if need be, go as a substitute for a man.

To the *Register*'s reply that it could see no reason why a different rule should apply to woman as a voter than to man, Annie Savery, in a second letter published on January 30, quoted the following couplet which an exasperated mother had once flung at Horace Greeley, editor of the *New York Tribune:*

> What right has woman, safe from wars alarms,
> To cast a ballot when she don't bear arms?
>
> For shame!, shouts Mrs. Huff in lofty dudgeon,
> For shame! Go to! Get out, you old curmudgeon!
>
> What right have you, with all your talk bewilderin,
> To cast a ballot when you don't bear children.

NO COMPROMISE WITH ERROR

EARLY IN THE SESSION it became evident that the leaders of the Polk County Woman Suffrage Society who considered Annie Savery a free lover because of her defense of Victoria Woodhull were making strenuous efforts to silence her and drive her from the suffrage ranks. This movement was led from behind the scenes by Martha Callanan, treasurer of the society. Maria Gray Pitman, president, was the chief spokesman. During a meeting at the courthouse on February 1 Mrs. Pitman, in a speech which was subsequently published in full in both the *Des Moines Register* and the *Des Moines Review,* declared that the once pure suffrage movement had become infiltrated with persons who were perhaps correct in theory but wonderfully deficient in matters of greater importance and who went around proclaiming to the world "Victory to Victoria." "We must insist that the only door we intend to open is purely woman suffrage and that we want no side-shows such as 'political social' or 'sciento-religious parties' following in its wake," said Mrs. Pitman. "When those who hold themselves aloof from us realize that among our real leaders there is *not* a spirit of compromising with error in any form, then we may expect to see thousands rush to our ranks." Mrs. Pitman expressed the earnest hope that "the wise and skillful ones aboard the suffrage craft would be permitted to guide the helm and bring their charge safely into port."

A letter published in the February 17 issue of the *Des Moines Review* under the initials of Martha Callanan took issue with Mrs. Savery's contention that women would be willing to serve as soldiers.

In this letter, which is one of her rare public statements, Mrs. Callanan said that she did not believe that even one woman in a thousand should shoulder a musket. "Woman's province is essentially at her own hearthstone," Mrs. Callanan said. "Her services are needed at home in time of war where she can and should perform many kinds of labor usually and properly done by man, that his stronger arms and steadier nerves may be spared to march to the front."

Unperturbed by her opponents within the suffrage ranks, Mrs. Savery continued to work wholeheartedly to persuade the legislators to approve the woman-suffrage amendment. Not only did she confer with individual legislators but on February 16 she gave an elegant reception in her home for all the members and their families. "To-morrow night the apple of discord is to be thrown into the Hesperidean garden of the Assembly by the first socio-politico party of the season," wrote the correspondent for the *Davenport Democrat* on February 15. "It is a soirée given by Mrs. Annie Savery, whose charms of person are only equalled by her intellectual acquirements, and who is one of the most fascinating firebrands ever yet added to the strong-minded woman's party of this or any other state. She entertains in grand style, and the rush for number nine kids [white kid gloves] by the members of both houses is something awful." This writer went on to say that the burden of the song, "Beware, beware, young man she's fooling thee" would doubtless attach to but one or two among the members of this session, as most were married men; and the divine influence of women had become blunted by constant contact. It is interesting to note that not a single Des Moines paper mentioned the Savery party.

By February 22 the hostility of the Polk County society toward Mrs. Savery had reached such proportions that the Des Moines correspondent of the *Dubuque Times* was led to comment that "some of the suffrage women were not only disgusting the best friends of the movement but also making foolish virgins of themselves." This writer, obviously an admirer of Annie Savery's, observed that the quarrel within the suffrage ranks amounted in essence "to a contest twixt heads with brains of power and heads otherwise. Because some women are endowed with faculties superior to others they can, by pen and words 'put a head on' any of the attacking party and win station thereby." He warned the women that until they could learn that in cohesion of forces lies the way to success, their bluster would amount to nothing. He could not help but think that a "few melancholy, sudden and positive funerals would be very advantageous."

This war within the suffrage ranks intensified as the session progressed. Because Annie Savery refused to be silent and the Polk County faction had no one to equal her speaking or writing ability, it was forced to look for spokesmen among the advocates in other states. This search, led by Martha Callanan, was not an easy task. Gone were the heroes and heroines of yesteryear. Theodore Tilton, who had spoken so eloquently for woman suffrage, was now an outcast because of his association with Victoria Woodhull. Anna Dickinson, the queen of the lyceum, was now past her zenith on the lecture platform; in 1872 she booked no lectures in Iowa—the first season she had missed since her initial appearance in 1866.

Elizabeth Cady Stanton and Susan B. Anthony, not welcome in Iowa because of their association with Victoria Woodhull, had been asked by the suffragists to stay out of the state while the legislature was in session. Miss Anthony obeyed orders; but Elizabeth Cady Stanton, who prided herself on never bowing to expediency, booked at least one Iowa lecture in 1872—at West Liberty on March 11. However, shortly before this date Mrs. Stanton was called to her home at Tenafly, New Jersey, because of the illness of her daughter Harriet. Kate Stanton, a cousin, substituted for Mrs. Stanton at West Liberty.

In addition to nursing her daughter while at Tenafly, Mrs. Stanton also came to the defense of Victoria Woodhull, who was currently under renewed attack because of a speech titled "The Impending Revolution," in which she declared herself a thoroughgoing communist and boldly attacked both capitalism and individual capitalists, including her erstwhile friend, Commodore Vanderbilt.[2] Meanwhile, suffragists in Iowa trembled for fear Mrs. Woodhull, who had announced a nationwide tour, might decide to speak in Des Moines.

Lucy Stone, as leader of the conservative, anti-Woodhull American Woman Suffrage Association, would have been welcome in Iowa; but she was tied down in Boston, where she not only had the responsibility for the *Woman's Journal*, which Mary Livermore had abandoned after one year as editor, but also the task of rebuilding her home which had recently been destroyed by fire.

Mary Livermore, now a professional lyceum lecturer, received an urgent invitation from Martha Callanan to come to Des Moines,

2. Although Mrs. Stanton continued to give Mrs. Woodhull her wholehearted support, Miss Anthony by 1872 was thoroughly disillusioned with her. "Mrs. Woodhull has the advantage of us because she has the newspaper, and she persistently means to run our craft into her port and none other," Miss Anthony wrote Mrs. Stanton on March 13. "If she were influenced by *women* spirits, either in the body or out of it, in the direction she steers, I might consent to be a mere sail-hoister for her; but as it is she is wholly owned and dominated by men spirits and I spurn the control of the whole lot of them. . . ."

which reached her while she was lecturing in Michigan. She immediately wired her old friend John Irish, asking, "Shall I come to Des Moines to lecture on Mrs. Callanan's invitation?" "No, nor on anybody's," Irish replied. "Keep all hands quiet and we'll carry the bill." Remembering that the Polk County society had failed to pay her guaranteed fee when she spoke under its auspices the previous year, Mrs. Livermore was only too glad to obey Irish's orders.

Mrs. Callanan was eventually able to enlist the help of Phoebe Couzins of St. Louis, the young woman who had lectured in Dubuque in 1869 and had recently been graduated with great pomp and

Phoebe Couzins, the first woman admitted to a law school in the United States, was brought as a lecturer to Des Moines by Mrs. Callanan in 1872.

ceremony from law school in St. Louis—the first woman in the United States to receive a law degree. Miss Couzins, a demure, petite, and pretty young woman, arrived in Des Moines on February 29 and spent a week as a guest in Mrs. Callanan's home. During her stay in the city she delivered two lectures at the courthouse, one on "The Legal Disabilities of Woman" and one on "The Bible Argument Against Woman Suffrage." Although a number of legislators attended her lectures, Miss Couzins was neither a sensational nor a brilliant speaker and failed to arouse much interest in the community. In her honor Mr. and Mrs. Callanan held an evening reception to which members of the legislature were invited. "A choice selection of friends," as the *Des Moines Review* expressed it, was also included. The paper was doubtless inferring that Mrs. Savery was not among the chosen. But even Miss Couzins was not immune from free-love charges, and her sponsors in the city were forced to announce prior to her first lecture that she had "no sympathy with the pretenders of the Woodhull school as has been suggested by the opponents of the cause." In mid-March, the Polk County society obtained the services of Jane Swisshelm, a well-known journalist and woman's rights pioneer.

JANE SWISSHELM, fifty-seven years old, was born in the frontier village of Pittsburgh, Pennsylvania, in 1815. A small, rather fragile woman, only five feet tall and weighing less than 100 pounds, she had delicate features accented by a sharp, pointed nose. Her pungent journalism combined with her prickly personality often led newspaper commentators to quip that her pen was as sharp as her beak.

Mrs. Swisshelm was best known for her writing in the Pittsburgh *Saturday Visiter* [sic], a lively reform journal which she launched in 1848, the year of the Seneca Falls convention. During her five years as editor she was widely quoted in papers from coast to coast, her name becoming a household word even to frontier families in Iowa. Although she advocated woman's rights in the *Saturday Visiter*, her association with other woman's rights advocates had been both fitful and stormy over the years. She attended her first woman's rights convention at Akron, Ohio, in 1851—a meeting presided over by Frances Dana Gage, who three years later lectured in Iowa. Mrs. Swisshelm announced after the Akron meeting that she found it so poorly managed that she would have nothing more to do with woman's rights conventions. For the next twenty years she did not attend another woman's rights meeting. The Woodhull storm, however, brought Mrs. Swisshelm back into action. In February 1871, while staying with her daughter in Chicago, she appeared at the annual meeting of the Illinois Woman Suffrage Association. There she delivered a lengthy antifree-love lecture, and a month later when the Illinois association split over the free-love issue Mrs. Swisshelm emerged as president of the anti-Woodhull, antidivorce, religiously orthodox Illinois Christian Woman Suffrage Association. Ironically, Mrs. Swisshelm herself was a divorcée.

Mrs. Swisshelm remained in Des Moines until after the legislature adjourned and delivered several lectures at the Polk County courthouse during the course of her stay. The reporter for the *Des Moines Review* found her to be "a fine looking old lady," who addressed her audience while seated in the judge's armchair. "She spoke with a certain air of freedom that bordered on nonchalance, and in a desultory way" he said of her first lecture. "In the main" he found "her points were well made, some of which abounded in sarcasm, while occasionally there was a sparkling of wit in her terse language." Mrs. Swisshelm was also granted the privilege of speaking in the hall of the House of Representatives on two different evenings, addressing audiences of legislators on woman suffrage and temperance. Here she delivered her lectures in a conversational tone while seated in the Speaker's chair.

Mrs. Swisshelm had not been in Des Moines long before people were commenting on her well-known propensity for scandalmongering. A letter dated March 16 and written by the Des Moines correspondent of the *Dubuque Times* noted that "Jane is a good, kindhearted gossiper, for orator you cannot call her, and tells a story quite cleverly. . . . She gives satisfaction to her audiences publicly," this writer said, "but in private conversation she lends herself easily and quite industriously to the general circulation of slanders of public men hatched by liars who look upon poor deluded Westerners who have confidence in General Grant and his administration as in a horribly lost condition. According to the venerable Jane, 'all sensible people in the East oppose Grant.'" This writer had also learned through Jane that "Mrs. Grant is a *reb*-el, and that she is one of the worst of that kind of people." He was sure it would be news to the warrior Ulysses to know that he had a rebel for a bedfellow. He was sorry Jane had "taken to peddling goods of so cheap and so flimsy a texture."

Iowa newspapers were also soon taunting Mrs. Swisshelm about her marital status. "Where or what is Mr. Jane G.?" asked the *Cedar Rapids Times* on March 21. "If the *Times* really wants to know, we presume Mrs. S. can tell us," retorted the *Des Moines Register*.

FIRST EXPERIENCE AS LOBBYISTS

SUFFRAGE WOMEN had been working seriously for many months, trying to prepare the ground for favorable action in the 1872 General Assembly despite the discouraging course of events. When the Republican state convention met in Des Moines in June 1871, a group of Des Moines women, armed with a petition asking for a woman-suffrage plank in the party platform, tried to secure a hearing before the delegates. However, when the women arrived at the convention hall early in the morning, they were told the crowd was so dense that it would be impossible for them to enter. When they returned at noon, they were informed that the convention had already adopted a platform and it was too late for them to present their petition. "The fact of the matter is that we were crowded out," declared Elizabeth Boynton Harbert in a letter to the *Woman's Journal*. She noted that the convention had now become "*his*-story" with never so much as a word in regard to *her*.

Despite the failure of the 1871 Republican state convention to endorse woman suffrage, Iowa women were still hopeful that the Republicans in the 1872 General Assembly would honor their pledge to submit the woman-suffrage amendment. "The present session of the Legislature, the advocates of woman suffrage think, is one fraught with deep import to their cause," commented the *Des Moines Leader* soon after the legislature convened in January. "For two years the women have been preparing for the onslaught on the law givers when they should assemble. Petitions have been in active circulation at the hands of long haired men and women. . . . The Legislature is now here and already we seem to hear the tramp of thousands as in crinoline and dimity they move forward in solid phalanx to demand their rights, the ballot or an office(er)," quipped this paper.

Although it was to be many years before Iowa women were ready to march in numbers for woman suffrage,[3] the dedicated pioneers of 1872 were eager to do all they could to advance their cause with the legislators. In mid-January Mrs. Bloomer came to Des Moines to attend a meeting of the executive committee of the Iowa Woman Suffrage Association—the first meeting of the leaders of the state association since the ill-fated October convention. The women at this time issued a statement reaffirming the morality of the woman-suffrage movement but refusing to denounce any suffragist because of social theories or religious affiliation. They also conferred with legislative leaders to ascertain the most advisable course of action. John Irish assured them that he could steer the woman-suffrage amendment through both the House and the Senate, but he urged the women to stay out of the way and let him handle the matter without their help. House majority leader John Kasson also pledged his cooperation. In response to an inquiry from Mrs. Bloomer about the possibility of her being permitted to address a joint session of the legislature, Kasson subsequently wrote that if the women should decide to press the suffrage question to a vote during the current session he would suggest that she ask for a hearing on February 16, at which time the House

3. One of the earliest woman-suffrage parades in the United States was held in Boone, Iowa, in 1908 at the time of the thirty-eighth annual convention of the Iowa Woman Suffrage Association.

would be willing to resolve itself into a committee of the whole to hear her and, at the same time, members of the Senate could also attend.

Mrs. Bloomer, however, did not act on this suggestion. Probably her natural timidity coupled with the hostility of the Polk County society deterred her from appearing. Whatever the reason Mrs. Bloomer remained in Council Bluffs for the rest of the session, leaving Annie Savery and others in Des Moines to make the strategic decisions and carry on the campaign.

EQUIVOCAL ACTION BY THE HOUSE

MEANWHILE, despite early assurances by legislative leaders that the General Assembly would approve the woman-suffrage amendment if the women wished it submitted during the current year, no one made a move to introduce the measure in either house prior to the legislative recess on February 1. Both John Irish, champion of woman suffrage in the 1870 General Assembly, and John Green, chief Republican spokesman for the measure, "are in a fix about their record on the Woodhull–free-love–Tilton platform," commented the correspondent for the *Davenport Democrat* on January 19, at a time when the executive committee of the Iowa Woman Suffrage Association was meeting in Des Moines. "They see that the great mass of the people have got over the *ardor femme*, and would, if possible, back out," this writer said, "but the pernicious petticoats are wrapped around them and the bluff Bloomer, the natty Sanford and the amiable Savery are convulsively pressing them to their capacious bosoms, determined that they shall not escape the leading strings of masculine maternity."

Finally, on February 14 after the legislature reconvened following its two-week recess, John Irish—apparently to the surprise of his colleagues—introduced the woman-suffrage amendment in the House along with a bill providing for its submission at the next general election. "Nothing short of a severe course of matrimonial felicity will ever beneficially effect John P. Irish," stated the correspondent for the *Democrat*, terming Irish's action as an opening of the wound. "Irish," this correspondent said, "is just as impulsive, witty, generous, caustic, sly, and fearless as ever, and was the first in the House to take the bull by the horns which from Green's silence must have gored him sadly."

The Des Moines correspondent for the *Keokuk Constitution*, in reporting Irish's action, thought it very doubtful that the current

General Assembly would approve the woman-suffrage amendment. "A number of members in the last Assembly voted in favor of the resolution regarding it as a good joke; but now when the carrying out of the joke a second time necessitates the submission of the question to a vote of the people, it becomes a serious joke," he said. The legislators, this writer predicted, would study the matter over seriously before playing the game any further.

Three days after Irish introduced the woman-suffrage amendment in the House, John Green, reporting for the Committee on Constitutional Amendments, recommended its approval. The measure was made a special order of business for four days later, Friday afternoon, February 21, at 2:30 P.M. It was evident that the House wished to dispose of this matter as quickly as possible.

This session was one of major interest to the women of Des Moines; one reporter estimated that there was an audience of 300. According to the *Council Bluffs Nonpareil:* "Ere the sun had passed the meridian, bevies of ladies might have been seen wending their way from all quarters to the Capitol—all anxious to get seats and to hear the debates—and by two o'clock the lobby, aisles and all sitting room—including many of the members' seats—were occupied by the beauty and fashion of Des Moines. The crowd which attended the Governor's inaugural was very large but this far exceeded it." These women had expected to hear a lively debate; but much to their surprise and bewilderment as soon as Irish made a motion to approve the amendment, Frank Leahy, a Republican bachelor, moved the previous question. This was a prearranged trick to cut off debate; and despite the seemingly earnest protests of Irish and a few others, the roll was taken and the amendment approved by a vote of 58 to 39. Irish then moved that the rules be suspended and an immediate vote be taken on the bill to submit the amendment at the next general election. After first defeating Irish's motion, the House reversed its action and approved the bill for submission by a substantial majority. John Green did not even attend the session on February 21. He was reportedly ill and confined to his room at the Savery Hotel. One wit later commented "that it was not suffering but suffrage that ailed him."

"The real fact of the matter is that the female question is decidedly being dodged and neither Green, Irish, nor any of its champions are in earnest," commented the Des Moines correspondent for the *Davenport Democrat.* These men, he said, were eagerly looking for its defeat in the Senate.

Indeed there was not a newspaper in the state which predicted victory for the woman-suffrage amendment in the Senate. "We had presumed that the chances were in favor of the Senate's agreeing to the action of the House" said the *Des Moines Register* on February 22, "but parties who have been canvassing the positions of the different Senators say the chances are the other way and that the vote will be close at best." According to the *Register* a large majority of the senators were opposed to woman suffrage, but at least a few of these men would vote for submission so that the voters themselves could make the final decision.

The House, however, did not completely trust the Senate to defeat the woman-suffrage amendment; and on March 6, just two weeks after approving the measure, it reconsidered the bill providing for submission of the amendment at the next general election and without debate voted to send it back to committee. This action left the House in the equivocal position of having approved a woman-suffrage amendment while at the same time withholding the means of providing for its ratification. It is interesting to note that John Irish was conspicuous for his absence from the House on the day this action was taken. "The men of the House now say they intend to see what the men of the Senate shall do," reported the *Register* the following day. This paper consoled the women by pointing out that the motion to recommit had carried by only a small majority. "Now is the time to make hay," quipped the *Register*. "If any real serious work is intended to be done, this is the golden hour and the darling opportunity."

When the House, contrary to the prediction of the skeptics, approved the woman-suffrage amendment on February 21, the women immediately went to work with renewed zeal to obtain a favorable vote in the Senate. Although it was generally agreed that most senators were against woman suffrage, it was hoped that a majority could be persuaded to vote for submission, so that the people themselves could make the final decision. This was the argument that the Radicals had used in persuading the legislature to submit the Negro-suffrage amendment, and it seemed only fair to the women that they should have the same opportunity as had been granted the colored man to take their cause to the voters.

On February 29 the *Des Moines Register* announced that friends of woman suffrage, who had made a careful canvass of the senators, claimed to have 27 votes for certain—one more than required for the suffrage amendment to pass. "Some of the ladies prominent in the lists of workers made no secret of their slates yesterday," the *Register* said, "showing in the Senate chamber lists of the names of Senators for and against to all who desire to see them." The paper trusted the ladies were not counting on a false hope.

DRAMA IN THE SENATE

MEANWHILE, Annie Savery was busy doing what she could to rescue the woman-suffrage amendment from its increasingly dismal prospects of approval by the General Assembly. Since Mrs. Bloomer was unwilling to come to Des Moines to speak, Mrs. Savery decided that she would sound out her friends in the Senate regarding the possibility of addressing that body herself in a committee of the whole. Mrs. Harbert was willing to appear with her if she could arrange for a hearing. Mrs. Savery's friends in the Senate advised her that she should not ask for a hearing if her request were likely to meet with serious opposition. At their suggestion she sounded out the leaders of the opposition as to their willingness to support a motion to hear her and Mrs. Harbert and found without exception that they were willing to do so. She singled out Senator Richards of Dubuque, a man who prided himself as a special champion of freedom of speech, as the most prominent among the opposition and asked him not only to support a motion to hear her but also to make the motion himself. Richards gallantly assented to Mrs. Savery's request. The afternoon of March 22, when the committee on constitutional amendments was scheduled to report on the woman-suffrage amendment, was set as the time for the women to appear.

When Mrs. Savery and Mrs. Harbert, with speeches carefully prepared, went to the capitol that day, they did not dream that the Senators would renege on their promise. However, just as the chairman of the committee on constitutional amendments was about to make this report, Senator Richards came over to Mrs. Savery and said he thought she should ask someone else to make the motion to hear her. He said he was not quite sure he was in favor of it, and in any event he intended to vote against it. When Mrs. Savery protested that it was too late to find another sponsor for the motion to hear her, Richards agreed to carry out his promise. He even assured Mrs. Savery that though he might vote against his own motion he would not speak against it.

As soon as the committee report was given (a majority favoring submission of the woman-suffrage amendment) and the Senate had made the amendment a special order of business for the following Friday, March 29, Senator Richards rose and moved that the Senate go into a committee of the whole to consider the amendment and that

Mrs. Savery and Mrs. Harbert be permitted to address them on the subject. Richards stated that he made the motion because he had been earnestly solicited to do so but that, nonetheless, he intended to vote against it. In the lively discussion that ensued, Richards was accused of providing the women with a barren fulfillment of an Indian promise.

Richards denied that he had betrayed any trust; but despite his promise not to speak against his own motion, he then went on at length railing against woman suffrage in an emotional speech in which he declared it would be perfidy for the legislature to submit the suffrage amendment, since a majority of the members were opposed to the measure in principle. Any senator voting for submission of the amendment who at the same time intended to vote against it at the polls would be violating his oath of office, Richards stated. In his opinion woman suffrage would be a dire calamity for Iowa; the state would be disgraced. "For the sake of the family ordained by Heaven itself to be the source and spring of all that is good in our Christian civilization—all that is worth a thought in this round world of ours," he hoped the proposition would be voted down.

After further discussion Richards' motion to hear Mrs. Savery and Mrs. Harbert lost by a vote of 20 to 24. "So it went on record that the Iowa Senate met and vanquished women," quipped the correspondent for the *Keokuk Gate City*.[4]

The humiliation of Mrs. Savery and Mrs. Harbert in the Senate set the whole city of Des Moines to buzzing. Why had they asked Richards, an opponent of woman suffrage, to sponsor their appearance? Why had he agreed to do so? Was the Polk County society to blame for his having gone back on his promise?

The first two questions were answered by Mrs. Savery in a letter to the *Des Moines Register*, written the day after the fiasco in the

---

4. In the Iowa chapter of the *History of Woman Suffrage,* vol. 3, p. 619; Mrs. Stanton used her editorial scissors and paste pot on the material furnished by Mrs. Bloomer to make it appear that Mrs. Savery and Mrs. Harbert did speak to the legislature in 1872. The *History* quotes Mrs. Bloomer as saying: "Notwithstanding this kind proposal of Mr. Kasson [for her to speak to the House on February 16], I did not act upon his suggestion. But Mrs. Harbert and Mrs. Savery, feeling that something must be done, had the courage and the conscience, on their individual responsibility, to call a mass meeting at the Capitol on the evening previous to the day appointed for the vote on the amendment in the House. Mrs. Harbert presided and opened the meeting with an earnest appeal; Mrs. Savery, Mr. C. P. Holmes, Senator Converse, and Governor Carpenter made eloquent speeches. . . . On the following day when the amendment came up in the House for the final vote, it was carried by 58 to 39." The passage beginning "to call a mass meeting" actually relates to a meeting held in 1874. The vote in the House that year was 56 to 38.

Senate, in which she explained the facts of her "earnest solicitation" of Senator Richards.

If Senator Richards was justified in changing his mind and taking "this sudden departure" from an expressed agreement, Mrs. Savery said in conclusion, then other senators would have been equally justified in disregarding their promise instead of strictly adhering to it as they did. "In his argument against woman's enfranchisement the gentleman arrogates to himself a sort of knight-errantry. He is so anxious to save woman from the dishonor of politics that he is ready to sacrifice himself 'in the last ditch' of public office rather than subject her to any such temptation." This he has a perfect right to do, said Mrs. Savery, but for one woman, she was not willing that this Sir Knight should break lance over her head in the name of chivalry.

Two days after Annie Savery's letter was published in the *Register*, a letter from Jane Swisshelm appeared that shed light on the role of the Polk County society in the affair. Mrs. Swisshelm stated that since the action of the Senate in refusing to hear Mrs. Savery and Mrs. Harbert was likely to be greatly misunderstood she thought it advisable to offer the following explanation:

> The addresses were a measure on which there was a decided difference of opinion among the friends of suffrage. The ladies who proposed to speak are both members of the State Association, whose actions in the last convention have generally been understood as endorsing FREE LOVE; or, at least, compromising with it; and those two ladies are believed to have acted with a majority, which made the ugly mistake.
>
> The POLK COUNTY ASSOCIATION, on the contrary, has placed itself squarely on the record as opposed to any weakening of the marriage bond; and was unwilling that the cause should be represented before the legislature by any one about whose sentiments, on this vital question, any doubt could be raised, and for this reason opposed the hearing.
>
> Earnest friends of equal suffrage voted against the resolution, proposing to grant it; while some of its enemies voted for it. So, that vote is no test on the main question, neither is it a test as to the ability or soundness of the proposed speakers. The first is unquestioned, or at least I have found no one who does not acknowledge that Mrs. Savery or Mrs. Harbert would have presented the question ably and eloquently, as they have often done before.
>
> The opinion seems to be equally unanimous that whatever seeming approval of the new 'social freedom' doctrine the state association gave, it was only seeming; and was induced by

charity which thinketh no evil, even of evil; but the charge
having recently been made against it, the other society which
has left no room for misunderstanding, would not consent to
appear before the legislature and the people, by attorneys who
affiliate with the state association, and some senators voted
against the resolution at the request of suffragists. Others,
perhaps the larger number, voted against such a departure
from legislative usage.

The people were supposed to elect the speakers in legislative
bodies, and it was questionable whether they had a moral or constitutional right to admit outsiders, Mrs. Swisshelm said in conclusion.
The rule was certainly against it, and she had known but one instance of its suspension. To her mind neither the ladies to whom the
unusual privilege was refused nor the friends of the cause in which
they generously prepared to use their gifts, without fee or reward,
had any reason for discouragement in this action of the Senate.

Refusing to be drawn into any public argument with her fellow
suffragists, Mrs. Savery took no notice of Mrs. Swisshelm's letter.
However, a few days after her humiliating experience in the Senate
she did express her irritation with Senator Richards in a letter published in the *Register,* in which she took him to task for his sickening
sentimentality about women. "Iowa disgraced by granting freedom
to its women!" Mrs. Savery exclaimed. "Why, sir, in the case of the
black woman subject to her master, we said that *slavery* was the
cause of her social sin. But in the case of the *white* woman you declare
that *freedom* is dangerous to her morality! Is *this* the secret of your
opposition? Are then the women of Iowa *so corrupt, so inherently
immoral* that they cannot be trusted with the ballot?" Mrs. Savery
asked. According to the newspapers, Mrs. Savery said, forty thousand
of the demimonde in New York alone were supported principally
by married men. "Are the homes which these men represent 'the
Heaven appointed homes' of which the Senator speaks so pathetically,
where woman's sphere is limited, and where she is taught subordi-
nation and subjection, according to his *beau ideal!* If 'such Heaven
appointed homes' beget only angels, why is it that so many married
men get away from them as much as possible? . . ." she asked. "Away
with this sickening sentimentality about 'women angels' who preside
over Heavenly homes, until these prating theorists can themselves become saints!" Mrs. Savery declared. These theorists had yet to learn
that it takes something besides a woman—though she were indeed an
angel—to make a "Heaven appointed home" on "this round world of
ours!"

"The Goddess of Reason and Other Irrepressible Women" was the title of a final lecture delivered by Mrs. Swisshelm at the court-house on the evening of March 28, the day before the Senate was to vote on the woman-suffrage amendment. This speech, for which no admission was charged,[5] doubtless dealt with the "irrepressible" Annie Savery. The reporter for the *Register*, who noted that the hall was "filled beyond the point of comfort," stayed for only two minutes. He was "definitely not enchanted."

While all this activity was going on in Des Moines, little or nothing was heard from suffragists in the rest of the state. The infant suffrage societies so hopefully organized over the past three years were either immobilized by internal friction or already dissolved in the wake of the free-love storm. "What is the matter hereabouts that there seems to be so little done or doing for the advancement of Female Suffrage?" the *Mount Pleasant Journal* taunted its "progressive women" on March 29. "Miss Couzins of St. Louis has lectured twice in Des Moines. Mrs. Swisshelm has been laboring there for a week addressing the Legislature and working up public sentiment," while in Mount Pleasant, "the birthplace of the State organization, not a movement has been made to second the unceasing activities at the center of the State."

And unceasing the activities of the Des Moines women seemed to be. On the morning of March 29, the fateful day set for Senate action on the woman-suffrage amendment, a letter from Annie Savery addressed to "The Honorable, the Members of the Iowa Senate Now in Session" appeared in the *Des Moines Register*. In a final attempt to persuade the senators to vote for submission of the woman-suffrage amendment, Mrs. Savery took issue with Senator Richard's contention that for a member to vote to submit the proposed amendment to the people while intending at the same time to vote against it at the polls is perjury.

"With profound deference to the distinguished Senator," Mrs. Savery wrote, "may even a woman be allowed to express the opinion that if it has come to *this*, that a servant of the people, holding his place by the suffrage of the people, commits perjury in granting a petitioner the right of going to the people with a constitutional question, then if this be so, our boasted constitutional liberty is a *farce* and '76 must come again!"

Mrs. Savery went on to quote from the debates of the 1857 constitutional convention to prove that it was manifestly the intention of

5. Mrs. Callanan probably financed Mrs. Swisshelm's stay in Des Moines.

the framers of the Iowa constitution that the people should have the controlling voice in any constitutional change. In the present instance, she argued, "The Legislature two years ago passed a resolution to submit an amendment to the people, to strike the word *male* from the constitution. The people have had the subject under consideration for two years. There is not a newspaper in the State but has discussed the question in all its bearings, and that, too, at a time in the history of the woman's cause when *everything* but justice has been against her. The result has been that the people have heard all." Yet, not a local or a state political convention had said to its candidates "that we disprove the action of the last Legislature and command you—our representatives—to stop it before it goes to the people." For this reason Mrs. Savery argued that any candid, fair-minded man in the General Assembly could be safe in saying that the people, by their silence at least, had said, "We are still in doubt upon this question. We would prefer that the people should express their opinion at the ballot box."

"You have given the ballot to every male descendent of a Pilgrim ancestry," Mrs. Savery told the senators. "You have picked up every waif of masculine degradation that ever landed upon our shores and linked him to the nation. You have taken up a whole race, to whom you deny social and domestic equality, and you have made them our political superiors. We therefore ask of you, the honorable representatives of the people, to take down the barrier, and let us go to those by whose suffrage you are here, that we may say to them, as you said to your party struggles—'Come, let us reason together' upon the question that concerns us all, and, if after the people have listened to our petition, they should reject our claims, then, we may at least have the satisfaction of knowing that you, gentlemen, have granted us an impartial hearing."

Alongside Mrs. Savery's letter to the members of the Iowa Senate was a letter written by Elizabeth Boynton Harbert, advising the women of Iowa to keep a copy of the fatal "nays" and the brave "yeas" as they were recorded in the Senate that day. Women were fast assuming the balance of power in politics, Mrs. Harbert said; and although they did not yet possess the franchise, still they could exert a great influence with pen and voice. She pointed out that Mary Livermore had recently campaigned for the Republicans in Vermont, and it was rumored that Iowa women would be invited to take part in the coming campaign.[6] Surely then and there they could use their influence

---

6. Matilda Fletcher of Council Bluffs, who had begun her lyceum career in 1869 with a poetic discourse on woman suffrage titled "Unclose the Door," was hired by the Republican party in 1872 to campaign for Grant. Wherever she spoke, she drew tremendous audiences who were curious to see and hear a woman political orator.

for the men who in the Senate and House had so gallantly tilted a lance in their favor and against those men who had opposed their enfranchisement.

"We bide our time and wait and watch to ascertain if the men of Iowa will continue to keep their mothers, wives, and daughters knocking and begging for justice and political equality," Mrs. Harbert said, "or if like loyal sons of true mothers they will welcome us to a seat on the Republican throne, give to us the badge of royalty and throw over us the purple."

THE LAST ACT

THE LAST ACT of the suffrage drama enacted in the Senate chamber on this morning of March 29 played to a house that was full to overflowing. The visitors' gallery was jammed; extra chairs had been put in every spare inch of space on the Senate floor; many senators had given their seats to women; and in the doorways and anterooms members of the lower house leaned over one another's shoulders, as they strained to watch the proceedings.

Promptly at ten o'clock Senator Bullis, president of the Senate, facetiously announced that the time had arrived for consideration of the joint resolution for striking "males" out of the state constitution. His announcement was greeted with hearty laughter by the men in the chamber.

Then Senator Beardsley was recognized. Principal spokesman for the women, he argued that the true question was not whether the senators favored a change in the constitution but whether they would allow the people to make the final decision. He pointed out that when the 1868 General Assembly submitted the proposal to strike the word "white" from the constitution "the number of people in the State who favored that amendment was not so large as the number who desire this change." Yet, the General Assembly at that time manifested no hesitancy in performing its duty. The present General Assembly, he said, should not do less for woman than a previous legislature had been willing to do for the Negro.

The next speaker was Senator Claussen, Republican of Davenport and a native of Schleswig-Holstein with a heavy German accent. The principal spokesman for the opposition, Claussen argued that "the foundations of our government are broad enough now. The State might wisely restrict but should not vastly extend the number of ignorant and indifferent voters" nor should it give to woman "whose very name is frailty" the right to make decisions relating to war and peace. Claussen asserted that if women had possessed the ballot in

1864 they would have voted to end the Civil War and make a dishonorable peace with the South.

Beardsley, who heatedly denounced Claussen for falsely accusing the women, was called to order by Bullis for insulting his fellow senator.

After brief remarks by two other senators, a roll call was taken on a motion to engross the suffrage resolution. This motion carried by a vote of 26 to 20. The women in the audience, regarding this vote as an omen of final success, breathed a sigh of relief. Then came a dead silence as the clerk called the roll on the main motion. First on the list was B. F. Allen, the Des Moines banker, who took the women completely by surprise when he voted a loud "No." This man of wealth and influence, who had voted for the amendment in the Thirteenth General Assembly, had been considered by the women to be a staunch friend of the measure.[7] Two other senators who had voted for the amendment in 1870 followed Allen's lead and went with the opposition. After a seemingly endless time in which the room was intensely quiet, the clerk reached the last three names on the roll—Willet, "no"; Wonn, "no"; Young, "yes." The final tally—ayes, 22; nays, 24; absent or not voting, 4. "Lost" buzzed around the chamber.

In describing the scene in the Senate that day, the Des Moines correspondent for the *Chicago Post* observed that "the ladies looked so regretful over the defeat of their pet measure" he almost pitied them. "Mrs. Savery, the high priestess of suffrage in Iowa, sat within three feet of the clerk with some of her intimate friends each side of her. She colored and paled alternately; looked as though she felt bad enough to cry—looked as though her idol had been dashed to pieces by ruthless men's lips and she would like to dash them to pieces. Aunty Swisshelm happened to be there and appeared to be thinking how much wormwood and gall was left in her inkstand. Mrs. Pitman, Mrs. Dickinson,[8] and Mrs. Coggeshall had fire in their eyes," and he imagined they wanted to fight. "One dear old lady over by the stove became considerably excited, and with a fist expounded to a Senator what she would have done if *she* was a man. That ended the play," this reporter concluded, "and the curtain dropped."

Another reporter noted among the women in the audience "Mrs. Lizzie Boynton Harbert, excellent in social life as she is eloquent

7. Mrs. B. F. Allen had been elected in absentia first president of the Polk County Woman Suffrage Society in October 1870, and had refused the office because she was opposed to woman suffrage.

8. Mrs. W. H. Dickinson was the wife of a homeopathic physician. They settled in Des Moines in 1858.

and efficient at the desk and rostrum." When Mrs. Harbert went home after the morning's proceedings, she dashed off a letter to the *Woman's Journal* venting her anger at the Iowa Senate. "I wish that all men and women, who like fair play, could have seen and heard the rulings of the president of the Senate, L. M. Bullis," she wrote. "Violently opposed to the measure himself, he was guilty of unpardonable partiality in his rulings." She also denounced Senator Allen, "the money-king of the State, a man who has always been a friend to the measure" who, in voting against it, "voted himself a lower place in the estimation of hosts of friends—friends who had pointed with pride to him as a man possessed of sufficient moral courage to vote according to his conscience." Mrs. Harbert also castigated Senator Claussen, "a man so foreign to our country that he could scarcely make himself understood who had the audacity to arraign all American women for *disloyalty*. Women, widowed and childless, because they gave husband and children to save their country, listened to such statements and knew that no woman could stand upon that floor and refute them in the name of woman," Mrs. Harbert indignantly declared.

"Let the coming women of Iowa remember her *champions* and her assailants," Mrs. Harbert advised. "We must see to it that we use all honorable means and influences for keeping our friends in power, and to prevent the re-election of Senators who persistently ignore our claims."

The *Woman's Journal* published the roll of the votes in the Iowa Senate on the woman-suffrage amendment "as a part of the historic record, which will some day be sought."

But it was Jane Swisshelm, with still some "wormwood and gall left in her inkstand," who had the last word. In a letter addressed "To the Women of Iowa"—which appeared in the *Des Moines Register* on March 31, the day after the defeat of the woman-suffrage amendment in the Senate—Mrs. Swisshelm wrote, "At the risk of seeming to hinder or oppose a cause to which my life has principally been devoted let me say that it is unwise, if not wicked, for the friends of woman's enfranchisement to urge members of the Legislature to vote for submitting a constitutional amendment to the vote of the people while they themselves do not approve of that amendment." After a study of the Iowa constitution, it was plain to her mind that "every legislator is bound by his oath not to submit any measure which he does not approve just as much as to submit one which he may believe to be for the public welfare. . . . Shall we, who propose to purify the government by our participation in it, use our influence, now, to teach men to trifle with their conscience, to violate their oaths?" she asked. "By all that it is dear to us, let the answer be NO! Let us not seek the right by unworthy means but rather continue to suffer than do wrong. Let us not ask anyone to do evil that good may come, but learn to labor and to wait, knowing that the right will triumph in God's good time."

On April 15, shortly before the legislature adjourned, the irrepressible John Irish furnished an epilogue to the 1872 suffrage drama by introducing a bill to confer upon women in Iowa the right to vote for presidential electors. This bill was received and filed without comment.

In late April the Fourteenth General Assembly adjourned to meet in special session in January 1873 for the purpose of revising the Code of Iowa. At the closing ceremonies a jesting resolution was adopted whereby the senators bequeathed to four well-financed but ostensibly impecunious railroad lobbyists all the "waste paper, old newspapers, etc., from under the desks of the members, also the rejected railroad tariff bill, Beardsley's speech on Female Suffrage and Claussen's reply. . . ."

SLAIN IN THE HOUSE
OF ITS FRIENDS

" 'THE WOMEN KILLED IT.' 'The bill was slaughtered by its own friends and advocates.' These are the statements made throughout the country," wrote Mary Livermore to Elizabeth Boynton Harbert after the defeat of the woman-suffrage amendment in the Iowa legislature.

Mrs. Livermore said she had found this defeat the hardest rebuff the woman's cause had yet received, and she had wept over it in her locked room as if she had received news of the death of a dear friend. It was the first failure that had really discouraged her. "Women everywhere, who were interested in the cause, felt the blow deeply," she told Mrs. Harbert. "The Michigan papers, one of the Chicago papers, and some of the Eastern papers, say plainly that if the Iowa *women* had been content to allow the Iowa *men* in the Legislature friendly to woman suffrage to manage the affair, the cause would have triumphed."

Mrs. Livermore's longtime friend John Irish, whom she considered as true as steel to the cause, had written her after the defeat that, before anyone had interfered, he had worked the matter up in the House and had it passed before anybody had been bored. In the same way he had 26 votes pledged for it in the Senate—even the vote of Senator Kinne, author of the adverse minority report, as well as others whose votes finally killed it. The women who consulted him should have believed him when he assured them of the entire safety of the measure; for before the vote was taken in the House, he had shown them his slate and they knew that every vote was cast exactly as he had predicted. But the determination of Mrs. Savery and Mrs. Harbert to address the Senate in a committee of the whole, combined with Mrs. Savery's savage newspaper attack on Senator Richards—an attack which "enraged his friendly colleagues, many of whom were pledged to go for the bill, and who then would not—were the beginning of the defeat. And just when matters were at the worst, Mrs. Swisshelm swooped down and began to scold—and then came the end, which damaged the entire cause everywhere, more even than the infernal Mrs. Woodhull.

"I am happy to tell you that the offensive alliance between Mrs. Stanton, Mrs. Hooker, and Miss Anthony and Mrs. Woodhull is at an end," Mrs. Livermore informed Mrs. Harbert. "They became convinced that she was all that we had told them, finally. A more stupendous fraud than Mrs. Woodhull never lived. Lying, blackmailing, and Heaven only knows what else were charged upon her. I will spare details. Enough that our friends are disenchanted and that we are, at last, all reunited. At any time you may read of us all in convention together." However, the two factions did not unite until 1890.

The *Des Moines Register,* in commenting on the defeat of woman suffrage in the Iowa legislature, was sorry that the amendment had not been submitted. The Republican party had its own record to meet on this issue and the women should have been given the same consideration as the Negro. The *Register,* however, blamed the women for their setback. "The West is not such an overgrown and ill-taught child that it must have Eastern wisdom imparted to make it go straight." Furthermore, the Iowa women might have been more judicious—opening a book of debits and credits, praising the "coming men," and threatening all others were not the best ways in the world to drum up votes.

The *Keokuk Gate City* called the death of the woman-suffrage amendment in the Senate "a clear case of the tedious results of overwork. The House early in the session, before the ladies had burdened ears and columns with their homilies and diatribes and arguments, passed this bill quietly and easily, but in order to make the thing sure fire in the Senate, Miss Couzins, Mrs. Swisshelm, Mrs. Savery, Mrs. Harbert, and others have labored in season and out of season, have poured their theories into ears Senatorial and un-Senatorial, till, when, in their opinion, the time had come to strike the great blow for liberty, the yeas were called, and lo! the vote was against them. Alas Poor Savery! Poor Woodhull! Poor Stanton! Poor Yorick! This suffrage matter was slain in the house of its friends."

A SOP FOR THE WOMEN

THE FOURTEENTH GENERAL ASSEMBLY, meeting in special session in January 1873, quietly and without oratory, abolished the legal disabilities of married women in its revision of the Code. This Code, whose provisions relating to husband and wife remain substantially the same to this day, provides that the wife cannot be held liable for the debts of her husband contracted either before or after marriage. She may hold property and conduct a business on her separate account and she may sue and be sued without her husband joining with her. She may bring suit against her husband for the protection of her separate property, and on the death of her husband she becomes guardian of their children. The wife inherits the same portion of her husband's estate as he would of hers if she had predeceased him; that is, one-third if they have children and one-half if they have none. The estate of dower was abolished, thus assuring the wife outright ownership of her portion of the inheritance rather than a life interest in the same.

"Surely the women may justly claim Iowa as the most liberal and progressive of all the States in its dealing with their property rights," declared Dexter Bloomer in an article in the *Council Bluffs Republican* concerning this revision of the Code. "But little remains to be conceded to them except the ballot," he noted, "and it has been shrewdly said that it is because this has been refused, that our legislators have gone as far as they have in conceding property rights to woman."

Carrie Chapman Catt leading the woman-suffrage parade in New York City November 1917 prior to the first referendum victory for woman suffrage east of the Mississippi.

Carrie Chapman Catt at the time of her marriage to Leo Chapman in Mason City in 1885.

10

1872–1920

Carrie Chapman Catt

W HEN SUSAN B. ANTHONY retired at the age of 80 as president of the National Woman Suffrage Association in February 1900, she took deep satisfaction in knowing that her successor, forty-one-year-old Carrie Chapman Catt, was ideally suited to take the helm of her beloved suffrage craft. Mrs. Catt, reared and educated in Iowa, began her suffrage work with the pioneer Iowa suffragists Mary Jane Coggeshall and Martha Callanan as her mentors. She was destined to lead the woman-suffrage forces of the United States to final victory in 1920 with the ratification of the Nineteenth Amendment to the federal Constitution.

AN IDEAL LEADER

BECAUSE MRS. CATT was a former Mason City resident, the convention in Washington, D.C., at which she was elected president of the National Association was of particular interest to the citizens of this community. One of them (probably a delegate to the convention) who served as a special correspondent for the *Mason City Republican* observed that "no person could see the remarkable interest that has been taken in this convention, the immense crowds that have thronged the doors of the church where the meetings were held, and could hear the brainy speeches from their platform and read the account of the ovation that was given their leader, Miss Susan B. Anthony, at the close of fifty years she has given the cause . . . without realizing that the woman's suffrage movement has 'come to stay.' "

This writer goes on to quote the *Washington Star*'s description of the dramatic scene when Miss Anthony presented their new president to the delegates: "The women went wild as Miss Anthony, erect and alert, with her snow white hair walked to the front of the platform, holding the hand of her young co-worker of whom she expects great things. Miss Anthony's eyes were tear-dimmed and her tones were uneven, as she presented to the convention its choice of a leader and paid her tribute of praise to the woman who had been her 'right-hand man' for so many years. It was such a tribute as most people get only after the sun of another world dawns on them. It was a tribute freighted with love and tender solicitude and rich with reminiscences of the past and full of hope for the future of Mrs. Catt and her work."

"In Mrs. Catt you have my ideal leader. I present you my successor," Miss Anthony concluded. By this time, reported the *Star*, "half the women were using their handkerchiefs on their eyes and the other half were waving handkerchiefs in the air. Mrs. Catt said quickly, 'Your president if you please, but Miss Anthony's successor, never! There is but one Miss Anthony and she could have no successor.' "

A handsome, vigorous, dynamic woman with a quick sense of humor, Mrs. Catt was highly skilled both as a presiding officer and a public speaker. For the preceding five years she had done outstanding work as chairman of the organization committee of the National Association.

Of medium height, Mrs. Catt had a dignified and erect bearing, a fair complexion, deep blue eyes, resolute chin, and light brown hair streaked with gray. She dressed tastefully but elegantly, usually in a shade of blue which accented the color of her eyes. "Mrs. Catt is fortune favored," the *Mason City Globe* had commented the previous October. "She possesses both physical charms and intellectual endowments. Always regarded as a handsome woman, she is more charming than ever."

A STRONG-MINDED GIRL

CARRIE LANE WAS BORN in Wisconsin in 1859 and came with her parents to Iowa in 1866, where they settled on a farm near Charles City. As a thirteen-year-old farm girl in 1872—the year that a woman-suffrage amendment met its first defeat in the Iowa legislature —Carrie Lane began her career as an outspoken feminist.

One afternoon during this summer her mother overheard a heated argument between Carrie and a male contemporary, as their words drifted into the house from the orchard where the young people were arguing. "Women can't fight, why should they vote?" the boy asked. Carrie countered by naming all the physically defective men in the neighborhood who were permitted to vote but were not able to fight. "If they can vote, why shouldn't women have the same privilege?" she asked.

"Where does that girl get her outlandish notions?" asked Mr. Lane when his wife told him about their daughter's encounter. "She'll never get married, I'm afraid!"

As the year 1872 progressed, Carrie followed with great interest the election campaign in which Horace Greeley, editor of the *New York Tribune,* headed an insurgent liberal Republican ticket in an effort to defeat Ulysses S. Grant for a second presidential term. Carrie's parents were Greeley supporters, and she was dismayed on election day when her father and the hired man went off to vote leaving her mother behind. Upon her father's return she challenged him about this. Mr. Lane explained that he owned the farm and therefore should have the responsibility of voting. Carrie countered that her mother through her labor had helped pay for the property. Her father then said that men know more than women. Carrie retorted that the hired man didn't know half as much as her mother. In recalling this incident in 1916, when campaigning for woman suffrage in Iowa, Carrie Chapman Catt told her audiences that she became a suffragist then and there. She also made a suffragist of her father.

After graduation from Charles City High School, Carrie went to the State Agricultural College at Ames, where in 1880 she graduated with top honors—the only girl among the seventeen members of her class. The following year she settled in Mason City, a community of 3,500, where she had been appointed principal of the high school. She subsequently was promoted to superintendent of schools. On February 12, 1885, Carrie, who had given up her school position the previous fall, married Leo Chapman, twenty-eight-year-old editor of the *Mason City Republican*, a weekly paper which he had purchased in 1883 after serving four years' apprenticeship with the *Des Moines Register*. Chapman, a native of Indiana who had come with his parents to Marshalltown, Iowa, in 1870, was an ardent, reform-minded young man who promptly made his wife a coeditor of the paper, carrying her name on the masthead along with his.

"WOMAN'S WORLD"

ON MARCH 19, 1885—four weeks after their marriage—a new feature entitled "Woman's World"[1] was added to the *Republican*, and its editor, Carrie Chapman, announced it would be "devoted to the discussion of such questions as purport to the welfare, the social, the political and intellectual position of women." Correspondence would be welcomed.

The following week a welcoming letter from a "Mrs. S. E." was published in the "Woman's World" which noted that "there are plenty of suffragists in this county but the absence of any organization deprives them of influence." She hoped the column would promote the cause. On April 9 a second letter, signed "Philes," endorsed the idea of a local suffrage society. "Nearly all other counties and towns have them," this writer asserted. "There is also a State Association. . . ." However, the time did not seem ripe for a suffrage society in Mason City. At least the "Woman's World" made no further mention of a local suffrage organization, nor did it carry any more correspondence from its readers on this or any other subject.

Carrie Chapman, nonetheless, was not to be easily discouraged in her woman's rights crusade. A firm believer in the theory of social evolution, she regarded any setback to the woman-suffrage cause as only a temporary rebuff. Commenting on the veto of a woman-suffrage bill by the governor of the Dakota Territory, she wrote on April 9, "Reforms of all kinds have grown sluggishly and public sentiment is slowly educated. No step of progress was ever made but its advocates fought dearly for victory. Such a

1. This column was modeled after a column titled "Woman's Kingdom" which Elizabeth Boynton Harbert edited for the *Chicago Interocean* during 1877–1884. The Lanes were subscribers, and Carrie was deeply impressed with Mrs. Harbert's woman's rights views.

reform as this . . . was never accomplished in a single generation. That women will have a voice in governmental affairs is inevitable."

On May 28 the "Woman's World" carried a long excerpt from a speech delivered by Mary Jane Coggeshall at the annual meeting of the Polk County Woman Suffrage Society. During the summer other columns defended women's right to strike for better pay and working conditions; deplored the "pernicious habit of calling a girl who remains unmarried until 25 an 'old maid' "; attacked the usual columns "devoted to women" which "are composed of quibs upon ridiculous subjects that ordinary people would not consider worth reading. Poodle dogs, hair pins, ice cream eaters and 'mashes' being specimens of the subjects treated." A series of columns was devoted to answering arguments against woman suffrage. "It is the duty of all women to inform themselves about suffrage," Carrie Chapman declared. "For a woman to say she does not know the results to be obtained from suffrage is to acquire knowledge that she has no interest in the welfare of women."

In the October 15 "Woman's World" Carrie Chapman gave an enthusiastic report about her visit the previous week to Des Moines, where she attended the Woman's Congress—a three-day convention sponsored by the Association for the Advancement of Women, an organization founded in 1873 for their cultural, social, economic, and political advancement.[2] This meeting was chaired by the association's illustrious president, Julia Ward Howe of Boston—author of "Battle Hymn of the Republic" and first president of the New England Woman Suffrage Association. Other notable women who attended this meeting were Mary Livermore, leader of the Northwest Sanitary Commission during the Civil War and former editor of the *Woman's Journal;* Frances Willard, president of the WCTU; Reverend Antoinette Blackwell, pioneer woman minister in the United States; and Elizabeth Boynton Harbert, former Des Moines resident living in Evanston, Illinois, who was well known in the Middle West for her writing on woman's rights. Among the Iowa women attending the meeting were a number of prominent suffrage advocates, including Amelia Bloomer, Mary Newbury Adams, Mattie Griffiths Davenport, Martha Callanan, and Mary Jane Coggeshall.

2. The Association for the Advancement of Women was an outgrowth of Sorosis, pioneer New York woman's club established in 1868. The Des Moines congress sparked the organization of the Des Moines Woman's Club, organized October 14, 1885, by twenty-two women meeting at the home of its first president, Dr. Margaret Cleaves, an 1873 graduate of the University of Iowa Medical School.

"It was not a convention of mannish women or men-haters, who met to bewail their fate in common, as many Iowa people seemed to suppose, but an Association the superior of which in point of intellectual quality and praiseworthy achievements does not exist," reported Carrie Chapman. "No woman could listen to the masterly papers and able discussion without forming a higher ideal of life and receiving a strength to help her realize it. . . . As the advancement of women is complicated with many theories and principles of political and social economy," Mrs. Chapman explained, "its object is more properly the solution of any political, social, moral, sociological, or psychological problem which may come before it. . . ." Despite this enthusiastic report, Carrie Chapman in later years confessed that she had felt a sense of frustration about this meeting. Here were too many fields to explore, no well-defined focus.

FIRST SUFFRAGE WORK

ON NOVEMBER 9 Carrie Chapman reported in the "Woman's World" about her first woman-suffrage meeting—the annual convention of the Iowa association at Cedar Rapids, which she had attended on October 20 and 21. About sixty-five delegates from different parts of the state were in attendance along with two out-of-state visitors—the sixty-seven-year-old suffrage pioneer Lucy Stone and her husband Henry Blackwell, who was the only man present. Lucy Stone, who "made one of her matchless addresses," was described by Mrs. Chapman as "a quaint appearing little old woman with round face wreathed in smiles and a demeanor so motherly and attractive as to win the hearts of all at a glance."

The plan adopted by the Iowa association for the coming year, Carrie Chapman told her readers, was the circulation of three petitions to be presented to the 1886 General Assembly: "One asking for a statute giving women municipal suffrage, one for a statute giving presidential suffrage to women, and one for an amendment removing all political disabilities from women."

The petitions asking for statutes giving presidential and municipal suffrage to women reflected the increasing discouragement among the suffragists of Iowa over their failure to persuade the Iowa legislature to submit a constitutional amendment, a process which required approval by two successive sessions. Only twice since the General Assembly first approved a woman-suffrage amendment in 1870 had the legislature again approved such an amendment, and in intervening years the measure had been killed in the House or the Senate, always by one or two unexpected votes.

Looking for a quicker and easier method of enfranchisement, suffragists in 1880 began a campaign for a law giving women the right to vote in municipal and school elections. This effort (which paralleled similar efforts by women in other states) met with very limited success in Iowa in 1894 when the General Assembly granted women the privilege of voting in elections involving the issuing of bonds, borrowing money, or increasing the tax levy.

Meanwhile, in 1886 during the session following the Cedar Rapids convention,[3] when Carrie Chapman learned that a municipal-suffrage bill had been introduced in the legislature, she organized a house-to-house canvass through which she succeeded in securing the signatures of all but ten Mason City women on a petition asking for favorable action on this bill. For the rest of her suffrage career this successful canvass was to be Carrie's stock answer to those who claimed that women did not want to vote.

A FUNEREAL DEPARTURE

DARK CLOUDS were looming on the horizon for Carrie and Leo Chapman, who were too ardent in their reform activities to suit the taste of some of their fellow citizens in Mason City. During the election campaign of 1885 Leo Chapman had antagonized the local Republican hierarchy by opposing for reelection the party's nominee for county auditor whom he charged with feathering his nest with the proceeds of office. Chapman's choice for the office was an independent candidate who was also endorsed by the Democrats. Despite Chapman's vigorous campaign against the regular party nominee (some said because of it) he was returned to office by a small majority. The auditor and his friends subsequently secured an indictment for crim-

3. Mrs. Catt in later years recalled that this petition was circulated prior to attending her first woman-suffrage convention. If this were so, it would mean that the petition was circulated during the 1884 General Assembly while Mrs. Catt was superintendent of schools in Mason City. In 1939, when eighty years old, Mrs. Catt wrote to Mary Hunter: "I did not know any suffragists anywhere when I read in the paper that a certain representative had introduced a bill granting municipal suffrage to women. This must have been in 1885 or 1886. So I organized a committee and we surveyed the town, asking women only to sign our petition for the passage of this measure. We did not approve municipal suffrage, but that was the bill. We got every woman in the town to sign that petition except ten and the story of these ten was amusing, so I wrote a letter telling about the ten who did not sign, and sent the petition to the man who had introduced the bill. He showed that letter to some of the suffragists who were working in the Capitol. . . ."

inal libel against Leo Chapman. Judging from future events, it seems evident that their intention was to run him out of town.

At first Chapman was jaunty about the affair; but when the matter came before the court in the spring of 1886 and the judge upheld the indictment over Chapman's demurrer, it was announced a few days later that Chapman had severed his connection with the *Mason City Republican* because of "failing health." The *Mason City Times,* a Democratic weekly, warned the new owner of the *Republican* "lest he too stumble into the pitfall that so completely engulfed his predecessors that their trumpeted coming was only equalled by their funereal departure. They flashed as the rocket," the *Times* said, "and fell as the stick." The *Times* suggested that Chapman's successor leave the shaping of the city and its destiny to "the good old pioneers and their sons." This debacle was so traumatic for Carrie Chapman that she never mentioned it in any of her biographical reminiscences, and it would have remained buried in history were it not for old newspaper files and court records.

After disposing of the *Mason City Republican,* Leo Chapman went to San Francisco, intending to buy a paper in that area. However, in August 1886 he was stricken with typhoid fever and died before Carrie, who was spending the summer with her parents on their farm near Charles City, could reach his bedside. The next year was a despondent one for Carrie Chapman. Reaching San Francisco after Leo's death, she stayed on to work as a newspaper reporter but felt that her life was without purpose or meaning. By the fall of 1877 she had determined to devote her life to the enfranchisement of women and with this in mind returned to Iowa, where she had family and friends. To earn a living, she began a career as a professional lecturer.

STATE ORGANIZER

CARRIE CHAPMAN's full involvement with the woman-suffrage movement began in October 1889 when she attended the annual meeting of the Iowa Woman Suffrage Association in Oskaloosa. Here she delivered an address which the *Woman's Standard* (an Iowa woman-suffrage paper established by Martha Callanan of Des Moines in 1886) described as "scholarly, witty, and convincing." Mrs. Chapman, the *Woman's Standard* said, "gave the fullest evidence of being a thorough student of the question and a woman who will make her individual force felt among the people of Iowa."

Iowa Woman Suffrage Association convention, Oskaloosa, 1889.
Carrie Chapman Catt is in the first row center, wearing cape. The
man in the second row is Henry Blackwell, and the woman to
his left is his wife Lucy Stone. Martha Callanan is seated on
Blackwell's right, and Mary Jane Coggeshall is seated second from
the left in this row. It was at this convention that Mrs. Catt was
persuaded to become an organizer for the Iowa Association.

Carrie Chapman was elected to the office of secretary of the Iowa association for the coming year and was also persuaded to try her hand at organizing. She lost no time in getting to work, starting at Sioux City on November 19, where she organized a Political Equality Club. From there, according to the *Woman's Standard,* she was scheduled to go to Cherokee, Aurelia, Alta, Fonda, Fort Dodge, Humboldt, Webster City, Williamson, Allen, Iowa Falls, Ackley, Waterloo, and Manchester. She also visited Independence, where she organized a Political Equality Club to replace Iowa's first Equal Suffrage Society which John L. Loomis had organized in 1867 and which had died in the wake of the free-love furor of 1872.

In February 1890, three months after the Oskaloosa meeting, Mrs. Chapman traveled to Washington, D.C., with Martha Callanan and other Iowa delegates to the national woman-suffrage convention. Here she delivered a speech which the *Woman's Standard* reported "did our state credit." However, the appearance of this new worker on the national platform was of minor importance to the delegates at this meeting whose interest was centered on the ceremonies marking the unification, after more than twenty years separation, of the two factions in the suffrage movement—one led by Lucy Stone under the banner of the American Woman Suffrage Association and the other by Elizabeth Cady Stanton and Susan B. Anthony under the banner of the National Woman Suffrage Association. A merger of the two organizations, under the name of National-American Woman Suffrage Association,[4] was headed by seventy-five-year-old Elizabeth Cady Stanton, who attended the convention only long enough to make a witty and eloquent speech and then left for England with her daughter Harriet Stanton Blatch. Susan B. Anthony, seventy-year-old vice-president of the new association, continued to carry the work load; and upon Mrs. Stanton's retirement as president in 1892 she was elected to that office. Seventy-two-year-old Lucy Stone was ill and did not attend the 1890 convention but was elected chairman of the executive committee, a purely honorary position as her days of active work were nearing an end. She died in 1893.

"SHE WENT OFF AND GOT MARRIED"

AFTER HER RETURN from the national convention, Carrie Chapman made another organization trip sponsored by the Iowa Woman Suf-

4. Although the official name of the national association after 1900 was National-American Woman Suffrage Association, it was usually referred to as the National Association. For the sake of brevity, it will be referred to in this chapter as the National Association.

frage Association. In June, however, she gave up her Iowa residence when she married George Catt of Seattle, Washington, a native Iowan who had graduated from the State Agricultural College at Ames in 1882 and was a successful engineer with a widespread business on the West Coast. In accordance with the terms of a written prenuptial agreement Carrie was to continue to use the name Carrie Lane Chapman, but after a few years she found it more convenient to use her husband's name and became known to the world as Carrie Chapman Catt. More important, the agreement also stipulated that she was free to devote at least two months each spring and each fall to suffrage work. As a matter of fact, she continued to devote more time than this to the cause. In the fall of 1891 Carrie and George Catt moved from Seattle to Boston; and the following spring they settled in the New York City area, where Carrie continued to reside after her husband's death in 1905. Since George Catt was a man of means, this marriage enabled Carrie to continue her suffrage work without financial worries; and at his death she was left an independently wealthy woman, able to support the suffrage cause with liberality.

Carrie Chapman's marriage to George Catt was distressing to the suffragists in Iowa. "I went around town with Mrs. Ankeny and begged money to keep Mrs. Chapman working, and then she went off and got married," Margaret Campbell,[5] president of the Iowa association, complained to Lucy Stone in a letter written July 30, 1890. "She promised to come back and work in September for us, but Miss Anthony has secured her for the South Dakota campaign. She still thinks she can come to Iowa for six or seven weeks before Christmas so the money is kept in reserve for her work. We are in a rather hard place here now," Mrs. Campbell lamented, "the loss of Mrs. Chapman after I had taken so much pains to secure her help for the State is very discouraging."

The South Dakota campaign referred to by Mrs. Campbell was Carrie Chapman's first campaign experience. Here, where a woman-suffrage amendment was submitted to a referendum at the November 5 elections, Carrie worked for two months, traveling under the most difficult conditions in this new, sparsely settled, and poverty-stricken state. The campaign had begun with high hopes for success, but Carrie soon saw that the women were fighting a hopeless battle. On election day they were beaten by a vote of two to one.

5. Margaret Campbell, fifty-nine-year-old native of Maine who had lived for a number of years in Massachusetts, was a close friend of Lucy Stone's and other New England suffrage leaders. She and her husband John canvassed Colorado during a campaign for a constitutional amendment for woman suffrage in 1877. In 1879 they settled in Des Moines, where Mrs. Campbell was active in Iowa suffrage work until 1901 when she and her husband moved to Joliet, Illinois.

A CLEAR-HEADED YOUNG WOMAN

WEARY AS SHE WAS after her South Dakota experience, Carrie Chapman made good her promise to the Iowa suffragists and returned to carry on her organizing work for the Iowa Woman Suffrage Association. At the annual convention of the Iowa association held in Des Moines on December 5, Mrs. Chapman, who was described by the *Des Moines Register* as a "clear-headed young woman with a business-like manner and energetic ways," outlined a plan for holding a convention in each of the state's ninety-nine counties, using these meetings as springboards for organizing local societies.

"There was a lively discussion over the plan of work," the *Register* reported. "The principle difference of opinion being over the formation of societies. Some weak sisters thought it was indecent to put forward the name of suffragists too much. . . ." These women preferred to work quietly in their churches until there was more sentiment in favor of the cause. But Mrs. Chapman in "a ringing speech frequently interrupted with applause contended there was no use to wait for more sentiment. The sentiment was here in every county in Iowa and she herself felt sure she could organize a convention in each of them. What was needed was the organization and crystallization of this sentiment so that when the Legislature met, the member would know that some of his constituents wanted him to vote for woman suffrage and that if he didn't he would be defeated. That was the only way to get anything done." Carrie Chapman's motion that the Iowa association arrange for a convention in every Iowa county was carried, and Mrs. Chapman was engaged to come back and work in the state during the coming April and May. The convention closed with the adoption of the following resolution: "That we are greatly pleased by the good work done by our lecturer and organizer, Carrie Lane Chapman, and regret her departure from our State, and our love and good wishes go with her to her new home."

"SHE HAS DONE US PROUD"

MRS. CHAPMAN, as agreed, returned to Iowa in the spring of 1891 and again in the fall of that year. She also worked in the state during the summer of 1892, taking the lead in organizing a four-day Mississippi Valley conference held in Des Moines in late September in conjunction with the annual convention of the Iowa Woman Suffrage Association. The convention met in the auditorium of the YMCA on 4th and High streets. Flying from the east window of the convention hall and extending out over 4th Street was a suffrage flag—a replica of the red, white, and blue flag of the United States except that it carried a single white star on the field of blue. This lone star represented Wyoming, which had been admitted to statehood in 1890 and was the one state in the Union where women had equal suffrage rights with men.

Delegates from fourteen states attended the Mississippi Valley conference—Iowa, Minnesota, Missouri, Wisconsin, South Dakota, Kentucky, Illinois, Indiana, Kansas, Nebraska, Florida, Mississippi, New York, and Massachusetts. In fact, the meeting had been so carefully planned and widely publicized that the officers of the National Association feared that Mrs. Chapman and her Iowa associates were trying to organize a rival society. "They put the chief blame on me," Mrs. Catt recalled in later years, but all the Iowa officers came in for a little distress. . . . I was very much disturbed about it for of course, such a motive did not exist."

The first program of the meeting was devoted to a panel discussion on the following question: "The growth of the work demands more money. How shall we raise it?" Mrs. Chapman, a member of the panel, told about methods of raising money which she had used successfully in Iowa. Miss Anthony, who had come to Des Moines to protect the interests of the National Association, was so delighted with Mrs. Chapman's interest and ability to raise money that she appointed her finance chairman of the National Association.

Another session of the Mississippi Valley conference was devoted to outlining a work plan which Carrie Chapman had used as state organizer in Iowa. This plan, which revealed to the delegates that a dynamo was at work in the suffrage ranks, included the following:

1. Groups to be organized by voting districts.
2. Work to indoctrinate all community leaders.
3. Suffrage lectures to be given before each teacher's institute.
4. Working women to promote suffrage for their own protection.
5. Suffrage cause to be presented at various meetings and conventions.
6. Itemized blanks to be furnished each society for the purpose of uniform reporting at annual conventions.
7. County woman-suffrage conventions to be organized at the same time as county fairs.
8. Each society to open an enrollment book and to make a systematic annual canvass of each district.
9. Cooperation to be invited from the WCTU, Women's Relief Corps of the GAR, and all other women's organizations.

A dinner for the delegates at the Kirkwood (former Savery) Hotel on the second day of the convention was, according to the *Register,* "perhaps the most elegant banquet ever given in Des Moines." The decorations which were "the finest ever seen on a Des Moines banquet board" consisted of "nasturtiums, goldenrod, wild sunflower, turned leaves of sumac." The programs were handsomely designed and beautifully printed in yellow. And climaxing all, were the after-dinner speakers "seldom equalled for brilliance." Carrie Chapman who served as toastmaster for the occasion, rushed off after the banquet (which ended at 1:00 A.M.) to speak at the Mills County Fair the following day, returning to Des Moines in time for the last day of the meeting. At the conclusion of the conference, the *Register* paid tribute to Carrie Lane Chapman's "queenly grace and charming voice, her eloquence and logic. . . . We may claim her as our very own," this paper said. "She has done us proud."

Two Heads in the Country, Two upon the Hearth, Two in the Tangled Business of the World.

Programme.

Toast Master ....Carrie Lane Chapman

Happy a woman's voice may do some good—here's
a woman will speak .... Catherine Waugh McCullock

Individual Rights... John J. Hamilton

The Dangers of an Irresponsible Educated Class .... Alice Stone Blackwell

The Ideal Woman—"Let your ideal run before you, and do you
run after it"... Rev. Ida C. Hultin

Either Sex alone is but half itself..................................Hon. M. B. Castle

Is Housekeeping one of the Industries .... Mrs. A L. Frisbie

The Stone which the Builders rejected the same has become
the head of the corner.......................................Rev. H. O. Breeden

Our Wage-Working Women.......................................Susan B Anthony

Attend to the Women ....Prest. B. O. Aylesworth

Are Men Responsible for the Present Situation ....Henry B. Blackwell

Good-will to Men ....Emma Smith DeVoe

Woman's Sphere is Bounded alone by Woman's Duty.............Hon. J. S. Polk

More Father in the Family, More Mother in the Councils of
the Nation..Rev. Olympia Brown

Menu.

BLUE POINTS, ON HALF SHELL

CELERY

CONSOMME ROYALE, EN TASSE

OLIVES   PICKLED

SWEET BREAD PATTIES, A LA REINE

SUPREME OF CHICKEN, A LA PRINCESSE

GREEN PEAS   POTATO CROQO

ORANGE SHERBET

COLD HAM   COLD TONGUE

TOMATOES, MAYONNAISE

ANGEL CAKE   MERINGUES   MACARO

ICE CREAM, AUX FRUITS

PEARS   GRAPES   PEAC

NUTS   RAISINS

COFFEE

Program and menu for the Mississippi Valley woman-suffrage conference $1.00-a-plate banquet held in the Kirkwood Hotel in Des Moines in 1892.

CAMPAIGNS IN THE WEST

AFTER 1892 Mrs. Chapman no longer served as organizer for the Iowa association. Her interest in the state, however, did not wane despite her increasing involvement with suffrage work elsewhere. Coming directly to Iowa from Colorado on November 10, 1893, Mrs. Chapman was able to report to the delegates at the state convention in Webster City about the Colorado campaign, where woman suffrage had been endorsed by the voters just three days previously. This was the first referendum victory in the history of woman suffrage; and Carrie Chapman, who had stumped the state for two months prior to the election, was the heroine of the Colorado campaign. The principle reasons why the cause was successful in Colorado, Mrs. Chapman told the Iowa convention, was "because it had been recognized by all political parties; then too the inhabitants were mostly miners who had emigrated to the West at the time eastern capitalists had imported foreign labor, and these men formed labor unions which universally advocate equal wages for men and women." In addition the fact that Wyoming, a woman-suffrage state, was adjacent to Colorado was also a favorable influence on the Colorado electors.

Mrs. Chapman's success in Colorado marked her as an outstanding worker among the suffragists of the country and brought urgent requests for her help wherever there was a campaign in progress. During 1894 she participated in two major campaigns, New York and Kansas. Both resulted in disappointing defeats for the women.

In August 1896 Carrie Chapman Catt (by 1895 she was using this name) helped organize a campaign in Idaho, where she persuaded four political parties—Gold Republican, Silver Republican, Democratic, and Populist—to endorse a woman-suffrage amendment which was to be submitted at the November elections. The referendum resulted in a victory for the women, and Idaho became the third suffrage state in the country. (Utah, where women had voted from 1870 to 1887, had become the second suffrage state when it was admitted to the Union the previous January.)

From Idaho Mrs. Catt went to California, where a suffrage amendment was also to be voted on in November. Here she worked for two months in one of the best organized campaigns in woman-suffrage history. Nonetheless, the women met defeat in the election, adverse majorities in San Francisco and Oakland overcoming favorable majorities in the rest of the state. The California defeat was a heart-

This photograph of Carrie Chapman Catt was taken in Los Angeles in 1896 during the California referendum campaign and gives a good idea of the elegance of dress for which she was noted.

breaking experience and left the state suffrage organization exhausted and in debt. Many years passed before it recovered to fight again.

But Mrs. Catt never wasted a moment bemoaning a defeat; she headed east with Miss Anthony after the California election, stopping en route to visit several state conventions. She returned to New York shortly before Christmas to entertain the board of the National Association whom she had invited to her spacious home at Bensonhurst, Long Island. At this meeting she outlined the ensuing year's plans for the organization committee of which she was chairman.

A WOMAN OF SUPREME ABILITY

THIS COMMITTEE, she told the board, planned to launch intensive campaigns in several states, one of them Iowa, where it was hoped enough sentiment could be created to force the legislature to submit a suffrage amendment to the voters of the state. Two-day conventions, presided over by workers from the National Association, were being scheduled in each of the state's ninety-nine counties—two adjoining counties to hold simultaneous meetings so that speakers could be exchanged. The northern half of the state would be covered in the spring and the southern half in the fall, ending with a state convention in Des Moines where headquarters would be opened prior to the 1898 session of the General Assembly.

The Iowa campaign which Mrs. Catt outlined to the board was launched in late January 1897 when the National Association held its annual convention in Des Moines. This was the first convention of the National Association held west of the Mississippi and only the second held outside the city of Washington. The Central Christian Church, where the delegates met, was decorated with green palms and the suffrage flag which now displayed four stars, representing, in addition to Wyoming, the new suffrage states of Colorado, Idaho, and Utah. Susan B. Anthony, the association's revered and stalwart seventy-six-year-old president, presided over the convention; and Carrie Chapman Catt took a prominent part in the proceedings. "Iowa has done more for the National Association and suffrage work throughout the country than any other state," Alice Stone Blackwell, Lucy Stone's daughter, told the delegates. "She has made the most valuable present of twenty years or more to the Association when she gave it Carrie Lane Chapman Catt."

"Some people feel that progress is slow, and some of our enemies feel that our progress is so slow that they can take courage. But it is not slow, for the evolution of society is ever gradual," Carrie Chap-

The *woman-suffrage flag with four stars representing Wyoming,*
Utah, Colorado, and Idaho—the first four states to give woman
the vote—was used from 1896 to 1910, when a fifth star was added
representing the state of Washington.

man Catt told the convention. "Our movement is not so far behind
as may be supposed. In fifty years thirty states have granted partial
suffrage to women," she pointed out. She was ashamed that Iowa
(where women had tax and bond suffrage only) had granted the most
limited privilege of any of these states.

Miss Anthony, who told the delegates that the Iowa legislature
had played with the woman-suffrage question "like a cat plays with a
mouse," urged the suffragists of the state to have suffrage planks inserted in the platforms of the political parties and "from that it will
be an easy step to submission by the Legislature. . . . To the four
states in our banner today," she said, "we expect to add in 1898
California, Nevada, Oregon, Washington, and Montana." By 1900

she expected a tenth star to be added to the flag representing Iowa.[6]

The Iowa legislature was meeting in special session at the time of the national convention in Des Moines in 1897, and an invitation was extended to the delegates to appear before the Senate. (The House refused to invite the women.) Miss Anthony acted as master of ceremonies for the occasion and presented speakers representing each of the four suffrage states as well as Mrs. Catt, who told the legislators that even though not a single member favored woman suffrage it was the duty of the General Assembly to submit the question to the voters of the state. She pointed out that even in a referendum only men could vote.

Following the national convention Mrs. Catt proceeded to put her plan for Iowa into action. The *Woman's Standard* in April 1897 listed fifty-eight county conventions which were scheduled between March 29 and June 18. Two national workers were in the state to help with this program. Mrs. Catt herself conducted the Cerro Gordo County convention which met in Mason City on May 20. Here the *Republican,* which she and Leo Chapman had once owned, paid glowing tribute to this woman of "supreme ability" and devoted nine full columns to reporting the convention.

Mrs. Catt returned to Iowa again in October to attend the annual convention of the Iowa Woman Suffrage Association in Des Moines, after which she chaired several county conventions. An ecstatic reporter for the *Woman's Standard* called Mrs. Catt's speech at the state convention "one of the most beauiful addresses we have ever heard. This beautiful woman in her elegant attire as she stood before that interested audience made a picture never to be forgotten."

At the Linn County convention in Cedar Rapids on October 23 Mrs. Catt reported that "we have succeeded admirably in our work in Iowa, and before the end of the year we hope to have every county in the state organized." At that time there were in existence eighty-five county societies and 150 local clubs all "in flourishing condition." This plan, she said, "gives us strength in every locality in Iowa and

6. There were no new suffrage states from 1896 when Idaho women were enfranchised to 1910 when a woman-suffrage amendment was adopted in the state of Washington. In 1969 the Iowa constitution still carries the word "male" as a qualification for voting. However, the 63rd General Assembly has given second approval to a constitutional amendment providing for changes in residence requirements for voters. This amendment, which will be submitted at the general election in 1970, brings the amendment in line with federal law by deleting the word "male" as a qualification for voters.

places us in a position to influence members of the Legislature directly. . . . We expect to be able to submit a suffrage amendment to the people of Iowa in 1900. . . . Once we get the measure before the people we have not much doubt as to what the result will be."

In accordance with Mrs. Catt's plan a state office was opened in Des Moines prior to the 1898 General Assembly, and on February 3 the women were granted a hearing before the House and Senate committees on constitutional amendments. Mrs. Coggeshall, president of the Des Moines Equal Suffrage Club; Mrs. Belden of Sioux City, the vivacious and witty president of the Iowa association, and other suffragists spoke. For the first time the antisuffragists were also represented at this hearing by several prominent women who protested that they were appearing only out of a deep sense of duty, as they preferred to remain quietly at home. All during this session, petitions for woman suffrage poured into the legislature, with as many as fifty being presented in a single day.

The legislature's response to all this activity was a refusal by either house to approve the woman-suffrage amendment. The amendment also met the same fate in the 1900 General Assembly, despite a deluge of petitions carrying more than 100,000 signatures. These defeats after so much work left the Iowa woman-suffrage movement exhausted and despairing for a number of years. But Mrs. Catt, with her firm faith in the evolution of society toward greater perfection, regarded these defeats as only temporary setbacks and kept on working at the same driving pace.

PRESIDENT OF THE NATIONAL ASSOCIATION

WHEN INSTALLED as president of the National Woman Suffrage Association in February 1900, Carrie Chapman Catt was universally considered to be the ideal successor to Susan B. Anthony. "Mrs. Catt plans for the object she has in view and her plans are deep and broad," said the *Boston Transcript* in a story reprinted in the *Des Moines Leader* shortly after she took office. "Abounding health, her cheerful visage, and elastic step suggest a reserve fund of energy stored up in youth on a western farm. Mrs. Catt has acquired the art of wise conservation of time and energy," said the *Transcript*, "and is never hurried or disturbed in spirit by small annoyances. . . . She is able, as few people can, to plan campaigns on long lines, forming strong combinations and bringing her force to bear on strategic points with a minimum expenditure of time and effort. She is an exceedingly

ONCE MORE THE CASTLE IS BEING STORMED.

This cartoon by J. N. Darling appeared in the Des Moines Register *February 20, 1909, while the Iowa General Assembly was in session.*

Two English militants attending the annual Iowa woman-suffrage convention in Boone, Iowa, in 1908 instigated this early woman-suffrage parade.

practical woman and believes that nothing can be accomplished without organization."

Despite her organizational genius, not a single suffrage campaign was won while Mrs. Catt was president of the National Association, a position which she held from 1900 to 1904. The successful referenda in Colorado in 1892 and in Idaho in 1896 had stiffened the opponents of woman suffrage and they were able to hold off another suffrage victory until 1910. Mrs. Catt, saw three factors—ignorance (especially in the foreign-born voter), indifference, and fraud—as the greatest enemies of woman suffrage. In her farewell address as president of the National Association she proposed the formation of a nation-wide good-government committee to consider the following methods of improving democracy:

1. Establishing an educational qualification for the ballot.
2. Lengthening the five-year residency requirement for citizenship for the more ignorant classes of immigrants.
3. Amending existing naturalization laws which make possible the

forging of citizenship certificates and the addition of noncitizens to the voting lists.

4. Increasing the period of residence required where the system exists of importation of voters just before the election with the intention of adding their names to the corrupt voting lists.
5. Establishing a slight property qualification for the ballot.
6. Disfranchising both the bribed and the briber in voting frauds.
7. Disfranchising eligible voters who fail to vote.

"Yet with the curtailment of the irresponsible vote at the bottom and the indifferent or dishonest vote at the top, we would not have completed our task," Mrs. Catt warned the convention. "An education of public sentiment must be conducted through every school and college and church, through the press, the pulpit, and the platform, until a healthy, wholesome hatred has been created for the selling and buying of votes at the polls, the graft of municipalities, and the corrupt control of Legislatures. . . . We must galvanize the whole electorate with the spirit of public service, and bring back the old enthusiasm for democracy."

Anna Howard Shaw, president of the National Woman Suffrage Association spoke at 8th and Story streets in Boone after the 1908 parade. Street parades and meetings were a new and daring technique for propaganda at this time.

CUTS TIE WITH THE
NATIONAL ASSOCIATION

IN 1905 Mrs. Catt attended the national convention in Portland, Oregon, where the suffragists hoped to get a woman-suffrage referendum on the Oregon ballot in the fall. Delegates to the Portland meeting traveled west in three special cars. Mrs. Catt, who had been visiting her mother in Charles City, joined the train at Boone. Here members of the Boone Political Equality Club met the train with bouquets which they presented to Mrs. Catt, now a vice-president of the National Association; Anna Howard Shaw, president; and Susan B. Anthony, honorary president, who at the age of eighty-five was also making the trip. All three women delivered short speeches from the back platform of the train.

Among the Iowa delegates at the Portland meeting was sixty-seven-year-old Mary Jane Coggeshall, pioneer Iowa suffragist and long-time friend of Carrie Chapman Catt. "When I get discouraged I think of Mrs. Coggeshall," Mrs. Catt told the convention. "She has been one of my strongest inspirations."

Unable to get along with her successor Miss Shaw, who was a brilliant speaker but lacked organizational ability, Mrs. Catt cut her ties with the National Association after 1905. She did this so quietly that even her friends were puzzled. "Mrs. Coggeshall spent two days with me on her return from the national convention," Margaret Campbell, former president of the Iowa Woman Suffrage Association, wrote to Alice Stone Blackwell on February 25, 1907. "We wondered why Mrs. Catt was not at the convention and feel sure that something has gone wrong between her and the powers that be." Mrs. Campbell reported that she had read in the *Interocean* that Mrs. Catt had opened an office in New York City where she would work for woman suffrage, believing that the time had passed when great conventions would do much good.

As this letter indicates, Mrs. Catt never publicly quarreled with Miss Shaw; but beginning in 1907 she began to build a Woman Suffrage Party in New York State, an organization which succeeded in 1917 in winning the first and most important referendum victory east of the Mississippi.

In addition to her work in New York State, Mrs. Catt was busy, from 1904 to the outbreak of World War I in 1914, building up the International Woman Suffrage Alliance of which she was president. She traveled to Europe a number of times in the course of her work for this organization; and following a serious illness in 1911–1912, she made a tour around the world, visiting with woman-suffrage leaders wherever she went.

RESURGENCE OF THE WOMAN-SUFFRAGE MOVEMENT

MEANWHILE, despite the fact that the National Association was relatively ineffective under Miss Shaw's presidency—a position which she held from 1904 to 1915—there was a resurgence in the woman-suffrage movement during these years brought about by several factors: the upsurge of Progressivism, the rise of new leaders in many of the state organizations, and the emergence of a militant wing of the suffrage movement whose members were known as suffragettes.

Miss Flora Dunlap, forty-one-year-old social worker and close friend of Jane Addams, represented the new leadership in Iowa. A native of Ohio, she came to Des Moines in 1904 to head Roadside

Flora Dunlap was president of the Iowa Equal Suffrage Association during the referendum campaign of 1916 and the first president of the Iowa League of Women Voters in 1919.

Settlement House. On October 10, 1913, she was elected president of the Iowa Equal Suffrage Association (successor to the Iowa Woman Suffrage Association) by a vote of 49 to 35 at a stormy annual convention at Boone. According to the *Des Moines Register,* "So tense was the situation that when the ballots were being prepared for counting Mrs. Ida Wise Smith pleaded from the convention floor for the women to forget petty ambitions and personal bitterness of feeling and receive the announcement of the vote in silence. When Miss Dunlap was declared the presiding officer, the delegates in one accord rose and sang the hymn, 'Blest Be the Tie that Binds.' Many of the women in the audience wept, but Miss Dunlap calm and self-possessed, sang."

"In naming Miss Dunlap the woman suffrage movement of the state has taken a very important first step towards realization of their hopes," said the *Register* in an editorial the following day. "The newly elected president combines with a tactful disposition and perfect poise and self control, a much more thorough knowledge of the practical phases of the woman problem than any woman could possibly have who had not been meeting the world on its practical side as Miss Dunlap has been meeting it."

The rise of militancy in the suffrage movement came with frustration over lack of success with traditional campaign methods. This movement, which began in England in 1906, soon spread to the United States; methods included street meetings, parades, picketing, and civil disobedience. Mrs. Catt, with her faith in education and organization, had no sympathy with these tactics. The *Woman's Standard* of July 1909 quotes Mrs. Catt as saying she was a "suffragist" not a "suffragette." She denied ever having advocated militant methods and took a firm stand against suffrage parades. "We do not have to win sympathy by parading ourselves like the street cleaning department or the police," she said. Although Mrs. Catt never condoned the extreme tactics of the militants (such as picketing the White House), she did eventually accept the parade as a valuable publicity tool for the suffrage movement. In October 1915 Mrs. Catt was one of 30,000 women who marched up Fifth Avenue in New York City in the largest suffrage parade ever organized in the United States. Two years later, draped from head to foot in a white broadcloth military cape, Mrs. Catt led another New York City parade.

By 1915 the suffrage flag was proudly displaying fifteen stars—the eleven added since 1896 representing Washington (1910); California (1911); Oregon, Kansas, and Arizona (1912); The Territory of Alaska (1913); and Montana and Nevada (1914). In addition to these full-suffrage areas the Illinois legislature granted presidential suffrage to women in 1913. This was the first break in the solid opposition to woman suffrage east of the Mississippi. In 1915 the Iowa General Assembly at long last gave second approval to a woman-suffrage amendment and provided for its submission to the voters of the state at the primary elections in June of the following year.

On the national level the federal amendment—the Susan B. Anthony amendment which had lain dormant since it was first voted on in the Senate in 1887—was also coming to life. It was brought to

Hooray for Mother

These drawings of a 1912 woman-
suffrage parade in New York City
were made by John Sloan to illustrate an article for Collier's Weekly.

Aw Susie, Be Them Dishes Washed?

Women Marching

a second vote in the Senate in March 1914, and the following January it came to a vote for the very first time in the House of Representatives.

RETURN TO THE HELM

VICTORY at last seemed in sight for the woman-suffrage forces of the United States, but a strong leader was needed for the final push. Carrie Chapman Catt, who at fifty-six considered herself too old for the position, was nonetheless persuaded to again assume the presidency of the National Association to replace Anna Howard Shaw, who had permitted the organization to disintegrate into numerous factions, each nursing its own petty jealousies. Mrs. Catt took office in December 1915 at the annual convention in Washington, D.C.

IOWA REFERENDUM

ONE OF THE IMMEDIATE TASKS facing Mrs. Catt was to help the Iowa suffragists prepare for the referendum set for the following June. "At a secret conference held Thursday in Washington, D.C.," the

❋

A woman-suffrage parade in New York City in 1915 with 40,000 women dressed in white carrying 15,000 yellow banners was the largest in the history of the movement. The Iowa banner reads, "Iowa men will vote on a woman-suffrage amendment in 1916."

❋ *Iowa Equal Suffrage Association board of directors, 1915: From left to right: Mrs. H. W. Spaulding, Grinnell; Mrs. Jansen Haines, Des Moines; Mrs. A. J. McNeal, Des Moines; Rev. Effie McCollum Jones, Webster City; Mrs. Carrie Chapman Catt, New Rochelle, N.Y., president of the National Woman Suffrage Association; Miss Flora Dunlap, Des Moines, president of the Iowa Equal Suffrage Association; Mrs. James K. Devitt, Oskaloosa; Mrs. Harriet B. Evans, Corydon; Mrs. Ella Caldwell, Adel.*

Mason City Globe-Gazette reported on December 21, 1915, immediately after the national convention, "the suffrage situation in Iowa was canvassed. At this conference were Miss Dunlap and Mrs. Catt. Since Iowa is one of three suffrage campaign states next year it is understood the national board will vote a large campaign fund and send national workers to the State." The *Globe-Gazette* also reported that as evidence of her loyalty to Iowa Mrs. Catt was sending, at her own expense, a national suffrage worker who would spend five months in campaign work in the state.

Mrs. Catt devoted a great deal of her time and attention to the Iowa campaign in 1916, including three short visits to the state to consult with suffrage workers and a month devoted to intensive campaigning. On Sunday afternoon February 6, while in Des Moines to meet with the board of the Iowa Equal Suffrage Association, she addressed a public meeting at the University Christian Church, where old friends and acquaintances as well as suffrage supporters flocked to hear her. "It was an impressive homecoming back to Iowa where she grew up . . . when Mrs. Carrie Chapman Catt, international suffrage leader, walked to the platform yesterday, . . ." said the *Des Moines Register* of this occasion. "Mrs. Catt who has addressed thousands of persons in this and other lands . . . was moved almost to tears as she faced the men and women, many of whom had been her school and college companions. . . . There were before her gray-haired men and women who were her classmates thirty-five years ago at the Iowa State College at Ames; middle-aged men and women who were her pupils in Mason City thirty-two years ago; a few of the small band of women who invited Mrs. Catt to give her maiden speech here twenty-five years ago; pioneers of Iowa who remembered her as a slip of a girl on a farm near Charles City. These together with leaders in the suffrage movement in the State and enthusiastic suffrage supporters gave her welcome."

Mrs. Catt told the audience, the *Register* continued, that "a bunch of violets in her room at the hotel that morning had brought back old memories. . . . She could see herself a child of eight again standing for the first time in front of their new frontier home and looking over the unbroken and violet carpeted prairie. . . . She told of the hardships experienced by the early pioneers in Iowa . . . and of her first suffrage work which was a house to house canvass in Mason City." After reviewing the development of suffrage in the United States, Mrs. Catt outlined the plan of attack of the organized opposition, paying special "respects to the anti-suffragists at work in Iowa in a tone that was cool and controlled but the words were caustic." This opposition, she said, was allied with the liquor interests and the unscrupulous railways of the country.

From the middle of April to the middle of May Mrs. Catt worked in Iowa, conducting training sessions for workers and lecturing in all the major cities. In Council Bluffs, where she spoke on April 16, the auditorium was completely filled. "It was the biggest affair of the kind ever staged in southwest Iowa," the *Council Bluffs Nonpareil* reported. "When all is said and done, there is really just one argument in favor of woman suffrage," Mrs. Catt told her audience, "that

POPULATION DIAGRAM

Women Suffrage States

Illinois

Male Suffrage States in which Question has not been Voted Upon

Male Suffrage States Recently Voting No

Within the last four years eleven states, with a combined population of 38,209,950, have rejected Woman Suffrage by overwhelming majorities at the polls.

Twenty other states, with a combined population of 34,695,088, have refused so far even to submit the question to the voters.

Eleven states, with a combined population of 8,189,469, have full suffrage for women, and in Illinois, with a population of 5,638,591, the suffragists have secured "Statutory" suffrage through action of the Legislature.

The substance of the demand for a Federal suffrage amendment, therefore, is that Congress shall force Woman Suffrage upon the Union in defiance of the will of nearly three-fourths of the States containing more than four-fifths of Uncle Sam's inhabitants!

What would be left of the doctrine of "state" rights" and of the principle of democracy if Congress should accede to this extraordinary demand?

Issued by the Iowa Association Opposed to Woman Suffrage.

"When a Fellow Needs a Friend"

"A VOTE FOR MOTHER IS A VOTE FOR A BETTER WORLD FOR ME DAD"

Courtesy of New York Tribune.

Suffrage Department
W. C. T. U. OF IOWA

Propaganda for woman suffrage included a blotter (below) put out by the Iowa Woman Suffrage Association in 1910 and a post-card (upper right) circulated by the WCTU of Iowa, date un-known. "Population Diagram" (upper left) is a postcard circu-lated in 1916 by the Dubuque Association Opposed to Woman Suffrage.

VOTES FOR WOMEN

On the Road to Woman Suffrage
STATIONS MADE IN 1910

JULY 8—Men's League for Woman Suffrage organized in Des Moines with 79 charter members.

AUG. 31 State Fair Woman Suffrage Rally. Lander's Band wears "Votes for Women" at Des Moines.

SEPT. 30—Carpenters and Joiners International Convention at Des Moines, representing 200,000 members, endorses woman suffrage resolutions, 300 to 40.

NOV. 6 Sunday, Mrs. Mary E. Craigie, Supt. Church Work of National Suffrage Association, speaks in Des Moines in First Baptist Church, morning service and in Plymouth church in afternoon.

NOV. 15, 16, 17—State Convention at Corydon. Dr. Barton O. Aylesworth, National Woman Suffrage Organizer, chief speaker.

is that we are part of the nation; we obey its laws and we pay our taxes; and we are entitled to a part in making the laws that regulate our welfare."

In Waterloo, where Mrs. Catt spoke to a crowd of 1,400 on May 4, she told her audience, "Some dead men vote as do some who have never been born and yet the women are not let in. They are allowed to go to schools and universities with the boys and yet when they want to have free speech they can only have it 100 feet from the polls on election day."

In Dubuque, where Mrs. Catt spoke at the Grand Opera House on May 21, "the audience filled the seats, boxes, packed the aisles and left men and women standing at the doors. . . . Twenty-five years from now woman suffrage will be a forgotten issue," she said. "Suffrage is coming from every direction. You can't stop it."

Touring the state at the same time as Mrs. Catt was another former Iowan, John Irish of California, champion of woman suffrage in the 1870 Iowa General Assembly. A professional antisuffrage campaigner since 1911, Irish drew only small audiences wherever he went in the state. His sponsorship was never announced, although it was generally assumed to be the liquor interests. Irish had alarming tales to tell about the dire effects of the woman-suffrage "experiment" in his home state of California, where women had voted since 1911. Not only had woman suffrage resulted in increased taxation but it had caused increased delinquency among women and children and given rise to the corrupt woman politician. If this were not enough to convince his audiences, Irish also warned that suffrage had put lines in women's faces and that men no longer took off their hats in elevators.

"It is really too bad that so many estimable people begin to see everything going wrong at about the time their own blood begins to cool," said the *Des Moines Register* of the seventy-three-year-old Irish. The *Register,* now a firm friend of woman suffrage under the editorship of Harvey Ingham—son of Algona's pioneer advocate Caroline Ingham—favored "youthful minds in old bodies. Every extension of liberty has vindicated itself," the *Register* declared. "The more rights the people have the more responsibilities they assume. No nation ever went upon the rocks because of liberty."

Despite a well-organized and well-financed campaign supported by a majority of the papers in Iowa, the woman-suffrage amendment was defeated on June 5 by a total of 10,341 votes, the four "wet" counties on the eastern border of the state—Scott, Clinton, Dubuque, and Des Moines—returning a large adverse vote which overcame favorable majorities in the rest of the state. Most astonishing was the fact that there were 29,341 more votes cast on the equal-suffrage amendment than the total cast for all candidates for governor.

An investigation by the WCTU subsequently revealed that victory was literally stolen from the women in Iowa. Thousands of unregistered votes were cast on the amendment despite the fact that registration was required by law. No record was kept of ballots officially issued to each precinct, and in most cases no unused ballots were returned. In fifteen counties there were 8,067 more ballots on the amendment than voters checked as having voted. Suffragists were advised, however, that even if fraud could be proved there was no way the election could be declared invalid.

THE PROMISED LAND

THE IOWA SITUATION, coupled with similar experiences in other states, convinced Mrs. Catt that women faced insurmountable odds in most state referenda and that the time had come to concentrate on an amendment to the federal Constitution. At a meeting of the executive committee of the national board, prior to a special "emergency" convention of the National Association held in Atlantic City in September 1916, Mrs. Catt laid out what came to be known as her winning plan. The state auxiliaries were to be divided into four groups, with each assigned to a particular task.

1. The twelve states where women could vote for presidential electors were to secure from the next sessions of their legislatures resolutions asking Congress to submit a woman-suffrage amendment.
2. The few states where there was a chance of carrying a state constitutional amendment were to try for that.
3. The largest group of states was to work for presidential suffrage.
4. Southern states, where the primary virtually determined the election, were to try for primary suffrage.

"When we filed out of the room at the close of that meeting, I thought I understood how Moses felt on the mountain top after he was shown the Promised Land," Maude Wood Park, congressional leader of the woman-suffrage forces, later recalled. "For the first time our goal looked possible of attainment in the near future."

The state organizations did their work so well that by May 1919 four new stars representing New York, Michigan, South Dakota, and Oklahoma had been added to the suffrage flag. Thirteen legislatures,

TO THE IOWA FARMER!--REMEMBER!

WOMAN SUFFRAGE
MEANS HIGH TAXES

TAX RATE IS BOUND TO INCREASE

The History of Equal Suffrage States is the Story of Taxpayers' Money Wasted---Money Thrown Away in Hysterical Legislation, Useless Commissions, Uncalled for Bond Issues, Increased Election Costs---Taxes are Squandered Because of a Catering of Legislative Interests to the Irresponsible Elements Among Voters.　Compare this Government Report:

Non-Suffrage States	Tax per $1,000	Equal Suffrage States	Tax per $1,000
Wisconsin	$11.80	Washington	$31.00
New Hampshire	16.00	Colorado	40.10
Vermont	18.83	Utah	32.60
Missouri	19.00	Wyoming	32.40
Massachusetts	17.30	California	21.50
IOWA	12.04	Idaho	41.50

(*Vol. 1, p. 761—Taxation Statistics Census Report.")

TAX RIDDEN CALIFORNIA

During the first four years of Woman Suffrage in California, 1911 to 1915, state taxes were increased from 18 to 36 millions, or 100 per-cent increase. The cost of county government is the highest of any state in the Union. Los Angeles alone cost the taxpayers 42 millions. Los Angeles Times says: "10 millions is political plunder."

DO YOU WANT THIS IN IOWA?

COLORADO'S EXPERIENCE

Denver has the highest tax rate of any city of its size in the world—$26.00 for every man, woman and child in the city. Colorado has the highest state tax in the Union. The Denver Post protests that "Public funds are notoriously wasted through useless commissions, and loose political methods."

DO YOU WANT THIS IN IOWA?

TAX CRISIS IN IOWA

Taxpayers of Iowa today are entering a Protest against the Squandering of Public Funds.　The Cost of running the State of Iowa has been for the Biennial Periods:
Ending June 30, 1895, **$3,624,000.** Ending June 30, 1914, **$11,996,000.**
Note this Enormous Increase in Taxes with no Increase in Population.
Facing this Critical Situation It Is No Time to Increase State Expenses by adopting Woman Suffrage and assuming Additional Election Expenses of a Million Dollars.

VOTE "NO" ON JUNE 5

The Farmers of Iowa should remember that the granting of Woman Suffrage means the doubling of the city vote in Iowa which has no thought of their interests and does not materially increase the farm vote.　"It is not your wife and daughter who will vote, but the women of towns and cities who have easy access to the polls and axes to grind."

YOU, MR. FARMER, MUST PAY THE BILL.　CAN YOU AFFORD THIS EXPERIMENT AT THIS TIME?

IOWA ASSOCIATION OPPOSED TO WOMAN SUFFRAGE　　　　DES MOINES, IOWA

THIS ADVERTISEMENT PAID FOR BY POPULAR SUBSCRIPTION AMONG PATRIOTIC IOWANS

Full-page advertisement in the Iowa Homestead, *May 25, 1916. According to Carrie Chapman Catt, when James M. Pierce woman-suffrage advocate and editor of the* Homestead, *was chided for his act to perfidy in publishing this ad, he meekly replied, "I got $600 for it."*

including Iowa, had granted presidential suffrage to women, and two had given primary suffrage. In less than three years the number of presidential electors for whom women could vote had jumped from 91 to 339. The suffragists had at last achieved enough political power to get favorable action in Congress.

The presidential suffrage bill which passed the Iowa Senate on April 4, 1919, passed the House on April 19 in the closing hours of the session. This session of the General Assembly had previously defeated a primary suffrage bill. The *Des Moines Capital* on Sunday, April 6, 1919, carried the following story:

> Iowa, one of the first states to consider equal suffrage, and now certain to be one of the last states to adopt it. That's a new Iowa record, set up when the Senate a few days ago defeated a measure proposing equal suffrage at primary elections and substituted for it a State constitutional amendment to drag itself wearily through a succeeding General Assembly and a statewide balloting.
>
> To the suffragists it represents fifty-one years of unceasing effort come to naught, and their movement done to death, at that, by those who seemed to be its best friends. The suffrage bill [amendment] passed the House again in 1917 but failure of the office of Secretary of State to publish the notice within the stipulated time nullified the Legislature's action. In order to avoid delay, the women substituted a bill providing for suffrage in primaries. It was this bill that was recently lost in the Senate.
>
> "On what ground do the legislators oppose the bill?" Miss Dunlap [president of the Iowa Equal Suffrage Association] was asked.
>
> "Because it would be such a shame for woman, sacred woman, to have her soil her fair hands with the sordid machinery of politics."
>
> "And the real reason?"
>
> "Politics. They are afraid it will mean trouble for the Republican party if the women get the vote. But it's only occasionally that they will admit it. Woman suffrage became a political issue in 1912 when Roosevelt put it in the platform of the Progressive party, and it has bulked large in the minds of politicians ever since. Of course they keep on spouting the old pedestal idea, while they beat their wives at home, I suppose."

On May 21, 1919, three days after the Sixty-sixth Congress convened, the woman-suffrage amendment was brought up in the House (where it had been defeated three times in the past four years) and was approved by a comfortable majority. On June 4 the amendment was brought up in the Senate (where it had been defeated four times in the past five years) and was passed by a narrow margin—five senators who had previously voted "no" changing to the winning side because of suffrage gains in their states. After the Senate vote Vice President Marshall, the presiding officer and an opponent of woman suffrage, gave the chair to ardent proponent Senator Albert Cummins of Iowa, so that he could make the victory announcement. Senator Cummins' voice trembled, Maude Wood Park recalled, as he declared the joint resolution for the Nineteenth Amendment to have received the affirmative vote of more than two-thirds of the senators present and voting. This amendment reads: "The right of the citizens of the United States to vote shall not be denied or abridged by the United States or by any State on account of sex."

Within an hour after the Nineteenth Amendment had been approved by the Senate, Mrs. Catt, waiting in New York where the suffrage headquarters were located, had sent telegrams to the governors of all states asking them to take immediate steps to secure ratification of the amendment. On July 2 Iowa became the tenth state to ratify when the legislature approved the amendment in a special session lasting just one hour and forty minutes, the shortest session in Iowa history.

"It was a short-sleeved, perspiring Legislature, closely flanked by a solid bank of georgette-clad femininity, which wore the smile of triumph earned by long and persistent effort," said the *Des Moines Capital* of this occasion. "The legislators took their dose without a grimace. Of course, it was not unpleasant to a large proportion of them, but there were some, notably in the Senate who were traditionally opposed to suffrage, who nevertheless voted 'yes' with smiling faces. It was entirely apparent that none of the politically ambitious was overlooking the fact that probably at the next election a body of voters will be added to the Iowa electorate fully two-thirds as large as the present voting strength."

"It was a wonderful moment," wrote Lillian Crawley (corresponding secretary of the Iowa Equal Suffrage Association) to the *Woman Citizen*. "The joyous expressions of these men who had taken hot and dusty rides on day trains, from their farms and stores in the scorching July weather that is Iowa's best corn grower, to come and cast their votes for ratification assured us of victory. So the work begun in 1868 by the women of Iowa is finished in 1919," Mrs. Crawley said. "It may have been a good thing that we have had this long, hard struggle, for we have learned many things in getting an insight into politics."

On August 26, 1920—following ratification by Tennessee,[7] the thirty-sixth state to fall into line—the Secretary of State of the United States proclaimed the Nineteenth Amendment the law of the land. On August 27 Mrs. Jens Thuesen of Grundy County, Iowa, became the first woman in the state to vote under the Nineteenth Amendment (and perhaps the first in the United States) when she cast her ballot in an election to establish a consolidated school district carved out of Black Hawk and Grundy counties. A total of seventy-seven women cast their ballots in this election.

"That vote of yours has cost millions of dollars and the lives of thousands of women," Mrs. Catt reminded the women of America in a message in the *Woman Citizen*. "The vote has been costly," Mrs. Catt declared. "Prize it. . . . Understand what it means and what it can do for your country. No soldier in the great suffrage army has labored and suffered to get a *place* for you. Their motive has always been the hope that women would aim higher than their own selfish ambitions; that they would *serve* the common good."

"The vote is won. Seventy-two years the battle for this privilege has waged, but human affairs with their eternal change move on without pause.

"Progress is calling on you to make no pause. Act."

❖

7. On August 31, 1920, John Irish wrote to George Parker, an Iowa friend: "I think the perjury of the Tennessee Legislature has finished the destruction of States Rights and slaughtered the element of personal honor. What a pity that the great dust of Andrew Johnson [a native of Tennessee] has to rest under the sod of a state so craven."

BIOGRAPHICAL NOTES

1872-1920

❉

THESE NOTES are presented for the reader who is curious about the later lives of those women who were leaders in the Iowa woman-suffrage movement during the Reconstruction era. Some who might have been included have been necessarily omitted because of lack of information.

MARY NEWBURY ADAMS

Born—Peru, Indiana, 1837; *died*—Dubuque, Iowa, August 5, 1901.

MRS. ADAMS, one of the leaders in founding the Northern Iowa Woman Suffrage Society in 1869, came increasingly to believe that women needed a broad education prior to gaining the ballot. Living in Dubuque, a city with a large Catholic population, she was particularly concerned about the influence of the Catholic church on women. "I for one, am afraid to have women vote throughout the United States till this government is on as free a basis as its founders wished it to be," Mrs. Adams wrote to Amelia Bloomer in 1877. "The women would vote as their pastors directed, rather than their husbands—and the church, as history shows, . . . is and must be opposed to Republicanism and to individual rights. I do not wish to discuss this abroad, but I want women . . . to prove that they can see for themselves what the ages teach before they hold so great a power. Men are for state and district schools; women for denominational. This tells its own story."

A pioneer worker in the Iowa Federation of Women's Clubs, Mrs. Adams thought that unless women were trained for the best thinking they could not appreciate comprehensive national affairs. "Organize all the women in Iowa into Women's Clubs leaving them free to choose what they work for," she said. "When they are properly educated they will be prepared to secure their full rights," she told Mrs. Bloomer.

263

Mrs. Adams was associated with a number of cultural and scientific organizations, including the Association for the Advancement of Women, the Social Science Association, the Anthropological Society, and the National Science Foundation. She was an intense student of religion and in later years turned to Theosophy.

AMELIA BLOOMER

Born—Cortlandt County, New York, May 27, 1818; *died*—Council Bluffs, Iowa, December 30, 1894.

MRS. BLOOMER, elected president of the Iowa Woman Suffrage Association at its ill-fated second annual convention in October 1871, held office until the third annual convention which did not meet until March 1873. Although subsequently elected from time to time to an office in the Iowa association, Mrs. Bloomer was never again active in state organization work. Always more at home with the pen than on the platform, she continued to be a vigorous defender of woman suffrage by means of letters to newspapers.

In 1880 Mrs. Bloomer was asked by Mrs. Stanton and Miss Anthony to write the Iowa chapter for a three-volume *History of Woman Suffrage* which they were preparing. Not until the publication of volume III in 1888 did the Iowa material appear. While for the most part the Iowa chapter is factually correct, it has many sins of omission; in particular, it fails to tell the story of the internecine warfare that paralyzed the early suffrage societies in Iowa. Excerpts from Mrs. Bloomer's correspondence regarding the *History* are of interest to the student of woman suffrage.

> *January 7, 1881, Susan B. Anthony to Amelia Bloomer:* Of course you must take note of that neat streak of camaraderie that split Iowa Suffrage Society as it did all others—I do not see how it can be avoided. . . . Give a fair sketch of all especially don't forget the Legislature's zig-zags in submitting our question. . . .

> *February 9, 1881, Susan B. Anthony to Amelia Bloomer:* You *must* tell of the Woodhull—and you had better put in the Executive Committee's circular you sent to all the papers. . . . [The circular referred to is the one prepared by Annie Savery stating the position of the Iowa Woman Suffrage Association on free love. There is no mention of either the circular or Mrs. Woodhull in the Iowa chapter.]

> *June 1885, Susan B. Anthony to Amelia Bloomer:* I think you had better strike out the *Woodhull* mentionings. We have given her all the importance she deserves in the Fourteenth Amendment chapter of Volume II and it seems to me unwise for the state chapters to give her the prominence of a mention.

> *June 29, 1885, Amelia Bloomer to Mary Jane Coggeshall:* Three or four years ago I was asked to write the Iowa chapter for the Woman Suffrage History. . . . I had the proof of my chapter but it has been so pruned down and altered, and sometimes I

was misrepresented in some of my statements, Mrs. Stanton making it read as she would like it to be and not as facts made it—that I was disgusted and disheartened. . . . Now I have a letter from Miss Anthony saying they are going on with the third volume and asking me to fix up my proof. . . . I feel that the thing ought to be rewritten. . . . It is all very discouraging, for they will leave in and take out whatever they please, and one don't know how it will come out. . . .

August 10, 1885, Susan B. Anthony to Amelia Bloomer: All I have to say is—make the Iowa chapter tell the truth, and nothing but the truth—in as concise a manner as possible. . . . Nor praise Des Moines [the Polk County Society] a word more than you think justice demands. . . . Mrs. Stanton and I tried to *condense* not to falsify—so tell the facts briefly.

September 9, 1887, Mary Jane Coggeshall to Amelia Bloomer: Your kind letter came this morning and the roll of manuscript. I will give it house room, tho' like you I take very little stock in the Woman Suffrage History. . . . Who cares yet for the history of this movement? I think the *future* historian will have to deal with the names of many of you early martyrs. . . .

In 1940 Mary Hunter wrote to Olive Cole Smith of Mount Pleasant, "Mrs. Bloomer furnished the material for the Iowa section in the *History of Woman Suffrage.* I know the *best* friends of the suffrage association were furious about some of her material and grieved that she omitted other important facts. I never refer to it without hearing in memory some of the remarks I have heard."

Mrs. Bloomer and her husband during their lives in Council Bluffs continued to live in the same house (several times remodeled and enlarged) in which they settled when they came to Iowa in 1855. Here they celebrated their golden wedding anniversary in 1890, and here Mrs. Bloomer passed away four years later. In 1895, a year after her death, Dexter Bloomer published the *Life and Writings of Amelia Bloomer.*

MARTHA CALLANAN

Born—near Albany, New York, May 18, 1826; *died*—Des Moines, Iowa, August 16, 1901, from injuries sustained when her carriage overturned.

THE WAR BETWEEN the liberals and the conservatives within the Iowa woman-suffrage movement culminated in victory for the conservatives in 1875 when James Callanan, Mrs. Callanan's husband, was elected president of the Iowa Woman Suffrage Association. In 1876 Mrs. Callanan succeeded her husband as president and continued to hold this office for four successive terms. She was succeeded in 1880 by Caroline Ingham of Algona. Mrs. Callanan was reelected at the 1879 convention only by virtue of casting a ballot for herself which broke a tie in a contest for the presidency. At this convention the Iowa Association abandoned its independent status and voted to ally itself with the American Woman Suffrage Association.

Echoes of the bitterness toward Mrs. Callanan are found in several letters of the period:

"Mrs. Callanan is utterly hostile to me but I shall work with her if I can; if she will not allow me the opportunity, I shall work independently," wrote Elizabeth Boynton Harbert, newly elected president of the Iowa Woman Suffrage Association, to Amelia Bloomer in the fall of 1874.

"*MONEY* not brains . . . has carried Mrs. Callanan to the very head of the movement," Maria Orwig of Des Moines wrote to Amelia Bloomer after the 1875 state convention. Mrs. Orwig, who was replaced by Mrs. Callanan as corresponding secretary, said that Mrs. Callanan was so determined to put her out of the state society "that she stepped down from the high position of chairman of the Executive Committee and *requested* the office of corresponding secretary! She knows how utterly I detest her and acts according to the dictates of her small nature." Mrs. Orwig went on to say that Mrs. Callanan had not only put her husband at the head of the organization but she had also put "a woman over whom she has entire control as chairman of the Executive Committee."

"I have always believed Mrs. Callanan at the bottom of Mrs. Savery's persecution, for it amounted to that," wrote Susan B. Anthony to Amelia Bloomer in December 1880.

Mrs. Callanan's devotion to the woman-suffrage cause was as steadfast and determined as was her drive to rid the movement of those whom she considered undesirable. In 1886 she launched the *Woman's Standard,* an Iowa woman-suffrage paper which she published for thirteen years and continued to support financially as long as she lived. "None but God and herself know how many days and nights in her little 'den' at home were spent in directing and sending suffrage literature over the State; writing for the *Woman's Standard,* the little state paper which she called her 'baby'; making routes for speakers (and paying their salaries); and writing to the county and local clubs for their encouragement," said Mrs. Coggeshall at the time of Mrs. Callanan's death. Active to the end, Mrs. Callanan entertained the Des Moines Woman Suffrage Society at her home only a few days before her fatal accident.

Mrs. Callanan was active in WCTU work from the time of the organization of the Des Moines chapter in 1874 until her death in 1901. She was instrumental in founding the Benedict Home, a WCTU institution for "fallen women," and for many years she served on its board of managers. In 1887 Mrs. Callanan was elected chairman of the franchise department of the Iowa WCTU, a position which she held until 1890. "Mrs. Callanan is so busy running the franchise department of the State WCTU that she leaves the *Standard* to me," wrote Mary Jane Coggeshall to Amelia Bloomer in September 1887. "She is having Miss Shaw [Anna Howard Shaw] of Boston for a month's work in Iowa, for the Unions, for franchise. . . . Mrs. Callanan is stirring them up on this subject with a very sharp stick. . . ."

Mrs. Callanan was a charter member of the Des Moines Woman's Club, a founder and long-time worker for the Home for the Aged, and an active supporter of the Business Women's Home.

"Quiet and unobtrusive, she was endowed with strength of character and fixity of purpose that seldom yielded to obstacles," said one commentator at the time of her death. "She always manifested an interest in public questions, often with a breadth and scope that surprised those who came in contact with her. She was a firm believer in the theory that wealth brings great responsibility to those who attain it."

In her will Mrs. Callanan left $10,000 to the Home for the Aged, $20,000 to Tuskegee Institute, $500 to the WCTU of Iowa, and $1,000 to Mrs. Whitney of Waterloo for the *Woman's Standard*. Her entire estate, after payment of taxes, amounted to about $40,500. Mr. Callanan (a very wealthy man) contested the will under the Iowa law which specifies that not more than one quarter of an estate may be left to nonprofit corporations. He succeeded in having his wife's bequests cut proportionately. When Mr. Callanan died in 1904, among many bequests to philanthropic organizations, he left $3,000 to the Iowa Woman Suffrage Association.

MARY JANE COGGESHALL

Born—Milton, Wayne County, Indiana, January 17, 1836; *died*—Des Moines, Iowa, December 22, 1911.

Mrs. COGGESHALL, the faithful secretary of the Polk County Woman Suffrage Society during its early years, continued to be a quiet and devoted worker for woman suffrage the rest of her life. She served as editor of the *Woman's Standard* (Mrs. Callanan lists herself as publisher) from 1886 to 1888 and continued to write for this paper long after her name was removed from the masthead. Mrs. Coggeshall served as president of the Iowa Woman Suffrage Association in 1890 and 1891 and again from 1903 to 1905. For the last six years of her life she served as honorary president of the state association, in which position she reluctantly but resolutely marched behind the brass band at the head of the suffrage parade (one of the first in the United States)[1] in Boone in 1908. "It wasn't so bad after all," she remarked with a sigh of relief when the parade ended.

The only one of the older generation of Iowa woman-suffrage workers to take a prominent part in national suffrage affairs, Mrs. Coggeshall was elected to the board of the National-American Woman Suffrage Association in 1895, a position which she held for a number of years. At national conventions this quiet Quaker lady with snow-white hair and demure face invariably captivated her audiences with her dry sense of humor, her brilliant repartee, and her sharp arguments. In dedicating the Iowa Woman Suffrage Memorial in 1936 Carrie Chapman Catt recalled a speech which Mrs. Coggeshall had given at a national convention in 1904 on the "Iowa Idea" which, as interpreted by her, was to lead the suffragists up to victory by rosy promises and then, within sight of the goal, defeat them by one or two unexpected votes.

Despite continual discouragement, Mrs. Coggeshall never wavered in her devoted work for woman suffrage. "Twenty-five years has but deepened our conviction that this reform is the need of the age," said Mrs. Coggeshall at the twenty-fifth anniversary of the Polk County Woman Suffrage Society in 1895. "We have learned that *our* work must be upon

1. The first woman suffrage parade in the United States was in New York City on February 16, 1908; the second parade was in California; and the third in Boone.

long lines," she said. "We who have toiled up the steps of the old Capitol only to see our bills defeated upon final vote. We who took our baby boys with us to those early meetings, now find these boys are voters, while their mothers are still asking for freedom. We only hope that the next generation of women may find their work made easier because we have trodden the path before them."

However by 1911, when the Iowa legislature once again rejected the woman-suffrage amendment, the strain of continual discouragement overcame Mrs. Coggeshall's usual fortitude in the face of defeat, as she saw a lifetime of work apparently spent to no avail. Her friends later recalled how she left the Capitol with pale face, broken look, and trembling lip. "Friends," said this seventy-four-year-old lady, "it does test the mettle of women to walk steadily forward year after year and be misunderstood."

When Mrs. Coggeshall died later this same year, she left $15,000 to the suffrage cause—$10,000 to the National Association and $5,000 to the Iowa association. Carrie Chapman Catt considered Mrs. Coggeshall her greatest inspiration, and in her book *Woman Suffrage and Politics* she calls her "The Mother of Woman Suffrage in Iowa."

MARY DARWIN

Born—Milford, Connecticut, November 12, 1821; *died*—Burlington, Iowa, July 30, 1886.

ALLIED WITH Mrs. Bloomer and Mrs. Savery in refusing to endorse the antifree-love resolution at the 1871 state woman-suffrage convention, Mrs. Darwin was for several years thereafter persona non grata with the conservatives in the Iowa Woman Suffrage Association. In 1876 she left Burlington for a four-year sojourn in Washington, D.C., where her eldest son lived. When she returned to her home in Iowa in 1880, she immediately became active in the WCTU. Mrs. Darwin attended the state WCTU convention in Council Bluffs in 1880, hoping to visit with Amelia Bloomer and find out what was going on in suffrage circles, but much to her disappointment Mrs. Bloomer was out of town. At the 1883 state convention of the WCTU, Mrs. Darwin made an eloquent plea for the members of the Union to realize the necessity of asking for the ballot if they were to be effective in achieving their reform goals. The following year the Iowa WCTU established a franchise department.

In 1884 Mrs. Darwin went to California to care for her sister who was ill. A few months after she returned to Burlington in 1886, she died of an apparent heart attack.

"Mrs. Darwin has been an active and prominent worker in philanthropic, temperance, and religious movements," said her obituary in the *Burlington Hawkeye*. "She was one of the trustees of the Iowa hospital for the insane at Mt. Pleasant; president of the Women's Christian Temperance Union; and identified with several religious, educational and benevolent and reform movements for the promotion of the welfare of society. She was a member of the Congregational Church and led a life of marked piety and religious zeal." There is no mention of her work for woman suffrage in this column-long obituary.

Mrs. Darwin's husband Ben, from whom she was separated in 1866 (they were later divorced), died in an insane asylum in Napa, California, in 1901.

Mary Darwin's Oberlin College B.A. diploma (1845) and her M.A. diploma (1855)—in the nineteenth century masters' degrees were usually granted without further schooling—are now in the Oberlin College Library. They arrived there under unusual circumstances. Miss Lelia Holloway, Oberlin reference librarian who gave these diplomas to the library, never knew Mrs. Darwin or her family. They came into her possession through her parents, who bought a house in Ottumwa, Iowa, in about 1900. The entire building was empty except for a lead case, under a window sill in the attic, which contained the precious diplomas. How they happened to be left there, Miss Holloway has never discovered.

MATTIE GRIFFITH DAVENPORT

Born—Pennsylvania, 1842; *died*—Butte, Montana, April 27, 1928

FOLLOWING HER MARRIAGE to Francis M. Davenport of Oskaloosa in 1870, Mattie Griffith of Mount Pleasant, one of the pioneer Iowa women to lecture on woman suffrage, served as principal of the Oskaloosa High School for two years. In 1874 her only child Warren was born. "On account of baby, poor health, and home cares I have been on the rostrum but little of late years and that little in the temperance work and a little suffrage thrown in incidentally," Mrs. Davenport wrote to Amelia Bloomer in 1880.

According to a report in the *Woman's Journal* of September 4, 1875, Mrs. Davenport "a member of the Women's Temperance Band" and also a vice-president of the Iowa Woman Suffrage Association, had been selected by her Republican township caucus as one of its delegates to the county convention. The convention by a vote of 36 to 17 refused to seat Mrs. Davenport. It is interesting to note that Mrs. Davenport's husband was a prominent Democrat in Oskaloosa.

In 1887 Mrs. Davenport was state treasurer of the WCTU. She was also a member of the board of managers of the WCTU Benedict Home for "fallen women." This same year her husband, unsuccessful in his law practice in Oskaloosa, went to Greene County where he farmed for five years. The couple later settled in Mount Pleasant. Davenport eventually went to Montana, where he homesteaded with his son. He died in Butte in 1921 and was buried in Montana.

Mrs. Davenport, who apparently stayed on in Mount Pleasant for several years after her husband went west, went to live with her son in Montana in 1918 when failing eyesight made it impossible for her to live alone. When she died in 1928, her body was brought back to Mount Pleasant for burial in the Griffith family plot, the Reverend Laura Galer of the Universalist Church officiating at her funeral.

"Mrs. Davenport was actively associated with many organizations especially the W.C.T.U.," says her obituary in the *Mount Pleasant Journal*. No mention is made of her work for woman suffrage.

ELIZABETH BOYNTON HARBERT

Born—Crawfordsville, Indiana, April 15, 1843; *died*—Pasadena, California, January 19, 1925.

MRS. HARBERT, who with Mrs. Savery was so rudely refused a hearing before the Iowa Senate in 1872, secured permission in 1874 for the Polk County Society to hold a suffrage rally in the hall of the House of Representatives the evening before the vote on woman suffrage in the House. Principal speakers of the evening were Mrs. Harbert and Senator Converse of Butler County. Mrs. Savery and Governor Carpenter, who were not scheduled to speak, made extemporaneous addresses at the request of the audience. In July 1874 Mrs. Harbert secured a hearing before the platform committee of the Republican state convention and succeeded in persuading the party to adopt its first woman-suffrage plank. Although the Republicans did not endorse woman suffrage per se, they did go on record favoring "a final submission of the question of amending the constitution so as to extend the right of suffrage to women."

In September 1874 Mrs. Harbert was elected president of the Iowa Woman Suffrage Association at its fourth annual convention, which was held in Des Moines. "I was unable to attend the convention and was very much surprised to hear that I had been elected president," Mrs. Harbert, in bed with a bad cold, wrote Mrs. Bloomer the day after the meeting. The previous week, she said, she had made an earnest talk to the Polk County society telling the ladies to look the subject squarely in the face and see how the society had deteriorated since it had allowed such workers as Mrs. Bloomer, Mrs. Darwin, Mrs. Savery, and others to withdraw. This little talk so offended some of the women that they refused by one vote to even send her as a delegate to the state convention, Mrs. Harbert told Mrs. Bloomer. However, at the convention, her friends rallied to her defense and she was unanimously elected president.

A few months after her election as president of the Iowa Woman Suffrage Association, Mrs. Harbert and her family moved to Chicago and soon afterwards to Evanston, Illinois. For eight years (1876–1884) she was president of the Illinois Equal Suffrage Association. For seven years (1877–1884) she edited "The Woman's Kingdom," a column in the *Chicago Interocean,* a paper which, because of its wide circulation in the Midwest, made Mrs. Harbert's name a household word throughout the region.

"When I was a young girl in Iowa, you were editor of the woman's column in the *Interocean* which came weekly to our home. I never failed to read those columns and I have always felt that your words at that time made a very great impression upon me in determining to work for woman suffrage," Carrie Chapman Catt wrote to Mrs. Harbert in January 1921. "I have therefore, always held you in reverence and gratitude. I think I must have told you this many times before but I want to repeat it again for these things cannot be said too often."

In addition to her lifelong suffrage activities Mrs. Harbert was a founder of the Evanston Woman's Club and served as its president for seven years. For two years she served as president of the Social Science Association of Illinois. She was a member of the board of managers of the

Girl's Industrial School of South Evanston and was active in the Woman's Congress, an association for the advancement of women.

In later life Mrs. Harbert lived in California (where women were enfranchised in 1911). She was an officer in the Woman's Civic League of Pasadena and the Woman's Press Association of southern California.

ARABELLA MANSFIELD

Born—Des Moines County, Iowa, May 23, 1846; *died*—Aurora, Illinois, August 1, 1911.

MRS. MANSFIELD who chaired the first Iowa woman-suffrage convention in Mount Pleasant in June 1870 is still a subject for journalists because she was the pioneer woman lawyer in the United States.[2] Admitted to the Iowa bar in 1869, Mrs. Mansfield's legal career, if she had any at all, was short. In 1872 she and her husband went to Europe, where they spent a year studying in England, France, and Germany. When they returned to Mount Pleasant in 1873, they again associated themselves with Iowa Wesleyan College. In 1879 John Mansfield accepted a position at DePauw University in Greencastle, Indiana, where he taught until 1883 when he retired because of ill health. Mrs. Mansfield, however, continued to teach in Mount Pleasant until 1886—four years at Iowa Wesleyan and a year as principal of the Mount Pleasant High School. She spent part of each year with her husband in Greencastle. In 1886 Mrs. Mansfield became a member of the faculty of DePauw, where she taught until her retirement in 1910, filling a variety of positions including those of registrar, preceptress of the ladies hall (Mansfield Hall, a woman's dormitory at DePauw is named in her honor), professor of history, and dean of the school of art and music. During the years she taught at DePauw, Mrs. Mansfield continued her close association with Iowa, spending her summers in Mount Pleasant, where she lived with her brother and his family and gave lectures at the Henry County Normal Institute and at summer church assemblies.

Biographical materials about Mrs. Mansfield do not indicate any reason for her failure to move to Greencastle during her husband's teaching years at DePauw or for her return each summer to her brother's home in Mount Pleasant during her years as a member of the DePauw faculty. An obituary notice in the *Mount Pleasant Journal* at the time of John Mansfield's death in 1894 gives a clue to the problem which she faced. John Mansfield, the obituary reveals, died at the insane asylum at Napa, California. "For many years his [Mansfield's] mind has been seriously affected and it became impossible for him to remain any length of time in any one place," President John of DePauw was quoted as saying. "During all this period his heroic wife stood unflinchingly at her post as professor in DePauw University faithfully providing means by which her afflicted husband might have the best medical attention and other care which he so much needed. She has had during these dark years the sincere

2. See "First Woman Lawyer from Mt. Pleasant," *The Iowan*, summer issue, 1967. "Honor First Woman Lawyer in U.S., an Iowan," *Des Moines Register*, April 27, 1969.

sympathy of the few friends who knew her silent and secret sorrow. . . ." From that time to the present, no mention is made in any of the material about Mrs. Mansfield of the "secret sorrow" in her life.

LIZZIE BUNNELL READ

Born—Syracuse, New York, December 24, 1834; *died*—Fayetteville, Arkansas, May 16, 1909.

LIZZIE BUNNELL READ was elected president of the Iowa Woman Suffrage Association at its third annual convention in Des Moines in March 1873. She was unable to attend the meeting, however, because a heavy snowstorm blocked the roads in northern Iowa. A picture of Mrs. Read, titled "President Iowa Woman's Suffrage Society" bravely shines forth on the bottom of page 74 of Andreas' *Atlas of Iowa* (1875)—the only woman's picture among the more than 200 men portrayed in this large volume.

Mrs. Read's greatest contribution to woman suffrage was through her writing, especially in the *Mayflower,* which she published in Indiana during the Civil War, and in the *Woman's Standard,* the paper Mrs. Callanan established in 1886. Mrs. Read's contributions to the *Standard,* however, lack the sparkle and freshness of her earlier writing.

Essentially an introvert, Lizzie Bunnell Read became increasingly withdrawn as she grew older. "She is fond of friends, and likes an occasional venture into society, but generally prefers to look on from a retired background," states an Iowa *Biographical Dictionary* published in 1878. "Contact with many people, she thinks robs her of herself; makes her tired and exhausted; disturbs and breaks up her electrical atmosphere; takes away from her more than she is able to get in return at the time, though subsequent digestion restores the equilibrium and generally shows something gained."   .

In 1897, a few years after her husband's death, Mrs. Read moved to Arkansas where she passed away in 1909.

Mrs. Read (perhaps because she was a partisan of the American Woman Suffrage Association) received only passing notice in the Iowa chapter of Miss Anthony's and Mrs. Stanton's *History of Woman Suffrage;* and no mention is made of her whatsoever in the material on Indiana, although her paper, the *Mayflower,* which she published while living in that state, was a unique contribution to the woman's rights movement. Among the books and papers left in Mrs. Callanan's home at the time it was sold for a mental hospital in 1904 were thirty-one issues of the *Mayflower,* which are now in the possession of the author. Only two other copies of this paper are preserved. These are in the Indiana Historical Society.

NETTIE SANFORD CHAPIN

Born—Portage County, Ohio, March 28, 1830; *died*—Marshalltown, Iowa, August 20, 1901.

NETTIE SANFORD of Marshalltown, whose sponsorship of the antifree-love resolution at the 1871 Iowa woman-suffrage convention brought her much credit for having smoked out the free lovers at this meeting. was subsequently persona non grata with both the liberals and the conservatives in the Iowa association. In 1873, she attended the third annual convention of the Iowa Woman Suffrage Association in Des Moines, at which Mrs. Bloomer again presided. "The old fight of the last convention was brought up again and much bad blood and more bad feeling engendered thereby," reported the *Des Moines Register*. Mrs. Sanford's name is notable for its absence from the list of the sixteen officers elected by this convention.

In October 1875 Mrs. Sanford began publication of a semimonthly paper —*The Ladies Bureau*—devoted to "Society Matters, Equal Rights and Reform," which continued publication until November 1877. At this time Mrs. Sanford, a widow since 1873, went to California, where she published the *San Gabriel Valley News* for six months. However, this venture failed, and she returned to Marshalltown with only $20 in her pocket. From 1879 to 1886 Mrs. Sanford lived in Washington, D.C., where she worked as a clerk in the Treasury Department and also served as a special correspondent for Iowa papers. Selections from her dispatches were later published in book form under the title *American Court Gossip or Life at the National Capitol*.

Upon her return to Iowa in 1886 Mrs. Sanford married E. N. Chapin, editor of the *Marshall County Times*. In May 1888 Nettie Sanford Chapin embarrassed the regular suffrage forces in Iowa when she chaired a national convention of the Equal Rights Party—a group of woman's rights extremists— which met in the YMCA in Des Moines. This meeting, which the *Des Moines Register* quipped, "made up in enthusiasm what it lacked in numbers," nominated Mrs. Belva Lockwood, a Washington, D.C., lawyer and woman-suffrage advocate, for its candidate for president of the United States. Iowa suffragists promptly disavowed any connection with this convention.[3]

A maverick all her life, Nettie Sanford Chapin wrote an *anti*prohibition tract in 1890 titled "The Iowa Cranks," which (according to her obituary) she published under her husband's name on the advice of an Episcopal minister.

In her later years, Mrs. Sanford was active in the Women's Relief Corps of the GAR. At the time of her death in 1903 she was engaged in publishing *The Pioneer,* a monthly paper devoted to Marshall County history.

ANNIE N. SAVERY

Born—London, England, 1831; *died*—New York City, April 14, 1891.

THE CAMPAIGN of 1872 marked the end of Annie Savery's work for the Iowa Woman Suffrage Association. At the annual convention of the Association held in Des Moines in March 1873, Mrs. Harbert read a letter from Mrs. Savery written from Washington, D.C. In this letter, concluding "Yours for harmony and unity," Mrs. Savery expressed the hope that women would "not continue to take counsel of their *fears* and by their lack of moral courage prove that they were not yet ready for the ballot."

In March of the following year Mrs. Savery—as a spectator—attended the rally of the Polk County Woman Suffrage Society, held in the hall of

3. Victoria Woodhull (a resident of England since 1877 and married to the wealthy and highly respectable Englishman, John Biddulph Martin) was also—for the fourth time—a candidate for president of the United States in 1888.

the House of Representatives, which was addressed by Mrs. Harbert and Senator Converse. When called for by the audience, Mrs. Savery consented to speak. "I made a rather happy extemporaneous address," wrote Annie Savery to Amelia Bloomer after the meeting. "At any rate, I got the applause at which Mrs. Harbert rejoiced." In her impromptu speech, which received widespread newspaper coverage, Mrs. Savery praised the Grangers for their liberal attitude toward women and took the antimonopolists to task for ignoring their claims to the ballot. "The anti-monopolists are opposed to bank monopolies and all other monopolies, but fail to discern that the greatest of all monopolies is the ballot monopoly," Mrs. Savery told her audience.

Although inactive in Iowa woman-suffrage affairs after 1872, Mrs. Savery continued her association with the National Woman Suffrage Association for several years. She attended its convention in Washington, D.C., in January 1873, and as late as 1878 her name is listed as a member of the executive committee of the National Association. (Such a position was often nominal.) In March 1874 Mrs. Savery wrote Amelia Bloomer that she was thinking of going to Michigan (where a woman-suffrage referendum was to be held in the fall) to help with the campaign there. There is no record, however, of whether or not Mrs. Savery actually did campaign in Michigan.

Annie Savery's broad vision, her daring and imagination, as well as her willingness to use her personal wealth to put her ideas into action led her into a multifaceted effort to improve the status of women. In 1871 she organized the Iowa-Italian Bee Company in partnership with Ellen Tupper, an Iowa woman who was a nationally known apiarist. Mrs. Savery supplied the capital for the operation—$10,000—and Mrs. Tupper, the know-how. At the national bee convention in Cincinnati that fall Mrs. Savery explained that she had undertaken the business as an example to other women, both rich and poor. Despite an auspicious beginning the Iowa-Italian Bee Company soon ran into trouble, and it probably came to a sudden end in March 1874 when a fire in the Savery home destroyed the hives which were wintering in the basement.

While in Washington during the winter of 1873 Mrs. Savery sought appointment to the position of United States Consul to Le Havre, France. She solicited and received the recommendation of the entire Iowa delegation to Congress and also congressmen from five other states. This bold step on Mrs. Savery's part raised a new storm of protest among her enemies in Iowa. In answer, in part, to these people Mrs. Savery explained her purpose in seeking the position in her letter, which was read to the annual convention of the Iowa Woman Suffrage Association in March of that year: "The interest of the cause demands an advanced step on the part of women, instead of being discouraged at theoretical reverses. . . . The wisdom of the step I will leave with you. It is quite enough for me personally that my petitioners are those who sit high among the governing class . . . and when such a jury have decided that woman is fitted, and entitled to positions of this kind, I feel that whether or not successful *at this time* . . . I can well afford, in behalf of women, to be used as a test by the heroic men of the Republican party, and can endure the assaults and selfishness of its mercenary partisans. The individual is nothing; but *woman,* to whom this special recognition of her rights belongs, is *everything*."

When Mrs. Savery's bid for a foreign post was rejected, she turned to the study of law, not with the intention of entering active practice, but to understand and trace the history of the rights of women more fully. She attended the law school at the University of Iowa during the 1874–1875 session (law was a one-year course at that time), graduating with honors in a class of seventy-two men and two women.[4] Her dissertation "Woman's Relation to Civil Government," delivered at the graduation ceremonies in June 1875, was printed in full in the *Des Moines Register*. Mrs. Savery's law school diploma along with her certificate of admission to the Iowa bar are preserved in the Iowa State Historical Building in Des Moines (presented by Mary Savery, Mr. Savery's second wife).

Personal troubles dogged Mrs. Savery all during the 1870's. In March 1874 her elegant home in Des Moines burned and she lost most of her wardrobe (including gowns and laces from Paris); her library, one of the finest in the state, was badly damaged; many works of art were damaged or destroyed; an expensive watch stolen; and the safe in the house broken into by looters, and all her silver taken. With no insurance and unable to rebuild, the Savery's moved into rooms in the Savery Hotel. "Of course I feel the loss of my home very much but I don't intend to let it grieve me," Annie Savery wrote to Amelia Bloomer soon after the fire. Mrs. Savery said her friends and acquaintances in Des Moines had been so kind and sympathetic since her misfortune as to quite surprise her. She would never again think the world—so called—cold and selfish. "Every house has been opened to us with pressing invitations to come and spend weeks with them. You would smile if you knew from all sources and people these invitations come, some of them you think my enemies. 'Oh Thestorides, of all things hidden from the knowledge of man, there is nothing so incomprehensible as the human heart,' " Mrs. Savery once again exclaimed.

The depression in the late 1870's brought financial disaster to her husband James Savery, and in October 1878 he and Mrs. Savery along with B. F. Allen, who had also lost his fortune (Mrs. Allen died the previous year), went to Montana. Within a few years Savery had recouped enough to come back to Des Moines, where in partnership with James Callanan he bought the assets of the American Emigrant Company, a business with which he had been associated since the 1850's. As in the past the Saverys continued to spend a great deal of time in the East. They established a residence in New York about 1883, but they continued to consider Des Moines their real home.

During the last fifteen years of her life Mrs. Savery devoted a great deal of time to the study of religion, joining with the Theosophists in their exploration of the thought of the great religious leaders of the world—both oriental and occidental. Her studies convinced her that there was a life after death and that those who studied faithfully to understand God and to live up to His highest teachings would be advanced in the afterlife beyond those who failed to understand and practice those teachings fully.

These religious convictions sustained Annie Savery during the last years of her life when, because of heart trouble, her health rapidly declined.

4. The first woman to be graduated from the University of Iowa Law Department was Miss Mary B. Hickey of Newton, who received her degree in 1873. The next two women to be granted law degrees from this university were Mrs. Savery and her classmate Mrs. Mary Emily Haddock of Iowa City, who were graduated in 1875.

Death had no fears for her—it was simply a transition to a purer, higher, better life—and she talked about it with a cheerfulness which amazed her friends. She only regretted that she had accomplished so little in this life.

When Mrs. Savery died in April 1891, her body was brought back to Des Moines for burial. In accordance with her wishes there was no sign of mourning at her funeral, which was held in parlors in the new Savery Hotel.[5] Friends and neighbors in Des Moines decorated the parlors with an abundance of smilax and red roses which festooned the archways and windows and even hung from the door knobs. The pallbearers wore roses on their sleeves in place of crepe, and each woman was given a rose as an expression of appreciation for her sympathy and kindness. After a short religious service old friends of Mrs. Savery's paid tribute to her. Judge Hubbard of Cedar Rapids, who spoke at length about Mrs. Savery's life, introduced his remarks by saying that since Mrs. Savery "believed that she would be present on this very occasion, observing all that we might do and listening to all that we shall say of her," he would speak of her with the assumption that she was present and would endeavor to say nothing that he would not say in her earthly presence.

The Des Moines papers devoted an unusual amount of space to Mrs. Savery at the time of her death. Her obituary in the *Des Moines Register* was a full column long, and the account of her funeral occupied three columns. The *Des Moines Leader* devoted an equal amount of space. In addition to her eulogies in these papers the *Des Moines Capital* honored her with an editorial, and the *Des Moines News* paid her a glowing tribute.

"In the earlier years of the city she was the moving spirit in literary circles—ambitious to make society what it should be—a coming together for mutual exchange of thought, to lift the burden of care and to elevate mankind," said the *Des Moines Capital* in its tribute to Annie Savery.

"She grasped any problem with a comprehension which could only come from habits of study rare among men and women . . ." said the *Des Moines Leader.* "In Des Moines she is remembered for her first modest home on Second Street . . . but much more for the hospitality of her home on Grand Avenue. Here she was accustomed to entertain old and young, rich and poor, and all with a freedom and cordiality which marked her as a friend of all."

"It will be old Des Moines that will stand about the grave," the *Des Moines News* said. "But young and new in Des Moines will gain worthiness and grace by turning aside from its daily pursuits to learn from the story of Anna N. Savery how much one person can do for the happiness of others, and how effectively large heartedness works in promoting a noble style of character and helpful modes of living. There were many elements of strength in Mrs. Savery's character," the *News* said. "Naturally brilliant and forceful, she added to unusual inborn energy a social grace and power that was extraordinary. Though a native of London, Mrs. Savery was truly American and genuinely western in spontaneous and hearty enthusiasms that America and the West develop."

5. The original Savery Hotel which James Savery lost in 1878 was later renamed the Kirkwood. The new Savery, predecessor to the present Savery Hotel, was built in 1877.

Mrs. Savery's "benevolences were very extensive but were almost always in secret," said the *Des Moines Register*. "She had an open hand and a ready purse for deserving charity, and was never without many protégés. Her contributions to educational and charitable institutions were large and numerous. . . . Her relatives and friends who were many, always found Mrs. Savery a generous benefactor. In recent years she has been very liberal in her contributions to religious institutions in New York although not a member of a church herself."

"She had a strong vigorous mind and never hesitated to grapple with any problem and solve it; *yet she was very far from a strong-minded woman* [emphasis added] and her tastes were domestic and always womanly," said the *Register*. "She labored for the uplifting of woman but she never became one of the extremists. . . . Her home was always tastefully furnished and indeed, the domestic side of her nature was very strong and not in the least overshadowed by her intellectual pursuits."

The *Woman's Standard*, Mrs. Callanan's suffrage paper, never mentioned the name of Annie Savery—either during her life or at the time of her death. And in all her eulogies in the daily papers there is only one direct reference to Mrs. Savery's work for woman suffrage. "She believed in and made some study of woman's suffrage and made some speeches in favor of it, but finally abandoned it as perhaps at present impractical and inexpedient," said Judge Hubbard at her funeral.

Mrs. Savery's mortal remains rest in the Savery mausoleum in Woodland Cemetery in Des Moines. If she is still watching over this world (and I have no doubt she is), may she take some satisfaction in this book which in a small measure brings to light the record of a gallant and able pioneer worker for woman suffrage in Iowa.

APPENDIX A

☙

WOMAN'S DECLARATION OF INDEPENDENCE
ADOPTED BY THE FIRST WOMAN'S RIGHTS CONVENTION
Seneca Falls, New York, July 1848

1. DECLARATION OF SENTIMENTS

WHEN, in the course of human events, it becomes necessary for one portion of the family of man to assume among the people of the earth a position different from that which they have hitherto occupied, but one to which the laws of nature and of nature's God entitle them, a decent respect to the opinions of mankind requires that they should declare the causes that impel them to such a course.

We hold these truths to be self-evident: that all men and women are created equal; that they are endowed by their Creator with certain inalienable rights; that among these are life, liberty, and the pursuit of happiness; that to secure these rights governments are instituted, deriving their just powers from the consent of the governed. Whenever any form of government becomes destructive of these ends, it is the right of those who suffer from it to refuse allegiance to it, and to insist upon the institution of a new government, laying its foundation on such principles, and organizing its powers in such form, as to them shall seem most likely to effect their safety and happiness. Prudence, indeed, will dictate that governments long established should not be changed for light and transient causes; and accordingly all experience hath shown that mankind are more disposed to suffer while evils are sufferable, than to right themselves by abolishing the forms to which they are accustomed. But when a long train of abuses and usurpations, pursuing invariably the same object, evinces a design to reduce them under absolute despotism, it is their duty to throw off such government, and to provide new guards for their future security. Such has been the patient sufferance of the women under this government, and such is now the necessity which constrains them to demand the equal station to which they are entitled.

The history of mankind is a history of repeated injuries and usurpations on the part of man toward woman, having in direct object the establishment of an absolute tyranny over her. To prove this, let facts be submitted to a candid world.

He has never permitted her to exercise her inalienable right to the elective franchise.

He has compelled her to submit to laws, in the formation of which she had no voice.

He has withheld from her rights which are given to the most ignorant and degraded men—both natives and foreigners.

Having deprived her of this first right of a citizen, the elective franchise, thereby leaving her without representation in the halls of legislation, he has oppressed her on all sides.

He has made her, if married, in the eyes of the law, civilly dead.

He has taken from her all right in property, even to the wages she earns.

He has made her, morally, an irresponsible being, as she can commit many crimes with impunity, provided they be done in the presence of her husband. In the covenant of marriage, she is compelled to promise obedience to her husband, he becoming, to all intents and purposes, her master—the law giving him power to deprive her of her liberty, and to administer chastisement.

He has so framed the laws of divorce, as to what shall be the proper causes, and in case of separation, to whom the guardianship of the children shall be given, as to be wholly regardless of the happiness of women—the law, in all cases, going upon a false supposition of the supremacy of man, and giving all power into his hands.

After depriving her of all rights as a married woman, if single, and the owner of property, he has taxed her to support a government which recognizes her only when her property can be made profitable to it.

He has monopolized nearly all the profitable employments, and from those she is permitted to follow, she receives but a scanty remuneration. He closes against her all the avenues to wealth and distinction which he considers most honorable to himself. As a teacher of theology, medicine, or law, she is not known.

He has denied her the facilities for obtaining a thorough education, all colleges being closed against her.

He allows her in Church, as well as State, but a subordinate position, claiming Apostolic authority for her exclusion from the ministry, and, with some exceptions, from any public participation in the affairs of the Church.

He has created a false public sentiment by giving to the world a different code of morals for men and women, by which moral delinquencies which exclude women from society, are not only tolerated, but deemed of little account in man.

He has usurped the prerogative of Jehovah himself, claiming it as his right to assign for her a sphere of action, when that belongs to her conscience and to her God.

He has endeavored, in every way that he could, to destroy her confidence in her own powers, to lessen her self-respect and to make her willing to lead a dependent and abject life.

Now, in view of this entire disfranchisement of one-half the people of this country, their social and religious degradation—in view of the unjust laws above mentioned, and because women do feel themselves aggrieved, oppressed, and fraudulently deprived of their most sacred rights, we insist that they have immediate admission to all the rights and privileges which belong to them as citizens of the United States.

In entering upon the great work before us, we anticipate no small amount of misconception, misrepresentation, and ridicule; but we shall use every instrumentality within our power to effect our object. We shall employ agents, circulate tracts, petition the State and National legislatures, and endeavor to enlist the pulpit and the press in our behalf. We hope this Convention will be followed by a series of Conventions embracing every part of the country.

2. RESOLUTIONS

Whereas, The great precept of nature is conceded to be, that "man shall pursue his own true and substantial happiness." Blackstone in his Commentaries remarks, that this law of Nature being coeval with mankind, and dictated by God himself, is of course superior in obligation to any other. It is binding over all the globe, in all countries and at all times; no human laws are of any validity if contrary to this, and such of them as are valid, derive all their force, and all their validity, and all their authority, mediately and immediately, from this original; therefore,

Resolved, That all laws which prevent woman from occupying such a station in society as her conscience shall dictate, or which place her in a position inferior to that of man, are contrary to the great precept of nature, and therefore of no force or authority.

Resolved, That woman is man's equal—was intended to be so by the Creator, and the highest good of the race demands that she should be recognized as such.

Resolved, That the women of this country ought to be enlightened in regard to the laws under which they live, that they may no longer publish their degradation by declaring themselves satisfied with their present position, nor their ignorance, by asserting that they have all the rights they want.

Resolved, That inasmuch as man, while claiming for himself intellectual superiority, does accord to woman moral superiority, it is pre-eminently his duty to encourage her to speak and teach, as she has an opportunity in all religious assemblies.

Resolved, That the same amount of virtue, delicacy, and refinement of behavior that is required of woman in the social state, should also be required of man, and the same transgressions should be visited with equal severity on both man and woman.

Resolved, That the objection of indelicacy and impropriety, which is so often brought against woman when she addresses a public audience, comes with a very ill-grace from those who encourage, by their attendance, her appearance on the stage, in the concert, or in feats of the circus.

Resolved, That woman has too long rested satisfied in the circum-scribed limits which corrupt customs and a perverted application of the

Scriptures have marked out for her, and that it is time she should move in the enlarged sphere which her great Creator has assigned her.

Resolved, That it is the duty of the women of this country to secure to themselves their sacred rights to the elective franchise.

Resolved, That the speedy success of our cause depends upon the zealous and untiring efforts of both men and women, for the overthrow of the monopoly of the pulpit, and for the securing to women an equal participation with men in the various trades, professions and commerce.

Resolved, therefore, That, being invested by the Creator with the same capabilities, and the same consciousness of responsibility for their exercise, it is demonstrably the right and duty of woman, equally with man, to promote every righteous cause by every righteous means; and especially in regard to the great subjects of morals and religion, it is self-evidently her right to participate with her brother in teaching them, both in private and in public, by writing and by speaking, by any instrumentalities proper to be used, and in any assemblies proper to be held; and this being a self-evident truth growing out of the divinely implanted principles of human nature, any custom or authority adverse to it, whether modern or wearing the hoary sanction of antiquity, is to be regarded as a self-evident falsehood, and at war with mankind.

APPENDIX B

REPORT OF THE 1870 IOWA WOMAN-SUFFRAGE CONVENTION AT MOUNT PLEASANT

In *The Revolution,* July 1870

Iowa Up and Doing —Proceedings of the State Convention —Mr. E. A. Studwell's Reception

MOUNT PLEASANT, IOWA, Friday, June 17.

The State Woman's Suffrage Association convened in this city yesterday. Mount Pleasant, you know, has been named by visitors as well as natives, the "Athens of the West," and with good reason.

Nearly every county of the State had its representatives, and, with the local attendance, filled Sander's Hall to overflowing.

OPENING OF THE MEETING

The meeting was called to order by I. B. Teter, presiding elder of the Methodist Church in this vicinity, and opened with prayer by the Rev. Mr. Broderick. The veteran reformer, Joseph A. Dugdale, was chosen temporary chairman. The above-mentioned gentleman was the prime mover in the Convention—an old Garrisonian Abolitionist, and loved and reverenced by all who know him. E. A. Vancise, a lawyer of some repute, was then chosen Secretary. After this a Committee was appointed on Permanent Organization, and, while the committee were out, Attorney-General O'Connor was called upon for a speech, and for half an hour succeeded in carrying the audience with him. He was both eloquent and earnest, and reminded his listeners of Phillips in his palmiest days. The Committee on Organization reported the following persons:

THE ORGANIZATION

PRESIDENT—Mrs. Belle Mansfield of Mount Pleasant.
VICE-PRESIDENTS—Dr. Holmes of Muscatine, and several others.
SECRETARIES—Frank Hatton, Editor *Mount Pleasant Journal*, and Mr. Lowry of Marshall County.

Mrs. Mansfield, on taking the Chair, was received with great applause, showing her popularity, which seems to have resulted more from an earnest strength of purpose than any real eloquence the lady might bring to the platform. She then thanked the association in a few well-timed remarks for their kindness and preference, and the society proceeded to business.

Another committee was appointed to consider the expediency of forming a State organization, and to report a constitution for same.

Hon. Charles Beardsley, editor, *Burlington Hawkeye*, was appointed Chairman of a committee on business, or, more properly speaking, on resolutions. The Chair, in selecting the names, added Miss Susan B. Anthony, who was expected to be present. The mention of this name brought to her feet an old worker of national fame [Amelia Bloomer], who desired to know why Miss Anthony's name should be thrust upon the State, or upon its business committee. She hoped and believed that the State had workers enough to engineer their own Convention, as well as do their own speaking. These indications of personal pique and animosity did not pass unobserved by the attentive and intelligent audience, and the lady, although well-known and highly respected by the citizens of Mount Pleasant, did not add a single feather to her cap, by this strange assumption of superiority.

Thus early the young and gifted chairman was compelled to contend with a combative element, annoying if nothing more. Elder Teter objected to having the president made accountable for this choice of name. After a long and rambling debate, with reconsiderations and amendments *ad libitum*, reminding us of your New York gatherings, a committee was appointed with Mrs. Amelia Bloomer as its chairman.

PERSONAL

During this excitement, Mrs. Dr. Tracy Cutler of Ohio, the representative of the American Society, was busily engaged taking notes, with her "friends" in a body at her back, acting in concert. At the left of the speakers Edwin A. Studwell was seated between Elder Teter and Friend Dugdale, watching every contest with a coolness that inspired the friends of the Union Society with confidence, although their forces were not acting in concert, and were seriously scattered. At the adjournment of the morning session, Mr. Studwell greeted Mrs. Cutler with an air reminding one of a prize-ring contest, where the antagonists shake hands before they encounter.

AFTERNOON SESSION

The Unionists had apparently been drilled by someone between the sessions, for when Mr. Beardsley reported the constitution and moved its adoption, it was found to be nearly word for word that of the Union Suffrage Society. When the committee on resolutions reported through its chairman, Mrs. Bloomer found, much to her astonishment, that she had introduced a resolution concerning the organization of a state association, but too late; the convention had adopted its constitution and also appointed a committee on permanent officers, again with the Hon. Mr. Beardsley as its chairman. During the absence of the committee Mrs. Cutler delivered an able address, crammed with logic and careful study, at the close of which the committee reported the following officers for the state Society, which were accepted:

ANOTHER ORGANIZATION

PRESIDENT—Hon. Henry O'Connor, Vice-President of the Union W. S. S.
VICE-PRESIDENTS—Amelia Bloomer, Joseph A. Dugdale, and many others.
RECORDING SECRETARY—Mrs. Belle Mansfield.
CORRESPONDING SECRETARY—Mrs. J. C. Savery.
TREASURER—L. W. Vale.
EXECUTIVE COMMITTEE—Mrs. Prof. M. A. P. Darwin, Hon. Chas. W. Beardsley, and others.

Mr. Beardsley was selected as Chairman of the Committee and also represented the Executive Committee of the Union Suffrage Society.

So far the Convention seemed pledged to "Union." The ground had again been pretty thoroughly canvassed between the sessions, wires had been silently pulled from the commencement, individuals gently led to their duty, and all was now apparently going to the tune of marriage bells. It was now just discovered by the majority of the audience that Mr. Studwell was present, and loud calls for a speech were heard on every side. The gentleman was, however, *non est comatibus* and Mrs. Bloomer took up the time by a manuscript address, followed by Mrs. Cutler and others.

MORNING SESSION

Hall again crowded. Vociferous calls for Studwell, and strangely enough, at the same time, yells were heard for "Susan," "Susan," "Miss Anthony," and then again Studwell. It was rumored through the audience that the old maid had at last succumbed to Cupid in the person of Studwell, but it was afterwards contradicted, as the gentleman is at least twenty-five years her junior and married at that. At this late hour of the convention, the ablest woman of our State, so considered by friends and enemies, Mrs. Prof. Mary A. P. Darwin, of Burlington College, spoke for at least an hour, and was listened to eagerly during the whole time. This lady is a natural logician, as well as an eloquent speaker, reminding one of Mrs. Stanton in her best efforts. At the conclusion, Col. George B. Corkhill, of Mount Pleasant, said:

Mrs. President—I am sure that no one in this large audience who has listened to the eloquent words we have just heard, can fail to appreciate in the highest degree the importance of the subject, and the cause so ably and earnestly defended by the lady who has just addressed us. Such a speech, so forcible in argument, so eloquent in appeal, and so beautiful in delivery, must of necessity command not only the attention and consideration of all who heard it, but will afford food for reflection that will bear fruit after this convention has adjourned.

FORTHCOMING SPEECHES

I learn, Mrs. President, that Mrs. Darwin intends speaking throughout the State of Iowa on the Suffrage question, under the auspices of the Union Woman's Suffrage Society, and that Mr. Edwin A. Studwell, with his proverbial clear-headedness, has appointed her as the general agent of *The Revolution* in this State. I am also informed that you, Mrs. President, and Mrs. R. Anna Canby, have generously offered your services to promote the circulation of that journal in this locality.

THE RESOLUTION

Mrs. Darwin intends, not only addressing the masses of the people in conventions, but to endeavor to see that in each home in our State a copy of the valuable paper is taken. Those who are oldest and most experienced in this movement deem it important to the success of the cause that *The Revolution,* so ably edited and conducted, should be disseminated broadcast throughout the State. I do not claim to speak with any authority on this subject, but from the remarks of those around me here, and from the fact that Mrs. Darwin, who is a member of the executive committee of their State Association, has undertaken in her love for the cause, to specially circulate this paper in the state, and that you, Mrs. President, and your associate, Mrs. Canby, have undertaken to represent it specially here in our own community, I presume it is recognized by you all as your special favorite, advocate, and representative paper. I therefore offer the following resolution, and move its adoption:

Resolved, That this convention heartily endorse the steps taken by Mrs. Prof. Darwin, as the general agent of *The Revolution* in this State, and trust she will be as fortunate in other localities in finding earnest working friends as have been secured for this city in the persons of Mrs. Belle Mansfield and Mrs. R. Anna Canby.

The resolution was unanimously adopted.[1]

1. Mrs. Cutler's account of this incident as reported to the *Woman's Journal* is as follows: "The State society had declared itself independent, but after Mrs. Darwin's speech a resolution was introduced, commending Mrs. Darwin to the confidence of the people of Iowa, and stating that she would travel through the State, and organize societies, acting at the same time as the agent of the Union Suffrage Society and *The Revolution.* The resolution was passed without thought by the audience, but directly Rev. Wm. Cole of Mt. Pleasant rose, and proposed that any agent of the *Woman's Journal* should be received with like confidence and cordiality. This was proposed, and then Mrs. Cutler proposed the *Advocate,* published at Dayton, and a Western paper, which was also adopted."

OBJECTIONS TO WOMAN'S SUFFRAGE

At this juncture the President wished to hear from any person in the audience who objected to the ballot for women. Loud calls for "Palmer," "Judge Palmer," resounded through the hall. At last the Judge took the platform and argued for an hour against Woman's Suffrage. His remarks seemed to be honest and free from the least taint of demagoguism. It was then arranged that the above-mentioned gentleman should argue the point after recess with Mrs. Cutler. The hall was again crowded. The Judge did well, but Mrs. Cutler did better—and brilliantly vanquished her opponent.

Thus ended a convention of five crowded sessions, which was complete in its conception, its constitution, and its officers.

BIBLIOGRAPHY

✿

THIS BIBLIOGRAPHY has three objectives: to indicate the sources which formed the basis for this book, to serve as a tool for other historians of the woman's rights movement, and to convey to the general reader some of the interest and excitement which the author experienced in locating material.

NEWSPAPERS AND PERIODICALS

Newspapers

For purposes of simplicity and clarity the place of publication has been substituted for official names of newspapers where these names do not indicate the place of publication; e.g., *Des Moines Register* for *Iowa State Register, Iowa City State Press* for *Iowa State Press, Marshalltown Times* for *Marshall County Times.*

Approximately fifty Iowa newspapers were searched for the information which forms the framework of this study. The *Des Moines Register* was consistently the most useful. Other papers which carried important parts of the Iowa woman's rights story are the *Marshalltown Times,* the *Dubuque Times,* the *Independence Bulletin,* the *Council Bluffs Nonpareil,* the *Mount Pleasant Journal,* and the *Burlington Hawkeye.* The largest collection of Iowa newspapers is in the Iowa State Department of History and Archives in Des Moines. The State Historical Society of Iowa at Iowa City also has a valuable collection. For the most part, papers not available in these collections are on microfilm. Exceptions are the *Mount Pleasant Journal* which is in the library of Iowa Wesleyan College at Mount Pleasant, and the *Council Bluffs Times* and the *Council Bluffs Republican* which are in the free public library in Council Bluffs. A search for information about the woman-suffrage bill presented to the Iowa legislature in 1866 by John Crookham of Oskaloosa led to the Antiquarian Society, Worcester, Massachusetts, where a single issue of the *Oskaloosa Herald* (Jan. 25, 1866) in the Society's collection carries a letter from Crookham explaining his reasons for proposing woman suffrage.

Out-of-state newspapers which provided useful information include the *New York Times,* the *New York Herald,* the *New York Tribune,* the *New York World,* the *Washington* (D.C.) *Star,* the *Chicago Tribune,* the *Chicago Journal* and the *Chicago Legal News.* [A file of the *Legal News* is in the Iowa State Law Library.]

Reform and Religious Periodicals

American Phrenological Journal
Banner of Light [spiritualist]
Boston Investigator [free thought]
Golden Age
National Anti-Slavery Standard
New York Independent
The Liberator [antislavery]
The Standard [successor to the *National Anti-Slavery Standard*]
Religio-philosophical Journal [spiritualist]
Water-Cure Journal [health]

Woman's Rights Periodicals

The Agitator. Chicago, Mar. 13, 1869–Jan.. 1870. [Merged with the *Woman's Journal.*]

The Chicago Sorosis. Cynthia Leonard and Delia Waterman, eds. Chicago, 1868. [This was probably a short-lived paper. Vol. 1, no. 1, Dec. 12, 1868, is in the collection of the Chicago Historical Society.]

The Ladies Bureau. Nettie Sanford, ed. Marshalltown, Iowa, Oct. 6, 1875–Nov. 1877. [A single issue of this paper, dated Feb. 29, 1876, is in the collection of the Chicago Historical Society. A clipping from vol. 1, no. 1 is in the woman-suffrage collection, Iowa Department of History and Archives.]

The Lily. Seneca Falls, N.Y.; Mount Vernon, Ohio; and Richmond, Ind., Jan. 1849–Dec. 15, 1856.

The Mayflower. Peru and Columbia City, Ind., 1861–1864. [Microfilm, Schlesinger Library, Radcliffe College.]

The Revolution. New York City, Jan. 1868–Feb. 1872.

The Sorosis. M. L. Walker, ed. Chicago, Oct. 1868–Mar. 1869. [Merged with *The Agitator.* Vol. 1, no. 7, Nov. 14, 1868; and vol. 1, no. 12, Dec. 19, 1868, are in the collection of the Chicago Historical Society.]

The Una. Providence, R.I., and Boston, Feb. 1853–Oct. 1855. [Bound volume is in the State Traveling Library, Historical Building, Des Moines.]

Woman Citizen. 1917–1927. [Successor to the *Woman's Journal.*]

Woman's Advocate. New York City, Jan. 1869–May 1870.

The Woman's Hour. Des Moines, 1887–1888. [A weekly paper published by the Polk County Woman Suffrage Association. Two issues of this paper are in the woman-suffrage collection, Iowa Department of History and Archives: vol. 1, no. 1, Sept. 26, 1877; vol. 2, no. 3, Sept. 17, 1878.]

Woman's Journal. Boston, Jan. 1870–May 1917.

Woman's Standard. Des Moines, Sutherland, and Waterloo, Iowa, Sept. 1886–Nov. 1911. [Bound volumes of this paper, 1886–1908, are in the Newspaper Division, Iowa Department of History and Archives, Des Moines. Unbound copies, 1908–1911, are in the woman-suffrage collection, Iowa Department of History and Archives, Des Moines.]

Woodhull and Claflin's Weekly. New York City, May 1870–June 1876.

BOOKS, ARTICLES, AND THESES

General Background

Beecher, Catherine E., and Stowe, Harriet Beecher. *The American Woman's Home; or, Principles of Domestic Science; Being a Guide to the Formation and Maintenance of Economical, Healthful, Beautiful, and Christian Homes.* New York, 1869.

Bestor, Arthur Eugene. *Backwoods Utopias.* Univ. of Pa. Press, 1950.

Bowers, Claude G. *The Tragic Era.* Cambridge, Mass., 1929.

Branch, E. Douglas. *The Sentimental Years, 1830–1860.* New York, 1934.

Brockett, L. P., M.D. *Men of Our Day.* Philadelphia, 1869.

Caldwell, Martha B. "The Attitude of Kansas toward Reconstruction of the South." Ph.D. dissertation, Univ. of Kans., 1933. Unpublished.

Calhoun, Arthur W. *A Social History of the American Family.* New York, 1918.

Commager, Henry Steele. *The Era of Reform, 1830–1860.* Princeton, N.J., 1960.

Croly, Mrs. J. C. *The History of the Woman's Club Movement in America.* New York, 1898.

Curti, Merle. *The Growth of American Thought.* New York, 1943.

Degler, Carl N. *Out of Our Past, the Forces that Shaped Modern America.* New York, 1959.

Donald, David. *The Politics of Reconstruction, 1863–1867.* La. State Univ. Press, 1965.

Filler, Louis. *The Crusade against Slavery, 1830–1860.* New York, 1960.

Foner, Philip S. *Frederick Douglass.* New York, 1950.

Gillette, J. William. "The Power of the Ballot: The Politics of the Passage and Ratification of the Fifteenth Amendment." Ph.D. dissertation, Princeton Univ., 1963. Unpublished.

Hibben, Paxton. *Henry Ward Beecher, an American Portrait.* New York, 1927.

Holbrook, Stewart H. *Dreamers of the American Dream.* New York, 1957.

Lomask, Milton. *Andrew Johnson: President on Trial.* New York, 1960.

Martin, E. W. *History of the Grange Movement or the Farmer's War against Monopoly.* Saint Louis, 1873.

Miller, Marian Mills, ed. *Great Debates in American History,* vols. 7, 8, *Congressional Debates on Woman Suffrage and Negro Suffrage, 1866–1872.* New York, 1913.

Nevins, Allan. *The Emergence of Modern America, 1865–1878.* New York, 1927.

Nichols, Thomas Law. *Forty Years of American Life, 1821–1861.* New York, 1937.

Nordhoff, Charles. *The Communistic Societies of the United States.* New York, 1875.

Noyes, John Humphrey. *History of American Socialisms.* Philadelphia, 1870.

Parke, Michael St. John. *The Life of John Stuart Mill.* New York, 1954.

Shaplen, Robert. *Free Love and Heavenly Sinners.* New York, 1954.

Stampp, Kenneth M. *The Era of Reconstruction.* New York, 1965.

Thomas, John L. *The Liberator, William Lloyd Garrison.* Boston, 1963.

Tyler, Alice Felt. *Freedom's Ferment.* Univ. of Minn. Press, 1944.

General Background, Iowa

Andreas, A. T. *Illustrated Historical Atlas of the State of Iowa.* Chicago, 1875.

Bergmann, Leola N. "The Negro in Iowa." *Iowa Journal of History,* vol. 46, Jan. 1948.

Berrier, G. Galin. "The Negro Suffrage Issue in Iowa—1865–1868." *Annals of Iowa,* vol. 39, ser. 3, spring 1968.

Blair, Laird W., ed. *Debates of the Constitutional Convention of the State of Iowa Assembled at Iowa City, Monday, January 19, 1857.* Davenport, Iowa, 1857.

Bloomer, D. C. "Notes on the History of Pottawattamie County." *Annals of Iowa,* vol. 9, 1871; vol. 10, 1872; vol. 11, 1873; vol. 12, 1874.

Brigham, Johnson. *History of Des Moines and Polk County.* Chicago, 1911.

Brown, Harriet Connor. *Grandmother Brown's Hundred Years—1827–1927.* Boston, 1929.

Chapin, Mrs. E. N. (Nettie Sanford Chapin). *American Court Gossip or Life at the National Capitol.* Marshalltown, Iowa, 1887.

Chapin, E. N. *Iowa Cranks; or, The Beauties of Prohibition.* Marshalltown, Iowa, 1893. [This booklet was written by Nettie Sanford Chapin but published under her husband's name.]

Cowles, Florence Call. *Early Algona. The Story of Our Pioneers, 1854–1874.* Des Moines, 1929.

Dixon, J. M. *The Valley and the Shadow, Comprising the Experiences of a Blind Ex-editor, Literary Biography, Humorous Autobiographical Sketches, a Chapter on Iowa Journalism.* New York, 1868.

Gallaher, Ruth A. "The Liquor Merry-Go-Round." *Palimpsest,* vol. 14, June 1933.

Gue, Benjamin F. *History of Iowa,* 4 vols. New York, 1903.

Hansen, Millard W. "Early History of the College of Law." *Iowa Law Review,* vol. 30, Nov. 1944.

Hussey, Tacitus. *Reminiscences of Early Des Moines.* Des Moines, 1919.

Ingham, Harvey. *Father Taylor, a Story of Missionary Beginnings,* [n.p., n.d.] [Education in Algona.]

———. *The Algona Bee, a Story of Newspaper Beginnings,* [n.p., n.d.]

Iowa Census—1850, 1856, 1860, 1870, 1880. Unpublished.

Iowa Historical and Comparative Census, 1836–1880. Des Moines, 1883.

Iowa Supreme Court Decisions. 1 Iowa (1849) through *35 Iowa* (1872).

Journals of the House of the Territory of Iowa. 1 T. A. (1838) through 8 T. A. (1846).

Journals of the Council of the Territory of Iowa. 1 T. A. (1838) through 8 T. A. (1846).

Journals of the House of the State of Iowa. 1 G. A. (1848) through 14 G. A. (1873).

Journals of the Senate of the State of Iowa. 1 G. A. (1848) through 14 G. A. (1873).

Laws of the Territory of Iowa. *Statute Laws,* 1838–1839; *Session Laws,* 1840–1846. (Reprint, Des Moines, 1912).

Laws of the State of Iowa. *Session Laws,* 1 G. A. (Jan. 3, 1848) through 14 G. A. (Jan. 15, 1873, adjourned session); *Code 1851; Revision of 1860; Code 1873.*

Legislative Supplement. Des Moines Bulletin, Jan. 10, 1870–Apr. 12, 1870. Des Moines, 1870.

Martin, Dick. "Paradise Valley: The Remains of E. G. Potter's Unique Empire, Built One Hundred Twenty-Two Years Ago Near Bellevue, Includes Iowa's First Library." *The Iowan,* vol. 13, winter 1964–1965.

Mills, Frank Moody. *Early Days in a College Town . . . with Autobiographical Reminiscences.* Sioux Falls, S.D., 1929.

———. *Something about the Mills Family and its Collateral Branches with Auto-biographical Reminiscences.* Sioux Falls, S.D., 1911.

Phillips, Semira A. *Mahaska County: A Story of the Early Days.* Oskaloosa, Iowa, 1900.

Quick, Herbert. *One Man's Life.* Indianapolis, 1925.

Ross, Earle A., ed. *Diary of Benjamin Gue in Rural New York and Pioneer Iowa, 1847–1856.* Iowa State Univ. Press, 1962.

Ross, Russell M. "The Development of the Constitution of 1857," and "Contemporary Editorial Opinion of the 1857 Constitution." *Iowa Journal of History,* vol. 55, Apr. 1957.

Shambaugh, Benjamin F. *The Constitutions of Iowa.* State Historical Society of Iowa, Iowa City, 1934.

Smith, Olive Cole. *Mt. Pleasant Recalls Some of the Happenings of Her First Hundred Years.* Mount Pleasant, Iowa, 1942. [The author is the daughter of Rev. William R. Cole.]

Stanton, Gerrit Smith. *When the Wildwood Was in Flower. A Narrative Covering the Fifteen Years Experiences of a Stockman on the Western Plains.* New York, c. 1909. [The author is the son of Elizabeth Cady Stanton.]

State of Iowa Official Register, 1941–1942. Des Moines, 1942. [This volume is useful because of the list of members of the General Assembly from 1846–1941.]

Stiles, Edward H. *Recollections and Sketches of Notable Lawyers and Public Men of Early Iowa.* Des Moines, 1916.

Woman's Christian Temperance Union of Iowa. Annual reports, 1875–1890. Published in Cedar Rapids with the exception of 1877, 1878, Iowa City; 1879, Burlington; 1880, 1881, 1882, 1884, Des Moines.

[County histories have also proved an invaluable source of information.]

Lecturing

Bode, Carl. *The American Lyceum*. New York, 1906.

Hoeltje, Hubert H. "Notes on the History of Lecturing in Iowa, 1855–1885." *Iowa Journal of History and Politics,* vol. 25, Jan. 1927.

————. "Ralph Waldo Emerson in Iowa." *Iowa Journal of History and Politics,* vol. 25, Apr. 1927.

————. "Some Iowa Lectures and Conversations of Amos Bronson Alcott." *Iowa Journal of History and Politics,* vol. 29, July, 1931.

Holland, J. G. *Plain Talks by J. G. Holland*. New York, 1883.

Pond, James Burton. *Eccentricities of Genius, Memories of Famous Men and Women of the Platform and Stage*. New York, 1900.

Wright, Luella M. "Culture through Lectures." *Iowa Journal of History and Politics,* vol. 38, Apr. 1940.

Marriage, Morals, and Sex

Andrews, Stephen Pearl, ed. *Love, Marriage, and Divorce and the Sovereignty of the Individual: A Discussion by Henry James, Horace Greeley, and Stephen Pearl Andrews*. New York, 1853.

Banks, J. A., and Banks, Olive. *Feminism and Family Planning in Victorian England*. New York, 1964.

Ditzion, Sidney. *Marriage, Morals, and Sex in America*. New York, 1953.

Ellis, John B. *Free Love and Its Votaries*. New York, 1870.

Foote, E. B., M.D. *Plain Home Talk and Medical Common Sense*. New York, 1868. [This book (page 921) reprints the following endorsement from *The Revolution:* "It should not be a *sensational* work, but it is, and *must* be, for the reason that it treats of the social, sexual, marital, and parental relations *as no other has.* . . . It is a book which everybody who sees will seize, read, and devour, and then probably secretly approve in the main, if openly condemning."]

Fryer, Peter. *The Birth Controllers*. New York, 1966.

Himes, Norman E. *Medical History of Contraception*. Baltimore, 1936.

Powell, Aaron M. *State Regulation of Vice*. New York, 1878.

Trall, R. T. *Sexual Physiology: A Scientific and Popular Exposition of the Fundamental Problems in Sociology*. New York, 1866. [A copy of this book is in the library of E. G. Potter, Iowa pioneer and free thinker who came to the state in 1842.]

Vreeland, Francis McLennon. "The Process of Reform with Especial Reference to Reform Groups in the Field of Population." Ph.D. dissertation, Univ. of Mich., 1929. Unpublished.

Religion and Free Thought

Chapin, Rev. Augusta. "History of the Universalist Church of Iowa." [This document was placed in the cornerstone of the Iowa City Universalist Church, Jan. 12, 1873, and is now in the collection of the State Historical Society of Iowa, Iowa City.]

Cross, Whitney R. *The Burned-Over District: The Social and Intellectual History of Enthusiastic Religion in Western New York, 1800–1850*. Cornell Univ. Press, 1950. [Excellent discussion of spiritualism.]

Marty, Martin E. *The Infidel, Freethought, and American Religion.* Cleveland, 1961.

Proceedings of Congregational Friends, Waterloo, N.Y., June 4–6, 1849; June 3–5, 1850; June 1–3, 1851. [Society of Friends, Records Committee, 15 Rutherford Place, New York, N.Y.]

Proceedings of Congregational Friends. Waterloo, N.Y., 1857. [A letter "signed on behalf of the Meeting of Progressive Friends held at Eden, Clinton County, Iowa, by Weltha Mix, May 18, 1857," is printed in this report. Society of Friends, Records Committee, 15 Rutherford Place, New York, N.Y.]

Putnam, Samuel P. *Four Hundred Years of Free Thought.* New York, 1894.

Tucker, Elva L. "History of the Universalist Church in Iowa, 1843–1943." M.A. dissertation, Univ. of Iowa, 1944. Unpublished.

Wahl, Albert J. "The Progressive Friends of Longwood." *Bulletin of Friends Historical Society,* vol. 32, spring 1953.

Worrell, Emma. "Memories of Longwood Meeting." *Friends Intelligencer,* vol. 75, Aug. 31, 1918.

Woman's Work in the Civil War

Brockett, L. P., and Vaughan, Mary C. *Woman's Work in the Civil War.* Philadelphia, 1867.

Fullbrook, Earl S. "Relief Work in Iowa during the Civil War." *Iowa Journal of History and Politics,* vol. 16, 1918.

Gallaher, Ruth A. "Annie Turner Wittenmyer." *The Palimpsest,* vol. 33, Apr. 1957.

———. "Annie Turner Wittenmyer." *Iowa Journal of History and Politics,* vol. 29, 1931.

Livermore, Mary E. *My Story of the War.* Hartford, 1892.

"Mrs. Ann E. Harlan." *Annals of Iowa,* vol. 2, ser. 3, Oct. 1896.

Moore, Frank. *Women of the War.* Hartford, 1866.

Young, Agatha. *The Women and the Crisis.* New York, 1959.

Antiwoman-Suffrage Literature

Beecher, Catherine E. *A Treatise on Domestic Economy.* Boston, 1843. [Chapter 1, "The Peculiar Responsibilities of American Women," is an antiwoman's rights argument.]

———. *Woman Suffrage and Woman's Profession.* Hartford, Conn., 1871.

Brockett, L. P. *Woman: Her Rights, Wrongs, Privileges, and Responsibilities, including . . . Woman Suffrage, Its Folly and Inexpediency, and the Injury and Deterioration which It Would Cause in her Character.* Hartford, 1870.

Bushnell, Horace. *Women's Suffrage: The Reform against Nature.* New York, 1869.

Curts, Ariana Wormeley. *The Spirit of Seventy-Six; or, The Coming Woman, A Prophetic Drama.* "A Play Written for Amateur Performance." Chestnut Hill, Mass., Mar. 1868. [Copy in University of Iowa Libraries.]

Fowler, O. S. *Creative and Sexual Science . . . As Taught by Phrenology and Physiology,* n.p., 1870.

The True Woman. [A periodical published in Baltimore from March 1871 to October 1873. Widener Library, Harvard University.]

Woman's Rights—History and Arguments

Bjorkman, Frances M., and Poritt, Annie G., eds. *Woman Suffrage: History, Arguments, and Results.* New York, 1916.

Booth, Edmund. "Reminiscences of Twenty-Seven Years Ago." *Annals of Iowa,* vol. 9, July 1871.

Bull, Mary S. "Woman's Rights and other 'Reforms' in Seneca Falls." *Good Companion,* vol. 5, 1880.

Catt, Carrie Chapman. *Then and Now.* New York, 1939. [Speech.]

Catt, Carrie Chapman, and Shuler, Nettie Rogers. *Woman Suffrage and Politics.* New York, 1923.

Claflin, Tennessee. *Constitutional Equality, a Right of Woman.* New York, 1871.

Coggeshall, Mary Jane. *History of the Polk County Woman Suffrage Association (1870–1895).* [Manuscript in the Woman Suffrage Collection, Iowa Department of History and Archives.]

———. "Woman's Suffrage Society," in Will Porter, *Annals of Polk County, Iowa, and City of Des Moines.* Des Moines, 1898, ch. 34.

Cutler, Mrs. H. M. Tracy, M.D. *Phillipia, or a Woman's Question.* Dwight, Ill., 1886.

Davis, Paulina W., ed. *A History of the National Woman's Rights Movement for Twenty Years [1850–1870] with the Proceedings of the Decade Meeting Held at Apollo Hall, October 20, 1870; with an Appendix Containing the History of the Movement during the Winter of 1871 in the National Capitol.* New York, 1871.

Dixon, J. M. "Woman Suffrage Association," *Centennial History of Polk County, Iowa.* Des Moines, Iowa, 1876, pp. 239–41.

Finch, Marianne. *An Englishwoman's Experience in America.* London, 1853.

Flexner, Eleanor. *Century of Struggle.* Harvard Univ. Press, 1959.

Gallaher, Ruth A. *Legal and Political Status of Women in Iowa.* State Historical Society of Iowa, Iowa City, 1918.

Harbert, Lizzie Boynton. *Out of Her Sphere.* Des Moines, 1871.

Harper, Ida Husted. *History of Woman Suffrage.* Vols. 5, 6, New York, 1922. [Iowa chapter in vol. 6 by Flora Dunlap.]

Harper, Ida Husted, and Anthony, Susan B. *History of Woman Suffrage.* Vol. 4, 1902. [Iowa chapter by Clara M. Richey.]

Hooker, Isabella B., Tilton, Theodore, et al. "Extracts, Letters, and Remarks . . . Intended for Circulation among the Friends (only) of Victoria Woodhull—In No Wise for the General Public." [Pamphlet probably published by Victoria Woodhull, 1871. Olympia Brown papers, Schlesinger Library, Radcliffe College.]

Horack, Frank E. "Equal Suffrage in Iowa," in Benjamin F. Shambaugh, ed., *Applied History,* vol. 2. State Historical Society of Iowa, Iowa City, 1914.

Hunter, Mrs. Fred, Crowley, Mrs. Fred, Lingenfelter, Mrs. E. A., et al. "Iowa Suffrage Memorial Commission." *Annals of Iowa,* vol. 14, ser. 3, Apr. 1924.

"Letters Written by John P. Irish to George F. Parker." *Iowa Journal of History and Politics,* vol. 31, July 1933.

Mill, John Stuart. *The Subjection of Women.* Philadelphia, 1869. [A copy of this book, presented to the author by B. D. Crane of Mount Pleasant, Iowa, was purchased by Orson Van Cise at the Crane Book Store in Mount Pleasant in 1869 and bears the following inscription: "July 30th, 1869. I know that you, Watson and Lizzie, are as much interested in the success of the cause herein advocated as Your bro. Orson."]

Miller, Helen Hill. *Carrie Chapman Catt: The Power of an Idea.* Carrie Chapman Catt Memorial Fund, 1958, pamphlet.

Report of the International Council of Women Assembled by the National Woman Suffrage Association, Washington, D.C., March 25–April 1, 1888. Washington, D.C., 1888. [This volume contains many reminiscences of woman's rights pioneers.]

Riegel, Robert E. *American Feminists.* Univ. of Kans. Press, 1963.

Robinson, Harriet H. *Massachusetts in the Woman Suffrage Movement.* Boston, 1881.

Stanton, Elizabeth Cady, Anthony, Susan B., and Gage, Matilda Joslyn. *History of Woman Suffrage.* New York, vol. 1, 1881; vol. 2, 1882; vol. 3, 1887. [Iowa chapter in vol. 3 by Amelia Bloomer, edited by Elizabeth Cady Stanton.]

Strachey, Ray. *The Struggle. A Short History of the Women's Movement in Great Britain.* London, 1928.

Studwell, Edwin A., and Canby, R. A. *Dottings from the Writings of Margaret Fuller Ossoli.* Brooklyn, 1869.

Train, George Francis. *The Great Epigram Campaign of Kansas.* Leavenworth, Kans., 1867, pamphlet. [Copy in Rare Book Room, Library of Congress with comment in longhand by Susan B. Anthony.]

Victory: How Women Won It—1840–1940. New York, 1940. [A centennial symposium published by the National American Woman Suffrage Association.]

Volume of woman-suffrage tracts, 1870. [State Traveling Library, Des Moines.]

Volume of woman-suffrage documents with index in Martha Callanan's handwriting, 1848–1871. [Includes a copy of the antifree-love resolution adopted by the Polk County Woman Suffrage Association, Nov. 2, 1871; and "Political Justice," a lecture delivered before the Polk County Woman Suffrage Association by Louis Rutkay, Dec. 20, 1870. State Traveling Library, Des Moines.]

Walker, Mary E., M.D. *Hit.* New York, 1871.

Woodhull, Victoria Claflin. *The Origin, Tendencies, and Principles of Government: A Review of the Rise and Fall of Nations from Early Time to the Present, with Special Consideration Regarding the Future of the United States as the Representative Government of the World.* New York, 1871.

Woodhull, Victoria Claflin, and Claflin, T. C. *The Human Body the Temple of God: or The Philosophy of Sociology, together with other Essays, etc., and Press Notices of the Extemporaneous Lectures Delivered throughout America and England from 1869 to 1882.* London, 1910.

Biographies of Women

SUSAN B. ANTHONY:
Dorr, Rheta Childe. *Susan B. Anthony.* New York, 1928.
Harper, Ida Husted. *The Life and Work of Susan B. Anthony.* Vols. 1, 2, Indianapolis, 1898; vol. 3, Indianapolis, 1908.
Lutz, Alma. *Susan B. Anthony, Rebel, Crusader, and Humanitarian.* Boston, 1959.

CATHERINE E. BEECHER:
Harveson, Mae Elizabeth. *Catherine Esther Beecher, Pioneer Educator.* Philadelphia, 1932.

AMELIA BLOOMER:
Bloomer, D. C. *Life and Writings of Amelia Bloomer.* Boston, 1895.
"Character and Biography of Amelia Bloomer." *American Phrenological Journal,* vol. 17, Mar. 1853.
Jordon, Philip D. "Amelia Jenks Bloomer." *The Palimpsest,* vol. 33, Apr. 1957.
Keatley, John H. "Amelia Bloomer." *Annals of Iowa,* vol. 12, July 1874.

CARRIE CHAPMAN CATT:
Peck, Mary Gray. *Carrie Chapman Catt.* New York, 1944.

ELIZABETH BUFFUM CHACE:
Chace, Lillie Buffum, and Wyman, Arthur Crawford. *Elizabeth Buffum Chace.* Boston, 1914.

CORDELIA THROOP COLE:
Throop, Addison James, ed. *George Addison Throop; Deborah Goldsmith, Ancestral Charts.* Compiled by Olive Cole Smith. East St. Louis, Ill., 1934. [This volume contains correspondence of Cordelia Throop Cole and her husband William R. Cole, 1846–1863.]

HANNAH TRACY CUTLER:
Burleigh, Celia. "People Worth Knowing: Mrs. H. M. Tracy Cutler." *Woman's Journal,* July 6, July 30, Aug. 6, Sept. 24, 1870.
Cutler, Hannah M. Tracy. "Reminiscences of Early Woman Suffrage Work." *Woman's Journal,* Sept. 19, Sept. 26, Oct. 3, Oct. 10, 1896.

ANNA DICKINSON:
Chester, Giraud. *Embattled Maiden, the Life of Anna Dickinson.* New York, 1951.

ISABELLA BEECHER HOOKER:
Stowe, Lyman Beecher. *Saints, Sinners, and Beechers.* Indianapolis, 1934.

JULIA WARD HOWE:
Howe, Julia Ward. *Reminiscences, 1819–1889.* Boston, 1900.

MARY LIVERMORE:
Livermore, Mary A. *The Story of My Life*. Hartford, 1899.

BELVA LOCKWOOD:
Kerr, Laura. *The Girl Who Ran for President*. New York, 1947.

ARABELLA MANSFIELD:
Williams, M. Romdall. "From Mount Pleasant; Nation's First Woman Lawyer." *The Iowan*, vol. 15, summer 1967.

LUCRETIA MOTT:
Cromwell, Otelia. *Lucretia Mott*. Harvard Univ. Press, 1958.
Hallowell, Anna Davis, ed. *James and Lucretia Mott, Life and Letters*. Boston, 1884.

ERNESTINE ROSE:
Suhl, Yuri. *Ernestine L. Rose and the Battle for Human Rights*. New York, 1959.

ANNIE SAVERY:
"Annie N. Savery." *Annuals of Iowa*, vol. 16, ser. 3, Oct. 1928.

ANNA HOWARD SHAW:
Shaw, Anna Howard, D.D., M.D. *The Story of a Pioneer*. New York, 1915.

ELIZABETH CADY STANTON:
Lutz, Alma. *Created Equal, a Biography of Elizabeth Cady Stanton*. New York, 1940.
Stanton, Elizabeth Cady. *Eighty Years and More*. New York, 1898.
Stanton, Theodore, and Blatch, Harriot, eds. *Elizabeth Cady Stanton as Revealed in Her Letters, Diary, and Reminiscences*. New York, 1922.

LUCY STONE:
Blackwell, Alice Stone. *Lucy Stone, Pioneer of Woman's Rights*. Norwood, Mass., 1930.
Hays, Elinor Rice. *Morning Star, a Biography of Lucy Stone*. New York, 1961.

JANE G. SWISSHELM:
Larsen, Arthur J., ed. *Crusader and Feminist, Letters of Jane Grey Swisshelm*. Minnesota Historical Society, 1934.
Swisshelm, Jane Grey. *Half a Century*. Chicago, 1880.

MARY WALKER:
Snyder, Charles McCool. *Dr. Mary Walker*. New York, 1962.

FRANCES WILLARD:
Earhart, Mary. *Frances Willard*. Univ. of Chicago Press, 1944.

VICTORIA WOODHULL:

Sachs, Emanie. *The Terrible Siren, Victoria Woodhull, 1838–1927*. New York, 1928.

Tilton, Theodore. "The Golden Age Tracts No. 3. *Victoria Woodhull. A Biographical Sketch by Theodore Tilton.*" New York, 1871. Pamphlet.

Dictionary of American Biography, 20 vols., supplements and index. New York, 1928 to date.

Gue, Benjamin F. "Biographical Sketches of Notable Iowa Men and Women." *History of Iowa*, vol. 4, New York, 1903.

Hanaford, Phoebe. *Daughters of America*, n.p., 1882.

Hanson, E. R. *Our Woman Workers. Biographical Sketches of Women Eminent in the Universalist Church.* Chicago, 1881.

"Men and Women of Iowa Biographies." Scrapbook series. 1909 to date. [Public library of Des Moines.]

Parton, James; Greeley, Horace et al. *Eminent Women of the Age.* Hartford, 1869.

Reeves, Winona Evans, ed. *The Blue Book of Iowa Women.* Mexico, Mo., 1914.

Stowe, Harriet Beecher, and Cooke, Rose Terry. *Our Famous Women.* Hartford, 1884.

Thorp, Margaret Farrand. *Female Persuasion, Six Strong-Minded Women.* Yale Univ. Press, 1949.

United States Biographical Dictionary and Portrait Gallery of Eminent and Self-made Men. Iowa vol. New York, 1878. [Information about wives is included in many of the biographical sketches.]

Willard, Frances E., and Livermore, Mary A., eds. *American Women—Fifteen Hundred Biographies.* New York, 1897.

[See also biographies of women in the Woman Suffrage Collection, Iowa State Department of History and Archives, Des Moines.]

LETTERS, DOCUMENTS, AND SCRAPBOOKS

Free Public Library, Council Bluffs, Iowa

Amelia Bloomer scrapbook.

Approximately 100 letters written to Amelia Bloomer including:

Henry Blackwell (Boston, Feb. 8, 1870).

Mrs. A. Frazier (Leon, Iowa, April 3, 1870) which reads in part:

I notice in the *Woman's Journal* that you are our Iowa Vice-president for the American Woman Suffrage Association. We are living so far south no one ever seems to think of us for we have not heard but very little about the woman suffrage movement. A few of us are trying to organize a woman's club, not under the name of woman's rights however. We want to meet and talk over our household affairs and discuss various topics so that we may learn to express our opinions publicly, as men do, according to our abilities. Would it be asking too much of you to write something to be read in our meeting for our encouragement and inspire into our little body more energy to go ahead and carry on our undertaking? Women have demanded a good deal of the Iowa Legislature. Now they demand of us that we do what we can to carry them out in what they have done for us. . . . Let us work with a will.

Martha Brown Haven (Des Moines, Mar. 12, 1870).
Mary A. Livermore (Chicago, Nov. 15, 1870).
J. L. Loomis (Independence, Iowa, Apr. 26, 1870).
Eleven letters from Annie Savery (Des Moines, Dec. 11, 1869; Dec. 19, 1869; Jan. 25, 1870; Feb. 6, 1870; Feb. 10, 1870; Feb. 14, 1870; Mar. 1, 1870; Mar. 26, 1870; Apr. 12, 1870; Mar. 1, 1871; Apr. 23, 1874). Mrs. Savery's letter of Feb. 14, 1870, reads in part:

I have said that I lectured only on compulsion. I now wish to say that I feel inwardly compelled to stump this State pretty thoroughly in the next two years. This question must be discussed by every man, woman, and child, before another Session. It *must be,* and dear Mrs. Bloomer, I hope you will be spared in the full vigor of your intellect to see this cause, in which you startled the people of Iowa fourteen years ago, finally triumphant in all demands! The Angels are whispering to me that we will prevail. . . . I do not know but you will smile at my enthusiasm, but it is a fact that I cannot talk upon this subject and have my pulses keep their wanted time. . . .

And now there is another matter which just occurs to me. In a former letter you spoke of not entertaining in style. I should be sorry to hear you disappointed in this respect in my house. We live in a cottage that was built twelve years ago, hence you can readily imagine that it cannot be extra fine. *Au contraire!* It is plain, but comfortable. For twelve years I have been travelling with Mr. Savery a good part of the time; abroad two years, and in New York or Washington every winter. Our house has been rented nine years out of that twelve. *I need say no more!* Therefore expect to find a plain house and a plain woman, but a warm welcome.

Three letters from Lucy Stone (Kennebunkport, Maine, Aug. 19, 1869; Waverly, N.Y., Feb. 13, 1870; New York City, May 16, 1870).

Friends Historical Library of Swarthmore College, Swarthmore, Pennsylvania

Dugdale correspondence including:
   Lydia Maria Child (Wayland, Mass., May 30, 1870). [Letter to Joseph Dugdale along with a message for the Iowa Woman Suffrage Convention.]
   Joseph Dugdale (Mount Pleasant, Jan. 15, 1870). Letter to Samuel M. Janney, which reads in part:

That thou art laboring faithfully in the responsible field assigned thee I have not a doubt and my prayers are mingled with the many friends of the oppressed and deeply wronged Aboriginees that even at this late date the remaining scattered tribes may (*many* of them at least) be preserved from utter extermination. After living to see the infamous system of American slavery thrown over the battlements and destroyed, one ought not to doubt the power of love in its all-controlling power to sway the uncivilized Indian. What a vast work is on the wheel! The next great question will be that of woman. There, not 3,000,000 but half the human race are disfranchised.

Lucretia and James Mott letters to the Dugdale family: Lucretia Mott to Sarah Dugdale (Joseph's mother), Philadelphia, Oct. 7, 1845; Lucretia Mott to Joseph and Ruth Dugdale, Philadelphia, Mar. 28, 1849; Lucretia Mott to Joseph and Ruth Dugdale, Auburn, N.Y., July 12, 1850; James Mott to Joseph Dugdale, Philadelphia, Sept. 11, 1841; James Mott to Joseph Dugdale, Philadelphia, Apr. 30, 1850.

Theodore Tilton (New York, Mar. 1870). [Note asking Ruth and Joseph Dugdale to sign accompanying appeal for formation of a Union Woman Suffrage Society.]

Grinnell College Library, Grinnell, Iowa

Record book of the "Literary Phalanx," Springdale, Iowa, 1856–1857. [The question debated on Oct. 8, 1856 was "Resolved: that the Woman Wrights [*sic*] movement is the offspring of restless and dissatisfied minds and is impracticable and subversive of the principles of Nature." Resolution was lost by a unanimous vote. The question debated on Feb. 4, 1857 was "Resolved: that we believe the doctrine of Free Love as advocated by Dr. and Mrs. Nickels (Thomas Law and Mary Gove Nichols) to be the great means of elevating and dignifying the race and hastening the good time coming when Righteousness shall cover the earth as the waters do the seas." Resolution was laid on the table following debate "to be taken up and discussed at any other time."]

Iowa State Department of History and Archives, Des Moines

Aldrich Autograph Collection:
Letter from Elizabeth Cady Stanton (New York, Apr. 5, 1866) to Amelia Bloomer.
Photographs and letters of Iowa woman-suffrage leaders, probably collected by Martha Callanan, include Mary Newbury Adams, Mary Darwin, and Rowena Guthrie Large.

Iowa Historical Library, Manuscript Division:
Mary Newbury Adams papers relating to women's clubs in Iowa prior to 1885.
Dexter Bloomer diaries and journal.
J. Callanan, Jr., scrapbook.
Corydon E. Fuller scrapbook. [Contains copy of "An Address De-

livered Before the State Convention of the Friends of Woman Suffrage," Oct. 1871.]

Annie Savery diploma, Bachelor of Law degree, State University of Iowa, 1875; certificate of admission to Supreme Court of Iowa, June 29, 1875.

Annie Wittenmyer war correspondence, 8 vols.

Record book of "Excelsior Debating Society," Anamosa, 1859. [The question debated on October 18, 1859, was "Resolved: that Woman should have the same rights and privileges as Man." Decided in favor of the negative.]

Iowa State Archives:

Petitions for woman suffrage presented to the Iowa General Assembly, 1874 and later.

Woman Suffrage Collection arranged by Mary A. Hunter (not catalogued) includes fifteen letters written to Joseph Dugdale regarding the June 1870 woman-suffrage and peace conventions in Mount Pleasant, among them:

Susan B. Anthony (Hornellsville, N.Y., May 19, 1870).

Joel Bean (West Branch, Iowa, May 8, 1870). [Joel Bean and his wife Hannah were neighbors of Herbert Hoover's grandparents and teachers of his parents, Jesse and Huldah Hoover.] His letter reads in part:

Thy letter of 24 ult. is before me. It was very kind in thee to remember us in connection with the proposed meeting. It will not be practicable for us to be in Mt. Pleasant at the time thou mentioned. . . . On the subject of Peace our sympathies are with all its advocates. . . . On the other subject, that of Woman's Suffrage, we are not yet ourselves proselytes to the movement. We might possibly get *convinced ourselves* but could not help at all in convincing others, by being with you. It is a movement with which I have had little to do, either in advancing or opposing, but have honest doubts about the fitness of wives and mothers entering the arena of politics and offices of State. I have my fears about it amounting almost to anxiety as to the result, but while I see the many good people entertaining a different view and strongly advocating it, I gather what comfort I can from the thought that their sight may be clearer, and their judgment better than mine on this subject, which is indeed one of great magnitude. . . .

Amelia Bloomer (Council Bluffs, Iowa, May 7, 1870).

J. L. Loomis (Independence, Iowa, June 14, 1870).

Henry O'Connor (Des Moines, May 10, 1870).

Other material in the Woman Suffrage Collection includes: Letter from Lucy Stone (New York, Nov. 13, 1869) to B. F. Gue urging him to come to the Cleveland meeting of the American Woman Suffrage Association; letters from Carrie Chapman Catt (1930–1939) to Mary A. Hunter; records of the Iowa Woman Suffrage Association (1887–1920) including minutes of the first meeting of the Iowa League of Women Voters; photographs, biographies, and reminiscences of Iowa woman-suffrage workers; newspaper clippings.

Library of Congress, Washington, D.C.

Susan B. Anthony diaries.

Blackwell papers:

Correspondence of Henry Blackwell and Lucy Stone written during the Kansas campaign of 1867.

Letters from Margaret Campbell to members of the Blackwell family, including: Lucy Stone (Des Moines, July 30, 1890); Alice Stone Blackwell (Joliet, Ill., Feb. 25, 1907); Henry Blackwell (Des Moines, May 14, 1900). The May 14 letter reads in part:

> We have been obliged to look on during the session of the Legislature in Iowa the past winter to see many things done that we abhorred and that was a misrepresentation of most of the suffragists of the State. I could not help wondering what Lucy Stone would have thought to have seen the special representative of the cause she gave her life to promenading in low neck and arms bare to the shoulder, at the Governor's reception, only a few days before the vote was taken in the House. It was common talk about town that the exhibition lost us four votes. . . . I have tried to keep silence but my heart has been sore grieved. . . .

Carrie Chapman Catt papers, including letters and photographs.

Anna Dickinson papers. Giraud, in *Embattled Maiden,* says of Anna Dickinson's last days:

> Six days before her ninetieth birthday, on October 22, 1932, two weeks before Franklin D. Roosevelt was elected President, Anna Dickinson, a frail, withered, defeated, forgotten woman drew her last breath, without heirs, without fame, without friends. Forgotten by public and history, she was quietly laid to rest. . . . Yet with her sense of history and drama, Anna must have known that someday her story would be told and her career resurrected. In all the long years of solitude and longing, of ever-deepening obscurity . . . Anna held on to all the records of the past that retold her life and that she alone possessed—the clippings, the letters, the memorabilia. . . . [Fortunately the probate judge in Orange County, N.Y., who was confronted with the task of disposing of these documents sensed their historical value and offered them to the Library of Congress.]

The Dickinson papers include the following letters which are pertinent to this book:

Susan B. Anthony (Lawrence, Kans., Sept. 23, 1867) to Anna Dickinson.

Edwin Lee Brown, Corresponding Secretary Associated Western Literary Societies (Chicago, Sept. 13, 1866) to Anna Dickinson.

Ruth Dugdale ("Near Mt. Pleasant," Iowa, Mar. 29, 1868) to Anna Dickinson.

Elizabeth Boynton Harbert (Crawfordsville, Ind., Sept. 20, 1868) to Anna Dickinson.

Mary E. M. McPherson (Iowa City, Mar. 9, 1869) to Anna Dickinson.

Anna Dickinson (Iowa City, Sept. 29, 1869) to her mother, Mary Dickinson:

Here I are—a speech made last night—a speech to be made tonight.—I slept so long—I ate at such a time—and took a little drive—I was cooked in such a hall—So I will only send kind regards. [A postcript to this note reads]: "I have had two regular bona fide offers this summer—one from a M.C. [The M.C. was William B. Allison of Dubuque who was elected Senator from Iowa in 1872.]

Anna Dickinson (Ottumwa, Iowa, May 23, 1871) to her mother:

I will say, here and now, for the benefit of whom it may concern, and for future reference in the writing of a book on natural history, that in the item of *fleas*, the biggest, strongest and finest it was ever my unhappy fate to meet, do literally swarm in this house. . . .

At Mt. Pleasant . . . I spent a pleasant little time with my friends, the Dugdales. I drove out with them in the afternoon to see their mother who lives with a married daughter seven miles in the country. . . . The son and daughter are old Pennsylvania farmers and it was pleasant to see their home "porched" as we say at home, round the house, covered with vine—doors and windows wide open—fine damask table cloth, such butter and cottage cheese and cream and fruit and homemade bread as are to be gotten nowhere out of a Pennsylvania-bred farmer's home (of the right sort).

There is nothing to tell of Ottumwa. . . . It too, is *Western* in the ugly way. More grog shops than grocery stores. . . . Nine thousand people in the place and but one school. My audience was a decent one as to numbers—concerning the intelligence and culture, I have nothing to say since it possessed neither.

Anna Dickinson (Grinnell, Iowa, May 26, 1871) to her mother:

I had a most delightful audience,—almost the first that has really pleased me since I came into the State. The town is thoroughly New England. That is one thing. Another is they are all enthusiastic about "Billy" [William Allison] for their next Senator and they apparently think it is a good thing to be decidedly in the good grace of their "next Senator's lady,"—as one of the city fathers informed me, with gravity becoming so momentous a statement. All this tickles me hugely, seeing that I would as soon marry our John as Billy. . . .

Anna Dickinson (Cedar Rapids, Iowa, May 30, 1871) to her mother:

At Marshalltown I fell into another "Quaker Meeting" half my audience seemingly being of that method of faith—were very nice people and very devoted to me—which, of course, demonstrated them sensible. . . .

National-American Woman Suffrage Association papers; letters and reports. Elizabeth Cady Stanton papers.

National Archives, Washington, D.C.

Four petitions to Congress from Iowa citizens asking for woman suffrage, referred: Jan. 29, 1869; Apr. 7, 1869; Feb. 14, 1870; Feb. 1, 1871.
One petition to Congress from Iowa women protesting the extension of suffrage to women, referred: Mar. 12, 1872.

New York Historical Society, New York City

Amelia Bloomer letters, including:
Amelia Bloomer (Council Bluffs, Feb. 9, 1872) to Mrs. R. A. S. Janney:

At the time of the passage of the Resolution two years ago and even up to six months ago, the friends of the cause were very sanguine of success both in the Legislature and at the polls. . . . But I am sorry to say that the cloud now rests upon us here as everywhere. . . .

New York Public Library

Carrie Chapman Catt papers, including a manuscript copy of a speech, "Zenobia," which was Mrs. Catt's first public lecture in 1887.

Radcliffe College, Cambridge, Massachusetts: The Arthur and Elizabeth Schlesinger Library on the History of Women in America

Olympia Brown papers, including material relating to the Kansas campaign of 1867 and the Chicago woman-suffrage convention, February 1869.
Elizabeth Boynton Harbert papers, including:
Letter from Mary Livermore (Boston, summer 1872, first page missing) to Mrs. Harbert concerning the defeat of woman suffrage in the Iowa legislature.
Scrapbook.
Letter from Lucy Stone (Cincinnati, Ohio, June 14, 1870) to her lecture agent, Charles Mumford, stating that she wanted bookings in Iowa and Michigan during the coming lecture season.

Seneca Falls Historical Society, Seneca Falls, New York

Amelia Bloomer papers, including:
Two speeches in longhand and sewn into booklet form.
J. L. Loomis letter (Independence, Iowa, Oct. 14, 1871) to Amelia Bloomer concerning the October 1871 Iowa woman-suffrage convention.
Letters from Susan B. Anthony and Elizabeth Cady Stanton to Amelia Bloomer concerning the Iowa chapter of the *History of Woman Suffrage*.
Letters from Iowa women to Amelia Bloomer in response to her request for material for the Iowa chapter of the *History of Woman Suffrage*.
Miscellaneous letters from Iowa women, for example, Mrs. P. G. Orwig (Des Moines, Dec. 31, 1875) to Amelia Bloomer:

I shall answer your *last* question *first*. Viz: Why did I not make myself, and my interest in the cause, known to you when you were so often in our city? Ans: Because I was under a cloud through my husband's misfortunes, and the ladies of Des Moines who were prominent in the suffrage movement *did not want me.* . . . Mrs. James Savery was my next door neighbor but she never thought of inviting me to call upon you as her guest or even asking me to take part in the suffrage cause. . . . But I never blamed Mrs. Savery. She only acted as the others did. And although I never admired her very much as a neighbor—I gave her due credit for what she accomplished in behalf of suffrage. She worked *nobly,* and was treated shamefully! I could have cried with mortification in that convention over which you presided with such Christian dignity and womanly consistency! But it would have availed nothing—those women were a disgrace to the name and sex. And yet *MONEY* not *brains* . . . has carried Mrs. James Callanan to the very head of the movement. . . ."

Smith College Library, Northampton, Massachusetts: Sophia Smith Collection

Letters relating to Miss Anthony's and Mrs. Stanton's visit to Iowa in June 1871:
Susan B. Anthony (Rochester, N.Y., May 30, 1871) to Martha Wright.
Susan B. Anthony (Sioux City, Iowa, June 14, 1871) to Martha Wright:

I think this from Mrs. Hooker . . . will interest you. What efforts more than Herculean [on the part of the Boston faction] to save themselves from contamination from touching even the hem of the Woodhull garments. It is too sick!! When will they begin the *washing* of their *men* champions and workers? It is high time.

We are having pleasant times. . . . I have with much hard work persuaded Mrs. Stanton to give all her letters to *The Revolution.* . . . She is at Council Bluffs with Mrs. Bloomer today. . . . Ask Eliza if she thinks Mrs. Stanton's 180 avoirdupois will break the back of the Yosemite Mustang? She is bound to try it anyhow. I should love to know dear Lucretia Mott's impressions of the Boston pure and unadulterated meeting.

State Historical Society of Iowa, Iowa City

Record book of "Young Men's Debating Club of Muscatine," 1853–1854. [The question debated on Jan. 7, 1854, was, "Are the Rights of Women Duly Respected in the United States?" Question was decided in the affirmative. Henry O'Connor, first president of the Iowa Woman Suffrage Association, was a member of this club.]

State Historical Society of Wisconsin, Madison, Wisconsin

Mathilde Anneke papers. [Correspondence with woman-suffrage leaders.]

State University of Iowa Libraries, Iowa City

Note written by Amelia Bloomer to editor of *Council Bluffs Nonpareil* relating to the state convention in Mount Pleasant (June 1870):

> Will you oblige me and other friends of Woman's cause as well as gratify your readers by giving place to the resolutions, constitution and list of officers enclosed—also to O'Connor's speech? If not all at one time, then separately as you may find most convenient. I shall esteem it a personal favor if you grant this request.

Vassar College Library, Poughkeepsie, New York: Alma Lutz Collection

Susan B. Anthony—Two letters written from Brown's Hotel, Cedar Rapids, Iowa, Feb. 9, 1871. One is to Mrs. Oliver Dennett thanking her for a contribution to be used toward paying off *The Revolution* debt. The other, which is to A. J. Grover, says in part:

> I with tonight's receipts shall be able to pay out the last dollar of my *interest money* for 1871 and my next check will be a *pull* down of the pile of thousands. I am sorry enough not to be in Chicago yesterday and today to help swell the chorus for *"Women already Voters under the 14th and 15th Amendments."* Oh, I am so glad Mrs. Woodhull has power to compel Congress to heed that point. Mrs. Stanton and all of us *failed* to do it last winter. . . .

INDEX

❇

Abolitionists, 8, 13n, 32, 41, 62, 83, 87, 90, 101, 104, 283; American Anti-Slavery Society, 32, 62, 79
Abortion, 81, 105, 110
Ackley, Iowa, 234
Adair County, Iowa, 86
Adams, Austin, 114, 115
Adams, Mary Newbury (Mrs. Austin), 99n, 110, 112, 113–16, 119, 139, 229, 263–64
Addams, Jane, 249
Addington, Julia, 141
Advocate (Dayton), 286n
Agitator, 107, 109, 111
Akron, Ohio, 205
Alaska Territory, 250
Albany, N.Y., 9, 150, 265
Alcott, Bronson, 8, 114
Alcott, Louisa May, 115
Algona, Iowa, 189, 256, 265
Algona Equal Rights Association, 120
Allen, Benjamin F., 126, 150, 218, 219, 275
Allen, Iowa, 234
Allen, Kitty (Mrs. Benjamin), 149, 150, 155, 157n, 218n, 275
Alta, Iowa, 234
American Anti-Slavery Society, 32, 62, 79
American Emigrant Company, 92, 275
American Equal Rights Association, (formerly American Woman's Rights Association), 38, 71, 73, 77; conventions, 38, 69, 98, 104–5, 108–9, 112–13
American Equal Rights Association of Independence, Iowa, 73, 135

American Woman's Rights Association. *See* American Equal Rights Association
American Woman Suffrage Association, 108, 109, 136–37, 139, 148, 182, 203, 265; conventions, 110–11, 136. *See also* National Association; *Woman's Journal*
Ames, Iowa, 50, 234
Anamosa, Iowa, 95
Anamosa Eureka, 41
Anderson, Keziah ("Kizzie") (Mrs. Wallace F. Dorrance), 175, 175n
Anderson, William, 175
Andrews, Stephen Pearl, 171, 177, 178, 180, 191
Anthony, Daniel, 70
Anthony, Susan B., 13n, 19, 32, 86n, 176, 193, 195n, 284–85; early years, 9–10; 1865 woman-suffrage campaign, 36–39; in Midwest, 69–71, 71n, 77, 112–13, 119, 138, 141, 180–81; in Iowa, 77, 156, 242; and *The Revolution*, 80–84, 88, 94; and Congress, 103, 172–74; and Elizabeth Cady Stanton, 104–5; and Lucy Stone, 104–8, 137; and Mary Livermore, 107–8; as lecturer, 160–62; and Victoria Woodhull, 169, 178–80, 203, 221; and Amelia Bloomer, 264–65, 266; and Iowa Woman Suffrage Association, 284–85
Anthropological Society, 264
Antimonopolists, 274
Antislavery movement, 8, 10; in Massachusetts, 4; in Iowa, 32, 50, 83;

309

Antislavery movement, *(cont.)*
American Anti-Slavery Society, 32,
62, 79; Loyal Women's League, 32,
138; Frederick Douglass, 62, 104, 105.
See also Abolitionists
Anti-Slavery Standard, 36, 79
Antisuffragists, 31, 141–42, 145, 244,
254, 256, 287
Arizona, 250
Arkansas, 272
Association for the Advancement of
Women, 229, 264; Woman's Con-
gress, 229, 271
Association of Western Literary Soci-
eties, 62
Atchison, Kans., 69
"Athens of Iowa." *See* Mount Pleas-
ant, Iowa
Aurelia, Iowa, 234
Aurora, Ill., 271

B

Babb, Washington Irving, 144
Babb, Mrs. Washington I., 95
Baker, Nathaniel B., 24
Baldwin, H. C., 23
Ballou, Mrs. Addie L., 178n
Baltimore, Md., 185
Banner of Light, 178n
Barnum, Phineas T., 62
Barton, Clara (Clarissa Harlowe), 62,
90n
"Battle Hymn of the Republic," 88,
229
Beach, Myron, 121
Beach, Mrs. Myron, 121
Beardsley, Charles, 43, 123, 139, 145–
46, 217–18, 284, 285
Beavers, Mrs. Mary A., 95, 139
Bedford South West (Taylor County,
Iowa), 175
Beecher, Henry Ward, 111, 139, 169n,
182
Beecher-Tilton scandal, 182, 182n, 185,
193
Belden, Mrs. Evelyn H., 244
Bellevue (Iowa) *Journal*, 81n
Benedict Home, Des Moines, 266,
269
Benton County, Iowa, 131
Berkeley, Calif., 116
Bird, Alice (later Mrs. Washington I.
Babb), 95
Birdsall, Mary, 152
Birth control, 81, 105, 110, 178n, 182,
184, 186, 192
Black Hawk County, Iowa, 261
Blackwell, Alice Stone, 241, 248

Blackwell, Antoinette, 229
Blackwell, Henry Brown, 69, 79, 105,
136–37, 136n, 230
Blackwell, Mrs. Henry B. *See* Stone,
Lucy
Blairstown, Iowa, 98
Blatch, Harriet Stanton, 234
Blood, James Harvey (Dr. J. A. Harvey), 170, 177, 180
Bloomer, Amelia Jenks (Mrs. Dexter),
3, 29, 83, 112, 132, 137n, 141n, 154,
182n, 229, 269; early years, 12–20;
and Susan B. Anthony, 32, 160, 161–
62, 264–65, 266; and Elizabeth Cady
Stanton, 38, 181; and Annie Savery,
94, 130, 153, 275; and Mary Adams,
99n, 263; and Lucy Stone, 108–10;
and Iowa Woman Suffrage Associa-
tion, 133–42, 188–90, 193, 207–8, 270,
273–74, 284, 285; and *The Lily*, 151,
152; and free love, 187, 268; and
Iowa General Assembly, 211, 212n
Bloomer, Dexter Chamberlain, 12, 19,
19n, 83, 141n, 178n, 181, 222
Bloomer costume, 9, 17, 19
Boone, Iowa, 49, 98, 207, 248
Boone County Advocate, 95
Boston, Mass., 8, 84, 88, 106, 111, 181,
182, 203, 229, 235, 266
Boston Transcript, 244
Bradstreet, Maria Hill (Mrs. S. Y.), 119
Bradstreet, S. Y., 119
Bradwell, Myra, 128
Brinkerhoff, Mrs. Martha H., 70, 97–
99, 99n, 112, 113, 117
Brook Farm, 8
Brooklyn, N.Y., 72, 111, 138
Brooks, James, 37, 38, 80
Brown, John, 83
Brown's Hotel, Des Moines, 161
Buchanan County, Iowa, 73, 135
Buchanan County Bulletin, 69, 73, 74,
116–17
Bullis, Henry C., 217, 218
Bunnell, Lizzie. *See* Read, Lizzie Bun-
nell
Burlington, Iowa, 63, 160; Ben and
Mary Darwin, 29, 45, 46, 96, 146,
188, 190, 268; Mary Shelton, 75, 76,
76n, 77; Elizabeth Cady Stanton,
121, 122, 123
Burlington Argus, 145
Burlington Hawkeye, 43, 63, 107, 123,
145, 268, 284
Burlington Lecture Association, 96
Burlington Telegraph, 17
Burlington University, 146, 285
Burlington Woman Suffrage Society,
32, 77, 145, 147

Business Women's Home, Des Moines, 266
Butler, Benjamin, 167, 169, 172–73
Butte, Mont., 269

C

Cady, Daniel, 7
California, 116, 142, 239, 241, 242, 250, 256, 268, 270, 271, 273
Callanan, James C., 150–51, 265, 275
Callanan, Martha Coonley (Mrs. James C.), 150–51, 155, 180, 190, 201–4, 215n, 225, 229, 232, 265–67, 272, 277
Campbell, John, 235n
Campbell, Margaret (Mrs. John), 235, 235n, 248
Canby, Mrs. R. Anna, 138, 286
Carpenter, Cyrus C., 154, 212n, 270
Case, Mary, 24
Cass County, Iowa, 86
Catt, Mrs. Carrie Chapman (née Lane) (later Mrs. George), 225–61, 240, 268, 270
Catt, George, 235
Cattell, Deborah (Mrs. Jonathan), 153–54, 155, 157
Cattell, Jonathan, 154
Cedar County, Iowa, 48, 154
Cedar Falls (Iowa) Gazette, 40
Cedar Rapids, Iowa, 83, 98, 160, 230, 243, 276
Cedar Rapids Times, 194, 206
Central Christian Church, Des Moines, 241
Cerro Gordo County, Iowa, 243
Chace, Mrs. Sarah, 184
Chapin, Augusta, 142, 147, 163
Chapin, E. H., 194n, 273
Chapin, Mrs. E. H. See Sanford, Nettie
Chapman, Leo, 228, 231, 243
Charles City, Iowa, 227, 232, 248, 254
Cherokee, Iowa, 180, 234
Chester County, Pa., 134
Chicago, Ill., 106–7, 107n, 112, 122, 143, 150, 189, 205, 220, 270
Chicago Interocean, 143, 228, 248, 270
Chicago Journal, 125
Chicago Legal News, 128
Chicago Post, 218
Chicago Tribune, 107n, 116, 119
Chickasaw County, Iowa, 23, 24, 49
Cincinnati, Ohio, 145, 274
Civil War: women's role, 23–32, 154, 163; Iowa, 23–32, 28, 56, 73, 74; hospital service, 28, 31, 77; Clara Barton, 62, 90n. See also Wittenmyer, Annie Turner

Claflin, Buck, 169
Claflin, Roxanna, 169–70, 178
Claflin, Tennessee (Tennie C.), 170
Clarence, Iowa, 98
Clarinda, Iowa, 174–75
Clarinda Republican, 175
Clark County, Ohio, 134
Clarkson, James S. (Ret), 162, 200n
Claussen, Hans R., 217–18, 219
Cleaves, Margaret, 229n
Cleveland, Ohio, 110, 111, 127n
Clinton, Iowa, 49, 98, 107n, 160
Clinton County, Iowa, 44, 49, 50, 60, 125, 126, 256
Coggeshall, John Milton, 153, 155
Coggeshall, Mary Jane (Mrs. John M.), 153, 155, 156, 156n, 218, 225, 229, 244, 248, 264–65, 266, 267–68
Cole, C. C., 40
Cole, William R., 139, 188, 190, 286n
Colorado, 44, 235n, 239
Communism, 13n, 203
Concert Hall, Philadelphia, 60
Cones, W. W., 84
Confederate states, 68
Connecticut, 44, 47, 52, 61, 146, 154, 268
Converse, Alonzo, 212n, 270, 274
Cooper Institute, New York City, 32
Coppoc, Barclay and Edwin, 83, 83n
Corkhill, George B., 285
Cornell College, 98, 121, 126
Cortland County, N.Y., 74, 264
Cottonwood Falls, Kans., 69, 70
Council Bluffs, Iowa, 148, 160, 181, 182, 188n; Amelia Bloomer, 19n, 20, 108–9, 148, 208; Matilda Fletcher, 119n, 127; Annie Savery, 137, 144; Mary Darwin, 147, 268
Council Bluffs Bugle, 40
Council Bluffs Chronotype, 19
Council Bluffs Nonpareil, 88, 142, 160, 161–62, 182, 194, 209, 254
Council Bluffs Republican, 222
Council Bluffs Woman Suffrage Society, 142, 148, 188n
Couzins, Phoebe, 118–19, 204–5, 215, 221
Cowan, Edgar, 68
Crawfordsville, Ind., 158, 270
Crawley, Lillian, 260
Creerey, Mrs., 74
Crookham, James A. L., 42, 42n, 43, 44
Cross, Judson N., 111, 111n
Cummins, Albert B., 260
Cushman, Charlotte Saunders, 63
Cutler, Hannah Tracy, 16n, 32, 138–39, 141, 145, 147–48, 153, 155, 284–85, 286n, 287
Cutts, Marcellus, 130

D

Dartmouth College, 113
Darwin, Charles Ben, 17, 45, 49, 56, 146, 269
Darwin, Mary (Mrs. C. Ben) (née Mary Abigail Platt), 17, 29–31, 45, 58, 96, 139, 145–47, 187–88, 190, 268–69, 270, 285–86, 286n
Davenport, Francis M., 269
Davenport, Mrs. Francis M. *See* Griffith, Mattie
Davenport, Iowa, 31, 58, 62, 84, 130, 160, 189, 217
Davenport Democrat, 58, 86, 202, 208, 209
Davenport Gazette, 186
Davis County, Iowa, 87
Declaration of Independence, 47, 87, 118
Delaware County, Iowa, 118, 143
Delhi, Iowa, 143
Democrats, 37, 38, 68, 70, 71, 80, 81, 103, 104, 115, 125–31, 159, 191, 239. *See also* Iowa Democrats
DePauw University, 271
Des Moines, Iowa, 29, 90n, 125–26n, 147, 184, 203, 205, 249; woman-suffrage debate in, 46, 49, 53, 54; General Assembly, 84–85, 125; Annie Savery, 91–95, 144, 275–76; woman-suffrage conventions in, 112–13, 135–37, 187–97 *passim,* 243; Amelia Bloomer, 130, 132–33, 141, 207; Polk County Woman Suffrage Society, 149–58, 265, 267, 270; Susan B. Anthony, 161–62, 180; Mary Livermore, 163, 204; Carrie Chapman Catt, 229, 236, 238, 254
Des Moines Bulletin, 125n
Des Moines Capital, 154–55, 259, 260, 276
Des Moines County, Iowa, 143, 256, 271
Des Moines Equal Suffrage Club, 244, 266
Des Moines Law School, 54
Des Moines Leader, 207, 245, 276
Des Moines Lecture Association, 90n
Des Moines Library Association, 91, 93, 145
Des Moines News, 276
Des Moines Register, 31, 49, 53, 94, 126–27, 142, 155, 157, 184, 219, 249, 250, 256, 273; woman-suffrage legislation, 43–45, 128, 167, 174, 199, 200, 210, 221; on lecturers, 54, 61, 87, 95, 159–64 *passim,* 182, 201; on conventions, 74–75, 112, 113, 149, 192, 194;

Annie Savery, 91, 92n, 93, 144, 145, 168, 168n, 190, 196, 212–15 *passim,* 274–77; editors of, 110, 120, 143; "R.W.T.," 184, 192–95; Victoria Woodhull, 185, 186, 186n; Carrie Chapman Catt, 228, 238, 254
Des Moines Review, 162, 201, 204, 205
Des Moines River, 17
Des Moines Statesman, 29, 43
DeWitt (Iowa) *Observer,* 50, 88, 183, 186n
Dickinson, Anna Elizabeth, 27, 47, 52, 58–64, 70, 90n, 92, 95, 97, 107, 112, 117, 203
Dickinson, Mrs. W. H., 218n
Dillon, John F., 31
District of Columbia, 67, 68, 84, 103, 104
Divorce, 9, 81, 105, 110, 183, 184, 185n, 190, 192, 205
Dixon, J. M., 93, 93n, 143
Dorrance, Wallace F., 175n
Douglass, Frederick, 62, 104, 105
Drake University, 156n
Dress reform movement, 3, 9, 16, 17, 19, 108, 121
Dubuque, Iowa, 17, 27, 57, 90, 97, 99n, 106, 110–29 *passim,* 141, 163, 187, 204, 256, 264
Dubuque County, Iowa, 256
Dubuque Herald, 17, 40, 43, 68, 84, 90, 97, 112, 122, 163
Dubuque Lecture Association, 64
Dubuque Times, 17, 42, 44, 97, 112–21 *passim,* 128, 143, 174, 180, 202, 206
Dubuque Tribune, 16
Dugdale, John, 63
Dugdale, Joseph, 63, 133–35, 138, 139, 141, 147, 186, 188–89, 283, 284, 285
Dugdale, Mary (Mrs. John), 63
Dugdale, Ruth (Mrs. Joseph), 63, 134
Dunlap, Flora, 157n, 249–50, 253, 259

E

East, the, 69, 70, 77, 111, 112, 135, 136, 141, 206, 220, 221, 275
Eden Township, Iowa, 49, 50, 60
Edgarton, Lillian, 145, 161, 163
Education: Iowa, 50; women's, 4, 7, 8, 20, 50, 75, 76, 92n; coeducational, 75, 116, 121
Elliott Seminary, Burlington, Iowa, 76n
Emerson, Ralph Waldo, 8, 62, 90n, 115
Employment, women, 62, 63, 81; Civil War effect, 23–24; in Iowa, 76–77, 125–26n, 127, 156
England, 234, 250

Equal rights. *See* Woman's Rights movement; Woman-suffrage movement
Equal Rights Party, 273
Equal Suffrage Society, Independence, Iowa, 234
Erie, Pa., 113
Europe, 92, 93n, 135, 144, 248, 271
Evanston, Ill., 229, 270

F

Farmer's Legislative Club (Iowa), 46, 49, 50, 53
Farmington, Iowa, 17
Farmington, N.Y., 87
Feminists, 227. *See also* Woman's Rights movement; Woman-suffrage movement
Fifteenth Amendment, 68, 101, 103–10 *passim,* 129, 167–97
Fletcher, Anna, 142
Fletcher, Mrs. Matilda, 119n, 127, 163
Florida, 237
Floyd County, Iowa, 47
Folsom, Mrs. A. P., 119n
Fonda, Iowa, 234
Foote, Mrs. A. E., 24
Fort Des Moines, Iowa, 17, 29, 146
Fort Des Moines Journal, 17
Fort Dodge, Iowa, 97, 110, 180, 234
Fort Dodge North West, 87, 97, 110
Fourteenth Amendment, 36, 37, 38, 39, 102, 160, 167–97
Fourth of July speeches, 118
Fowler, Orso, 137n
Frank Leslie's Weekly, 172
Freedman's Relief Society, 61
Free-love controversy, 81, 96, 161, 188, 192–95 *passim,* 199; antifree-love resolution, 105–6, 152, 268, 272; Victoria Woodhull, 141, 170, 177–87, 178n, 190–91; Annie Savery, 201–6; Stephen Pearl Andrews, 171, 180
Friends, Society of. *See* Quakers
Fuller, Corydon E., 155, 156, 156n, 190
Fuller, Margaret, 8, 138

G

Gage, Frances Dana, 20, 153, 205
Galena, Ill., 112, 122
Galer, Laura, 269
Garrison, William Lloyd, 8, 79, 136n
GAR Women's Relief Corps, 273
Gaylord, Wilberforce P., 47–49
Glenwood, Iowa, 85, 144

Goff, Catherine S., 83
Golden Age, 185, 185n
Golden Age Pamphlet, 186
Gold Republicans (Idaho), 239
Gough, John, 62, 71
Grand Avenue (formerly Greenwood Avenue) Des Moines, 93, 150, 276
Grangers, 274
Grant, Ulysses S., 28, 84, 101, 122, 206, 216n, 227
Graves, J. K., 115
Graves, Lucy C. (Mrs. J. K.), 113, 115
Greeley, Horace, 62, 186, 201, 227
Green, John, 130, 208, 209
Greencastle, Ind., 271
Greene County, Iowa, 269
Green Plain Meeting of Hicksite Friends, 134
Greenwood, Grace, 62
Griffith, Mattie (later Mrs. Francis M. Davenport), 83, 83n, 84, 94–95, 110, 118, 147–48, 229, 269
Grinnell, Iowa, 163
Grinnell College, 93, 114, 115, 116, 146
Grundy County, Iowa, 162, 261
Gue, Benjamin F., 87, 87n, 97, 110
Gue, Mrs. Benjamin F., 110

H

Haddock, Mrs. Mary Emily, 275n
Halleck, Henry Wager, 28
Hancock, Carrie, 74
Harbert, Elizabeth Boynton (Mrs. W. S.), 158, 163, 180, 189, 207, 211, 212, 212n, 216–17, 218–21, 228n, 229, 266, 270–71, 273–74
Harlan, Ann E. (Mrs. James), 28
Harlan, James, 28, 157n
Harper's Ferry, Va., 83, 83n
Harvard University, 113, 139
Hastings, S. Clinton, 55
Hastings School of Law, University of California, 55
Hatton, Frank, 62, 122, 123, 284
Haven, Martha Brown (Mrs. Oscar D.), 151–52, 156–57, 162, 168n
Haven, Oscar D., 152
Henderson, John Brooks, 68
Henry County (Iowa) Normal Institute, 271
Henry County Woman Suffrage Society, 186
Henshaw, Edwin, 175
Hickey, Mary B., 275n
Hicksites, 50, 134. *See also* Quakers
Historical Building, Des Moines, 38
Hoge, James, 27
Holloway, Lelia, 269

Holmes, C. P., 212n
Home Colony, Washington, 178n
Home for the Aged, Des Moines, 266, 267
Homer, New York, 12
Homer, Ohio, 169
Hooker, Isabella Beecher, 169, 169n, 172, 221
Hopedale Academy (Ohio), 94
Howe, Julia Ward, 88, 104, 136, 229
Hubbard, Nathaniel M., 276
Hull, Moses, 178
Humboldt, Iowa, 234
Hungary, 156
Hunter, Mary Ankeny, 83n, 195n, 231n, 265
Huston, Emory S., 77
Huston, Mrs. Emory S., 75–77, 96

I

Idaho, 239, 243n
Illinois, 90, 116, 128, 158, 229, 235, 237, 250, 271
Illinois Christian Woman Suffrage Association, 205
Illinois Woman Suffrage Association, 205, 270
Independence, Iowa, 69, 73, 98, 116, 134–35, 187, 234
Independent, 62, 72, 75, 96, 136n, 185
Indiana, 19, 90, 102, 120, 138, 143, 148, 151–58 passim, 228, 237, 263, 267, 270–72
Indiana Historical Society, 272
Indianola, Iowa, 143
Ingham, Caroline (Mrs. William), 118, 120, 256, 265
Ingham, Harvey, 120, 256
Ingham, William, 120
Ingham Hall, Des Moines, 29
International Woman Suffrage Alliance, 248
Interocean, 143, 228, 248, 270
Iowa Agricultural College. See Iowa State University
Iowa Capitol, Des Moines, 268
Iowa Capitol, Iowa City, 56
Iowa City, Iowa, 50, 56, 92, 142, 147, 163, 275
Iowa City State Press, 40, 92, 142, 200
Iowa Code, 1851, 55; 1860, 56
Iowa Constitution, 41–45, 215–16; Constitutional Convention, 1857, 40–41; move to delete word "white," 41, 45, 87; resolution to delete word "male," 44, 87, 243n; Woman Suffrage Amendment, 128–32, 199–222
Iowa Democrats, 40–45 passim, 60, 84, 88, 113, 126, 128, 231–32, 269. See also Democrats
Iowa Equal Suffrage Association. See Iowa Woman Suffrage Association
Iowa Falls, Iowa, 234
Iowa Federation of Women's Clubs, 263
Iowa General Assembly, 39, 40; Tenth, 42; Eleventh, 42, 56, 84; Committee on Constitutional Amendments, 44, 45, 86, 87, 129–31; Eighth Territorial, 55; Third, 55; Twelfth, 84, 130; Committee on Domestic Manufactures, 85, 86; Thirteenth, 85, 125–33, 150, 218; Fourteenth, 127, 157, 206, and the Woman Suffrage Amendment, 199–222; House action, 208–11; Senate defeats amendment, 211–20; Fourteenth Special Session, 220, abolishes legal disabilities of married women, 222; 1897 special session invites woman-suffrage delegates to speak, 243; amendment fails in 1898 and 1900 sessions, 244; 1915 session approves same, 250; presidential woman suffrage granted, 1919, 259; Iowa ratifies Nineteenth Amendment, 260
Iowa Homestead (Des Moines), 46, 49
Iowa House, Fort Dodge, Iowa, 180–81
Iowa-Italian Bee Company, 274
Iowa League of Women Voters, 157n
Iowa Negro suffrage, 40–45, 73, 73n, 84–89; literacy limitation advocates, 44; and Anna Dickinson, 58; Negro-suffrage constitutional amendment, 45, 84; popular referendum, 1868, 84
Iowa population, 19n
Iowa Quakers, 20, 50, 53, 63, 116, 134, 142, 151, 153, 154, 267
Iowa railroads, 27, 49, 61; North Western Railroad, 49, 98; Anna Dickinson's special train, 59n, 64; Dubuque and Sioux City Railroad, 98
Iowa Republicans, 39, 60–97 passim, 115, 122, 141, 154, 175, 231–32, 269, 270, 274; on Negro suffrage, 39–49, 60; Radicals, 40, 44, 45, 60, 84, 210; Thirteenth General Assembly, 125–31; Fourteenth General Assembly, 206–22 passim. See also Republicans
Iowa Sanitary Commission, 31
Iowa social conditions and culture, 19, 43–44, 98–99, 153, 275, 276. See also Women, moral conditions
Iowa State Historical Building, 275
Iowa State University (formerly Iowa Agricultural College or Iowa State College), 50n, 127, 154, 227, 235, 254
Iowa Supreme Court, 56, 177

Iowa Wesleyan College, 75, 76n, 95, 121, 143, 144, 271

Iowa woman's rights movement, 45, 50, 90, 91, 95, 98, 114, 151, 153; national leaders, 3, 121; Amelia Bloomer, 16–20; war work, 29–32; Charles Beardsley, 43, 145; under law, 54–64, 113, 222; Theodore Tilton, 72–73, 74–77; publications, 83, 84; Mount Vernon Equal Rights Association, 98; Algona Equal Rights Association, 120; General Assembly, 1870, 125–33; Declaration of Independence, 118, 279–82

Iowa Woman Suffrage Association (later Iowa Equal Suffrage Association), 32, 94, 96, 133–49, 151, 163, 187–93 passim, 208, 234–45, 236, 248–73 passim; formed Mount Pleasant Convention, 1870, 139–49, 188, 189, 207, Appendix B, 283–87; conventions, 142, 145, 149, 159, 187, 189, 207, 232, 236, 243, 249, 273; resolution on woman-suffrage amendment to Iowa Constitution, 189; resolution disavowing responsibility for utterances or opinions foreign to woman-suffrage ballot, 189; officers elected, 189–90; palladium resolution tabled, 190; Mrs. Savery on free love, 190–92; "R.W.T." criticism and controversy on palladium resolution, 190–97; Mrs. Catt's Iowa plan, 236–44

Iowa woman-suffrage memorial, 267

Iowa woman-suffrage movement, 31, 32, 39–64, 69, 71–75, 83–99, 112–20, 187; The Revolution, 81; petitions to Twelfth General Assembly, 85; Thirteenth General Assembly, 125–33; debate on woman-suffrage amendment to Iowa Constitution, 128–32; conventions, 133, 135, 139, 162, 230; first meeting in Des Moines, 1870, 141; lecturing, 158–64; battle for woman-suffrage amendment in Fourteenth General Assembly, 199–222; lobbying, 206–8, 210; county conventions held, 243; suffrage referendum defeated 1916, 256; parades, 207n

Iowa woman-suffrage organizations: Burlington Woman Suffrage Society, 32, 77, 145, 147; Oskaloosa Woman Suffrage Association, 95; Marshall County Woman Suffrage Association, 96, 143, 195, 196; Northern Iowa Woman Suffrage Association, 112–20, 143, 163, 263; Monticello Woman Suffrage Society, 119; Council Bluffs Woman Suffrage Society, 142, 148, 188n; Iowa League of Women Voters, 157n; Mitchellville Woman Suffrage Society, 157, 188; Henry County Woman Suffrage Society, 186; Equal Suffrage Society, Independence, Iowa, 234; Des Moines Equal Suffrage Club, 244, 246. See also Iowa Woman Suffrage Association; Polk County Woman Suffrage Association

Iowa women in public office: county recorder, 23; notary public, 24; deputy clerk, 24; military secretary to governor, 24; clerk to adjutant general, 24; state sanitary agent, 28; engrossing clerk, House of Representatives, 125–27; superintendent of schools, 116, 141; school board member, 154, 157

Iowa women in the professions: law, 95, 128n, 144, 204; ministry, 142; college professor, 146; medicine, 189

Irish, the, 70, 71, 103, 140, 156

Irish, John P., 40, 85, 126, 129, 131, 142–43, 147, 163, 189–220 passim, 256, 261n

Irish, Mrs. John P. (nèe Anna Fletcher), 142

J

Jacobs, Mrs. C. A., 95

Jasper County Republican, 96

Johnson, Andrew, 35, 60, 67, 261n

Johnstown, N.Y., 7, 121

Johnstown Academy, 7

Joliet, Ill., 235n

Jones County, Iowa, 119, 131

Julian, George W., 102–3

K

Kansas, 17, 36, 42, 69–71, 84n, 97, 102, 173, 237, 239, 250

Kansas City, Mo., 173

Kansas Equal Rights Association, 69

Kasson, John Adam, 85, 129, 207, 212n

Kentucky, 154, 237

Keokuk, Iowa, 27, 122

Keokuk Constitution, 122, 208–9

Keokuk Gate City, 132, 212, 221

Keosauqua, Iowa, 154

Keosauqua Mirror, 41

Kilburne, Galen F., 86

Kilburne, Jennie A. (Mrs. Galen F.) (Mrs. S. A.), 86

King, William Fletcher, 121

King, Mrs. William Fletcher, 121

Kingsbury, Elizabeth A., 90–91, 91n

Kinne, Samuel H., 221

Kirkwood (formerly Savery) Hotel, Des Moines, 238, 276n
Knox County, Ohio, 145
Kossuth, Louis, 156
Kossuth County, Iowa, 120

L

Ladies Bureau, 273
Ladies State Sanitary Convention, Des Moines, 28–31, 45, 146
Lake, Harriet, 74
Lake, Jed, 74
Langworthy, Mrs. J. L., 17
Large, Rowena Guthrie (Mrs. William P.), 113, 116, 187
Large, William P., 115
Lawrence, Kans., 70
Lawton, Mrs. N. O., 74
Leahy, Frank, 209
Lecturing, 62, 113, 114, 133, 139, 140, 144, 156, 215; Lucy Stone, 4, 158–64; Elizabeth Cady Stanton, 8–9, 121–23, 180–84; Amelia Bloomer, 19–20; Mary Livermore, 27, 158–64, 203; Anna Dickinson, 52, 58–64, 89–99, 90n; lyceum, 60–64; Theodore Tilton, 72–73, 128; Susan B. Anthony, 77, 158–64, 180–84; Phoebe Couzins, 118–19, 204; Matilda Fletcher, 119n, 127–28, 216n; Carrie Chapman Catt, 232–48, 254–57
Lee, D. S., 73
Legal rights of women, 5, 106; in Iowa, 54–64, 113, 222
Leonard, Mrs. Cynthia, 107n
Lewis, Dio, 75, 76
Liberator, The, 79
Libraries, 61
Library Hall, Chicago, 106–7, 107, 112
Library of Congress, 162
Lily, The, 12, 16, 19, 151, 152
Lincoln, Abraham, 61
Lind, Jenny (Johanna Maria), 63
Linn County, Iowa, 243
Liquor interests, 254, 256
Little, E. C., 74
Livermore, Mary Ashton, 27, 28, 105–7, 110–19 passim, 136n, 156, 162–64, 163n, 203, 204, 216, 220, 221, 229
Locke, Mattie (later Mrs. J. K. Macomber), 127
Lockwood, Belva, 273
Logan, Olive, 108, 109, 161, 163
London, England, 8, 16n, 92, 273
Longwood Meeting House, Pa., 134

Longwood Meeting of Progressive Friends, 134
Loomis, John L., 69, 70, 73–75, 116, 118, 135, 187, 234
Loughridge, William, 172
Low Moor, Iowa, 44, 49, 50
Low Moor Farmer's Club, 50
Lowden, Iowa, 98
Lowry, Austin P., 139, 143, 195, 284
Loyal Women's League, 32, 138
Lyceum, 60–64
Lyons, Iowa, 111
Lyons Mirror, 150

M

McClaren, Dr., 121
McCreery, J. L., 116, 117–18, 143
McCreery, Loretta (Mrs. J. L.), 116, 143
McMartin, Duncan, 7
McMartin, Mrs. Madge Cady, 7
Madison County, N.Y., 73
Mahaska County, Iowa, 42, 116
Maine, 35n, 235
"Male" suffrage, 36, 38
Manchester, Iowa, 234
Mansfield, Belle (Arabella) (Mrs. John), 95, 110, 128n, 139, 143–44, 188, 271–72, 271n, 284, 285, 286
Mansfield, John M., 110, 144, 271
Mansfield Hall, DePauw University, 271
Marshall, Thomas Riley, 260
Marshall County, Iowa, 17, 96, 107n, 143
Marshall County Times, 273
Marshall County Woman Suffrage Association, 96, 143, 195, 196
Marshalltown, Iowa, 95, 107n, 119n, 140n, 143, 188, 189, 228, 272, 273
Marshalltown Pioneer, 273
Marshalltown Times, 88–89, 107n, 178n, 194, 194n, 196
Mason City, Iowa, 225, 227, 243, 254
Mason City Globe Gazette, 226, 253
Mason City Republican, 225–26, 227, 228, 232, 243
Mason City Times, 232
Massachusetts, 35n, 115, 152, 167, 235, 237
Massachusetts Anti-Slavery Society, 4
Mathews, Augusta (Mrs. A. E. Foote), 24
Maxwell, George M., 44, 46–47, 48
Mayflower, 24, 120, 151, 272
Mechanicsville, Iowa, 98
Meliss, David, 80, 81

Merrill, Samuel, 141
Metropolitan Hall, Davenport, 58
Mexico, 146
Michigan, 90, 99n, 114, 115, 121, 147, 174, 204, 220, 257, 274
Middlebrook, Anna M., 87
Midwest, the, 108, 112, 121, 170, 182, 229, 270
Milford, Conn., 146, 268
Mills, Frank M., 88, 92n, 110, 143, 200n
Mills, William, 129
Mills County Fair, 238
Milton, Ind., 267
Milwaukee, Wis., 147
Minneapolis, Minn., 111n
Minnesota, 44, 82, 82n, 85n, 111n, 121, 178n, 237
Minor, Francis, 168
Minor, Virginia (Mrs. Francis), 168, 176
Minor resolutions, 168, 168n
Mississippi, 237
Mississippi River, 115, 162, 250
Mississippi Valley (Suffrage) Conference, Des Moines, 236–38
Missouri, 68, 97, 237
Missouri River, 19, 19n
Missouri Valley, Iowa, 180
Missouri Woman Suffrage Association, 168, 176
Mitchell County, Iowa, 141
Mitchellville Woman Suffrage Society, 157, 188
Montana, 242, 250, 269
Montgomery County, Iowa, 86
Monticello, Iowa, 118, 119, 120
Monticello Woman Suffrage Association, 119
Moore's Hall, Des Moines, 145, 155, 159
Morgan County, Ohio, 115
Mott, Lucretia Coffin (Mrs. James), 8, 60, 134
Mount Pleasant, Iowa, 28, 32, 62, 75, 83–134 passim, 135–49, 136n, 160, 187, 188, 190, 215, 265, 269, 271, 284, 285, 286; "Athens of Iowa," 63
Mount Pleasant Journal, 62, 80, 89, 94, 122, 148, 186n, 215, 269, 271, 284
Mount Pleasant State Hospital, 268
Mount Vernon, Iowa, 98, 121
Mount Vernon Equal Rights Association, 98
Mozart Hall, Burlington, Iowa, 63
Murray, Benjamin F., 85
Muscatine, Iowa, 17, 55, 140, 144, 145
Muscatine Democrat, 17
Music Hall, Chicago, 107n

N

Napoleon Bonaparte, 93, 93n
National-American Woman Suffrage Association. See National Association
National Association, 234, 234n, 237, 241, 267, 268, 274; conventions, 225, 234, 241, 248, 252, 257; Mrs. Catt succeeds Miss Anthony as president, 225; Mrs. Catt proposes nationwide good-government committee, 1904, 247–48; Mrs. Catt retires as president, 247–48; Mrs. Catt resumes presidency, 1915, 252; Mrs. Catt's "winning plan," 257
National Party of the New America, 80
National Science Foundation, 264
National Woman Suffrage and Education Committee, 173, 173n, 177
National Woman Suffrage Association (formerly Woman Suffrage Association of America), 108, 111, 134, 151n, 173, 178n, 225. See also Union Woman Suffrage Association; National Association
Nebraska, 20, 68, 237
Negroes in Iowa, 39, 85n, 154. See also Antislavery movement; Douglass, Frederick; Negro suffrage
Negro suffrage, 32, 35, 35n, 36, 39, 71, 79, 84n, 85n; anti-Negro suffrage, 39, 71; "citizens of African descent," 42, 60; referendums, 44; in Congress, 67–69. See also Iowa Negro suffrage; Fifteenth Amendment
Nevada, 242, 250
Newbury, Samuel, 114
New England, 5, 44, 87, 107, 108, 115, 235
New England Freedman's Aid Society, 90
New England Woman Suffrage Association, 88, 91n, 104, 229
New Hampshire, 35n, 61
New Hampton, Iowa, 23
New Harmony, Ind., 16
New Jersey, 136
New Sharon, Iowa, 116
Newspapers. See names of individual newspapers
Newton, Iowa, 96, 275
New York, 16, 19, 35n, 37, 49, 69, 70n, 73, 87, 87n, 120, 237, 239, 257, 264, 272, 273
New York City, 19, 32, 71, 81, 171, 191; Elizabeth Cady Stanton, 9, 36, 182; meetings in, 38, 69, 108, 110, 112, 134, 177; Annie Savery, 92, 273, 275,

New York City, *(cont.)*
277; Carrie Chapman Catt, 235, 248, 250, 260
New York Tribune, 62, 186, 227
New York Woman Suffrage Party, 248
New York World, 155
Nineteenth Amendment, 84, 103, 156, 225, 259–61
North, the, 32, 46, 84, 101, 103
North Carolina, 154
Northern Iowa Woman Suffrage Association, 112–20, 143, 163, 263
Northwest, the, 107
Northwest Sanitary Commission, Chicago, 24, 27, 28–29, 31, 106, 229
Northwest Sanitary Fair, Chicago, 27, 61
Nourse, Charles C., 154, 157
Nourse, Rebecca (Mrs. Charles C.), 154–55

O

Oakland, Calif., 239
Oakland Times, 142
Oberlin College, 4, 7, 45, 110, 120, 146, 147, 159, 269
O'Connor, Henry, 128, 139, 140–41, 140n, 142, 159, 163, 187, 189, 283, 285
Ohio, 4, 19, 20, 27, 32, 84–115 *passim,* 134, 138, 145, 151, 153, 180, 205, 249, 272
Ohio Cultivator 153
Ohio Medical College, 145
Oklahoma, 257
Older, Mrs. E. B., 74
Omaha, Nebr., 20, 70, 71, 181
Opera House, Dubuque, Iowa, 121, 256
Orange, N.J., 5
Oregon, 242, 248, 250
Orphans home (Davenport, Iowa), 31
Orwig, Maria, 266
Osage, Iowa, 97
Oskaloosa, Iowa, 42, 95, 130, 141, 145, 147, 172, 188, 232, 269
Oskaloosa Herald, 43, 145
Oskaloosa Woman Suffrage Association, 95
Ottawa, Ill., 107n
Ottumwa, Iowa, 17, 141, 160, 269
Ottumwa Courier, 17
Owen, Robert, 16

P

Page County, Iowa, 175
"Palladium resolution" controversy, 190–97

Palmer, Benjamin, 44, 48, 49, 50
Palmer, Frank, 143
Palmer, Mrs. Frank, 143
Palmer, Phoebe (Mrs. Benjamin), 49–53
Paris, France, 81, 93, 93n
Paris, Tenn., 146
Park, Maude Wood, 257, 260
Parker, George, 261n
Parker, Theodore, 8
Pasadena, Calif., 270
Paulson, Mrs. Edna Snell. *See* Snell, Edna
Peace convention, Mount Pleasant, Iowa, 133, 141
P.E.O. Sisterhood, 95
Pella, Iowa, 141
Pennsylvania, 68, 94, 134, 205, 269
Perkins, W., 107n
Peru, Ind., 24, 263
Philadelphia, Pa., 8, 27, 60, 63, 92
Phillips, Wendell, 62, 79, 284
Pillsbury, Parker, 71n, 80
Pitman, Maria (nèe Maria Freeman) (Mrs. John H. Gray) (later Mrs. C. J. Pitman), 152, 157, 158, 180, 201, 218
Pittsburgh, Pa., 205
Political Equity Club, Boone, Iowa, 248
Political Equity Club, Independence, Iowa, 234
Political Equity Club, Sioux City, Iowa, 234
Polk County, Iowa, 150
Polk County courthouse, 54, 163, 205
Polk County Woman Suffrage Association, 53, 54n, 145, 149–58, 218, 229, 267, 270, 273; officers, 149–55, 180, 186; on free-love issue, 195, 201–6, 208, 212–14
Polygamists, 104n
Pomeroy, C. R., 156
Pomeroy, Charles, 110
Pomeroy, Mrs. Charles, 110
Pomeroy, Samuel C., 102
Populist Party (Idaho), 239
Portage County, Ohio, 272
Porter, Maria W., 189
Portland, Oreg., 248
Pottawattamie County, Iowa, 178n
Prairie Grove Meeting of Hicksite Friends, 134
Progressive Party, 259
Prohibitionists, 154. *See also* Temperance movement
Prostitution, 81, 105, 110, 181; in Iowa, 17, 19, 62, 76
Purvis, Robert, 71n

Q

Quakers, 8, 10, 12, 48, 60, 63, 83, 138, 191; Hicksites, 50, 134; Progressive Friends, or Congregational Friends, or Friends of Human Progress, 50, 87n, 134. *See also* Iowa Quakers

R

Radicals. *See* Republicans
Railroads, 19n, 27, 254. *See also* Iowa railroads
Ralley, Mary Coppoc, 83
Ramsey, Linda R. (later Mrs. Hartzell), 24
Rankin, Mrs. Samuel E., 157
Read, Lizzie Bunnell (Mrs. S. G. A.), 24, 120, 151, 189, 272
Read, S. G. A., 24, 120
Reconstruction Act, 1867, 68
Redhead, Wesley, 157
Reform movements. *See* Abortion; Birth control; Dress reform movement; Free-love controversy; Legal rights of women; Woman-suffrage movement; Woman's rights movement
Religion, 9, 10; Baptists, 86n; Catholics, 86n, 115, 140, 263; Christian denomination, 156n; Congregationalists, 145, 146, 268; Episcopalians, 13, 155; freethinkers, 13n, 93, 116; *Independent*, 62; Methodists, 75, 86n, 98, 121, 143, 152, 154, 156, 283; Mormons, 13, 13n, 83; Presbyterians, 9, 12, 86n, 114, 150; Theosophists, 264, 275; Transcendentalists, 115; Unitarians, 139, 153; Universalists, 106, 119n, 147, 157, 269. *See also* Quakers; Spiritualism.
Religio-Philosophical Journal, 188n
Republicans, 35–39 *passim*, 68–80 *passim*, 101–2, 104, 110, 115, 159, 191, 199, 216, 216n, 227, 263, 274; Radicals, 35, 39, 60, 67, 68, 69; Gold or Silver Republicans (Idaho), 239. *See also* Iowa Republicans
Revolution, The, 80–84, 87–108 *passim*, 118, 121, 122–23, 128, 138, 147–48, 160, 171, 174, 178, 184, 187, 283, 286
Rhode Island, 35n
Richards, Benjamin B., 211–13, 214, 221
Richmond, Ind., 152
Rising Sun, Iowa, 113
Roadside Settlement, Des Moines, 157n, 249

Robinson, Charles, 70
Robinson, Frank M., 115
Robinson, Laura G. (Mrs. Frank M.), 113, 115
Rochester, N.Y., 10, 176, 180
Rollins, Charles W., 98
Roosevelt, Theodore, 259
Rose, Ernestine, 105
Russell, John, 131
Russell, Lillian (Helen Louise Leonard), 107n
Rutkay, Louis, 156, 189
Rutland, Vt., 177
"R.W.T." (anonymous), 184, 192–94

S

St. Louis, Mo., 19, 19n, 28, 118, 168, 204, 215
St. Paul, Minn., 121
Salem, Mass., 115
Salter, William, 146
Sanford, Nettie (Mrs. Daniel Sanford) (later Mrs. E. H. Chapin), 95–96, 143, 188, 189, 190, 194n, 208, 272–73
San Francisco, Calif., 142, 152, 182, 183, 232, 239
San Francisco Chronicle, 182
San Gabriel Valley News (Calif.), 273
Sanitary Commission, 163
Sanitary Convention, Des Moines, 28–31, 45, 146
Sanitary Fair, Chicago, 27, 61
Saratoga, N.Y., 92
Saturday Visitor, 205
Saunders Hall, Mount Pleasant, Iowa, 139
Savery, Annie N. (Mrs. James C.), 160, 161, 180, 266, 268, 270, 273–77; lectures, 91–94, 139, 144, 163, 190, 190n; and Amelia Bloomer, 130, 132–33, 135–36, 137, 153; Polk County Woman Suffrage Society, 141, 145, 155, 158, 202–3, 208; Iowa Association, 145, 149, 187; letters to the *Des Moines Register*, 168, 193–94, 196–97, 200–201, 212–16; and General Assembly, 211–12, 212n, 218, 221–22
Savery, Mrs. Chester, 133
Savery, James C., 92, 162, 275
Savery, Mary (Mrs. James C.), 275
Savery Hotel, Des Moines, 92, 275, 276, 276n
Scott County, Iowa, 256
Seattle, Wash., 235
Seneca Falls, N.Y., 3, 4, 7, 8, 9, 10, 12, 13, 16, 19, 121, 134, 205, 279
Seneca Falls Courier, 13
Seneca Falls Historical Society, 184n

Sharman, Mrs. Susan, 156, 158
Shaw, Anna Howard, 248, 252, 266
Shelton, Amanda, 77
Shelton, Mary E. ("M.E.S.") (later Mrs. Emory S. Huston), 75–77, 96
Shelton, Ortus C., 76n
Sheridan, Philip Henry, 53
Sherman, William Tecumseh, 53
Sherman, Mrs. William Tecumseh, 185
Shiloh, Battle of, 28
Shoemaker, S. H., 88
Shoemaker, Will R., 188
Silver Republicans (Idaho), 239
Simpson College, 143
Sioux City, Iowa, 180, 234
Sioux City Journal, 160
Sixteenth Amendment, 103, 104, 122, 157, 157n, 169, 172, 174
Slavery. *See* Abolitionists; Antislavery movement; Negro suffrage
Smith, Ida B. Wise, 249
Smith, Olive Cole, 83, 265
Snell, Edna (later Mrs. Edna Snell Paulson), 110, 113, 115–16, 116n, 118
Snell, Mary, 116n
Snell Seminary, 116
Social Science Association, 264
Soldier's aid societies: Western Sanitary Commission, 28; Ladies State Sanitary Commission, 28–31, 45, 146; Iowa Sanitary Commission, 31; United Christian Commission, 31. *See also* Northwest Sanitary Commission
Soldier's Home, Marshalltown, Iowa, 140n
Sorosis, 107n, 229n. *See also* Association for the Advancement of Women
South, the, 35, 36, 39, 46, 101
South Adams, Mass., 10
South Dakota, 235, 237, 257
Sparr, Mary, 180
Spencer, Benjamin, 126
Spencer, Mary E., 125–27, 127n
Spiritualism and spiritualists, 86, 86n, 87, 107n, 119, 170, 178n; in Iowa, 178n, 188n. *See also* Andrews, Stephen Pearl; Free love; Woodhull, Victoria
Springdale, Iowa (Humboldt), 83, 154, 188
Stanton, Elizabeth Cady (Mrs. Henry B.), 3, 13, 13n, 16, 19, 32, 72, 103, 110, 138, 172; early years, 7–9, 60, 134; and Susan B. Anthony, 10, 36–39, 104–5, 107, 108, 111, 234, 264, 272; lecturing, 69–71, 71n, 91, 112, 120, 121–23, 128, 136, 182–84, 193; *The Revolution,* 80–83, 88, 89, 118; Victoria Woodhull, 173n, 174, 178,
180–82, 187, 203, 221
Stanton, Gerrit Smith, 7
Stanton, Harriet, 203
Stanton, Henry Brewster, 8, 9, 37
Stanton, Kate, 203
States rights, 261n
State University of Iowa, 50, 229n, 275, 275n
Stebbins, Emily Calkins, 23, 24
Stone, John Y., 85, 130
Stone, Lucy (Mrs. Henry B. Blackwell), 3, 9, 13n, 47, 79, 88, 119, 134, 146, 230, 235; early years, 3–4; lecturing, 19, 69–71, 136, 136n, 137, 141, 158–60, 162; as moderate, 80, 84, 104–11, 138, 181, 203, 234
Stone, William M., 24
Story County, Iowa, 44, 46, 50
Stowe, Harriet Beecher, 169n
Studwell, Edwin A., 138, 283, 285, 286
Suffragettes, 207n, 249, 250, 267, 267n
Suffragists. *See* Woman-suffrage movement
Susan B. Anthony amendment to U.S. Constitution, 250
Swisshelm, Jane G., 205–6, 213–14, 215, 215n, 218, 219–20, 221
Syracuse, N.Y., 272

T

Taylor County, Iowa, 175
Temperance movement, 10, 12, 13, 19, 20, 31, 93, 94, 95, 140, 141, 154. *See also The Lily*
Tenafly, N.J., 9, 203
Tennessee, 28, 146, 261n
Terrace Hill mansion, Des Moines, 150
Teter, I. B., 283
Texas, 119n
Thirteenth Amendment, 35
Thompson, George, 62
Thompson, Marianne (later Mrs. A. P. Folsom), 119n
Thuesen, Mrs. Jens, 261
Tilton, Elizabeth (Mrs. Theodore), 182
Tilton, Theodore, 62, 72–73, 96, 128, 136n, 138, 145, 173n, 182, 182n, 185, 186, 187, 200, 203
Tisdale, Gilbert J., 49
Toledo, Iowa, 160
Topeka, Kans., 69
Traer, John, 131
Train, George Francis, 70–71, 71n, 80, 81, 108–9, 173
Travel, modes of, 17, 19, 29, 31, 49, 61, 69, 70, 98, 121, 248. *See also* Railroads
Troy Female Seminary, 7, 114

True Woman, The, 185
Tuileries Palace, Paris, 93, 93n
Tupper, Ellen, 274
Tuskegee Institute, 267
Tweed-Murphy graft, New York City, 191

U

Union Relief Society, 154
Union Suffrage Society. *See* Union Woman Suffrage Association
Union Woman Suffrage Association (National Woman Suffrage Association), 138, 148, 173n, 284, 285, 286n, Appendix B, 283–87
United States Christian Commission, 31
United States Congress, 61, 80, 143, 181; 39th, 36, 67–68; 40th, 68–69, 101
United States Constitution, 36, 177; "male," move to insert in, 36, 38; suffrage amendments introduced, 68, 102, 103; Susan B. Anthony amendment, 250; Nineteenth Amendment passed, 259–61. *See also* Fifteenth Amendment; Fourteenth Amendment; Nineteenth Amendment; Thirteenth Amendment
United States Consul to Le Havre, France, 274
United State Supreme Court, 168, 176
Universalist Church: Dubuque, 97, 112; Mitchellville, 157
Universal suffrage, 79
University Christian Church, Des Moines, 254
University of California, 55
Upper Des Moines, 120
Utah, 13, 83, 104n, 239

V

Vale, L. W., 285
Vancise, E. A., 283
Vanderbilt, Cornelius, 170, 203
Vermont, 35n, 115, 136, 151, 177, 216
Vicksburg, siege of, 28, 74
Victoria, Queen, 54
Vineland, N.J., 90

W

Waistbrooker, Mrs. Lois, 178n
Walker, Mary, 108–9
Washington, D.C., 28, 61, 92, 103, 122, 127n, 171, 174, 174n, 225, 268, 273

Washington Star, 170, 226
Washington State, 235, 242, 243n, 250
Washington Territory, 146
Washington University, 118
Water-Cure Journal, 17
Waterloo, Iowa, 90, 234, 256
Waterloo, N.Y., 8, 12, 50, 134
Wayne County, Ind., 267
Webster City, Iowa, 234, 239
West, the, 72, 123, 146, 206, 221, 234, 276
West, Albert, 148
West, Kate (Mrs. Albert), 148
West Chester, Pa., 134
Western Sanitary Commission, St. Louis, 28
Western Woman Suffrage Association, 119
West Liberty, Iowa, 203
Weston, E. W., 50
Weston, Mrs. E. W., 44
Wharton, Henry, 48
Willard, Emma, 7, 114
Willard, Frances, 31, 229
Williamson, Iowa, 234
Wilson, David S., 113
Wilson, Henrietta E. (Mrs. David S.), 113, 116
Wilson, Thomas Stokeley, 57, 113
Wilson, William G., 87
Winterset, Iowa, 20, 84
Wisconsin, 44, 84n, 90, 121, 147, 227, 237
Withrow, Mrs. Thomas, 132
Wittenmyer, Annie Turner, 27–31, 45, 77, 96, 146
Woman Citizen (formerly *Woman's Journal*), 84, 260, 261
Woman's Congress, 229, 271
Woman's Journal, 84, 91n, 111, 132, 136, 139–63 *passim,* 174, 177, 184, 203, 207, 218, 229, 269, 286n
Woman's Declaration of Independence, 13, 279–82
Woman's Medical College, Philadelphia, 189
Woman's rights movement, 3, 4, 8–10, 13, 16, 17, 19, 20, 80–84, 104–11, 134, 159, 205; conventions, 4, 5, 7, 9, 10, 50, 60, 88, 134, 177, 205, 279; Woman's Declaration of Independence, 13, 279–82; Civil War halts movement, 23; Kansas Equal Rights Association, 69; Mount Vernon Equal Rights Association, 98; Algona Equal Rights Association, 120; labor unions, 239; Equal Rights Party, 273. *See also* American Equal Rights Association; Dress reform movement; Iowa woman's rights movement; Le-

Woman's rights movement, *(cont.)*
gal rights of women; *The Revolution*
Woman's Standard, 232, 234, 243, 250, 266, 267, 272, 277
Woman-suffrage campaigns, 36; in Kansas, 69–71; Texas, 119n; South Dakota, 235; Idaho, 239; Colorado, 239; California, 239–40; Iowa, 253–56
Woman-suffrage flag, 237, 241, 250, 257
Woman-suffrage movement, 20, 36, 37, 41, 42, 83–84, 102–11; and Congress, 67–69, 101–3; conventions, 106, 112, 119, 162, 168, 169; Kansas, 69–71, 173; woman-suffrage petitions to Congress, 103; household suffrage, 75; woman-suffrage petitions for District of Columbia and territories, 102; Vermont campaign, 136, 136n; movement for enfranchisement under Fourteenth and Fifteenth Amendments, 167–97; referendum victory in Colorado, 239; Sixty-sixth Congress passes woman-suffrage amendment, 1919, 259–60; Nineteenth Amendment becomes law, 1920, 261. *See also* American Woman Suffrage Association; Illinois Christian Woman Suffrage Association; Illinois Woman Suffrage Alliance; International Woman Suffrage Alliance; Iowa Woman Suffrage Association
Woman-suffrage parades, 207n, 250, 267, 267n
Women, moral conditions, 81, 105; "double standard," 180, 181
Women and politics, 37, 52, 61, 80, 81, 215–17. *See also* names of individual suffrage and woman's rights leaders
Women in public office. *See* Iowa women in public office

Women in public service: Civil War, 23–32, 77, 93. *See also* Civil War
Women's Christian Temperance Union, 31, 229, 257, 266, 268, 269
Women's clubs, 229n; Iowa, 114, 229, 266, 263
Wood, Sam, 69, 70
Woodhull, Victoria (nèe Claflin) (Mrs. Canning Woodhull), 77, 141, 167–97, 195n, 200, 201, 203, 203n, 205, 221, 222
"Woodhull-Claflin clique," 190–97
Woodhull-Claflin Murray Hill mansion, 171, 178
Woodhull and Claflin's Weekly, 171, 174, 182n, 184, 185, 186n
Woodhull memorial to Congress, 167, 169, 171–72, 173
Woodland Cemetery, Des Moines, 277
Worcester, Mass., 4, 5, 134
Work, Henry D., 154
Work, Mary (Mrs. Henry D.), 154
Wright, Ed H., 53, 155n
Wright, Mrs. Ed. H., 53, 155
Wright, Henry C., 87
Wright, James, 54, 156, 156n
Wright, M. C., 54, 57, 156n
Wright, Martha, 180, 181, 182
Wyoming, 103, 159, 237, 239

Y

Yonkers, N.Y., 127n
Young Men's Associations (variously called Young Men's Christian or Young Men's Library Associations), 61; Association of Western Literary Societies, 62; Young Men's Literary Association, 64

SPIRIT LAKE

ESTHER-
VILLE

OKOBOJI

ALGONA

PETERSON

SIOUX RAPIDS

CHEROKEE

STORM LAKE

SIOUX CITY

CORRECTIONVILLE

FT DODGE

SMITH LAND

BOONE

AMES

ONAWA

DENISON

CALIFORNIA JUNC.

MISSOURI VALLEY

MOORE'S HALL

ATLANTIC

OMAHA CITY

COUNCIL BLUFFS

SAVERY HOUSE

B.F. ALLEN

PLATTSMOUTH

CRESTON

OSCEOLA

VILLISCA

SIDNEY

CLARINDA

LEON

BEDFORD

CARRIE CHAPMAN C
CHARLES CI

IO

AMELIA BLOOMER HOME
COUNCIL BLUFFS

IOWA RAIL ROADS OF 1870
"THE ROADS RUN GENERALLY IN
PARALLEL LINES, NEVER LOOKING
AT OR SHAKING HANDS WITH EACH
OTHER..." ELIZABETH CADY STANTON
CEDAR RAPIDS · APRIL 7 1870

IO